The Handbook of
Multisource Feedback

The Handbook of Multisource Feedback

The Comprehensive Resource for Designing and Implementing MSF Processes

David W. Bracken

Carol W. Timmreck

Allan H. Church

Editors

Foreword by David Campbell

JOSSEY-BASS
A Wiley Company
San Francisco

Jossey-Bass books and products are available through most bookstores. To contact Jossey-Bass directly, call (888) 378-2537, fax to (800) 605-2665, or visit our website at www.josseybass.com.

Substantial discounts on bulk quantities of Jossey-Bass books are available to corporations, professional associations, and other organizations. For details and discount information, contact the special sales department at Jossey-Bass.

 Manufactured in the United States of America on Lyons Falls Turin Book. This paper is acid-free and 100 percent totally chlorine-free.

Library of Congress Cataloging-in-Publication Data

The handbook of multisource feedback : the comprehensive resource for designing and implementing MSF processes / by David W. Bracken, Carol W. Timmreck, Allan H. Church, editors.—1st ed.
    p. cm.—(The Jossey-Bass business & management series)
Includes bibliographical references and index.
ISBN 0-7879-5286-9
    1. Communication in organizations.   2. Organizational effectiveness—
Evaluation.   3. Communication in organizations—United States—Case studies.
4. Organizational effectiveness—United States—Evaluation—Case studies.
I. Bracken, David.   II. Timmreck, Carol W.   III. Church, Allan H.
IV. Title.   V. Series.
    HD30.3 .H3567 2000
    658.4'5—dc21   00-009883

FIRST EDITION
HB Printing   10 9 8 7 6 5 4 3 2 1

The Jossey-Bass
Business & Management Series

Contents

Part Three: Systems Forces in Multisource Feedback

Foreword

This is an excellent sourcebook on multisource feedback (MSF). It is intended for practitioners, researchers, consultants, and organizational clients who are trying to understand the MSF process. Refreshingly, the contributors are likewise drawn from these same categories. It is unusual to see such a wide range of formal credentials, practical experience, and thus varied viewpoints focused on one specific topic.

Multisource feedback, in its simplest form (which, as we shall see, is not so simple), has these basic components:

1. Some purpose for doing an assessment: "the project"
2. Some person to be assessed: "the ratee"
3. Some collection of people to do the assessing: "the raters"
4. Some specific characteristics to be assessed: "the items"
5. Some technique, either paper-and-pencil or electronic, for collecting the data: "the survey"
6. Some method for aggregating the raters' responses: "the data"
7. Some form for reporting the results: "the report"
8. Some process for providing the report to somebody: "the feedback"
9. Some actions to be taken, developmental or administrative or both: "the decisions"
10. Some procedure for determining if all of this was worthwhile: "the follow up"

For each point, myriad detailed questions come to mind. To take as an example point four (the items), a number of questions need to be addressed:

- What topics should be covered?
- How many items should there be?

- In what format should they be presented?
- How should they be displayed: on paper, by computer, or on the Internet?
- Are any of the items offensive to any demographic subgroup?
- Are the items legally defensible?
- Which language or languages should be used?
- Are there any copyright problems?

And on and on. A similar list can be generated for each of the points listed; indeed, the basic purpose of this book is to raise this long list of potential questions, and then to present quantitative data, case studies, reasoned opinions, and collected experience to arrive at defensible answers.

Historical Context

Multisource assessment and feedback has swept into the worlds of psychological assessment and performance management in the last three decades, and some historical context here may be useful for understanding where the process has come from so as to better appreciate where we are today and where we are likely to go next.

Standardized psychological assessment is generally considered to have started around 1900 in Paris through the efforts of a French physician, Alfred Binet. He was asked by the Paris School Board to develop a method of identifying students who could not profit from the usual classroom experience: slow learners, or learning disabled ("special education") students. For this purpose, Binet did two things that had never been done before. First, he standardized the questions, that is, each student was asked exactly the same questions, such as, "Here is a clock; what time is it?" Then he normed the responses, that is, he determined at which age the average student learned to tell time. The answers of subsequent students were compared with these norms, and the resulting scores were used to assign students to appropriate instructional methods.

Binet's two techniques—standardized items and normed responses—still underlie virtually all current methods of psychological assessment, including many multisource assessments. His techniques were brought to the United States by Lewis Terman of Stanford University with publication of the Stanford-Binet Intelligence Test in 1916. Shortly thereafter, in 1917–18, these techniques went to war with the establishment of the United States Army Personnel Classification Committee, which developed the Army Alpha (verbal) and Beta (nonverbal) tests for screening military recruits, again using standardized questions and normed responses. Hundreds of thousands of men were tested, and the results were used to assign recruits to appropriate classifications, especially in sorting out those recruits who were admitted to officer training programs. It is worth noting that all of these tests were scored by hand—a considerable constraint on how broadly they could be used.

This was the first large-scale application of psychological assessment techniques, and the success of this approach energized the civilian psychologists who had been drawn into the military to develop these programs. When they returned home after the war, they enthusiastically began to develop all sorts of new psychological measuring instruments.

Over the next four decades, the 1920s through the 1950s, a wide variety of psychological tests, surveys, inventories, and other assorted instruments were developed, all for the purpose of assessing individuals for administrative purposes, such as college entrance, therapeutic treatments, occupational classification, employment selection and placement, and, of course, military assignment. With virtually no exceptions, the purpose of the assessment was to serve the needs of the assessing institution—not those of the person being assessed, who typically was never even told the results. Even when the presumed purpose was therapy or vocational counseling, assessees were often not shown the results of the testing; rather, the therapist or counselor "interpreted" the results for the client. Most assuredly, the test results were deemed the property of the organization and remained in the client's files. There were no carbon copies to be taken home.

The assessments tended to fall into a few basic content categories: intelligence tests, tests of other specific traits such as mathematical or mechanical abilities, personality inventories, and career surveys. Progress was relatively slow, partly because there were only a few hundred psychologists in America (in 1950, there were roughly one thousand members of the American Psychological Association) and partly because data processing machines were so primitive. With the exception of a few specialized, *idiot savant* machines capable of scoring specific tests such as the College Boards, the Minnesota Multiphasic Personality Inventory, and the Strong Vocational Interest Blank, all test scoring methods were still essentially done by hand, again severely restricting their usage. Even the IBM 803 Test Scoring Machine, the first workhorse of the field and the machine that immortalized the number two pencil, had to be fed by hand, sheet by sheet.

In 1962, Harlan Ward, founder of National Computer Systems (NCS) in Minneapolis, tied together a high-speed paper transport, an optical scanner, and a digital computer for the first time, and the use of tests grew quickly and broadly. In 1969, shortly after NCS went public, I was invited to serve on the board of directors; NCS rapidly became the world's largest test processing company. Over the course of twenty-seven years, I became vividly aware of the direct connection between improvements in data processing hardware and software, and the growth of psychological assessment.

With increased usage came increased resistance. The 1960s saw rising resentment toward psychological testing, for at least two reasons. First, in the early days, essentially no attention had been paid to what is now termed "political correctness" in item selection. For example, incredibly, until 1969 one of the more widely used career inventories still asked respondents to indicate how much they liked working with "Negroes," and a popular managerial sentence-completion survey asked individuals to complete the sentence, "If I had to wear a suit and tie to work, I would feel. . . ." In addition, gender-specific vocabulary abounded: *policeman, salesman, waitress, stewardess.* Stereotypes were maintained and used in both selection and counseling.

Second, a substantial body of research accumulated to demonstrate that some demographic categories were being "adversely affected," that is, scores for some demographic categories were below the population mean. This suggested that the tests were biased toward these categories, either in item selection or in norming.

A third factor probably fueled this resentment toward psychological assessment, but in a much subtler and not widely recognized manner: the fact that psychological tests and surveys were still being used almost exclusively for the benefit of the assessing institution, not for the benefit of the individual. For the most part, individuals were still not being shown the results of their own assessments, even though important decisions were being made about them, based on their test results. The general professional stance was that assessees could not adequately understand their results, so they were better off being kept in the dark. There was somewhat more openness with career inventories, especially as the NCS high-speed printers now produced carbon copies that could be handed to the counselee; still there was a lot of professional skittishness about sharing the test results. The APA Code of Ethics still deemed it unethical to send test results to respondents through the mail.

(A personal note here demonstrating these policies: when I graduated from college in 1955, I went to work for Procter & Gamble, which had just been recognized by the National Association of Manufacturers as "the best-managed company in America." As part of the employment process, I completed a lengthy battery of tests. I never saw the results, and no one ever discussed them with me. When I went into the Army a year later, I completed the Army General Classification Test (AGCT), and I never saw those results either, until much later, when I was put in charge of the personnel folders of the unit that I was assigned to. Of course, the first thing I did was to look at my own file.)

In the 1960s, psychologists reacted quickly to these charges of political incorrectness and bias, first by cleaning up the test items, and second by focusing a great deal of attention on the issue of adverse impact. Although the problems with the latter issue have not been resolved, as a society we have at least learned to focus on the problem in a more sophisticated manner; several chapters in this book touch on the issue. Regarding sharing the assessment results with the assessed individual, progress came from an unexpected direction: from establishment of the Peace Corps, an initiative driven by President John F. Kennedy in the early 1960s. In this government-sponsored program, thousands of idealistic Americans volunteered to go overseas and help less developed countries adopt more advanced methods of sanitation, home construction, medical practices, agricultural methods, and the like.

It became quickly apparent that these ambassadors needed some personal preparation for succeeding in strange cultures, and the psychologists who were brought in to aid in this orientation began using psychological surveys to help the Peace Corps volunteers better understand themselves, under the theory that self-understanding would aid them in dealing with cultural change. For the first time, assessment was done for the benefit of the individual being assessed, although the results were also used by the Peace Corps committees that were in charge of volunteer assignments.

This change of sharing the assessment results with the individual being assessed sounds simple and obvious today, but it was not so at the time. Administering tests for the benefit of the individual instead of for the sponsoring organization was a sea change of policy, yet the new approach caught on very quickly because it was so popular with those being assessed.

(Another personal note to demonstrate the change. For reasons too complicated to discuss here, I remained in the Army Reserve until 1978, which essentially meant that I attended military training once a month, and two weeks each summer, for twenty-two years. Each year, my commanding officer filled out an Officer Efficiency Report (OER) on my performance. True to the times, I was never shown these reports, nor were they ever discussed with me. Of course, I knew they were being filled in, because I was filling them in on my own subordinates. However, the year before I retired, I noticed one day that I had been asked to initial my OER and thus could see the ratings. At the same time, I learned that this change in policy meant I could see all of my earlier reports, which were stored with thousands of others in a dusty Army warehouse in St. Louis. I made a special trip, visited the warehouse, and was ushered into a bleak, windowless cubicle with the proverbial naked light bulb hanging over the desk. I spent a couple of fascinating hours looking over twenty-two years of my OERs, noting what my commanding officers had thought of me. It was not necessarily a painful experience, but it was also not particularly exhilarating. In retrospect, there were a few themes running through the data that I might have worked on developmentally, had I known that they were an issue. A high-ranking military officer who looked over this Foreword for me insists that procedures were different in the active Army, and that OERs were shared, by regulation, with those being assessed. Could be.)

In the early 1970s, one of the psychologists working in these Peace Corps training programs, Robert Dorn, joined the staff of the Center for Creative Leadership and brought with him the Peace Corps concept of "assessment for development," which meant sharing assessment results with the assessee. This approach was immediately popular and effective in CCL's early leadership training program, although the initial approach used only self-reports, not multisource feedback. Such instruments did not then exist, nor, incidentally, were there any data-processing systems set up to handle them.

However, during the next few years (the mid-1970s), one of Dorn's staff members, an economist, Robert Bailey, began tinkering with a "multisource feedback" survey, and its usefulness in working with managers in leadership programs quickly became apparent. Perhaps Bailey was more successful in these early ventures because he was not bound by the same sort of blinders as were psychologists, who were still tied to self-reports. In retrospect, the idea of using systematic information from others in the standardized-questions, normed-responses format seems obvious, but it was not so at the time.

The Zeitgeist being what it is, I suspect there were other early experiments of this sort going on in other locations, but I was not aware of them. From my experience, I believe Dorn and Bailey were the pioneers of MSF, though they were probably not aware of breaking new ground. They were merely seeking better ways to give feedback to participants in CCL's leadership training programs.

Other reviewers of this Foreword cited several examples of MSF in their organizations in the 1970s; clearly it was an idea that was catching on. However, the spread of these techniques was slow, partially because of the normal inertia facing the adoption of any new technique, and partially because, for these purposes, data-processing facilities and software were still primitive. No professionally published, commercially available 360-degree feedback instruments had yet appeared.

All of this changed quickly in the 1980s as personal computers proliferated, and when, simultaneously, the value of MSF became more apparent—especially as noted in the enthusiasm of those receiving this personal information about themselves. Even when the data were painful, they were usually appreciated.

Contemporary Challenges of MSF

The resultant explosion of activities in the 1980s and 1990s is well documented by the chapters in this book. The most salient questions surrounding the ten core points listed earlier are addressed here, along with a wide range of commentary about many other aspects of multisource assessment and feedback. The volume and quality of work here make it clear that the pace of change is picking up, and the next few years will undoubtedly see many more changes— some of them unpredictable, especially those tied to future developments in data-processing techniques.

One can imagine, for example, a ballroom full of corporate managers all from the same company, each equipped with a palm-sized, infrared transmitter, all evaluating each other simultaneously, with the aggregate results being displayed in real time on a large screen in the front of the room, while each individual's personal results are being displayed privately on the handheld device. Other, even more extreme approaches are easy to imagine.

At the same time these new data-processing techniques are being developed, the content that is being assessed will surely also be more refined, and arguments over exactly which core competencies should be included in performance assessments will be resolved. The solutions are unlikely to be simple, since applications will undoubtedly proliferate in assessment areas that are at the moment unimaginable.

The diverse, collective efforts of the authors of the chapters in this book should help us understand not only how we arrived at where we are now but also where we are likely to go in this innovative future.

Colorado Springs, Colorado   DAVID CAMPBELL
October 2000

Preface

*Large-scale change occurs when a lot of people change
just a little.*
Unknown

A reference volume of this sort represents both a major undertaking and a significant contribution to the practice and research of feedback. No project of any worth, however, can be successfully completed without a vision of some sort. Our vision for a "handbook" of multisource feedback (MSF) originated from a number of observations of the field:

- Rapid proliferation of MSF processes is occurring amid a relative void of systematic research and discussion (Church and Bracken, 1997; Waldman, Atwater, and Antonioni, 1998).
- MSF processes are rarely evaluated from a systems perspective regarding success factors (Timmreck and Bracken, 1997).
- Other than two special journal issues (Church and Bracken, 1997; and Tornow, 1993) that focused primarily on research-related results, the literature is lacking a comprehensive review from multiple contributors engaging in feedback interventions and research that adequately captures the breadth of MSF practices, tools, and methods. The closest attempt to date has been the Tornow and London book (1998), which was authored exclusively by individuals associated with the Center for Creative Leadership—a valid but admittedly somewhat narrow perspective (Bracken, 1999).

For *The Handbook of Multisource Feedback,* we are very pleased to say that we have recruited and gained the support of a wide-ranging group of contributors from diverse backgrounds, including academics, practitioners, applied researchers, consultants, and some with backgrounds so broad as to defy classification. A primary criterion in seeking out contributors for this project was the extent to which each has made a substantive contribution to the MSF field through research, publication, or implementation. We believe strongly in the results of our efforts, and the list of contributors here clearly includes the thought leaders in the current and future practice of MSF.

Purpose

Despite its length and comprehensiveness, we must recognize that this handbook has its limitations in scope. We cannot address *all* approaches and issues found in processes that attempt to provide feedback to individuals from multiple feedback providers. In fact, we can envision an almost infinite number of permutations of methods by which that can be accomplished. Having said this, our biases are toward multiple source feedback systems applied across large segments of organizations, horizontally (for example, with supervisors), vertically (across a division or department), or some combination of each, including full-scale companywide implementations.

With this perspective in mind, our intent here is to focus on the issues surrounding designing and implementing MSF processes and, in turn, to minimize our coverage of potentially important determinants of successful feedback (however defined) determined by less systemic factors such as individual differences. We acknowledge and welcome, however, the large volume of research addressing characteristics of the rater and ratee in the feedback dyad that affect the quality and acceptance of feedback, such as personality, cultural background, race, gender, and so on. For good or bad, we view these factors as givens in large-scale MSF systems—that is, variables that we can and should acknowledge but that cannot be manipulated, changed, or even addressed in the sense of independent variables. In more individualized feedback settings (such as a one-on-one coaching or counseling situation), the implementer would probably find individual differences very useful, such as assessing the self-esteem of the recipient as an indicator of receptiveness to feedback. Such an approach is much less feasible when hundreds or thousands of feedback recipients are involved.

The purpose of this handbook is to address those variables or factors that we *can* manipulate (make informed decisions about) in designing and implementing large-scale MSF processes. Our objective, then, is to create a knowledge base for determining the consequences of these decisions, and hopefully identify best practices that increase the probability of success.

Given this broader "systems" perspective for MSF, for the purposes of the *Handbook* we have adopted as a definition of *success* "focused, sustained behavior change and/or skill improvement in a sufficient number of individuals so as to lead to increased organization effectiveness" (Bracken and Timmreck, 1999; Bracken, Timmreck, Fleenor and Summers, forthcoming). This definition is important because it helps to define the scope and purpose of the contents of this handbook by

- Implying that "focused" change is consistent with organizationally (as opposed to individually) defined objectives
- Assuming that the process is not an "event" but requires ongoing sustainability and integration to be effective (Tornow and London, 1998)
- Allowing for skill development in areas not necessarily measured by the instrument itself
- Requiring that feedback and behavior change occur within an organizational setting

Although we have not imposed any particular overriding philosophy on how such success is best accomplished (say, through using MSF for developmental rather than decision-making purposes), we have encouraged each of our contributors to provide a balanced treatment of his or her topic areas. The result, we feel, offers enough information that the reader can make his or her own conclusions about how best to use MSF tools and techniques.

Audience

Based on this perspective, it should be apparent that our intended audience is primarily practitioners: those who are charged with making decisions regarding designing and implementing MSF processes in organizational settings. We hope to extend assistance in the difficult task of weighing the pros and cons of each decision that must be made in such a complex process.

Given this primary audience, it should come as no surprise, then, that several chapters in this handbook come from internal practitioners themselves, among them offerings from Sears (Chapter Twenty-Four), Kaiser Permanente (Chapter Twenty-Five), and Shell (Chapter Ten). These chapters give us insight into the inevitable trade-offs that are inherent in MSF design and implementation. The experiences of those who are actively involved with MSF applications in their own organizations are clearly invaluable, but all too often inaccessible for a variety of reasons. Although this situation has led to formation of such consortia as the Multisource Feedback Forum (Timmreck and Bracken, 1997), where some individuals are able to share their experiences with others, we feel very fortunate to be able to offer the perspectives of these practitioners to others in the field in the context of the *Handbook*.

This type of information and shared experience is in turn supplemented by *researchers* in the field who provide systematic treatments of various methodological and instrumentation aspects of MSF that should be generalizable across multiple settings with the foundation of science and rigor. With these contributions in mind, we see the applied research community as another important audience for the *Handbook*. We hope that it serves as both a vehicle for sharing state-of-the-art thinking and an impetus for continued evolution of the future of the field in terms of practice and applied research.

A third and no less important audience for this book comprises those consultants who are in a position to make recommendations to their clients regarding design and implementation of MSF processes, or consultants who themselves engage in designing and delivering such tools and techniques for the benefit of their client organizations. As with many of the other chapters, these external practitioners are also well represented among the contributors, both as primary authors and in partnership with others (for example, academics).

Finally, we also hope that organizational clients—including the feedback sponsors and champions across leadership, management, and staff positions—are also able to make use of the contents of the *Handbook* to select, evaluate, and facilitate their work with their internal and external practitioners to better evaluate the capabilities advertised and advice being offered.

In short, this is a handbook for everyone involved in designing and implementing MSF tools, systems, and processes. One audience for which this book is not intended is the feedback participants themselves—the raters and the ratees. Specifically, we do not see this volume as a resource for recipients of feedback to help them get the most out of the process. This handbook recommends, however, how those resources can be best obtained through other sources.

MSF Terminology

Many terms have been used over the relatively short history of feedback methodology to refer to MSF processes. Perhaps most common among these is *360-degree feedback*. Although many people continue to use the term, relatively few are aware that it was actually trademarked by TEAMS International more than a decade ago. Other popular terms that have since emerged in the United States include *multirater assessment, multirater feedback, multisource assessment, full-circle feedback, upward feedback,* and various trademarked derivatives of these phrases.

In the interest of consistency, we have chosen to use the term *multisource feedback* throughout this handbook and have asked our contributors to do the same. We prefer this term multisource feedback because we feel it most accurately captures the process we are describing—that is, obtaining feedback (in whatever format) from more than one source. We prefer not to use other terms that imply inclusion of all possible feedback sources in a circle (since this is often not the case), or those connoting an evaluative rather than descriptive component (such as assessment). For ease of reference, we have also standardized on a pair of additional terms: *raters* as the providers of feedback, and *ratees* as the recipients of feedback efforts.

Lessons from Other Measurement Processes

The contributors to this handbook typically are industrial-organizational psychologists or those who have a related background by formal training or practice. This level of consistency is not by coincidence; in fact it reflects our strong bias that MSF, whether used for development or decision-making purposes, should be based on strong measurement principles. Moreover, without attention to measurement principles and concerns, such approaches are not "valid" in our opinion and are unlikely to result in success as defined above. Although the field of MSF—if it can even be called a field unto itself—is still struggling to accumulate enough research and experience to guide decision making in large-scale applications (Church and Bracken, 1997), the good news is that the applied organizational science community (including practitioners and researchers in industrial-organizational psychology, organization development, and organization behavior to name just a few of these areas) has a wealth of information in other areas that we can bring to bear on MSF processes.

As shown in Figure P.1, MSF can be viewed as having characteristics shared with three major areas of practice: assessment (for example, testing, assessment centers), performance management, and employee surveys. Each of these practice areas has considerable research and experience that can be applied to MSF, as shown in Table P.1.

Unfortunately, many MSF processes are saddled with some of the greatest challenges drawn from these three practice areas. This often results in an uncontrolled environment with a large number of feedback providers (of questionable skill and motivation) using instruments of marginal quality and spurious linkages to existing initiatives, under conditions of large-scale data collection that require 100 percent accuracy! We present this perspective on MSF as a reminder that it is not just "a test," or just "a survey," or just "feedback"; it is a complex combination of all these elements operating in a real-time environment in uncontrolled settings. We therefore expect that the reader will find the *Handbook* of most value over time after having read all or at least a cross section of the various chapters herein and having gotten a better understanding of how MSF works as a total system.

Customers of MSF

We have encouraged our contributors to make recommendations regarding MSF design and implementation, and in turn we encourage you, the reader, to make your decisions based on these

**Figure P.1. MSF as the Intersection
of Three Practice Areas.**

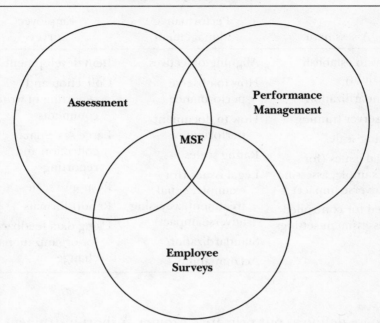

recommendations, your experience, and your situation. Amid all of this, we also strongly suggest that you consciously and deliberately consider your customers in each decision. We acknowledge that any business process ultimately has to serve constituencies such as stockholders and customers. But we also believe that a successful MSF process dutifully serves those purposes, and that success is best achieved through considering the impact and reactions of the raters, ratees, and management (and the organization as a whole as well). Bracken, Timmreck, Fleenor, and Summers (forthcoming) provide a systematic treatment of how each of these customers might differentially define success and the desirable characteristics of the process, and many of these characteristics are in direct conflict.

Let's take an example. One of the decisions in an MSF process is the length of the instrument, a decision that can be based on both science and philosophy. Part of the philosophy is a direct result of

Table P.1. Lessons Applied to MSF Design and Implementation.

Assessment	Performance Management	Employee Surveys
How to establish validity	Aligning objectives	Item development
Standardization	How to observe performance	Collection and reporting of write-in comments
Observer training	How to document performance	Large-scale data collection and reporting
Rating scales	Rating scales	
Legal issues (for example, assessing adverse impact)	Legal issues (for example, equal treatment, assessing adverse impact)	Response scales
Need for controlled assessment settings		Report formats
	Standardization	Using data feedback for organizational change
	Accountability	

who we define as our primary customer. A short instrument explicitly identifies the rater (and secondarily the organization) as the primary customer by stating that we are willing to sacrifice feedback richness in the interest of keeping the raters "happy" by making the task easy. Short also potentially equates to less time and expense. On the other hand, if the participant (ratee) is our primary customer, we should be inclined to provide feedback that is clear, specific, and comprehensive, characteristics that usually translate into longer instruments. Moreover, if the customer in this case is the senior leadership of the organization, its interest in tracking culture change over time, differentiating among higher and lower performers, or diagnosing various group differences, likely requires that certain demographic or background level data also be collected. Though common enough in practice, including such additional information can raise anxiety and suspicion regarding confidentiality of the process among raters and ratees.

In sum, we are suggesting that although you should try not to ignore any single customer group or stakeholder in a decision, usually one set of customer needs does take precedence over another.

As you make decisions based on what you read here, we suggest that you try to clearly and succinctly articulate to yourself the reason behind the MSF-related implementation and process decisions made, and the impact they have on each customer group, with the resulting effects on the success and sustainability of the total effort.

Handbook Themes

As the vision for this handbook took shape, we began with an outline of topics to cover and then identified leaders in the field to write the chapters. We were pleasantly surprised to find that, almost without exception, our authors were willing to take on our assigned topic. At the same time, we gave them considerable latitude when it came to crafting their contributions. Even though we did give each author some suggested topics to address and made suggestions during the editing phases, we purposely refrained from overtly imposing our views (and biases) on the content through editing or censoring; as a result, the *Handbook* does not have a cohesive point of view but instead presents a variety of often conflicting opinions for the reader to consider.

Given the freedom of the contributors, it is interesting to see what themes have emerged across the chapters. From our viewpoint, we suggest these are the most important themes emerging from the *Handbook:*

- *MSF is a process, not an event.* This is certainly not a new thought (Bracken and Timmreck, 1999; Church and Waclawski, 1998; Timmreck and Bracken, 1997; Tornow and London, 1998), but it is a theme taken from the abstract (Chapters One, Four, and Twenty-Two, and the Appendix) to very concrete examples regarding organizational realities (Chapters Twenty-Four and Twenty-Five), logistical challenges (Chapter Ten), user reactions (Chapter Fifteen), and organization development and change (Chapter Nineteen). Lurking within this theme is the notion of *sustainability* (Chapters Twenty-Two, Twenty-Six, Twenty-Nine, and Thirty), one of the differentiators of a process versus an event.
- *MSF is not a stand-alone process.* This theme is related to the first one; an MSF process is far more likely to be sustained if it is viewed as a business priority and integrated with other systems.

This is the central purpose of Chapter Twenty-Six, but it is also an important point in Chapters Four and Sixteen and all of Part Two.

• *Behavior change is the primary goal.* Perhaps stating this as a theme is stating the obvious, but we sense that this goal is lost in some applications of MSF. Again related to the belief that successful MSF processes are not events, some MSF processes make little or no provision for measuring behavior change. The need for behavior change is the central idea in our definition of success and further offered as the key to sustainability in Chapter Thirty. We also see behavior change addressed in terms of tools for creating and sustaining it (Chapters Fourteen and Twenty-Five) and then measuring it (Chapter Sixteen).

• *MSF as a tool for decision making.* Despite lingering resistance to using MSF in decision making (Bracken and others, 1997), many of our authors have expressed opinions as to when it is appropriate to use MSF for decisions and under what circumstances (Chapters Twenty, Twenty-One, and Twenty-Six, and the Appendix). This of course culminates in discussion of the "great debate" (Chapter Twenty-Three) and the increasingly accepted view that developmental and decision-making MSF processes can and probably should coexist.

• *The importance of rater training.* We highlight this activity as a theme because we see a substantial gap between the stated importance of rater training and its relatively rare implementation. As pointed out in the Appendix, we see rater training as an essential part of an MSF process used for decision making, closely followed by our opinion that those same guidelines improve development-only processes as well. The promise of rater training is central to Chapter Eight's treatment of improving rater performance. It is mentioned in many chapters as a desirable feature of successful MSF processes (Chapters One, Six, Seven, Eleven, Twenty, Twenty-One, Twenty-Three, Twenty-Nine, and Thirty) and arguably a legal requirement when used for decision making (Chapter Twenty-Eight).

• *MSF is grounded in measurement.* The types of MSF processes we have chosen to include in this handbook are based on data collected by questionnaires and are ultimately quantified, usually in terms of mean scores (Chapter Twelve). This quantification permits users to assess performance and skill gaps, track progress in behavior change, and make comparisons between individuals when decisions must be made. Such measurement places severe (and appropriate) pressure on the measurement process itself, a topic we asked Murphy, Cleveland, and Mohler to address directly in Chapter Nine. But measurement issues lurk in almost every phase of the process, from instrument design (Chapter Six) to rater performance (Chapter Eight), processing accuracy (Chapter Ten), the effect of technology (Chapter Eleven), and assessing impact (Chapter Sixteen). Ultimately, the measurement is no better than the quality of its use and the "decisions" made (even if only "developmental"), the subject of Part Two. Certainly there are legal issues that compel us to strive for sound measurement (Chapter Twenty-Eight), but more important, good measurement helps sustain the MSF process by generating data to support its value and creating fair and accepted decisions that users (including participants) will continue to support.

Organization of the *Handbook*

The Handbook of Multisource Feedback is organized into three major sections. Part One, "The Methodology of Multisource Feedback," addresses the nuts and bolts of MSF, that is, how to design and implement the data collection and reporting. The fact that this takes sixteen chapters should by itself speak to the complexity of this topic. Part One begins with a process model that leads the reader through sequential consideration of the various steps in a model MSF system. The rest of the first part of the book likewise uses an ordering that basically follows the same sequence. The context for Part One comes from a treatment of the history of MSF in Chapter Two. (Note also that David Campbell's Foreword contains a personalized view of the evolution of MSF.)

Part Two, "Applications of Multisource Feedback," reinforces our view that MSF is nothing more than a parlor game unless it is used to create behavior change. Five of the chapters in this part look at various "uses" of MSF, both developmental and decision making, drawn together with a concluding chapter on the "great debate" between the development-only and decision-making forces.

Systems forces operating to influence MSF processes are covered in Part Three (as foreshadowed in Chapter Four's acknowledgment of the importance of context). Part Three begins with perspectives offered by internal consultants in Sears and Kaiser Permanente, case studies addressing the realities that organizations impose on MSF practitioners. The remaining chapters in this section consider topics that permeate the entire MSF process and therefore should be considered at every step and with every decision made in design and implementation.

The *Handbook* closes with "Guidelines for Multisource Feedback When Used for Decision Making." These guidelines were a product of the Multisource Feedback Forum, a consortium of organizations having ongoing MSF processes, and were published in an earlier form in the *Industrial-Organizational Psychologist* (Bracken and Timmreck, 1999). Since that publication, we have continued to receive feedback and suggestions, and the version here reflects this input. The guidelines present best practices based on research and experience and are offered as a source for decision making during design and implementation. For those readers interested in additional rationale behind the guidelines, we refer you to Bracken, Timmreck, Fleenor, and Summers (forthcoming).

Although the *Handbook* contains a great deal of information, as the editors of this rather large volume (thirty chapters) we would like to point out that perhaps one should not feel *compelled* to read the entire contents straight through. Rather, we expect many readers to turn to the specific chapters or groups of chapters that are most relevant to their concerns or areas of interest. Along with the Index and the Table of Contents, information in many chapters takes the form of cross-references that should facilitate this process as well.

On the other hand, as editors we would also feel remiss in not encouraging our readers to at least peruse the entire volume. Moreover, given that one of the major themes of the *Handbook* is that MSF is indeed a process (a system), we expect that the reader will find it difficult to get a full perspective on a given topic without reading multiple chapters, and ideally the entire *Handbook*.

Summary

One of our frustrations has been in getting this book published before the information becomes obsolete; such is the nature of the publication process. With the help of our contributors and publisher, we hope to give our audience a resource that reflects the most up-to-date and progressive practices and thinking in this field.

This handbook is offered in the spirit of problem solving. Every MSF process has problems to be solved, but we believe that every problem has solutions. Part of what we offer here is a set of ways to diagnose your situation and choose from the many alternatives available to you, hopefully learning from the experience and expertise of others and applying it so that it works for your organization. As we have noted in other forums (Church and Bracken, 1997; Timmreck and Bracken, 1997), not every MSF process succeeds, and in some cases deservedly so. This has sometimes created a kind of pessimism whereby organizations are unwilling to venture into large-scale MSF implementations because of this fear of failure. We believe that MSF can succeed *under the right conditions,* and this book is dedicated to the proposition that it is possible to create those conditions and realize major benefits to the participants and the organization as a whole.

We hope that you the reader will find the contents of this handbook to be informative, stimulating, and helpful in your present and future work with MSF. Good luck; we hope to hear from you with your future experiences as we continue to learn how to make this powerful process even better.

October 2000

DAVID W. BRACKEN
New York, New York

CAROL W. TIMMRECK
Houston, Texas

ALLAN H. CHURCH
Pelham, New York

References

Bracken, D. W. "Review of *Maximizing the Value of 360-Degree Feedback.*" *Personnel Psychology,* 1999, *51,* 734–738.

Bracken, D. W., and Timmreck, C. W. "Guidelines for Multisource Feedback When Used for Decision Making." *Industrial-Organizational Psychologist,* 1999, *36*(4), 64–74.

Bracken, D. W., Timmreck, C. W., Fleenor, J. W., and Summers, L. "360 Feedback from Another Angle." *Human Resource Management Journal,* forthcoming.

Bracken, D. W., and others. *Should 360-Degree Feedback Be Used Only for Developmental Purposes?* Greensboro, N.C.: Center for Creative Leadership, 1997.

Church, A. H., and Bracken, D. W. "Advancing the State of the Art of 360-Degree Feedback: Guest Editors' Comments on the Research and Practice of Multirater Assessment Methods." *Group and Organization Management,* 1997, *22*(2), 149–161.

Church, A. H., and Waclawski, J. "Making Multirater Feedback Systems Work." *Quality Progress,* 1998, *31*(4), 81–89.

Timmreck, C. W., and Bracken, D. W. "Multisource Feedback: A Study of Its Use for Decision Making." *Employment Relations Today,* 1997, *24*(1), 21–27.

Tornow, W. W. "Editor's Note: Introduction to Special Issue on 360-Degree Feedback." *Human Resource Management,* 1993, *32*(2–3), 211–219.

Tornow, W. W., and London, M. (eds.). *Maximizing the Value of 360-Degree Feedback: A Process for Individual and Organizational Development.* San Francisco: Jossey-Bass, 1998.

Waldman, D. A., Atwater, L. E., and Antonioni, D. "Has 360-Degree Feedback Gone Amok?" *Academy of Management Executive,* 1998, *12*(20), 86–94.

The Contributors

DAVID W. BRACKEN is director of research consulting for Mercer Delta Consulting LLC in New York City. His prior work associations include Xerox, BellSouth, Towers Perrin, William M. Mercer, and dwbassessments, inc. Bracken has more than twenty years of corporate and consulting experience and is regarded as an authority in the use of multisource feedback for decision making. He received his B.A. degree from Dartmouth College and his M.S. and Ph.D. degrees in industrial/organizational psychology from Georgia Tech. Bracken is a licensed psychologist in Georgia.

CAROL W. TIMMRECK is an organizational consultant at Shell Oil, where she has been responsible for development and annual implementation of multisource feedback processes for nearly all of Shell's U.S. managers. She cofounded and cofacilitates the Multisource Feedback Forum, a consortium of large companies with active MSF processes. She has addressed numerous national audiences on the topic of multisource feedback. She received her Ph.D. degree in industrial/organizational psychology from the University of Houston and is a licensed psychologist in the state of Texas.

ALLAN H. CHURCH is a principal consultant in management consulting services at PricewaterhouseCoopers, LLP. He specializes in designing multisource feedback systems and organization surveys for change. He is also an adjunct professor at Columbia University, where he teaches these applications. Previously, he was employed for nine years at W. Warner Burke Associates, Inc., and three years at IBM in the personnel research and communications research departments. He received his Ph.D. in organizational psychology from Columbia University. He has published more than one hundred articles, many book chapters, and a recent book, coauthored with Janine Waclawski, titled *Designing and Using Organizational Surveys*. He is also the editor of the *Industrial-Organizational Psychologist* and the *Organization Development Journal*.

David Antonioni is an associate professor of management at the University of Wisconsin-Madison and chair of executive education with the School of Business. He has designed, implemented, and evaluated a model for multisource feedback, which has been adapted by Andersen Consulting. He consults with companies on MSF, and his research is published in a variety of journals.

Leanne E. Atwater is an associate professor of management at Arizona State University West. She has authored twenty-five journal publications, one of which, "Has 360-Degree Feedback Gone Amok?" won best paper award for 1998 in the *Academy of Management Executive*. She is also president of Atwater Management Consulting.

H. John Bernardin is the University Research Professor at Florida Atlantic University in Boca Raton, Florida. He received his Ph.D. in industrial/organizational psychology from Bowling Green State University. He is the former editor of *Human Resource Management Review* and has written or edited seven books and more than fifty articles on performance management.

Scott A. Birkeland is a research associate at Personnel Decisions Research Institutes and a doctoral student at the University of South Florida in industrial/organizational psychology. His applied experience includes developing and delivering assessment simulations and exercises, managerial coaching and training, and quantitative data analysis. His research focuses on assessment procedures for leadership development.

Walter C. Borman is chief executive officer of Personnel Decisions Research Institutes and professor of psychology at the University of South Florida. He is a fellow of the Society for Industrial and Organizational Psychology and a past president as well. He has more than 250 publications, including books, articles, chapters, papers, and technical reports on such topics as performance appraisal and selection.

Stéphane Brutus is an assistant professor of management at Concordia University in Montreal. After obtaining a Ph.D. in industrial/organizational psychology from Bowling Green State University, he completed a postdoctoral fellowship at the Center for Creative Leadership in Greensboro, North Carolina.

W. Warner Burke is professor of psychology and education and chair of the Department of Organization and Leadership at Teachers College, Columbia University. He has authored more than one hundred articles and book chapters, and thirteen books. His Ph.D. is from the University of Texas, Austin. He has been working in the field of organization development for more than thirty-five years.

Jeanette N. Cleveland is a professor of psychology at Pennsylvania State University. She has served on the editorial boards of numerous journals, including the *Academy of Management Journal, Journal of Applied Psychology,* and *Journal of Organizational Behavior,* and has published extensively in the areas of performance appraisal and diversity at work.

Victoria B. Crawshaw is director of performance and development processes at Sears. She earned her B.A. from Knox College in Galesburg, Illinois, and Ph.D. in industrial psychology from the University of Illinois, Chicago. She has been with Sears since 1994 and designs and manages the company's performance management and executive development processes.

Anthony T. Dalessio is an industrial/organizational psychologist in the IBM Global Employee Research department. He has been a senior specialist at Bell Atlantic, a director at LIMRA International, and a consultant to NASA. He is on the editorial board of *Personnel Psychology.* He received his Ph.D. from Bowling Green State University.

Maxine A. Dalton is director of global leadership research at the Center for Creative Leadership. She has used MSF surveys with groups and individuals in developmental programs conducted throughout the world. Her Ph.D. is in industrial psychology from the University of South Florida.

Mark R. Edwards serves as chief executive officer of TEAMS International, an automated assessment technology firm. He is also a professor at Arizona State University. His research focuses on small-sample metrics for measuring human performance. He has authored more than one hundred articles along with several books and has won numerous awards for teaching, speaking, writing, and innovative technologies.

Ann J. Ewen is CEO of Whitehat.com, a global high-tech direct marketing firm. She has worked with executives around the world on initiatives to enhance individual, team, and organizational performance. She has taught at Arizona State University, is widely published, and has won numerous awards for executive leadership and technology excellence. Her research interests include performance improvement, advanced technologies, diversity fairness, and community.

James L. Farr is professor of industrial/organizational psychology at Pennsylvania State University, having received his Ph.D. from the University of Maryland. A former president of the Society for Industrial and Organizational Psychology, he has been a visiting professor at Sheffield University, University of Western Australia, and Chinese University of Hong Kong.

John W. Fleenor is currently director of knowledge management at the Center for Creative Leadership. Formerly the head of the Center's research program on multisource feedback, he is coauthor of three books and numerous articles on MSF. His Ph.D. in industrial/organizational psychology is from North Carolina State University.

Marshall Goldsmith, founding director of Keilty, Goldsmith & Co., is one of the world's foremost authorities on helping leaders change behavior. He has been asked to work with more than fifty CEOs. He is coeditor of *The Leader of the Future* and *Leading Beyond the Walls.* He has been ranked as one of the top ten leadership consultants by the *Wall Street Journal.*

Glenn Hallam heads Creative Metrics, which creates unique measurement tools for high-tech companies. While at the Center for

Creative Leadership, he coauthored the Campbell-Hallam Team Leader Profile and Campbell-Hallam Team Development Survey. He holds a Ph.D. in industrial/organizational psychology (University of Minnesota) and B.A. in psychology (Stanford University).

Michael M. Harris is professor of management at the University of Missouri-St. Louis, College of Business Administration. He has written numerous book chapters and articles on performance management and assessment. He recently coedited the *Employment Interview Handbook* and is currently under contract to write a book on employee staffing.

Sally F. Hartmann is vice president, human resource planning and executive development at Sears, where she has worked since 1984. She holds a Ph.D. in industrial psychology from the University of Illinois, Chicago. Her team is accountable for selection, performance review, MSF, attitude surveys, succession planning, and executive development. She has been a member of the Society for Industrial and Organizational Psychology since 1984.

Jerry W. Hedge is president of Personnel Decisions Research Institutes. He is a fellow of the Society for Industrial and Organizational Psychology and the American Psychological Association. He received his Ph.D. in industrial/organizational psychology in 1982 from Old Dominion University. He has published extensively in the scientific literature and regularly presents at professional conferences.

Laura Heft is the manager of management and organizational development for the Anheuser-Busch Packaging Group, providing services that include coaching and development, MSF, organizational surveys, competency model development, team development, and training design and delivery. She received her Ph.D. in industrial/organizational psychology from the University of Missouri, St. Louis.

Mary Dee Hicks, formerly a senior vice president at Personnel Decisions International and member of the executive services team, has specialized in developing talent in organizations. She has written and spoken extensively on coaching and learning, coauthoring (with David B. Peterson) two books on the topic.

George P. Hollenbeck is an industrial/organizational psychologist specializing in leadership development. He has worked at IBM, the Psychological Corporation, Fidelity Investments, Harvard Business School, and as a human resources executive at Merrill Lynch. Based in Texas, he consults with individual executives, writes, and teaches about leadership.

Robert A. Jako is a consultant for Mercer Delta Consulting. He received his B.A. degree from the University of California, Berkeley, and his M.S. and Ph.D. degrees from Colorado State. He has held faculty positions at the University of Nebraska, Omaha, and the University of California, Berkeley, and senior positions in assessment and leadership development at Kaiser Permanente.

Richard Lepsinger, managing vice president of Right Manus and coauthor of *The Art and Science of 360-Degree Feedback* and *The Art and Science of Competency Models,* has been a management consultant for more than twenty years. He has extensive experience developing and implementing business strategy, assessment systems, and large-scale management simulations.

Jean Brittain Leslie is the manager of instrument development research and instructor of the Benchmarks Certification Workshop at the Center for Creative Leadership. She also manages translations of CCL instruments into other languages and their psychometric evaluations. She has an M.A. in sociology from the University of North Carolina at Greensboro.

Manuel London is director of the Center for Human Resource Management at the Harriman School for Management at the State University of New York, Stony Brook. His recent books are *Job Feedback* and *Maximizing the Value of 360-Degree Feedback* (coedited with Walter W. Tornow and published by Jossey-Bass, 1998).

Anntoinette D. Lucia, managing vice president of Right Manus and coauthor of *The Art and Science of 360-Degree Feedback* and *The Art and Science of Competency Models,* specializes in using feedback systems to help individual executives improve their effectiveness, facilitating strategic organizational change, and linking human resource plans to strategic plans.

Dana McDonald-Mann is a senior consultant at Data Decisions International. Prior to joining DDI, she managed Benchmarks, a 360-degree executive instrument, at the Center for Creative Leadership. She managed the first major content revision of the instrument and facilitated assessment-related workshops and feedback sessions for executives. She has also worked with senior executives on four continents.

Carolyn J. Mohler is a graduate student at Colorado State University. She is pursuing a joint Ph.D. in counseling and industrial/organizational psychology. She has conducted research on performance appraisal rating, multisource feedback, rater goals, and organizational support. Her other interests include reactions to feedback following individual assessment and coaching.

Kevin R. Murphy is a professor of psychology at Pennsylvania State University. He is the editor of the *Journal of Applied Psychology* and past president of the Society for Industrial and Organizational Psychology. He has published papers, chapters, and books in the areas of performance appraisal, psychological measurement, statistics, and gender and work.

Daniel A. Newman is a Ph.D. candidate in psychology at Pennsylvania State University. He received his B.A. in psychology from Rice University. His research interests include organizational and personal development, data analysis, and research methods.

David B. Peterson is senior vice president and worldwide practice leader for coaching services at Personnel Decisions International. Coauthor of two best-selling books, *Development FIRST* and *Leader as Coach,* he provides executive coaching and consultation for organizations seeking to create greater strategic advantage through faster learning and better people development.

Steven G. Rogelberg is an associate professor of industrial/organizational psychology at Bowling Green State University and the director of the Institute for Psychological Research and Application. He has published more than twenty-five articles and book chapters addressing issues such as survey design and measurement, team effectiveness, and employee morale and attitudes.

James W. Smither is a professor in the Management Department at La Salle University. He received his Ph.D. in industrial/organizational psychology from Stevens Institute of Technology. He is associate editor of *Personnel Psychology*. He worked previously in corporate human resources for AT&T and continues to consult for many large corporations.

Jeffrey D. Stoner is director of Multi-Rater Solutions for Personnel Decisions. His role as product developer, business developer, and consultant affords him the opportunity to apply his fifteen-plus years of broad human resource experience to developing high-impact development solutions for clients who use multirater feedback and assessment processes.

Lynn Summers is cofounder of Performaworks, an outsource provider of Web-based performance management services. A graduate of the University of South Florida's industrial/organizational psychology program, he has served as staff psychologist at Baltimore Gas & Electric, vice president of training at Hardee's Food Systems, head of the human resource program at Peace College, and book review editor of *Personnel Psychology*.

Carol Paradise Tornow is an adjunct staff member at the Center for Creative Leadership and consulting partner with the Tornow Partnership. She received her doctorate in industrial/organizational psychology from the University of Minnesota. She taught business strategy and continues to maintain a consulting practice in the areas of strategic management and human resource planning.

Walter W. Tornow most recently was a senior fellow and vice president at the Center for Creative Leadership. He received his Ph.D. in industrial/organizational psychology from the University of Minnesota. He has extensive applied research, consulting, teaching, and management experience and has published widely. He recently coedited, with Manuel London, *Maximizing the Value of 360-Degree Feedback* (Jossey-Bass, 1998).

Catherine L. Tyler is a doctoral student at Florida Atlantic University. Her research interests include performance appraisal, team development, and international human resources. Published works include book chapters on ethics in supervision and performance appraisal training. She has also presented works at national and international conferences.

Brian O. Underhill, senior consultant with Keilty, Goldsmith & Co., specializes in leadership development and MSF, executive coaching, and organizational culture. He develops leadership competency models and supporting multisource inventories for major organizations. His clients have included AT&T, Johnson & Johnson, Sun Microsystems, and U.S. West Wireless.

Ellen Van Velsor is group director of core research and development at the Center for Creative Leadership. She is coauthor of *Breaking the Glass Ceiling,* coeditor of the *Center for Creative Leadership Handbook of Leadership Development* (Jossey-Bass, 1998), and author of numerous other articles and reports. She holds an M.A. and Ph.D. in sociology from the University of Florida.

Nicholas L. Vasilopoulos is an assistant professor of psychology at George Washington University. He earned his Ph.D. from Stevens Institute of Technology. He has been a personnel researcher at the U.S. Immigration and Naturalization Service, where he developed entry-level and promotional assessment systems. He has coauthored articles on upward feedback and assessment.

Kiran Vendantam is a graduate student at Arizona State University, where he focuses on computer science and assessment technologies. He has conducted extensive research on automated software and innovated with advanced techniques to analyze MSF performance distributions across a variety of projects. He has also authored papers on international agribusiness policy for the USDA.

Janine Waclawski is a principal consultant in management consulting services at PricewaterhouseCoopers, LLP, and an adjunct professor at Columbia University. She previously was employed at W. Warner Burke Associates, Inc., and IBM. She received her B.A. in psychology from the State University of New York, Stony Brook, and her Ph.D. from Columbia University. She specializes in using surveys and MSF for organizational change and executive development.

David A. Waldman is a professor of management at Arizona State University West and affiliated faculty member of the Department of Management at Arizona State University Main. He has published more than sixty articles and book chapters, and a recent book (coauthored with Leanne E. Atwater) on MSF. Accomplishments include Fellow status in the Society for Industrial and Organizational Psychology.

Alan G. Walker is manager of personnel research for First Tennessee National Corporation, headquartered in Memphis. He received his M.A. in industrial/organizational psychology from Western Kentucky University. He was hired by First Tennessee in 1992 to develop, implement, and manage their upward-feedback, 360-degree, and employee opinion survey programs.

Tom Wentworth is president of Compendium, a multinational company providing processing and reporting services for multisource, employee, and customer assessments, and performance management systems in all paper and electronic media. Services are offered to corporations and consulting organizations, with multisource projects consisting of several participants to tens of thousands.

Alicia J. Winckler is the manager of testing and selection processes at Sears. She earned her M.A. in industrial psychology from the University of Colorado at Denver. Until recently, she managed MSF for Sears. Prior to Sears, she worked as a project manager for HR Avantis.

David J. Woehr is an associate professor of management at the University of Tennessee. He received his Ph.D. in industrial/organizational psychology from the Georgia Institute of Technology. His research on job performance measurement, work-related attitudes and behavior, training development, and quantitative methods has appeared in a variety of journals and as papers presented at professional meetings.

Francis J. Yammarino is professor of management and Fellow of the Center for Leadership Studies at the State University of New York, Binghamton. He earned his Ph.D. at the State University of New York, Buffalo. His research and consulting interests include superior-subordinate relationships, leadership, self-other agreement processes, and multiple levels of analysis issues.

The Handbook of
Multisource Feedback

The Methodology of Multisource Feedback

CHAPTER 1

Introduction
A Multisource Feedback Process Model

David W. Bracken
Carol W. Timmreck
Allan H. Church

In planning, organizing, and editing the contents of *The Handbook of Multisource Feedback,* we discovered that it would be very helpful if we had a normative model or framework to characterize the various steps in the types of multisource feedback (MSF) processes explored in this volume and in practice. Since we were unable to identify an existing model or framework of MSF that encompassed all of the variables we were interested in exploring, in true scientist-practitioner fashion we created one ourselves! After a number of iterations, thoughtful exchanges, occasionally heated debates, and initial presentations to other practitioners and colleagues, the culmination of this developmental effort was the Process Model of Multisource Feedback presented in Figure 1.1.

Although the model was certainly meaningful for us as editors, others (practitioners, academics, consultants, and clients of MSF systems) may find this model helpful as well when making use of certain chapters in the *Handbook* or when working with their own internal or external feedback processes. We think the model illustrates well the many elements, critical factors, and interdependences involved in most (if not all) MSF systems. As with most well-constructed frameworks, inherent in this model are several of

Figure 1.1. A Process Model of Multisource Feedback.

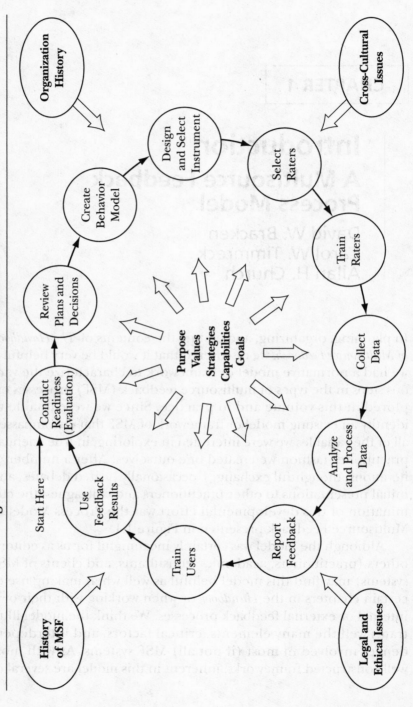

our core assumptions about MSF processes, which we hope will guide practice.

Using the Process Model of MSF

Aside from being a useful tool for thinking about MSF in general, the model is also intended to serve as a helpful framing mechanism for the contents of this handbook. Here is a brief description of how each of the various chapters in this work correspond or link to various elements in the model.

Conducting Readiness (Evaluation)

Note first that we conceptualize the entire MSF process as cyclical, that is, as a *repeating cycle,* consistent with our definition of *success* (see the Preface), which requires that the feedback process be sustained and repeated. This means that one cycle through the entire model represents *only* one administration of implementation of the feedback process. Although each step is clearly important in its own right and should be examined carefully by those individuals responsible for implementing the process, it is important to recognize that in repeated administrations certain steps may be minimized or perhaps even skipped entirely (for example, create behavior model, design or select instrument, train raters, etc.) if they are no longer needed or of less importance at that juncture in the MSF cycle.

We begin the very first cycle with an examination of readiness (Chapter Three). In future iterations, the notion of readiness is likely to be replaced by evaluation, that is, an examination of success and whether the MSF process can be repeated with or without modifications (Chapters Fifteen and Sixteen). Either way, however, the importance of some type of assessment regarding the MSF process itself (whether for readiness or for gauging success of an earlier iteration) is a critical step that is often missing in many MSF applications, as well as in many other types of organizational initiatives.

Clearly, not every organization is ready to begin (or should repeat) an MSF process. MSF "happens" within the context of the entire organization, which includes not only the prevailing culture, leadership, structure, mission and strategy, and existing development and performance management systems but also the cumulative history of the organization. All of these factors can serve to either help or hinder the process and thus need to be assessed or at least formally recognized at some level.

Planning and Decision Review

MSF processes (as covered in this handbook) are typically of such large scope, visibility, impact, and expense that they require very deliberate and well-communicated planning and decision-making efforts to support their implementation (this is highlighted in Chapters Three and Twenty-Four). We believe that the most important decision involved in establishing (or maintaining) an MSF process is to set the *purpose* of the effort, or more specifically, how the feedback data are used by the organization. This decision has an impact on almost every other aspect of the MSF process both initially and over time (Bracken, 1996). Thus, purpose is listed in the very center of the entire process model in Figure 1.1. Chapters Seventeen through Twenty-Two, Chapter Twenty-Six, and the Appendix detail a number of (sometimes competing) perspectives and approaches to the purposes and uses of MSF processes.

Behavioral Model Development

Another explicit assumption of our framework is that successful MSF processes must be based on a solid behavioral model. Such models may have components derived from many organizational sources (among them competencies, values, principles, practices, objectives, etc.) and may often have been created initially by an organization for purposes other than MSF, but the model used to guide MSF applications must meet two conditions. First, it must be aligned with organization objectives and strategies, that is, be valid and demonstrate linkages (Chapter Four). Second, it must consist of measurable behaviors that can be easily (and reliably) observed and assessed, meaning not those that represent inherent traits or complex or loosely defined concepts (Chapters Five and Six).

Instrument Development

Given some of our earlier comments regarding successful MSF efforts, we feel strongly that feedback data must be generated primarily from some type of instrumentation or questionnaire. Typically, such an instrument includes a combination of multiple-choice response items and short-answer or write-in comments. Whether based on a standard tool or custom-designed measure, since the data collected can only be as good as the questions asked, in this context solid instrument design and selection become the sine qua non of successful MSF processes. Chapters Five and Six are devoted specifically to the issues involved in selecting, developing, and evaluating good behaviorally based instrumentation for use in MSF applications.

Selecting Raters

When designing and implementing MSF processes, a number of important decisions regarding rater selection are required, among them who selects (and approves) the raters, what types of raters are appropriate for a given context, and how many raters should be selected. For example, if a manager has twenty direct reports and wants to receive some feedback, should data be collected from all twenty of these people, some randomized portion (say, five), or a particular subset selected specifically to highlight maximum variability (or perhaps maximum consistency) in the responses obtained? These are important questions that need to be answered in the context of the purpose. Decisions regarding rater selection, of course, also affect the design of the instrument, the method and process of implementation (for example, rater training and data collection), the complexity of analysis, and the nature of the reporting. Chapters Seven, Eleven, and Twelve address some of these issues and concerns in more detail.

Training Raters

It surprises us somewhat to note that although the potential benefit of rater training has typically been considered in the context of performance appraisal, it has actually been severely neglected in the context of MSF. Often rater training in developmental feedback efforts is simply written off as being too "impractical" or costly. This is particularly true with organizations that are designing new MSF systems and eager to initiate the process and start collecting feedback right away. Despite these barriers, we would challenge any researcher who studies and reports on the inherent "problems" with MSF (for instance, regarding rater honesty, response rates, or the arguments for and against using MSF for decision-making purposes) to consider the impact of rater training first as a partial solution before rejecting arguments of "practicality." A more balanced analysis of the impact of such training (and how it should best be delivered) is needed before comparing the potential costs and benefits of MSF as a larger process. Many of these issues are discussed directly in Chapter Eight and (as noted in the Preface) mentioned in numerous other chapters as well.

Collecting Feedback

The challenges of collecting the feedback using questionnaire formats has a long history, derived largely from employee surveys using external consulting firms or data-processing vendors (as reported in Chapter Ten). Although many organizations continue to use the more traditional and familiar methods of data collection (optical scan forms, paper-and-pencil questionnaires), there are now a range of exciting opportunities and options made potentially available through emerging technologies. As with organizational survey efforts, some of these technologies are disk-based, intranet, Internet, and even automated voice-response systems. Chapter Eleven is a detailed discussion of one new type of application that is growing in popularity and utility: Web-based data systems.

Data Processing

Actual processing and reporting of data, particularly in the volume typically required for large-scale MSF applications, is an important step in the cycle with its own set of unique challenges and complexities (just imagine the forms and coordination needed for oneself, five direct reports, five peers, one supervisor, five external clients, and five internal customers for a small company with, say, only five thousand managers). Our bias in this area is to use external resources (who may serve as MSF consultants or vendors) to play this role from the twin perspectives of data management and analysis expertise as well as the impact of such efforts on the perceived and real confidentiality and security of the highly sensitive data that are collected. Chapters Ten and Eleven discuss these issues in more detail.

Feedback of Results

Although making a feedback report may seem simple at first, as many first-time feedback practitioners have discovered this part of the process also has its own set of issues and complexities. Decisions made here can have major implications for the technology, logistics, and recipient (or user) receptivity when delivering results. Thus, it is very important to consider the specific needs of the individuals involved when planning this stage of the process. As noted earlier, the sheer volume of reports itself can be overwhelming, coupled with the requirement for 100 percent accuracy. At the same time, each report has a user (in some cases more than one) who has to be able to understand, interpret, and, most important, apply the results for the purpose (or purposes) for which the data were intended. Thus, it is important to always attend to finding the right balance, for a given set of users, between too much information and specificity on the one hand and ease of use and interpretability on the other (see Chapter Twelve).

In short, even if an MSF process is conducted for all the right reasons and is based on a good behavioral model, with appropriately trained raters and excellent instrumentation and administration methods, the process may still ultimately fail thanks to poor reporting. For example, if the report itself is uninterpretable by the user (the focal manager or feedback recipient), behavior change or skill development is extremely unlikely. The process simply cannot be successful where poor preparation and delivery of results are involved. Chapters Ten through Thirteen and Twenty-Five reflect some of the issues involved here.

Feedback Applied

To use a medical metaphor, we would argue that implementing an MSF process in an organization without a clear understanding of the intent in application (because it is the current management consulting fad, or because the competition is doing it) is akin to giving a prescription to a patient simply because it is for a popular drug. Both examples amount to a case of professional malpractice for not having done a proper diagnosis of the situation. Moreover, we would also argue that giving a diagnosis without a prescription— that is, saying feedback is needed without actually implementing it successfully—is irresponsible at best. Regardless of the purpose of MSF efforts, practitioners and consultants need to ensure that the feedback is used accurately and consistently, and aligned with organizational objectives and existing initiatives and systems. Chapters Fourteen, Seventeen through Twenty-Two, Twenty-Four, and Twenty-Five describe conditions and examples of how the process should work.

Evaluation

As noted earlier, it is our firm belief that every organizational intervention, whether large or small, should be formally evaluated for its degree of impact, and MSF systems are no exception. Evaluation in this context can reflect two separate but related realms.

One area is *impact:* Has the process achieved the desired results (such as significant behavior change, culture change, identification of useful information for personnel decision making, or performance improvement)? Two perspectives on the type of impact are relevant here. One treats behavior change as an independent variable, attempting to link it to some higher-order outcome (revenue, customer satisfaction, reduced turnover) under the umbrella of increased organization effectiveness (Chapter Sixteen). The other perspective treats behavior change as a dependent variable, asserting that MSF feedback can be used as a performance measure, and that individuals who exhibit more of the desired behaviors (for instance, values) are by definition successful (Byham and Moyer, 1998). Either way, these outcomes need to be formally articulated and ultimately assessed.

The second area or type of evaluation concerns the elements of the MSF system itself, which is to say, the *process*. Here the evaluation question concerns the quality, utility, and appropriateness of the goals, measures, communications, data-collection and analysis methods, rater training, reports, and applications (Chapter Fifteen). In other words, this is equivalent to an overall evaluation of attention to (and quality of) each of the elements described in the MSF process model in Figure 1.1.

MSF System Forces

As noted in the Preface, one of our core assumptions regarding MSF is the need to think in systems terms. It is always important to remember that MSF processes operate in real time with real people, and every decision made along the implementation path has iterative implications for multiple aspects of the MSF process. Most if not all of these decisions have the potential to make or break the success of the entire effort. The content of Chapters Nineteen, Twenty-Four, Twenty-Five, and Thirty and the Appendix reflect this systemic orientation to implementing MSF efforts. Our framework, as depicted in Figure 1.1, explicitly acknowledges the existence of several categories of forces that define the context in which the feedback process operates. We discuss the categories next.

Core Context

At the core of our model are several framing forces. The criticality of having a clear purpose for MSF applications has already been described earlier in this chapter. Additionally, organization values, strategies, and goals serve to frame and guide both the process and the content of MSF (Chapter Four). This alignment occurs either explicitly, when the process and content are designed to model and capture the letter or the spirit of espoused values and defined strategies, or implicitly, when the process as implemented reflects a given set of organization values, goals, or strategies. Chapters Nineteen and Twenty-Six address these issues in particular. In addition, organizational capabilities (Stalk, Evans, and Shulman, 1992) are also included as part of the core content here because these represent the larger strategic processes by which organizations design, deliver, and commit to their own success (Chapters Four, Six, Twenty-Four, and Twenty-Five).

Organization History

Every organization (and every organization member) has a history. These cumulative experiences, icons, and memories represent part of the fundamental underlying nature of an organization. The impact of history is indelibly stamped on the organization's culture, its systems and procedures, its leadership, and the way it manages change and complexity. There should be no surprise then, that history—what has gone before—can create both opportunities and significant barriers for MSF implementations as well (Bracken, Timmreck, Fleenor, and Summers, forthcoming). For example, prior experiences with failed organizational change or restructuring initiatives, poor survey or failed MSF efforts, breaches in confidentiality, lack of trust in management, and a whole host of other baggage can represent significant hurdles beyond those associated with designing the MSF process itself. Chapters Three and Twenty-Nine describe how such issues might be confronted.

Cross-Cultural Issues

Given the global nature of most large organizations today and the trend toward greater consolidation vis-à-vis megamergers and acquisitions, the potential impact of cross-cultural differences on MSF applications must also be taken into account. Organizations (and their members) typically operate in one or more cultures or parts of the world, and this fact have significant implications for the purpose of the effort, the type and acceptability of the instrumentation and method of data collection used, the necessity and perceived importance of rater training, and the overall degree of impact that might be expected. In some European countries, for example, it is often deemed inappropriate to ask clients for their feedback, and cultural effects are emerging even at the response rate level (Church, Rogelberg, and Waclawski, 2000). Chapter Twenty-Seven focuses on a number of these issues in more detail. If organizations are to truly incorporate MSF as a systemic process however—that is, throughout the entire organization—these issues must be identified and subsequently incorporated into the development and planning process.

Legal and Ethical Issues

Other aspects of the systemic context of MSF include both the legal environment and the ethical issues involved in collecting sensitive data and reporting back to individuals. Even though MSF applications have not yet been the primary target of many legislative decisions, litigation on performance appraisal suggests some guidance, and the future of work in this area is rapidly emerging in such outlets as the *Industrial-Organizational Psychologist* (for example, Gutman, 2000). Chapter Twenty-Eight concerns the current legal aspects of MSF processes and the possible future that may be in store for MSF applications.

History of MSF

Finally, no exploration of a process or field as complex and multifaceted as MSF would be complete without a clear understanding and review of its theoretical and historical origins. Although not necessarily a large contributor to the current application of MSF systems and processes, the values, norms, methods, and assumptions of such MSF systems are clearly based in a variety of fields, perspectives, and early research into organizational life. Chapter Two gives a thorough and well-documented overview of the history of MSF, which helps set the context and explain, at least in part, why practice and research in the field are so varied today. For example, the ongoing debate (even in this handbook; see Chapter Twenty-Three) on development only versus decision making in MSF stems in large part from the multiple influences and philosophical heritages.

Conclusion

In conclusion, it is our hope and intention that this model of MSF as a process helps serve as a lasting contribution to the field, one that assists both the readers of this handbook as well as practitioners, researchers, and managers in thinking about the complexities involved in implementing successful MSF systems. If the reader finds this model useful, then we have done our jobs as editors well.

References

Bracken, D. W. "Multisource (360-Degree) Feedback: Surveys for Individual and Organizational Development." In A. I. Kraut (ed.), *Organizational Surveys: Tools for Assessment and Change*. San Francisco: Jossey-Bass, 1996.

Bracken, D. W., Timmreck, C. W., Fleenor, J. W., and Summers, L. "Another Angle on 360-Degree Feedback." *Human Resource Management*, forthcoming.

Byham, W. C., and Moyer, R. P. *Using Competencies to Build a Successful Organization*. Pittsburgh, Pa.: Development Dimensions International, 1998.

Church, A. H., Rogelberg, S. G., and Waclawski, J. "Since When Is No News Good News? The Relationship Between Performance and Response Rates in Multirater Feedback." *Personnel Psychology*, 2000, *53*, 435–451.

Gutman, A. "Recent Supreme Court ADA Rulings: Mixed Messages from the Court." *Industrial-Organizational Psychologist*, 2000, *37*(3), 31–41.

Stalk, G., Evans, P., and Shulman, L. "Competing on Capabilities: The New Rules of Corporate Strategy." *Harvard Business Review*, Mar.–Apr. 1992, pp. 57–69.

CHAPTER 2

History and Development of Multisource Feedback as a Methodology

Jerry W. Hedge
Walter C. Borman
Scott A. Birkeland

Although the 1990s saw the burgeoning popularity of the multisource feedback (MSF) "movement," with its widespread visibility in the workplace, the methodology did not gain its popular status overnight. Rather, the origins can be traced back to the turn of the century. In this chapter, we examine one hundred years of ratings research and follow the evolution of the multisource perspective across industry, academic, and public sector environments.

Starting with the early days of rating-scale development, we follow accumulating evidence for the use of ratings in the private sector, across two world wars, and the explosion of research and application in the business world and government research laboratories. We also note the infusion of innovative thinking from the teacher-effectiveness research literature, and survey-based research and feedback domains. We then describe how the tenor of the times during the 1980s and early 1990s helped create the impetus for the multisource, or 360-degree, feedback movement. We close with some reflections on where the field has been and offer a few cautionary notes to consider as the MSF movement charges toward maturity.

Early Rating Research and Development: 1900–1941

Searching for the moment of MSF conception can be a tricky endeavor, and one certainly open to some debate. Nevertheless, if we consider the broader category of performance ratings, the beginning point was probably very early in the twentieth century, when supervisory ratings gained in popularity. With industrial psychology in its infancy, and the industrial revolution attracting a growing number of new workers to the cities, psychologists began to explore better ways to hire and train employees as well as measure performance on the job.

Paterson (1922) noted that Walter Dill Scott introduced the method of rating the abilities of workers in industry prior to World War I. He invented what became known as the man-to-man comparison scale, and as director of the Committee on Classification of Personnel in the United States Army modified that scale for use in rating the efficiency of army officers. This scale supplanted the seniority system of promotion in the army and initiated an era of promotion on the basis of merit.

There were inherent difficulties with applying the man-to-man system in industry (for example, multiple comparisons). Paterson (1922), working with employees of the Scott Company, developed a graphic scale to address these difficulties and described studies demonstrating the scale's reliability, consistency over time, usefulness, and practicality. Later, Bradshaw (1931) discussed improvements to the graphic rating scale that included "behaviorgrams" to anchor the scales and help better illustrate the trait.

Hayes and Paterson (1921) discussed the graphic rating scale's purposes in industry, including (1) educational impact on the rater and ratee as to what is important on the job; (2) uniformity of expressing the opinions of supervisors so as to avoid snap judgments and to attain standardization of what the company sees as essential for employees to possess; and (3) bringing to the attention of management the progress of the individual, to enable merit increases, promotions, transfers, and vocational counseling.

Scott (1932) suggested that the rating scale used for supervisors should include dimensions such as personality, originality, leadership, organizational ability, cooperativeness, ability to develop workers, and technical ability, while worker scales should include dimensions such as ability to learn, personal productivity (quantity), workmanship (quality), industriousness, initiative, cooperativeness, and knowledge of the work. He also noted that the scale developer should take care to define clearly the important qualities, and that raters must be thoroughly trained.

Certainly, ratings were frequently used during this time period as a criterion for selection-system validation. For example, Kornhauser (1923) developed a selection battery for billing machine operators and validated it against production records and supervisor ratings. Similarly, Shellow (1926) developed a selection device to use with streetcar motormen. Initially, Shellow used "chief instructor" ratings and those by a member of the "education department," but when the correlation between the two sources was found to be .05, he abandoned rating criteria and used turnover as a criterion.

Kornhauser (1923) suggested that there were two principal sources of criterion information that can be used: production records and ratings. Although production records were believed to be more objective, they were not always available, or even necessarily an adequate measure. He suggested that ratings were personal opinions and had many shortcomings and grave inaccuracies, but when properly administered and obtained from several executives independently, they proved to be more satisfactory than production records.

Thus, some applied psychologists were at the time supportive of ratings under certain conditions, but the method was not without its detractors. As far back as 1920, Link reported that some researchers believed the term *rating scale* was a misnomer because it implied qualities of accuracy that the scale obviously did not have; Link also noted that the term *opinion record* had been recommended instead.

Although the use of supervisors was almost universal as the choice of rating source during this time period, there were at least two exceptions that bear mention. Link (1920) noted that Shelton (1919) discussed a method referred to as "mutual rating," where every individual in the workgroup is rated (using secret ballot) by both subordinates and supervisors. Also, Cook and Manson (1926) described the use of customers as raters to evaluate salesclerks. This focus on customers was noted by Viteles (1928) as a significant addition to the literature on rating scales.

The War Years and the Postwar Boom in Rating Research and Application: 1942–1966

World War II brought with it unprecedented opportunities in personnel research, and great strides were made in developing criteria and predicting job performance. In reflecting on this time period, Flanagan (1948) suggested that perhaps the greatest contribution of industrial psychology was the successful demonstration to the military leaders of the appropriateness of psychological principles in areas such as prediction of job performance, classification of personnel, and motivational factors.

Even though criterion development received considerable attention during the course of the war, by necessity single, readily available measures were often used, most frequently for predictor validation (see Nagle, 1953). Nonetheless, innovative thinking about very practical ratings problems was evident. For example, Sisson (1948) devised the "forced choice" method of gathering supervisory ratings because the army needed to promote a large number of top-ranking officers to oversee the rapidly mobilizing forces. Their current officer evaluation system produced extremely inflated ratings, making it difficult to differentiate among officers' performance, but Sisson's forced-choice ratings were found to produce scores that were normally distributed, and the method was adopted for immediate use with army officers.

Rating Research and Application in the Military After World War II

After the war ended, the military services began to establish research laboratories to investigate "personnel issues." This proved to be a highly productive period of psychological research, and much progress in research and application occurred in examining a variety of rating sources and assessment techniques. For example, Flanagan (1954) described the conception of the "critical incident" technique as a method of criterion development whereby specific examples of job behavior were identified that described particularly effective or ineffective job performance.

One of the first studies of the predictive validity of peer ratings was conducted during this time (Williams and Leavitt, 1947), using Marine Corps officers. The authors concluded that peer evaluations were more valid predictors of success in officer candidate school than several objective tests, and were more valid predictors of future performance than were supervisor ratings. Wherry and Fryer (1949) concurred, suggesting that peer ratings might constitute the "purest" measure of leadership of the criteria that they tested (which included academic grades, instructor ratings, and peer ratings). Hollander (1954) carried out an extensive investigation of the peer-evaluation process and concluded that the research on "buddy ratings" offers compelling evidence in support of their reliability and validity; peer ratings predicted such diverse criteria as Officer Candidate School performance, success in flight training, and leadership effectiveness.

Other researchers began to examine the issue of criterion comparability. For example, Gaylor, Russell, Johnson, and Severin (1951) noted that supervisory ratings of army file clerks correlated only .48 to .55 with production records (even though they had the records available to them) and cautioned that the magnitude of the correlations was not sufficient to warrant substituting one criterion for the other. Peters and Campbell (1955) correlated self and supervisor proficiency ratings with scores on a diagnostic proficiency test of air force mechanics' job knowledge. Correlations ranged from .32 to .37 between ratings and the proficiency test, and the authors concluded that ratings were not sufficiently correlated with these test scores to justify substitution. Also, self-ratings correlated with first- and second-level supervisor ratings .30 and .23 respectively.

Hausman and Strupp (1953) collected supervisory and peer ratings of air force mechanics' performance and found the two to be correlated, .51 on average. However, they also found that peers were better able to differentiate between dimensions compared with the "halo" present in supervisory ratings. Berkeley (1955) compared supervisor, coworker, and self-ratings of air force enlisted personnel and found no differences between supervisors and coworker mean ratings; self-ratings showed only a small relationship to ratings by supervisors or coworkers.

Rating Research and Application in Industry

During this time, industry-based rating research and application began to grow and expand in a variety of directions. For example, Driver (1942) noted that some had argued for having supervisors rated by subordinates because "no one knows the boss like these individuals." Driver concluded, however, that such a plan would be impractical because subordinates (and peers) are not likely to be accurate. Zerga (1943) described increased use of merit ratings in the private sector, noting that American industry was gradually accepting the premise that periodic objective rating of employees was as important as scientific study of production processes.

Springer (1953) compared ratings of candidates for promotion made by supervisors with ratings made by coworkers. She found that coworker ratings were more lenient, higher reliabilities existed within source than across sources, and supervisor ratings were more reliable than peer ratings. Weitz (1958) tested the validity of peer evaluations obtained from life insurance agents as predictors of success at the assistant manager level. He concluded that peer evaluations were better than supervisor evaluations at predicting success. Hicks and Stone (1962) found similar results with managers, when comparing supervisor and peer ratings.

Maloney and Hinrichs (1959) reported on the development and use of a feedback tool for supervisors. The program, called "Rate Your Supervisor," gave supervisors a personal report showing both how each supervisor was rated and, for comparison purposes, how they were rated as a group. The tool, geared to self-development, consisted of thirty-seven personal traits (receptive to new ideas, indecisive, etc.), four "results" items geared toward how the supervisor's work group was performing (team spirit, creativity, etc.), twenty-six supervisory behaviors (uses subordinates' abilities fully, admits own errors, etc.), and five summary evaluation items that were open-ended questions (such as "Do you like working for him?").

In addition to research and application in the public and private sectors, this time period saw much energy devoted to conceptualizing about the criterion domain, with attention directed at, for example, multiple versus composite criteria, and criteria to evaluate criteria (see among others Dunnette, 1963; Guion, 1961; Weitz, 1961; Wherry, 1957). The prevailing research evidence during this period suggested that rating sources did not produce particularly comparable information about the ratee, and the general opinion about these findings was that all sources were therefore not equally "good."

However, some researchers and practitioners began to advance a different perspective. For example, Dunnette (1963) commented that if various measures correlate highly, we gain some confidence that we are measuring the core; yet this in turn reduces the need to combine data from multiple sources to form a single composite. Put another way, if the measures show low correlations, a researcher may be either concerned because of the apparent lack of unity in this job success construct or gratified that he or she is tapping rather independent dimensions of job success. In addition, Dunnette pointed to Thorndike's advice that "lack of correlation weakens faith in one or both measures, except in so far as each measures distinct aspects of performance for which there is no rational basis to expect intercorrelation" (1949, p. 124).

The Beginning of the Modern Multirater Perspective: 1967–1992

A major impetus using multiple rating perspectives came from research in the late 1960s and early 1970s that presented the "multi-trait-multirater" (MTMR) approach to measurement. Most notable in this regard was the publication of Lawler's 1967 article titled "The Multitrait-Multirater Approach to Measuring Managerial Job Performance." In the article, Lawler offered the MTMR approach as a worthwhile alternative to both the widely used supervisor rating and the variety of objective measures that were being touted as replacements (salary level, organizational level achieved, business game results); he then led the reader through analysis and interpretation of several data sets, demonstrating how the use of ratings from multiple sources can offer new and useful insights into the meaning of the results.

Lawler argued that considerably more information could be obtained about the meaning of ratings using an MTMR approach than could be obtained if a single rater or single trait was used. He also suggested that an individual's peers and subordinates were often in a better position to judge the incumbent's performance and potential for other jobs than was the individual's supervisor. Thus, improved decision quality should result from the additional relevant evaluations offered by other observers.

Four years later, Kavanagh, MacKinney, and Wolins (1971) continued with the multisource perspective, describing application of an analysis-of-variance approach to interpretation of multitrait-multimethod data where the methods were organizational-level rating sources. This approach yielded indices of the convergent and discriminant validity of multisource ratings.

Campbell, Dunnette, Lawler, and Weick (1970) and Borman (1974) noted that high interrater reliability between raters at different organizational levels should not necessarily be expected; raters at different levels may have different perspectives regarding ratee performance because they observe diverse samplings of ratee behavior as a result of their distinctive roles relative to the ratee. Landy and Farr (1980) added that one should expect only low to moderate correlations between ratings made by different raters and emphasized that "it cannot be stated that any one type of rater is more valid than any other" (p. 78). Thus, ideally each rating source may generate valid ratings from its own perspective, but because each source has a relatively unique perspective in relation to performance-related behavior observed and role relationship with the ratee, across-source interrater reliability is not high.

Such endorsements for use of a multiple-rater perspective helped establish a framework for examining the rapidly accumulating data on a variety of sources of appraisal. For example, Lewin and Zwany (1976) and Kane and Lawler (1978) reviewed the literature on peer assessment and found the data encouraging with respect to the reliability, validity, and freedom from bias of peer-assessment methods; they concluded that peer assessments are tapping important performance-related variance. However, McEvoy and Butler

(1987) noted that peer ratings are generally not well accepted by raters *or* ratees, except when they are used for developmental purposes, because of the potential for intragroup conflict resulting from peers assuming an administrative decision-making role.

Hegarty (1973, 1974) noted that subordinate ratings of supervisors proved useful (and acceptable) as a method of performance feedback to supervisors. Mabe and West (1982) performed a meta-analysis of relationships between self-assessments on trait dimensions and criteria relevant to those assessments. They found moderate validity for self-ratings. Bernardin (1992) provided some support for customer-based appraisals as a source of added and unique information beyond that from top-down appraisal.

Harris and Schaubroeck's meta-analysis (1988) of supervisor, peer, and self-rating studies found much stronger agreement between supervisors and peers than between self and peers and self and supervisors. In addition, analysis of job type found that self-supervisor and self-peer correlations were lower for managerial or professional employees than for blue-collar and service employees.

Borman (1991) summarized the large body of research evidence accumulating for multiple-rater perspectives, noting that each source has advantages in producing valid performance information. Experienced supervisors have reasonably good norms for performance, having observed relatively large numbers of employees working on the job, and thus have well-calibrated views of performance levels. Peers are usually exposed to a wide variety of performance information from fellow workers, and thus it may be difficult to hide one's actual performance level from coworkers. Self-ratings have a similar advantage in gathering performance-related information firsthand. Subordinates are likely to have relevant information about their supervisors' leadership skills.

Some disadvantages to each of these rating sources should be noted as well. Supervisors may not be in a good position to observe much of the day-to-day work performance of subordinates. Coworkers and subordinates often lack experience in making formal performance evaluations. Subordinates may be in a position to see only a relatively small portion of their supervisors' job performance. Finally, self-ratings may be distorted because of inflated evaluations of the rater's own performance.

Two Related, Influential Streams of Research

This section describes two other areas of research that influenced thinking and development activity within the MSF arena. First, we highlight work on survey research and feedback for individual development that emerged from the domain of organization development and change. Next, we briefly review findings from teaching effectiveness research as they pertain to sources of evaluation.

Data-Based Feedback and Organization Development

This chapter on the evolution of multisource feedback would not be complete without mentioning the survey and feedback work that grew out of the action research of Kurt Lewin. Mann ([1957] 1971) discussed some of the groundbreaking work done by the University of Michigan Survey Research Center starting in the late 1940s. It focused on "changing patterns of relationships between superiors and subordinates" by using survey results. This feedback process evolved as Mann and his colleagues learned how to apply findings from human relations research into organizations so that they would be understood and used in day-to-day operations.

The feedback process that was developed involved reporting major findings to senior company officers, and work sessions at the workgroup level, where supervisors and their subordinates would meet to review and interpret the data and formulate plans for constructive administrative actions. In addition, Mann ([1957]1971) and colleagues empirically evaluated the feedback program over a two-year period and found significant positive changes in employee attitudes and perceptions compared to a control group.

It is important also to highlight here Nadler's influential 1977 book on using data-based methods of feedback and organization development. The emphasis was on use of survey data to support organization change; at the time of its publication, only a few pieces had been written about using such data as a tool for working with organizations. (The influences of the organization development and change literatures and that somewhat different perspective are dealt with more thoroughly elsewhere in this handbook; see Chapter Nineteen.)

Before we leave the topic of feedback, it should be noted here that during this period two extensive reviews of the performance feedback process were published. Ilgen, Fisher, and Taylor (1979) and Nadler (1979) described empirical research underscoring the notion that performance feedback from others is an important determinant of both individual and group behavior in organizations.

Evaluations of Teaching Effectiveness

An entirely separate stream of research on evaluations of teaching effectiveness was being conducted in numerous colleges and universities, spanning a relatively broad period of time. This research stream is briefly cited here because the measurement issues dealt with (and conclusions drawn generally parallel those of) our mainstream rating research and may have influenced current thinking about the use of multiple rating sources. Doyle (1983) offered an historical perspective on teaching evaluation, noting that student rating programs to evaluate teachers began as far back as 1900, with a sharp increase in this activity beginning around 1927 and a resurgence of activity again in the 1970s.

Marsh (1987) in turn provided an extensive review of the student evaluation literature and described pioneering work undertaken by Remmers. As early as 1927, Remmers and Brandenburg discussed principles for evaluation instrument design, suggesting that (1) the number of traits must be small enough to reduce the possibility of halo and carelessness caused by rater boredom, (2) important traits must be agreed on by experts, and (3) traits must be observable and capable of being judged. Over the course of thirty years, Remmers conducted numerous studies that examined an extensive array of rating issues, including rating reliability, validity, generalizability, multiple purposes for ratings, and relationship among measures (see, for example, Remmers, 1934, 1958).

Although student ratings of teaching effectiveness have been the primary focus of research and development, certain alternative sources have been investigated. For example, Webb and Nolan (1955) reported good correspondence between student ratings and instructor self-evaluations, but neither of these indicators was positively correlated with supervisor ratings. Morsh, Burgess, and Smith (1956) correlated student ratings, student achievement, peer ratings, and supervisor ratings and found that student ratings correlated with achievement; peer and supervisor ratings correlated with each other but not with student ratings or student achievement.

Braskamp, Brandenburg, and Ory (1985) found that ratings by students and alumni were substantially correlated and that both were moderately correlated with self-evaluations. However, ratings by colleagues based on classroom observations were not related to the other three sources. Howard, Conway, and Maxwell (1985) found moderate correlations between student ratings and instructor self-evaluations, but ratings by colleagues were not significantly correlated with student ratings, self-evaluations, or the ratings of trained observers. They recommended that researchers collect as many measures of teaching effectiveness as possible to create a multisource index.

A Confluence of Movements and the MSF Zeitgeist

Although a move toward an employee-involved workplace can be traced back to the human relations and participative management movement of the 1950s and 1960s (see Likert, 1961; and McGregor, 1960), and even the leadership research of the 1940s and 1950s (for instance, Lewin, 1947), it was not until the 1980s and 1990s that such practices became much more mainstream in industry. Talk about "quality of work life" and "quality circles" evolved into "total quality management" (Cummings and Molloy, 1977; Lawler, 1987; Ledford, 1993), all emphasizing increased employee involvement.

The use of workteams has increased dramatically in the last decade. Many organizations have found that traditional hierarchical and functional approaches are inadequate, and they believe they can significantly improve their effectiveness by establishing teams. Frequently, the teams are described as "empowered" or "self-managed" because they perform for themselves many of the tasks management used to perform (such as self-monitoring; Mohrman, Cohen, and Mohrman, 1995).

The push for quality control and the continuing shift from a manufacturing economy to a service economy helped to direct increased attention toward customer satisfaction. This customer orientation is characterized by active involvement at all levels of the organization and a high level of measurement and feedback (Peters and Austin, 1985; Peters and Waterman, 1982). Together, these trends were an ideal foundation on which the MSF movement grew and prospered.

By the late 1970s, companies were beginning to invest substantial resources in standardized collection of behavioral feedback for managers. Morrison, McCall, and De Vries (1978) published a report from the Center for Creative Leadership that reviewed twenty-four survey feedback instruments then in use and offered advice to instrument developers and personnel managers about the strengths and weaknesses of these instruments. By the late 1980s, terminology such as "360-degree feedback" and "multisource feedback" began to be linked with these tools and procedures, and such labels were beginning to appear in the popular print media (see, for example, Bennett, 1990; Edwards, 1991; and Ludeman, 1991).

However, it was not until 1993 that these emerging tools and techniques received a unifying focus. In that year, Tornow edited a special issue of *Human Resource Management* on 360-degree feedback. This issue amounted to a platform for presentation of the concept and available research evidence, as well as a forum for debate about the merits of this process. Since that time, the field has grown exponentially; this handbook offers the most extensive and recent research and application available on the topic.

Conclusions

Research and (especially) application of multisource feedback systems continue to grow and evolve. In this review of one hundred years of research activity in the field, we have tried to demonstrate that although the terminology may be new, the concept of gathering and using data from multiple rating sources to gain insight into incumbent performance has a long history. As Hedge and Borman (1995) noted, reliance on more than one source of appraisal will become more and more of a necessity in the future, as technological advances and changing conceptions of the work environment make it unrealistic to assume that the supervisor may have the best—or only worthwhile—perspective on an employee's performance.

Anytime a tool or technique is embraced so broadly in a relatively short period of time, research typically lags behind practice, causing increased speculation about its ultimate worth (Fletcher and Baldry, 1999). Nonetheless, such widespread use can also foster increased research activity (see, for example, Conway and Huffcutt, 1996; Borman, 1997). In addition, continued collection of multisource data to the degree that is presently occurring as a result of such extensive adoption of the system offers tantalizing opportunities for future research activity. The chapters that follow should give the reader an opportunity for thoughtful reflection on the past, present, and future of multisource feedback.

References

Bennett, A. "Corporate Succession Gets a New Lexicon." *Wall Street Journal,* Oct. 4, 1990, p. 1B.

Berkeley, M. H. *Comparison of Supervisor, Co-Worker, and Self-Ratings of WAF Job Performance.* (Publication no. TN-55-25). Lackland Air Force Base, Tex.: Air Force Personnel and Training Research Center, 1955.

Bernardin, H. J. "An 'Analytic' Framework for Customer-Based Performance Content Development and Appraisal." *Human Resource Management Review,* 1992, *2*, 81–102.

Borman, W. C. "The Rating of Individuals in Organizations: An Alternate Approach." *Organizational Behavior and Human Performance,* 1974, *12*, 105–124.

Borman, W. C. "Job Behavior, Performance, and Effectiveness." In M. D. Dunnette and L. M. Hough (eds.), *Handbook of Industrial and Organizational Psychology.* Palo Alto, Calif.: Consulting Psychologists Press, 1991.

Borman, W. C. "360-Degree Ratings: An Analysis of Assumptions and a Research Agenda for Evaluating Their Validity." *Human Resource Management Review,* 1997, *7*, 299–315.

Bradshaw, F. F. "Revising Rating Techniques." *Personnel Journal,* 1931, *10*, 232–245.

Braskamp, L. A., Brandenburg, D. C., and Ory, J. C. *Evaluating Teaching Effectiveness: A Practical Guide.* Thousand Oaks, Calif.: Sage, 1985.

Campbell, J. P., Dunnette, M. D., Lawler, E. E., III, and Weick, K. E. *Managerial Behavior, Performance, and Effectiveness.* New York: McGraw-Hill, 1970.

Conway, J. M., and Huffcutt, A. I. "Testing Assumptions of 360-Degree Feedback: A Meta-Analysis of Supervisor, Peer, Subordinate, and Self-Ratings." Paper presented at the eleventh annual conference of the Society for Industrial and Organizational Psychology, San Diego, Calif., Apr. 1996.

Cook, H. D., and Manson. G. E. "Abilities Necessary in Effective Retail Selling and a Method of Evaluating Them." *Journal of Personnel Research*, 1926, *5*, 74–82.

Cummings, T. G., and Molloy, E. S. *Improving Productivity and the Quality of Work Life*. New York: Praeger, 1977.

Doyle, K. O. *Evaluating Teaching*. San Francisco: New Lexington Books, 1983.

Driver, R. S. "Training as a Means of Improving Employee Performance Rating." *Personnel*, 1942, *18*, 364–370.

Dunnette, M. D. "A Note on the Criterion." *Journal of Applied Psychology*, 1963, *47*, 251–254.

Edwards, M. R. "Accurate Performance Measurement Tools." *HRMagazine*, 1991, *36*, 95–100.

Flanagan, J. "Contributions of Research in the Armed Forces to Personnel Psychology." *Personnel Psychology*, 1948, *1*, 53–62.

Flanagan, J. "The Critical Incident Technique." *Psychological Bulletin*, 1954, *51*, 327–358.

Fletcher, C., and Baldry, C. "Multi-Source Feedback Systems: A Research Perspective." In G. Cooper and I. Robertson (eds.), *International Review of Industrial and Organizational Psychology* (Vol. 14). New York: Wiley, 1999.

Gaylor, R. H., Russell, E., Johnson, C., and Severin, D. "The Relation of Ratings to Production Records: An Empirical Study." *Personnel Psychology*, 1951, *4*, 363–371.

Guion, R. M. "Criterion Measurement and Personnel Judgments." *Personnel Psychology*, 1961, *14*, 141–149.

Harris, M. M., and Schaubroeck, J. "A Meta-Analysis of Self-Supervisor, Self-Peer, and Peer-Supervisor Ratings." *Personnel Psychology*, 1988, *41*, 43–62.

Hausman, H. J., and Strupp, H. H. *Non-Technical Factors in the Job Performance of Aircraft Mechanics*. HFORL Report No. 36. Washington, D.C.: Human Factors Operations Research Laboratories, Air Research and Development Command, 1953.

Hayes, M.H.S., and Paterson, D. G. "Experimental Development of the Graphic Rating Scale." *Psychological Bulletin*, 1921, *18*, 98–99.

Hedge, J. W., and Borman, W. C. "Changing Conceptions and Practices in Performance Appraisal." In A. Howard (ed.), *The Changing Nature of Work*. San Francisco: Jossey-Bass, 1995.

Hegarty, W. H. "Supervisors' Reactions to Subordinates' Appraisals." *Personnel*, 1973, *50*, 30–35.

Hegarty, W. H. "Using Subordinate Ratings to Elicit Behavioral Changes in Supervisors." *Journal of Applied Psychology*, 1974, *59*, 764–766.

Hicks, J. A., and Stone, J. B. "The Identification of Traits Related to Managerial Success." *Journal of Applied Psychology*, 1962, *46*, 428–432.

Hollander, E. P. "Buddy Ratings: Military Research and Industrial Implications." *Personnel Psychology*, 1954, *7*, 385–393.

Howard, G. S., Conway, C. G., and Maxwell, S. E. "Construct Validity of Measures of College Teaching Effectiveness." *Journal of Educational Psychology*, 1985, *77*, 187–196.

Ilgen, D. R., Fisher, C. D., and Taylor, M. S. "Consequences of Individual Feedback on Behavior in Organizations." *Journal of Applied Psychology*, 1979, *64*, 349–371.

Kane, J. S., and Lawler, E. E., III. "Methods of Peer Assessment." *Psychological Bulletin*, 1978, *85*, 555–586.

Kavanagh, M. J., MacKinney, A., and Wolins, L. "Issues in Managerial Performance: Multitrait-Multimethod Analyses of Ratings." *Psychological Bulletin*, 1971, *75*, 34–39.

Kornhauser, A. W. "A Statistical Study of a Group of Specialized Office Workers." *Journal of Personnel Research*, 1923, *2*, 103–123.

Landy, F. J., and Farr, J. L. "Performance Rating." *Psychological Bulletin*, 1980, *87*, 72–107.

Lawler, E. E., III. "The Multitrait-Multirater Approach to Measuring Managerial Job Performance." *Journal of Applied Psychology*, 1967, *51*, 369–381.

Lawler, E. E., III. "Transformation from Control to Involvement." In R. H. Kilmann, T. J. Covin, and Associates, *Corporate Transformation: Revitalizing Organizations for a Competitive World*. San Francisco: Jossey-Bass, 1987.

Ledford, G. E. "Employee Involvement: Lessons and Predictions." In J. R. Galbraith, E. E. Lawler III, and Associates, *Organizing for the Future: The New Logic for Managing Complex Organizations*. San Francisco: Jossey-Bass, 1993.

Lewin, A. Y., and Zwany, A. "Peer Nominations: A Model, Literature Critique, and a Paradigm for Research." *Personnel Psychology*, 1976, *29*, 423–447.

Lewin, K. "Frontiers in Group Dynamics: Concept, Method, and Reality in Social Science: Social Equilibria and Social Change." *Human Relations*, 1947, *1*, 5–42.

Likert, R. *New Patterns of Management*. New York: McGraw-Hill, 1961.

Link, H. C. "The Application of Psychology to Industry." *Psychological Bulletin*, 1920, *17*, 335–346.

Ludeman, K. "Customized Skills Assessment." *HRMagazine*, 1991, *36*, 67–72.

Mabe, P. A., and West, S. G. "Validity of Self-Evaluation of Ability: A Review and Meta-Analysis." *Journal of Applied Psychology*, 1982, *67*, 280–296.

Maloney, P. W., and Hinrichs, J. R. "A New Tool for Supervisory Self-Development." *Personnel,* 1959, *36,* 46–53.

Mann, F. C. "Studying and Creating Change: A Means to Understanding Social Organization." In H. Hornstein and others (eds.), *Social Intervention: A Behavioral Science Approach.* New York: Free Press, 1971. (Originally published 1957.)

Marsh, H. W. "Students' Evaluations of University Teaching: Research Findings, Methodological Issues, and Directions for Future Research." *International Journal of Educational Research,* 1987, *11,* 253–388.

McEvoy, G. M., and Butler, P. F. "User Acceptance of Peer Appraisals in an Industrial Setting." *Personnel Psychology,* 1987, *40,* 785–797.

McGregor, D. *The Human Side of Enterprise.* New York: McGraw-Hill, 1960.

Mohrman, S. A., Cohen, S. G., and Mohrman, A. M., Jr. *Designing Team-Based Organizations: New Forms for Knowledge Work.* San Francisco: Jossey-Bass, 1995.

Morrison, A. M., McCall, M. W., and De Vries, D. L. *Feedback to Managers: A Comprehensive Review of Twenty-Four Instruments.* Greensboro, N.C.: Center for Creative Leadership, 1978.

Morsh, J. E., Burgess, G. G., and Smith, P. N. "Student Achievement as a Measure of Instructional Effectiveness." *Journal of Educational Psychology,* 1956, *47,* 79–88.

Nadler, D. A. *Feedback and Organization Development: Using Data-Based Methods.* Reading, Mass.: Addison-Wesley, 1977.

Nadler, D. A. "The Effects of Feedback on Task Group Behavior: A Review of the Experimental Research." *Organizational Behavior and Human Performance,* 1979, *23,* 309–338.

Nagle, B. F. "Criterion Development." *Personnel Psychology,* 1953, *6,* 271–290.

Paterson, D. G. "The Scott Company Graphic Rating Scale." *Journal of Personnel Research,* 1922, *1,* 361–376.

Peters, R., and Campbell, J. T. *Diagnosis of Training Needs of B-29 Mechanics from Supervisory Ratings and Self-Ratings.* Publication no. TM-55-12. Lackland Air Force Base, Tex.: Air Force Personnel Research Laboratory, 1955.

Peters, T. J., and Austin, N. *A Passion for Excellence: The Leadership Difference.* New York: Random House, 1985.

Peters, T. J., and Waterman, R. H. *In Search of Excellence: Lessons from America's Best-Run Companies.* New York: HarperCollins, 1982.

Remmers, H. H. "Reliability and Halo Effect on High School and College Students' Judgments of Their Teachers." *Journal of Applied Psychology,* 1934, *18,* 619–630.

Remmers, H. H. "On Students' Perceptions of Teachers' Effectiveness." In W. McKeachie (ed.), *The Appraisal of Teaching in Large Universities.* Ann Arbor, Mich.: University of Michigan Press, 1958.

Remmers, H. H., and Brandenburg, G. C. "Experimental Data of the Purdue Rating Scale for Instructors." *Educational Administration and Supervision,* 1927, *13,* 519–527.

Scott, W. D. "Personnel Rating." *Industrial Relations,* 1932, *3,* 11–12.

Shellow, S. M. "Selection of Motormen: Further Data on Value of Tests in Milwaukee." *Journal of Personnel Research,* 1926, *5,* 183–188.

Shelton, H. "Wood Mutual Rating." *Bulletin of the Taylor Society,* 1919, *5.*

Sisson, E. D. "Forced Choice: The New Army Rating." *Personnel Psychology,* 1948, *1,* 365–381.

Springer, D. "Ratings of Candidates for Promotion by Co-Workers and Supervisors." *Journal of Applied Psychology,* 1953, *37,* 347–351.

Thorndike, R. L. *Personnel Selection: Test and Measurement Technique.* New York: Wiley, 1949.

Tornow, W. W. (ed.). "360-Degree Feedback." *Human Resource Management,* 1993, *32,* 211–384 (special issue).

Viteles, M. S. "Psychology in Industry." *Psychological Bulletin,* 1928, *25,* 309–340.

Webb, W. B., and Nolan, C. Y. "Student, Supervisor, and Self-Ratings of Instructional Proficiency." *Journal of Educational Psychology,* 1955, *46,* 42–46.

Weitz, J. "Selecting Supervisors with Peer Ratings." *Personnel Psychology,* 1958, *11,* 25–35.

Weitz, J. "Criteria for Criteria." *American Psychologist,* 1961, *16,* 228–231.

Wherry, R. J. "The Past and Future of Criterion Evaluation." *Personnel Psychology,* 1957, *10,* 1–5.

Wherry, R. J., and Fryer, D. C. "Buddy Ratings: Popularity Contest or Leadership Criterion?" *Personnel Psychology,* 1949, *2,* 147–159.

Williams, S. B., and Leavitt, H. J. "Group Opinion as a Predictor of Military Leadership." *Journal of Consulting Psychology,* 1947, *11,* 283–291.

Zerga, J. E. "Developing an Industrial Merit Rating Scale." *Journal of Applied Psychology,* 1943, *27,* 190–195.

CHAPTER 3

Readiness for Multisource Feedback

Ann J. Ewen
Mark R. Edwards

Many organizations considering implementing MSF struggle first with the question "Are we ready?" This chapter discusses MSF readiness by addressing another question: How ready is the organization to implement an MSF system?

The issue of readiness arises prior to implementation and concerns how prepared the organization is to change from a single-source feedback system to a multisource assessment process. Some organizations must address the issue of whether a change should be made from no feedback system to MSF. The readiness discussion focuses initially on organizational culture readiness, and then on infrastructure readiness.

User reactions may be examined using one of the variety of research methods available, such as surveys, interviews, focus groups, or staff meetings. A quick focus group that convenes organizational opinion leaders may be the most efficient and fastest way to assemble information about the process. However, surveys allow more structured input and may serve both as an important communication device and a baseline metric to support a culture change.

Recent MSF surveys of the Fortune 2000 indicate that more than 95 percent of these firms use some form of MSF somewhere in the organization (Edwards and Ewen, 1998). However, fewer than 6 percent of organizations established a baseline measure when they began the MSF project with a measure of readiness. We hope that the examples here will increase those percentages.

The Nature of MSF Systems

MSF systems are extremely flexible, so by their nature they occur in a variety of sizes and complexities. MSF systems may be compared with airplanes in that they are designed to accomplish many objectives. Some are fast, others slow. Some have large capacity, while others have modest capabilities. Although airplanes have identifiable physical attributes, MSF systems are human systems, so nearly every system is unique.

This uniqueness creates a range of MSF systems as presented by practitioners, HR professionals, and academics extending from informal, nonscientific systems that frankly do not work at all to sophisticated global networked systems that work easily and efficiently.

The variety in MSF system design is also reflected in process objectives and use. Some systems are used only for development. Others are designed and built to support a wide range of organizational needs, such as culture change, leadership training, employee development, TQM, teams, performance appraisal, pay, selection, and succession planning (Edwards, 1983). This discussion assumes that readiness and user reactions apply to scientifically designed MSF systems and not to trivial, informal feedback systems.

Readiness

How ready is an organization for MSF? *Readiness* is defined as the degree to which (1) the organizational norms are congruent with multisource feedback and (2) members, both leaders and individual contributors, believe the resulting behavioral feedback adds value.

Measures of readiness reflect attitudes and intentions. Employee and leadership attitudes—and especially intentions—tend to predict organizational behaviors or adoption of new processes (Fishbein and Aizen, 1975). Organizations where employees and leaders alike have a positive attitude toward participative leadership and intend to use the resulting information constructively typically have high readiness for MSF. High readiness means an organization is positioned to adopt MSF quickly and easily.

In theory, low readiness may mean MSF is relatively difficult to adopt, possibly because of a hierarchical, autocratic organization. Certainly it is assumed that leaders would seem unwilling to relinquish any of their control. In reality, an organization whose members are fed up with autocracy and associated problems such as unfairness, politics, and favoritism may quickly embrace MSF. It tends to break down autocratic command-and-control systems, replacing them with systems that reflect participative leadership and recognize and reward high performance rather than politics. For example, MSF has been adopted by many hierarchical organizations in Canada because it permits substantial improvements in distributive justice (Cohen, 1998).

Organizational readiness can be determined by querying stakeholders regarding their views (which they are willing and able to communicate) about MSF. We examine readiness at two levels to determine the degree to which stakeholders are willing to provide and receive feedback from multiple sources for two purposes: purely for their own development, and to assist in career development or serve as an input to performance management.

These two contrasting purposes may yield different results. In general, most organizations today find that stakeholders, executives, management, and employees show a definite preference for MSF. The concept behind MSF concerns whether employees would prefer to receive feedback from a single source—their supervisor alone—or from multiple sources (London and Beatty, 1993). However, stakeholders may not be as eager to receive feedback from multiple sources if they expect the results to be used for administrative decisions such as performance appraisal, pay, and promotion (Edwards, 1989).

Evolution of MSF Readiness Assessment

Employees were typically skeptical about MSF in the 1970s and 1980s (Edwards and Goodstein, 1982). Assessment methods such as focus groups, interviews, staff meetings, and surveys were confounded because the concept of MSF was hypothetical to many employees, managers, and executives. Since they had never experienced receiving or using feedback from multiple sources, they were naturally concerned. The MSF process was perceived as backward or upside down, relative to the way performance-related information should flow. In addition, since few people were familiar with successful MSF models, many others dismissed the idea entirely.

Asking employees about their preference for single-source or multisource feedback was like asking people who were familiar with traveling only in trains about their willingness to fly. Until they had experience or learned from the experience of others, the new method just did not make sense.

Today there are many success models for MSF; they have been published in nearly every HR journal and business magazine (Edwards and Ewen, 1995; Fleenor and Prince, 1997). As a result, nearly all managers in Fortune 2000 firms are familiar with MSF (Edwards and Ewen, 1998). Yet our focus groups and surveys in 1999 indicate that fewer than 50 percent of managers in small businesses and people in international firms are familiar with the concept of MSF. Therefore, readiness represents an important issue because even awareness does not necessarily correspond with readiness to adopt.

"Readiness I": Purely Development

Several approaches are available for assessing readiness for developmental feedback (the first of two purposes we examine in this chapter, the other being decision making). Four methods are described here.

Method One: Litmus Test

Readiness to receive MSF for pure development is easy to measure using a single question, presented in either a focus group or a survey, to capture the perception of readiness in terms of preference:

> Would you rather receive feedback from:
> A. Your boss or manager
> B. Multiple sources, including manager, colleagues, and other
>   work associates

Our research shows that most organizations, both public and private, find overwhelming support for the MSF model, as more than 80 percent of employees prefer multiple sources if asked directly. This represents a dramatic cultural shift from ten years ago, when typically fewer than 35 percent of employees indicated a preference for multiple sources before they had experienced such feedback. User support from a majority of organizational members indicates sufficient support to begin testing the MSF process, perhaps by way of a small pilot of twenty feedback receivers.

Method Two: Nominal Group

Another quick and effective method for determining readiness is to assemble a cross-functional focus group and then use nominal group technique to explore this question: "What advantages do you see in the multisource model of Figure 3.1, as compared to single source?"

The advantage of using the nominal group process is that the content developed from potential users' insights helps in communicating the benefits of the MSF system to others in the organization.

Figure 3.1. Comparison of Feedback Systems.

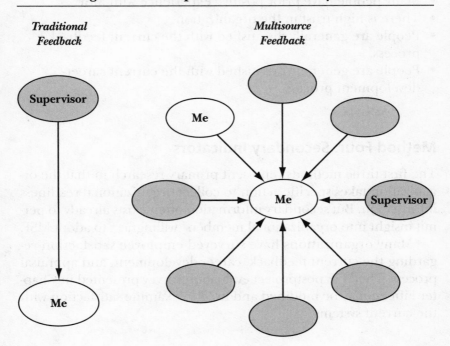

Traditional Feedback

Multisource Feedback

Focus-group members know what is going on in the organization and can identify the process attributes that are most aligned with organizational and employee needs. For example, some groups focus primarily on the need for MSF for reasons of organizational structure, such as wider spans of control, geographic distances, or a movement to teams. Others focus on such cultural factors as trust in leadership, fairness, organizational justice, diversity, and process credibility. Still others may emphasize continuous learning, motivating behavioral change, building emotional intelligence, moderating "plateaued" careers, or managing performance.

Method Three: Organizational Survey

Many organizations want stronger documentation to support readiness than is possible with these quick procedures. A readiness metric that gives a broader-based measure includes the assessment statements found in Table 3.1 (Edwards and Ewen, 1996b).

There are several other important readiness indicators:

- Many people have prior positive experience with MSF.
- There is high trust in the organization.
- People are generally dissatisfied with the current feedback process.
- People are generally dissatisfied with the current career-development process.

Method Four: Secondary Indicators

The first three methods represent primary research in that the organization takes specific action to collect organizational readiness information. But secondary information often exists already to permit insight into organizational members' willingness to adopt MSF.

Many organizations have surveyed employee satisfaction regarding the current feedback, career-development, and appraisal process. The MSF postproject evaluation survey presented in Chapter Fifteen may be modified and used to examine satisfaction with the current systems.

Table 3.1. Readiness Assessment for MSF.

Please indicate agreement using a 10-point scale, where 10 is high agreement and 1 is low agreement.

A. Management supports decisions at the lowest possible level. ____
B. Business results blend individual and team performance. ____
C. Policy supports performance-based management. ____
D. Management wishes to align vision, values, and job behaviors. ____
E. Managers are willing to serve as role models for receiving feedback. ____
F. How work gets done, as well as what gets done, is important. ____
G. Units or teams set shared objectives. ____
H. Developmental feedback is encouraged. ____
I. Employees are not satisfied with the current performance feedback. ____
J. Customer feedback and TQM measures are embraced. ____
K. Some managers already solicit feedback from others. ____
L. Managers talk to others to get input before making selection decisions. ____

Scoring. Add the scores from each question to get the total score.

Over 100: aligned. MSF will be embraced.

Over 80: support. MSF will find support but will need assistance for acceptance.

Under 80: uphill battle. MSF needs substantial communications and support.

Need for MSF

A variety of indicators may flag the need for, and consequently the relatively quick adoption of, MSF.

Employee Opinion

In many organizations, employee opinion surveys often indicate that fewer than 50 percent of employees are satisfied with the current performance feedback process. Many organizations—even the most admired companies—find fewer than 25 percent of employees satisfied with single-source feedback and appraisals (Edwards, Ewen, and Verdini, 1995).

Example of Employee Opinion Survey
Many organizations find an employee project team comes forward
with MSF as a solution to an organizational challenge. For example, an aerospace firm empowered project teams to address eight
broad areas to improve organizational effectiveness. The areas
were derived from their employee-satisfaction survey. Seven of the
eight project teams recommended MSF, for different reasons. The
project teams and recommendations (Table 3.2) were as follows:

1. *Leadership development.* Surveys, focus groups, or interviews
indicate that more than 33 percent of individual contributors or

Table 3.2. Sample Project Teams and Recommendations.

Project Team	Recommended MSF to Address
Continuous learning	Motivate learning and measure progress
Communications	Improve understanding of what behaviors are critical to business success
Teams	Create support and accountability for team-based organizational structures, including permanent and virtual teams
Nonperformance	Create a clear and credible method for identifying and addressing nonperformance, and upgrade performance standards
Diversity	Improve the fairness and accuracy of performance measures and talent metrics for all employees
Performance management	Develop enhancements to the performance management process that motivate high performance
Talent assessment and succession planning	Build assessment that measures talents, capabilities, and potential that may be used for development, selection, and succession

leaders indicate that leaders need development. For example, a national research laboratory found that their leaders were technically brilliant but "leadership challenged." MSF served as a bridge to provide developmental feedback to leaders and then to produce intelligence for selecting new leaders.

2. *Culture change.* An organization that announces a major culture change and desires alignment around a new vision and set of values behaviors presents an opportunity for immediate implementation of MSF.

3. *MSF champion.* Many organizations have adopted MSF because one or a few organizational members acted as change agents to initiate and support the MSF process. The champion often comes from an operational group (sales, production, finance, R&D). A single person can make a huge difference in an organization by introducing MSF to his or her workgroup as a pilot. Soon others follow.

4. *Span of reporting.* Organizations that increase the span of control beyond twelve to fifteen direct reports to a supervisor find that supervisors and direct reports are ready to adopt MSF. Many production, R&D, service, and health care organizations have spans of more than thirty-five, so no practical choice exists for evaluation and development other than MSF.

5. *Diversity management.* There have been several high-profile headlines concerning major corporations struggling with fairness and alleged failure to practice diversity. Texaco and Mitsubishi are recent examples. The pressure to change internal processes accelerates MSF adoption as a tool to drive behavioral change in a manner that is diversity-fair.

6. *Teams.* Organizations moving to team-based structures, such as Lands' End, GlaxoWellcome, and GMAC, find team members ready to use MSF because there is no other viable solution for accountability, development, and performance management.

7. *Legal concerns.* Several organizations have experienced litigation regarding the lack of fairness and accuracy of their supervisor-only appraisal system. They adopted MSF systems to enhance fairness and accuracy of performance data.

8. *Cronyism.* An aerospace firm that was very traditional and hierarchical found a backlash to selection decisions on the basis of friendship. Rewards, recognition, and promotions were given

based on politics rather than performance. MSF was a solution that moderated the problem of cronyism. No other solution, theoretical or practical, has been presented to confront cronyism.

Readiness for MSF may be measured using various methods. But readiness for using MSF for both development and performance represents a more complex measure.

Development and Performance

The use of MSF for development only represents a significant irony. Most organizations adopt MSF to improve fairness, accuracy, and credibility for organizational decisions (see Chapters Twenty and Twenty-One). Yet MSF used purely for development brings few of these advantages to the organization, leaders, or employees because the information goes only to the employee for career development. Because the process was not developed for performance evaluation use, it cannot be shared with the supervisor without raising legal or ethical considerations.

When used only for development, the organization gets little value for administration, time, and cost investment in MSF (for more on the debate surrounding this concern, see Chapter Twenty-Three). In addition, the organization is forced to continue two redundant processes: single-source, supervisor-only appraisal and MSF. Employees are confused by the two systems, with MSF generally receiving higher satisfaction marks and providing better information, yet not being used for appraisal. The organization seems to say that a process perceived as unfair and supervisory-only takes precedence over a process that gives better-quality feedback.

These measures are trivial in the sense that the feedback receiver has no *accountability* to use the intelligence gathered at nontrivial cost. Most organizations find their members lack the energy, interest, and time to support two evaluation processes. Consequently, if MSF is used purely for development for a large segment of organizational members, the process predictably evaporates after several iterations. Small, executive projects may be sustained longer because they often allow one-on-one consultative support and do not have to be sustained by greater organizational energy.

The issues associated with using MSF for performance tend to overwhelm people before they have experienced an MSF process.

It is hard to offer substantive input when people have no experience and are not trained in the MSF process. They do not know how to answer the performance question, which only confounds adoption of MSF.

"Readiness II": Development and Performance

Estimates of the level of MSF adoption for both development and performance vary. Robert Jako reported a Corporate Leadership Council study that indicated 80 percent of benchmarked companies were using MSF as their primary performance management tool (Jako, 1997). However, our research suggests substantially lower MSF adoption levels for performance management, about 32 percent (Edwards and Ewen, 1998).

Critical Success Factors

When MSF is introduced, a number of critical success factors are key to effective implementation and acceptance (Bracken, 1997; Edwards and Ewen, 1996a).

Experience

Users should have firsthand experience in receiving feedback through a first-phase MSF process for developmental use only, prior to integrating the information into the performance management system. MSF is like riding a bicycle: until you've ridden one, discussion about behavioral feedback is purely academic. Once you've done it, you understand what riding means, and questions about the experience make perfect sense.

Training

Experience with an MSF process, at a minimum, imparts experiential learning. Preferably, users should get training before and after the MSF to help them understand how to provide and receive feedback.

Safeguards

Both process and technology safeguards should be in place to address such predictable user concerns as process and content validity, technology accuracy, respondent anonymity, friendship bias, respondent collusion, differential evaluation-team rigor, and other potential sources of error (Edwards and Sproull, 1985).

Process Evaluation

The MSF process was used and then evaluated by those who were users (both feedback providers and receivers) for fairness, accuracy, credibility, and other issues. After initial use of MSF, people are trained and experienced in the process. They can then effectively answer the question, "Should MSF be used as an input to performance management?"

Segment Constituencies

MSF postprocess evaluations may be viewed very differently by such groups as executives, managers, supervisors, and independent contributors. All constituencies may be surveyed similarly, but the results for each group should be examined separately. If the MSF experience has been positive, what are user reactions to the MSF system? How can the MSF system be evaluated for its value-added capacity for the organization?

Implementation Strategies: Push Versus Pull

Experience shows that many organizations trying to impose MSF on employees to solve appraisals, pay, and other unresolved issues fail. Pushing MSF data on users typically fails as users push back. Unfortunately, data do not speak for themselves. The quality of MSF data may not be effectively self-interpreted by many users, including even scientists and engineers. Users have many questions that can only be answered by the experience of riding the bicycle. Hence, training support for first-time users is critical. In contrast to a push strategy, a "demand pull" strategy is usually quite successful. It works as follows:

1. Users try MSF.
2. They find the process enhances fairness, accuracy, simplicity, and trustworthiness of performance information.
3. Users then pull the MSF process into the organization with the request that it be used for both development and performance.

The demand-pull strategy follows the path of allowing users experiential learning from the MSF process before using it for evaluative or appraisal decision processes (Edwards and Goodstein, 1982).

Infrastructure Readiness

Our research suggests that large-scale MSF processes do not survive without supportive technology. Without technology support, the MSF process requires too much administrative time and organizational energy. Organizations tend to look to their HR staffs to administer these systems, and in today's overworked organization they find their HR staffs unable to respond.

Administrative Overhead

Numerous organizations, among them Ciba-Geigy, Westinghouse, Boeing, American Airlines, First Interstate Bank, and Pacific Gas and Electric, have built and then abandoned paper-based MSF systems because they were too burdensome. For example, our calculations for a seventeen-thousand-person MSF project at American Airlines in 1989 were that the global process required more than one million pages of paper. Each page of paper required such administrative actions as sorting, stuffing, scanning, tracking, scoring, reporting, packing, addressing, and mailing—outbound (surveys), inbound (completed surveys), and then outbound again (reports).

Technology support reduces administrative costs by as much as 80 percent because software takes over many of the administrative responsibilities. A critical constraint for technology applications is access to a PC (Bracken, Summers, and Fleenor, 1998). MSF data may be collected electronically on disk, at a kiosk, over a LAN, by client server, or on the Web. Most organizations are migrating to a Web strategy for data collection.

Many organizations find the current infrastructure insufficient for automated MSF, so they delay MSF installation until the infrastructure is ready. We are aware of no large-scale MSF projects that have survived more than a few years without automated solutions. The administrative burden and cost simply exceed the organization's capability to sustain the process. Hence, MSF readiness should include an audit of available infrastructure. Organizations should be realistic regarding the capabilities inherent in supporting technology-based MSF. (For more on this subject, see also Chapter Eleven.)

Summary

Does MSF readiness predict user reactions or process success? Unfortunately, these data do not offer a convincing answer because the readiness metrics were not connected directly to the measures of user satisfaction. Yet on an anecdotal basis, MSF readiness is clearly associated with project satisfaction. For example, the Hewlett-Packard culture in Utah was very positive and very high on readiness. They are the first (and only) MSF project we have supported with 100 percent of users being satisfied with the MSF process. However, some other organizations with low "readiness" exhibited very high satisfaction scores once they became users.

An organization's culture often provides an excellent metric for MSF readiness. Our research and experience indicate that organizations with reputations as Fortune "most admired" tend to have the easiest job in introducing a culturally upside-down feedback system. We have also seen low-trust, hierarchical, autocratic organizations find adoption to be quick if the employees desperately desire change.

References

Bracken, D. W. "Maximizing the Uses of Multirater Feedback." In D. W. Bracken and others, *Should 360-Degree Feedback Be Used Only for Developmental Purposes?* Greensboro, N.C.: Center for Creative Leadership, 1997.

Bracken, D. W., Summers, L., and Fleenor, J. W. "High-Tech 360." *Training and Development,* 1998, *52*(8), 42–45.

Cohen, D. "Multisource Assessment for Competency Management." Paper presented at the 360-Degree Feedback Global Users Conference, Orlando, Fla., May 1998.

Edwards, M. R. "Productivity Improvement Through Innovations in Performance Appraisal." *Public Personnel Management Journal,* 1983, *12,* 113–124.

Edwards, M. R. "Making Performance Appraisals Meaningful and Fair." *Business,* 1989, *39*(3), 17–22.

Edwards, M. R., and Ewen, A. J. "Moving Multisource Assessment Beyond Development: The Linkage Between 360-Degree Feedback, Performance Appraisal and Pay." *ACA Journal,* Winter 1995, pp. 2–13.

Edwards, M. R., and Ewen, A. J. *Providing 360-Degree Feedback: An Approach to Enhancing Individual and Organizational Performance.* Scottsdale, Ariz.: American Compensation Association, 1996a.

Edwards, M. R., and Ewen, A. J. *360-Degree Feedback: The Powerful New Model for Employee Assessment and Performance Management.* New York: AMACOM, 1996b.

Edwards, M. R., and Ewen, A. J. "Multisource Assessment Survey of Industry Practice." Paper presented at the 360-Degree Feedback Global Users Conference, Orlando, Fla., May 1998.

Edwards, M. R., Ewen, A. J., and Verdini, W. "Fair Performance Management and Pay Practices for Diverse Work Forces: The Promise of Multisource Assessment." *ACA Journal,* Spring 1995, pp. 50–63.

Edwards, M. R., and Goodstein, L. D. "Experiential Learning Can Improve the Performance Appraisal Process." *Human Resource Management,* 1982, *11,* 18–23.

Edwards, M. R., and Sproull, J. R. "Safeguarding Your Employee Rating System." *Business,* 1985, *35*(2), 17–27.

Fishbein, M., and Aizen, I. *Belief, Attitude, Intention and Behavior: An Introduction to Theory and Research.* Reading, Mass.: Addison-Wesley, 1975.

Fleenor, J. W., and Prince, J. M. *Using 360-Degree Feedback in Organizations: An Annotated Bibliography.* Greensboro, N.C.: Center for Creative Leadership, 1997.

Jako, R. A. "Fitting Multirater Feedback into Organizational Strategy." In D. W. Bracken and others, *Should 360-Degree Feedback Be Used Only for Developmental Purposes?* Greensboro, N.C.: Center for Creative Leadership, 1997.

London, M., and Beatty, R. W. "360-Degree Feedback as a Competitive Advantage." *Human Resource Management,* 1993, *32,* 353–372.

CHAPTER 4

Linking Multisource Feedback Content with Organizational Needs

Walter W. Tornow
Carol Paradise Tornow

A multisource feedback process (MSF) can be one of the most powerful of all tools for promoting both individual and organizational development and effectiveness (Tornow and London, 1998). However, its full potential can only be realized if there is linkage built between the organizational and the individual perspectives. It is through such linkage that establish a foundation for organizational relevance and individual usefulness for the MSF process.

MSF linkage is achieved by attending to three major areas of consideration, the three Cs:

1. Context: the organization's business environment and strategy, which frame and provide the purpose and rationale for the instrument
2. Content: the instrument's domain focus in terms of what is to be measured
3. Connectivity: the instrument's constituencies in terms of who should be "connected" or involved in the MSF process

As Figure 4.1 shows, these three considerations are interrelated and—as foundation blocks for organizational relevance and usefulness to the individual—represent critical success factors for effectively designing and implementing MSF.

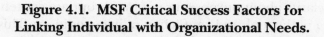

**Figure 4.1. MSF Critical Success Factors for
Linking Individual with Organizational Needs.**

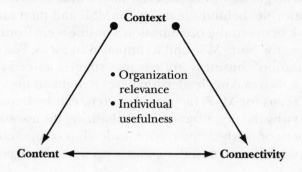

Context influences content; that is, organizational business needs and strategy are the motivational context for the instrument's application focus, purpose, and content domain. Also, context influences connectivity, where the business strategy and application focus create the rationale for determining who the relevant constituencies are that need to be connected up. In turn, content influences connectivity because understanding the application focus and content domain helps identify who the appropriate constituencies are to involve. Finally, connectivity influences content in that certain constituency groups are more appropriate sources for assessment and feedback for particular types of content.

This chapter describes the key defining elements for each of the three critical success factors; it also gives appropriate examples and considerations that can guide designing the MSF process.

Linkage Through Context

Attending to context is of primary importance because it guides the MSF design and thus helps ensure its organizational relevance. Context refers to the organization's business environment and strategy, which serve as a broad framework for the rationale, application focus, and purpose for MSF. It is for these reasons that considerations of context need to come first, before focusing on the instrument's content and connectivity. To do otherwise risks lack of clarity about purpose, use of inappropriate content or application of the tool, and conflicting rating conditions. This means taking a strategic view by being clear about what is driving organizational priorities behind the desire for MSF, and then making the critical link between the organization's business environment and the purpose for using MSF and its application focus. For example, an organization's business strategy may suggest a need for better leadership, thus making leadership development an important application focus for MSF. Its purpose, then, can be better understood as to why the organization is emphasizing the assessment and development of newly defined core leadership competencies, and the kind of feedback conditions that support such purpose.

Understanding Context: A Critical Success Factor

Understanding context and having it drive content and connectivity considerations helps the MSF instrument and process demonstrate organizational relevance. Furthermore, the usefulness of the instrument for individuals is helped because the content is related to what it takes to be successful—given the organization's business environment and strategy. In short, context is a critical success factor because it creates a strategic framework for understanding the need for MSF, offers a business rationale for its application focus and purpose, and thereby ensures the instrument's relevance to the organization and usefulness to the individuals. As the next section shows in more detail, contextual considerations can result in different purposes for the tool and application focus. In turn, these affect the type of instrument content and constituencies that need to be connected to the process.

Application Focus: An Important Contextual Consideration

Contextual considerations, including application focus and purpose, drive instrument content (what is to be measured) and target constituencies (who should be involved). Application focus and purpose also influence what is appropriate regarding the instrument's assessment and feedback conditions (data anonymity, confidentiality, ownership). To show the differential shaping effect contextual considerations can have, let us look at three major applications of MSF—individual or leadership development, culture change and alignment, and performance management—and how the respective application focus of each influences important variations in purpose, content, conditions, and target populations.

Individual or Leadership Development

By far the most frequent application of the MSF process is for individual development purposes—particularly, leadership development. Here, the MSF process serves as a core component for individual assessment and development (see Chapter Seventeen). It is a key learning tool that promotes greater self-awareness. This includes understanding how one is viewed by others and one's impact on others. More important, self-awareness is assumed to be a key part of personal development and a necessary condition for leadership effectiveness.

There are four conditions critical for success when using an MSF process for development:

1. *Anonymous feedback.* The multiple sources who are asked to provide feedback need to be guaranteed anonymity to ensure that their feedback is as open and candid as possible.

2. *Confidential feedback report.* Feedback recipients need to have assurance that no one else will see the information. This is to create a climate of "psychological safety," thus minimizing the potential for becoming defensive and maximizing the likelihood of the individual "owning" the feedback.

3. *"Ownership."* Recipients need to own their feedback, that is, take responsibility for the accuracy of the feedback and be willing to do something with it through an action or development plan.

4. *Climate for development.* The organization and the person's manager need to be committed to following up and supporting the person's action or development plan. Therefore, encouragement should be given for the recipient of the feedback to share the feedback and development plan with the manager for purposes of enlisting support and needed resources. However, the choice of sharing the information with the manager—although encouraged—cannot be coerced. It needs to be done voluntarily.

If these conditions of success are not present, then the likelihood of individual learning, growth, and change is significantly diminished.

Culture Change

A second major application of the MSF process is for culture-change purposes. Here, MSF can be used as a strategic vehicle to communicate new direction for the organization. For an example of communicating shared values and core competencies needed to implement a new direction, see Chapter Nineteen. The MSF process, through its instrumentation and feedback report, presents a common language that lets people assess whether they "walk the talk" and serves to facilitate organizational alignment and culture building. When the MSF process is used as a culture-change tool, it is more likely to be driven from the top down.

When using the MSF process for culture change, the feedback report can go not only to the individual member of a team or group but also to the team or group (without identifying any individual data in the team report). Team-level feedback—in addition to individual-level feedback—has the advantage of serving as an organizational diagnostic for monitoring the culture-change progress, as well as to facilitate sharing responsibility among the team members for creating and maintaining the new culture.

By integrating the culture-change purpose of MSF into the performance-management system, the organization can institutionalize the process of organizational alignment and ensure accountability. However, to be successful, a two-phase implementation plan should be considered for this use of MSF. Initially, the MSF process should be linked only to the development objective, and anonymity and confidentiality maintained as key feedback conditions. This serves to orient the organization's members to the new language and expectations. After sufficient trust in the new system has been built and there is adequate organizational readiness, integration into the performance management system for evaluation purposes can be considered. Linking MSF feedback to performance evaluation requires explicit communication about the change and broadening of purpose before the switch in conditions is to occur—specifically, that the feedback report is no longer confidential but shared with the manager as part of the performance appraisal and development planning discussions.

Performance Management

A third application focus for using the MSF process is linking it directly to the performance management process (see Chapter Twenty). This serves to integrate multiperspective feedback with performance planning, review, development, and reward. The goal is to involve in the feedback process the right constituencies, those who are vital to defining job success for the job incumbent. This becomes particularly important for those work situations where there is a high degree of interdependency for job success. Examples include project teams and other matrix management structures. The feedback recipient's manager usually is involved with the job incumbent in integrating and interpreting the feedback and the differences in perspectives that might emerge. In this application of MSF, the feedback conditions do not include confidentiality of the feedback report since it comes from and through the manager, and it may not include feedback-giver anonymity. For example, individuals who served in project manager roles may not remain anonymous when providing performance feedback for a project member; however, other project coworkers offering feedback may remain anonymous.

Using MSF for performance management is not without risk and controversy. The conditions for success when MSF is used "for development purposes only" are different from, and potentially at odds with, those when MSF is also used for performance appraisal purposes. That is, conditions of anonymity and confidentiality—which are central to MSF for development only—are not observed generally if MSF is used for appraisal purposes as well. As a result of changing these conditions, the concern is that achievement of the developmental objective may be jeopardized; that is, little learning, change, and growth may occur as a result of the MSF feedback because the conditions for success (anonymity, confidentiality, voluntary data sharing) were absent.

Another issue with using MSF for performance management revolves around candor and anonymity. Anonymity of ratings may promote candor, but it works against rating accountability. Although not having ratings be anonymous promotes accountability, this can detract from candor in an organization whose members are not skilled in giving and receiving feedback. Generally speaking, there must be a considerable amount of trust and organizational readiness before considering using MSF for both development and performance management purposes.

Table 4.1 is a summary framework for relating MSF applications to their different purpose, content, conditions, and target populations. Organizational readiness may differ depending on which of the three MSF applications are desired.

Table 4.1. Relating Application Focus to Purpose, Content, Conditions, and Populations.

Application Focus	Purpose	Content	Conditions	Target Population
Individual/ leadership development	Intrapersonal and inter-personal development via self-awareness	Leadership competencies	Anonymous feedback; confidential feedback report; voluntary sharing	Leaders, managers, high-potentials
Culture change and alignment	Communicate new competencies and facilitate organizational alignment	Core competencies; climate assessment	Anonymous feedback; confidential feedback report on first one or two trials	Top leaders, managers, professionals
Performance management	Performance expectations and feedback from key constituencies	Competency profile; performance plan; customer requirements	Feedback may not be anonymous; feedback not confidential, but shared by manager	Jobs that are highly interdependent; project work teams; matrix management

Linkage Through Content

Given a clear understanding of context, the second critical success factor for effectively designing and implementing MSF is its content. Content deals with the instrument's domain focus and coverage in terms of what is to be measured. Content can be expressed in several ways. For purposes of this chapter, with its emphasis on linkage, only three of the major content categories are described. For a more extensive description of item content considerations, Van Velsor (1998) provides further examples and guidelines (see also Chapter Six on instrument design).

Types of Content

Among the major content categories that MSF instruments use for organizational and individual development and effectiveness purposes are values, strategies, and goals; skills; and competencies. They differ in perspective and emphasis, yet they can also have important interrelationships if incorporated as part of an integrated MSF design.

Values, Strategies, Goals

The first form of content expression emphasizes broad directional commitments stemming from the organization's strategic intents. That is, they offer strategic direction as to where the organization is heading and thereby facilitate organizational alignment through specifying the mapping of behavioral expectations individuals need to meet. An example of this content category can be seen in one company's statement of its three core values:

1. Commitment to marketing ("We will respond creatively to customers' current and future needs")
2. Commitment to quality ("We will meet customers' expectations for value and service")
3. Commitment to people ("We will practice a management philosophy that empowers the people of this company to reach their full potential")

This form of content expression is especially helpful for ensuring organizational relevance of the MSF instrument, since it calls out quite explicitly the organizational values. Translating these values behaviorally makes the instrument more useful for individuals. Skills and competencies are two such ways of making the content behavioral.

Skills

This type of content expression reflects the specific listings of employee skill requirements that enable the behavioral expression contained in the broad specifications of values, strategies, and goals statements. These typically serve to define in explicit and micro fashion the key characteristics of individual difference that people need to possess for effectively meeting the behavioral expectations laid out by the organization.

Examples of skills can be found in one of the MSF instruments highlighted by Van Velsor (1998): analyzing issues, establishing plans, providing direction, leading courageously, fostering teamwork, motivating others, coaching and developing, championing change, and managing disagreements.

Competencies

Competencies make up an umbrella category spanning the first two perspectives. They represent a combination of skills, knowledge, abilities, values, and other individual difference characteristics that are necessary for effective performance. They typically represent in macro fashion the behavioral expression of this combination. An example of this type of content category can be found in a set of core competencies used by a major global organization: customer focus, results orientation, innovation, leadership, collaboration, change orientation, and communication. Each actually represents a competency cluster that includes a set of specific competencies. For example, *collaboration* includes relationship building, interpersonal understanding, and teamwork. Various types of job analysis techniques are available to give practitioners the necessary how-to's in building competency models relevant to their particular needs (Reilly and McGourty, 1998).

Which particular set of competencies are required in an organization is a function of its business strategy and the resulting organizational capability requirements. Many organizations adopt competency models for integration with their business strategy as a way of being sure that both human resource and MSF processes have demonstrable organizational relevance. Figure 4.2 is a conceptual model of the competency perspective and how business strategy drives competency requirements and MSF design to affect individual and organizational effectiveness outcomes.

Competency Models as Integrating Mechanisms

What makes competency models useful as strategic business tools is that they can serve as a framework for relating the competency requirements employees need for success to the capability requirements of the business. This causes us to link individual actions— such as training programs or development plans—to the needs of the business by focusing on those competencies important for success. They are also a mechanism for integrating the various HR processes and applications into a coherent and mutually supportive system by providing a common language for defining, communicating, and evaluating employee behavior.

As business needs change over time, so do the capabilities required for success. As organizational capability requirements change, so do the competency requirements of individual jobs. Therefore, competency profiles should be viewed as "living tools,"

**Figure 4.2. A Conceptual Model of How
Business Strategy Drives Competency
Requirements, MSF Design, and Outcomes.**

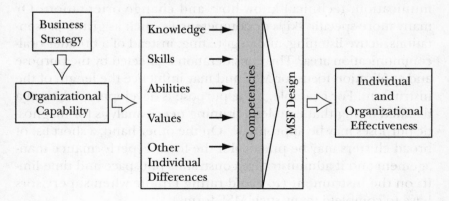

dynamic documents with specific competency requirements that may be expected to change over time. The organization's particular set of needed competencies may also evolve over time as human resources and line managers gain experience with these competencies in their actual practice and as the organization evolves in its capability requirements. This evolution of the competency model may take the form of refining definitions of specific existing competencies, adding new competencies, or changing existing ones.

Finally, competencies should have ongoing evaluation for their credibility and currency. For example, they should pass the test of line managers really believing that superior performance on the listed competencies indeed improves organizational performance. A second test of their credibility is to ask whether the organization's "stars" would score high on them, relative to those who are less successful.

Content Considerations

Several considerations influence MSF instrument content. Although related to application focus and purpose, they add another set of dimensions when deciding about the nature of the content. Three of the major ones are level of perspective, time frame for change, and human resource orientation.

Level of Perspective: Macro Versus Micro

What is the level of detail that should be covered by the instrument: a few, broad-brush skill or competency areas, such as communication, technical know-how, and change orientation? Or many more-specific skills or competencies, such as giving presentations, active listening, and negotiating, instead of a broader oral-communication area? This consideration is affected by the purpose and application focus for MSF and may influence the length of the instrument. For example, if the purpose is developmental, then a detailed listing that enables a training needs analysis for diagnostic purposes may be appropriate. On the other hand, a short list of broad clusters may be practical if the focus is performance management and if administrative constraints put space and time limits on the instrument (to avoid rating fatigue when supervisors have to complete many such MSF forms).

Time Frame: Short-Term Versus Long-Term

How quickly is change to be noted in the skill or competency areas: almost immediately, such as within three to six months? Or more lasting, deep change, which requires longer periods of time, follow-up, and resource commitment? Time frame consideration is also related to such factors as (1) the trainability of the particular skill or competency areas, (2) how quickly the organization needs to acquire the particular skills and competencies, and (3) the preferred human resource orientation in the organization. For example, if the application purpose is developmental, then the instrument might include only those skill and competency areas that are developable. On the other hand, an MSF instrument that is to be used for performance management purposes should probably include all the skill and competency areas important for job success, regardless of their trainability. This is even more important if selection becomes another focus for MSF application.

Human Resource Strategy: Selection Versus Development

Which is the preferred strategy in the organization: selection for immediate import of needed skill or competency areas, or training and development for longer-term, in-house growth of the needed capability requirements? For example, a selection orientation becomes appropriate when an organization adopts a business strategy that necessitates quick and drastic culture change, and where the current skill and competency set is inadequate to meet future business demands. On the other hand, development may be the preferred orientation if the organization wants to use its current workforce and therefore wishes to invest in them to ensure continued currency and competitiveness of skills and competencies. The type of human resource strategy is also related to how amenable skill or competency areas are to development. Therefore, the organization may go outside to hire people with the needed skills and competencies that are difficult to develop inside, while using a developmental approach for the other areas that are more amenable to in-house growth and change.

Relationship to Context and Connectivity

As indicated before, content is a function of context. Application focus and purpose influence what is covered by the instrument domain—such things as leadership competencies, core values, performance plans, and customer requirements. Content is also influenced by considerations of how detailed the assessment needs to be, how quickly change is to come about, and how developable specific content areas are.

Content areas also suggest the appropriate constituencies with whom to connect in the assessment and feedback process. Certain content areas are appropriate for bosses, others for peers, others for subordinates, and still others for customers. For example, customers are an appropriate constituency for providing content feedback in areas related to customer focus and quality of service, but less appropriate when the content deals with, say, delegating. Bosses have a good perspective typically when it comes to such content areas as planning and strategic thinking but usually are less well placed observationally to comment about subordinates' skills in delegating and coaching. Peers can be a good constituency to provide content feedback in such areas as collaboration and technical know-how, but they may be less so if the content deals with strategic planning and delegating skills (for more on rater selection, see Chapter Seven).

Linkage Through Connectivity

The final critical success factor in effectively designing and implementing MSF is connectivity. Connectivity focuses on what the appropriate constituencies are that need to be connected or involved in the MSF process. Connecting the appropriate constituencies also has a significant impact on perceptions of organizational relevance and usefulness to the individuals regarding MSF process and results.

Multiple Perspectives

People having varying status relationships with MSF recipients generally have different views of the recipients' skills and competencies. The reasons for such variations among these perspectives may include differences in expectations, kinds and amounts of interactions, behaviors toward certain groups, and observational opportunities. Feedback sources such as peers, bosses, direct reports, and customers can provide unique perspectives, some of which overlap while others complement, depending on content area and application focus.

Conflicting Roles and Conditions

Different driving purposes for MSF can influence what the appropriate rating conditions are for instrument administration, and the roles participants are asked to play. For example, the rating conditions regarding confidentiality, anonymity, and data ownership typically vary depending on whether the purpose is development only or appraisal. Furthermore, supervisors find it difficult to balance the potential conflict in role demands of playing both coach and judge when mixing MSF purposes of development with appraisal. Issues of rating reciprocity can also surface in a team or project management environment where participants play multiple roles for each other in providing and receiving feedback. These assessment and feedback issues are more likely to turn competitive if the purpose is appraisal (where there is a perception of a fixed pie regarding rating evaluations, pay, and promotion) than if it is for development.

Relating Connectivity to Context and Content

Application focus, purpose, and content influence which target constituencies should be involved for organizational relevance and fairness. For example, customers are a critical source for feedback regarding service quality and customer orientation (Paradise Tornow, 1998). Direct reports provide invaluable feedback when it comes to leadership-related issues, while peers are in a good position to assess content areas of cooperation, coordination, and technical know-how.

Situational demands for MSF are also inherent in highly interdependent work settings and therefore influence the feedback sources to be involved. Examples are teams, project management, and matrix management structures. R&D environments frequently incorporate this type of organizational form and offer an important opportunity for MSF application. Feedback sources here would need to represent all those constituencies who have a stake in the recipient's work and success, such as other project members, project managers, project customers, and functional boss.

Conclusion

In conclusion, understanding the linkage among MSF context, content, and connectivity is critical to effectively designing the MSF process and developing the items on which feedback is based. Specific item focus and content follow from a careful understanding of the unique strategic context, broad content objectives, and connectivity requirements of the organization.

References

Paradise Tornow, C. "The Competitive Advantage of Customer Involvement in 360-Degree Feedback." In W. W. Tornow and M. London (eds.), *Maximizing the Value of 360-Degree Feedback: A Process for Individual and Organizational Development*. San Francisco: Jossey-Bass, 1998.

Reilly, R. R., and McGourty, J. "Performance Appraisal in Team Settings." In J. W. Smither (ed.), *Performance Appraisal: State of the Art in Practice*. San Francisco: Jossey-Bass, 1998.

Tornow, W. W., and London, M. *Maximizing the Value of 360-Degree Feedback: A Process for Successful Individual and Organizational Development*. San Francisco: Jossey-Bass, 1998.

Van Velsor, E. "Designing 360-Degree Feedback to Enhance Involvement, Self-Determination, and Commitment." In W. W. Tornow and M. London (eds.), *Maximizing the Value of 360-Degree Feedback: A Process for Individual and Organizational Development*. San Francisco: Jossey-Bass, 1998.

CHAPTER 5

Selecting a Multisource Feedback Instrument

Ellen Van Velsor
Jean Brittain Leslie

With hundreds of multisource feedback (MSF) instruments on the market today, choosing the best instrument for your use can be a daunting task (Van Velsor, Leslie, and Fleenor, 1998). This chapter focuses on the general characteristics of "good" MSF instruments and offers guidelines for selecting the instrument that best meets your user needs. The chapter concludes with a discussion of the appropriate use of standard and customized instruments. Although we do not review specific multisource feedback instruments here, the reader interested in in-depth reviews is referred to *Feedback to Managers* (Leslie and Fleenor, 1998).

Characteristics of Quality MSF Instruments

Although there are a set of quality criteria that MSF instruments should meet (AERA, APA, and NCME, 1999), there is no one best instrument. A good instrument is one that meets these quality standards, is a good fit with the target audience and intended use in your organization, and is distributed by a vendor offering a full range of services to the user, as indicated in Exhibit 5.1. We discuss each of these points in turn.

Exhibit 5.1. Qualities of a Good MSF Instrument.

- Permits easy access to complete information about the product
- Fits with your organization's intended use
- Is well-constructed, with established reliability and validity
- Has an ongoing research program for continuous learning and instrument update
- Provides feedback in a format that is understandable and useful
- Provides guidelines for an administrative process that protects the anonymity of rater data and ensures confidentiality for the ratee
- Has complete interpretive materials available for both the facilitator and the feedback recipients
- Has a resource-rich development guide or a process available for action planning and follow-up

---

Easy Access to Complete Information

To choose the instrument that best meets your needs, you require several kinds of information. At a minimum, you should be able to secure all of the following:

- A listing of definitions for the domains assessed by the instrument
- A sample item for each domain
- A sample feedback report
- Information on what training or certification is available or required
- Cost information
- Information on available scoring options and translations
- Summaries of all psychometric research conducted on the instrument to date
- Descriptions of the research samples used in that research

A top-of-the-line vendor of MSF feedback instruments will have this information ready for delivery to you on request. In terms of psychometric research, what should be readily available to you are summaries of the results of factor analyses or other methods used to construct the feedback scales, results of studies conducted on item or scale test and retest reliability, internal consistency scale reliability, and criterion validity research.

If, after a couple of contacts with the vendor, all you can get your hands on is a brochure or address of a Website that describes the instrument in glowing terms, or if the vendor acts as if any of this information is proprietary, then shop elsewhere.

Good Fit with Intended Use

When reviewing MSF instruments as a careful buyer, you need to be clear about the fit between certain properties of the instrument and the intended use of that instrument in your organization. The four steps to assessing good fit, described in the sections that follow, have to do with (1) the domains assessed by the instrument, (2) the characteristics of the target audience, (3) the desire to measure change over time, and (4) the resources you have in your organization to implement multisource feedback.

The first step in making a good assessment of fit is to compare your understanding of the specific domains that are important to your organization to the definitions of the assessment domains that the vendor gives you.

The domains assessed by the instrument are important for two reasons. First, you want the instrument you choose to match, as closely as possible, the competency areas perceived or identified as important in your organization (see Chapter Four for more on this topic). Second, if you intend to use an instrument for development, you want the domains assessed to be behavioral domains that are amenable to change. We discuss this second issue later in the chapter.

In assessing fit between an instrument's domains and your company's needs, one source of potential confusion is the multiple meanings that assessment domains can have. An assessment domain such as "flexibility," for example, can be defined as "behaving in ways that are often seen as opposites" (Lombardo and McCauley, 1994), or it can mean "easily adjusts to change" (Campbell, 1998). Each of these flexibility scale definitions can be useful, but the meaning of *flexible* in each instance differs. So it is important to be sure you are getting domains that assess the qualities you are looking for, as closely as possible. If too few assessment domains on a particular instrument appear to measure the kinds of leadership capacities you are looking for, try other instruments.

The next step in making a good assessment of fit is to compare your understanding of the intended target audience, to whom the instrument will be administered, to good descriptions of the research samples used both in the development research on the instrument and in generating instrument norms (in terms of industry, managerial level, age, race, gender, and national culture). If you are using the instrument outside the United States, be aware of translations available and what is known abroad about the reliability and validity of the instrument.

For example, if you are looking for an instrument to use with middle-level managers in a financial services organization with several locations outside of the United States, be sure that the instrument you choose is applicable to this group. By *applicable*, we mean not only that the assessment domains are the right ones for your organization but also that the instrument has been developed for and/or tested on a group similar to the group that will be using it. If the research sample on which the items and scales were tested comprised students at a U.S. military academy and no further research has been done to test the instrument with other samples, then you do not have enough information to judge that it is suitable for your use in this instance. If subsequent research (let's say with male managers in domestic marketing firm and with female college presidents in the United States) has results that confirm the reliability and validity of the assessment domains, you are closer to being able to judge how useful the instrument is to you. If further studies have shown positive results for your industry, in countries representing your target population, having a gender mix of middle managers similar to your organization, then you have an instrument with a very good fit to your target audience.

Although you won't always find that research has been done on your exact population, especially if your group is culturally or racially diverse, most MSF instruments do use managerial populations in at least a significant portion of their research and development work. Look for an instrument that has been tested on a group as similar as possible to your target audience.

Preferably, the instrument you choose uses norms that focus on or include managers with characteristics similar to your target audience as well. Norms are the average scores to which individuals are compared, in presenting scored feedback.

If portions of your audience come from outside the United States, look for an instrument that has norms generated from a diverse sample or that has separate norms available for diverse groups. If possible, choose an instrument that has norms available for the target countries in your group. It is easy for people abroad to dismiss their results if they are compared to managers only from the United States (Leslie, Gryskiewicz, and Dalton, 1998). Similarly, if norms are generated only from white male managers and a proportion of your audience is female, African American, or from another ethnic group, reasonable questions about the applicability of the norms can be raised by members of these groups.

Finally, if you intend to use the instrument outside the United States, find out now about translations available and what is known about the reliability and validity of the instrument in the target countries (see Chapter Twenty-Seven for more on cross-cultural issues). Too often, a decision is made to adopt a particular instrument, only to find out later that it has not been translated into the languages needed to implement the process in all critical geographic areas. When done well, translations take time, and a last-minute effort to pull off this work can result in poorly constructed and invalid measures.

The third step in making a good assessment of fit is to consider whether there is a desire down the road for an assessment of change using the instrument. For example, if the instrument is used as part of a training program or long-term development effort, it may be desirable to plan to retest participants at some point in the future, so as to be able to evaluate the impact of the training or track behavior change or skill improvement over time. If measuring change will be an issue, check for test and retest reliability, and review the response scale used on the instrument. Test and retest reliability is particularly important for understanding the stability of scores over short periods of time. If you know that the item and scale scores do not change randomly owing to poor instrument construction, you can be sure that change that does show up over time is actual change in behavior or improvement in skills. Reliability is discussed more fully later on in this chapter (see also Chapter Nine).

If your intention is to use the instrument to measure change, it would also be wise to pay attention to the response scale used in the instrument. By *response scale*, we mean the response choices given to raters with each item on the test. Most MSF instruments use a frequency or magnitude response scale, where the choices represent the frequencies or degrees to which a behavior can occur. An example of this format would be "How *often* does the manager display the following behaviors?" with the response categories being "very frequently," "frequently," "sometimes," "occasionally," and "never." If an instrument has this type of response scale, its usefulness for assessing change over time lies in knowing whether the frequency of behaviors increases or decreases. However, if you are looking for improvement in quality of behavior or mastery of skills, frequency of behavior may not give you information you are looking for.

Another way to assess skills or behaviors is with a response scale that measures mastery or performance relative to others. An example of a mastery format would be "Compared to other managers at this level, how would you rate the skills and behaviors of this manager?" with response options being "among the best," "better than most," "somewhat above average," "about average," "somewhat below average," "lower than most," and "among the worst." This type of scale may better allow you to make inferences about change over time in the level or quality of individuals' skills. However, if a developmental intervention is organizationwide, this type of response scale may not show the change that is actually happening, because the standard of comparison may be raised if the group as a whole improves.

Assessing change using MSF can be complex and misleading. To date, few MSF instrument vendors have completed research showing that individuals change after feedback in the areas assessed by the instrument. We do know that regardless of the instrument used, change requires time and support processes beyond the feedback itself. If creating and measuring change is part of your plan, we advise that you do some additional reading, using some of the many good sources available on this topic (Martineau, 1998; see also Chapters Sixteen and Twenty-Two).

The final step in making a good assessment of fit is to review information about the expertise required of feedback facilitators, the comprehensiveness of support and interpretive materials available, the options for administration and scoring, and the costs of different versions of the MSF instrument package, in light of the staff and financial resources available in your organization for its administration.

MSF instruments vary with respect to how much guidance they give facilitators and feedback recipients. In general, the less experienced your facilitators, the more they benefit from training or certification and the more extensive the written guidelines and interpretive materials they need. If individual feedback recipients receive little or no facilitation of their feedback, clear and comprehensive interpretive materials must be available for feedback recipients. If an instrument is used by individuals not skilled in the English language, all materials should be available in translated form.

Once you have made an assessment of fit between your organization's intended use of an MSF instrument and the features and benefits offered by a variety of instruments, you have narrowed your search to a handful of possibilities. Considering the other criteria of quality MSF instruments, which follow, then helps you narrow your choice to the one best for you.

Good Instrument Construction

To get the best value in an instrument, choose an instrument that is well constructed and has demonstrated reliability and validity. Reliability and validity have to do with an instrument's ability to produce consistent, stable results, to actually measure what it claims to measure, and (with MSF instruments focused on managerial or leadership behaviors) to assess qualities that are related to a manager's effectiveness. A high-quality instrument has met or exceeded minimal test development standards; has publicly available reports on the psychometric properties of the instrument; and does not make claims about its properties, impact, or appropriate use that are not supported by research.

The psychometric properties that are particularly important for MSF instruments include test and retest reliability, internal consistency and validity with respect to the main inferences underlying the use of the instrument. If an instrument is too "new" or too early in its development for such research to have been done, it is not ready for public use. This section briefly explains each of these areas; we do not go into depth in any one area. (See Chapter Nine for more on this subject.)

Test and retest reliability refers to the stability of responses over short periods of time. If items are well constructed and unambiguous, but sufficient time has not elapsed to expect real change in behavior or skill, then individuals' responses to items should not change significantly from one administration to the next. However, if the meaning of an item is unclear or debatable, the lack of clarity can produce variations in response and you cannot be sure whether change on the item is due to actual change in the individual or to item instability. It is appropriate to eliminate unstable items from an instrument or to revise them to improve their stability.

In reviewing information about an instrument, you might find that test and retest reliability is reported for items (the actual questions people respond to on an instrument), or you may find that it is reported for scales (the assessment domains on which people receive feedback, comprising multiple items). Some may argue that the scale level of reporting is sufficient, in that the scales are the domains on which people receive feedback, but we believe it is important to review the item-level results as well. When people work on how to improve in a particular domain, they often look at the items as specific behaviors and understandably choose the lowest-rated items to work on. Test and retest reliability is important because you do not want managers trying to work on items that are unstable to begin with.

Although many statisticians believe a test and retest value of .7, over short periods of time, is sufficient, many MSF instruments do not achieve this result, especially at the item level. Raters are typically are not trained observers and therefore rely on their perceptions, which can change according to events or interactions over a short period of time. In general, items that are specific and behavioral have higher test and retest reliability than those that are general or that require raters to make inferences from their experience to values or traits that are not directly observable. So in considering an instrument for use, check to see that test and retest reliability is available, and that unstable items have been eliminated in the development process. But do not expect test and retest reliability results to be as high as those expected for internal consistency, which we describe below.

Homogeneity within scales is called internal consistency. You should find information about internal consistency reported for each scale on which feedback is received. Items that are included in the same scale are intended to measure the same construct. By studying the internal consistency of scales, we gather statistical evidence that this is so (rather than relying on the author's judgment that it is so). Most often, a statistic called Chronbach's alpha is reported for each assessment domain, with a value of .7 generally considered acceptable. Beware of using instruments reporting a disproportionate number of scales having alphas less than .6, as this indicates that one or more of the assessment scales on which people receive feedback may not be measuring the domain or domains with an acceptable level of precision.

Validity has mainly to do with the meaning that you want to attach to the scores on an instrument. People who use multisource feedback often put unquestioned faith in the products they use, making assumptions that have not been tested about the use of the product. One common assumption when looking at the scores on an instrument is that the scores measure what they claim to be measuring. For example, we assume that the "decisiveness" scale measures decisiveness and not some other competency. To support this assumption, we would want to see evidence that decisiveness scores on this instrument are correlated with decisiveness scores on another instrument, or with scores on personality measures related to decisiveness. We might also look for evidence that these decisiveness scores are uncorrelated with aspects of personality that we know to be unrelated to decisiveness; or we might want to know that people widely considered content experts in assessing decisiveness have reviewed and approved the items.

Another assumption we often make about assessment domains on an MSF instrument is that the scores on these domains are related to managerial effectiveness. After all, this is what we are trying to improve, by choosing certain competencies to focus on with an MSF process. So it is important to look for evidence that scores on these scales are actually related to effectiveness. A quality MSF instrument that has been on the market for some time will be able to boast many studies showing strong relationships between higher scores and greater effectiveness. You should not use an instrument that cannot produce even one such report.

Ongoing Research Program for Continuous Learning and Instrument Update

An MSF instrument is a measurement tool. As such, it is vital that it be as well tuned as possible to the domains it attempts to measure and to the context in which this measurement is carried out. Whenever a quality MSF instrument is released for sale, the psychometric properties of the most frequent intended use are available. This often means it has been tested on a sample of U.S. managers at one or more managerial levels (middle or upper management). Sometimes, but not always, this sample is gender- and racially diverse. Even so, the original research sample is necessarily bound by time. That is, the research and norm data, collected at one point in time, do not necessarily withstand the passage of time and organizational change. Thus research results need to go up for periodic reexamination. Once new or additional target audiences are identified, more research should be undertaken to establish the reliability and validity of use with these groups (for example, leaders in the education sector, or leaders in countries other than the United States).

Feedback in an Understandable and Useful Format

A quality MSF instrument displays feedback in a format that helps the individual sort through the large amounts of data generated in the MSF process. On an instrument that does not require training in use, the feedback display should be easily interpretable by the feedback recipient.

Good instruments usually employ a variety of techniques to help individuals understand their data (see Chapter Twelve). Comparing an individual's scores to norms (derived from a large sample of individuals who have taken the instrument previously) is a common practice, as is highlighting the highest or lowest scores received. Focusing the individual on self-rater discrepancies is a frequently used strategy, sometimes providing a listing of the scales showing the largest differences between self-perceptions and the ratings of others. Other strategies for helping people understand the meaning of their scores include comparison to an ideal (whereby individual scores are plotted against desired scores) or supplementing scores with rater perceptions of the specific areas where the managers should "do more" or "do less," for example, "do more listening" or "do less monitoring" (Leslie and Fleenor, 1998).

Guidelines to Protect Rater Anonymity and Ratee Confidentiality

Regardless of how an MSF instrument is used, trust and support are essential elements of the process (Chappelow, 1998; Van Velsor, 1998). If raters do not trust that their ratings are anonymous, they may not express their true views in their ratings. If the individuals being rated do not believe that their data are treated confidentially by those responsible for facilitating feedback and coaching them, they may not give accurate self-views or may refuse to participate in the process.

Ensuring anonymity and confidentiality in the MSF process has partly to do with how the instrument is constructed and scored and partly with how the data and feedback report are handled. Most MSF instruments break raters out into groups for purposes of feedback. That is, ratings from peers are averaged and displayed separately from ratings of direct reports. A good MSF instrument does not provide feedback in a rating category where there are fewer than three respondents. In other words, if an individual has had three forms completed by direct reports but only one or two forms completed by peers, a good instrument does not include separate feedback from peers. Instead, peer data might be combined with direct report data or simply not scored, so as to protect the anonymity of the one or two peers who did respond.

The one exception to this "rule" seems to be for the boss's feedback. Many high-quality MSF instruments now provide the boss's ratings separately from others, although we don't know as much as we need to know about whether removing the protection of anonymity from bosses' ratings changes the nature of those ratings.

The rationale for this practice is that people being rated are particularly interested in the boss's ratings. Yet recent research (Brutus, London, and Martineau, 1999) shows that managers pay most attention, in their feedback reports, to ratings provided by direct reports.

Although confidentiality of individuals' data is particularly critical in an environment where trust is low, it is always important and deserving of careful consideration in implementing MSF. A good MSF instrument features guidelines for setting up a process in your organization that ensures adequate confidentiality; or the vendor can give you references for learning more about how to create a safe climate for feedback (see Chapter Twenty-Four for an applied example).

Interpretive Materials for Facilitator and Feedback Recipient

Additionally, a good MSF instrument comes with supplemental materials that aid in using and interpreting the instrument. Extensive trainer guides or manuals, videos, toll-free telephone numbers, and training programs are all examples of support materials a user can expect from a quality vendor. A trainer's guide gives detailed information on the development of the instrument, norms for various subsamples, step-by-step administrative information, tips for designing a feedback session, exercises for understanding the results, and information about ongoing research. Certification training can ensure that the person using the instrument understands the process recommended by the vendor, the research on the instrument, the feedback display and results, and how to give feedback.

Resource-Rich Development Guide and Process for Action Planning and Follow-Up

Feedback without development or action planning often does not have impact. If you have chosen an instrument that displays the feedback in a understandable and useful format, participants in the MSF process have a clear idea about what their feedback is and what it means (often called respectively the "what" and the "so what"). To conclude the process (to get clear on the "now what"), people require resources for development planning. Vendors offer all sorts of developmental, planning, and follow-up resources, including guide books, workshops, toll-free hotlines, e-help, development planning worksheets or cards, and postassessments to measure change after a period of working to improve skills. A good MSF instrument comes with one or more development planning tools (in paper or electronic format, or conducted as part of a training seminar) to help people plan for action as a result of their feedback.

Appropriate Use of Standard and Custom MSF Instruments

This chapter has focused so far on selecting a standard, off-the-shelf MSF instrument, the most readily available and best-understood means of gaining access to multisource feedback tools that are reliable and valid. However, after close inspection of available instruments, you might find that there is no single off-the-shelf instrument that provides a good-enough fit for competencies you are trying to develop. In this case, consider customization as an option.

The customization option is one of the most exciting features of MSF available today. Customization can mean working with a vendor who alters a standard instrument for you, by adding new items to assess additional areas or by allowing you to choose only a subset of the scales. Customization can also mean purchasing a tool or process that lets *you* design an instrument from a pool of available items or scales. In either case, the process can allow you to assess only those areas you feel are important and can give you flexibility in how raters are broken out and how feedback is displayed— and even what the instrument is titled. These customized features may produce an instrument that results in increased buy-in, participation, and impact.

Yet MSF instruments with an "open architecture" (allowing clients to build an instrument with a pool of items or scales) are currently the subject of considerable debate. The main issue of concern is the degree to which customization reduces the overall integrity (reliability and validity) of the instrument. When using a high-quality, standard instrument, the buyer can be reasonably assured that the assessment scales are reliable in their measurement, measure what they say they measure, and are related to effectiveness as a leader.

But if an instrument is customized, the necessary psychometric research may not be part of the process. For example, if additional items are written to add to a standard MSF instrument, the user does not know whether those new items, and the scales created from these items, are reliable and valid, unless additional research is conducted. Similarly, if assessment domains are customized by eliminating or adding items to existing scales, the integrity of the original assessment may be compromised in ways that cannot be understood without further analysis. Some vendors who specialize in customization put together an instrument that meets client specifications without testing for reliability or validity, while others may be willing to conduct the research to create psychometrically sound instrument domains. This is an area where the buyer needs to beware. (For more on instrument development, see Chapter Six.)

To avoid many of these pitfalls, the best approach to customization, in our view, is for the customer to pick and choose among a pool of available assessment domains (that is, feedback scales, rather than individual items) that have established reliability and validity. If additional domains are needed, the items written to assess these domains should undergo comparable testing to establish basic knowledge about their psychometric properties. This process allows the customer to receive the benefits of customization, while still maintaining high quality standards. As with a standard instrument, information should be available on the reliability and validity of each of the scales in the database, the populations on which the scales have been tested, and the target managers for whom they are appropriate. Given the evolving state of technology, this documentation may be built into the same electronic platform on which the customization process resides, or made available in printed format.

Although customization is appealing to many, it does have limitations. An important one is the nonavailability of norms. Norms are built up as a standard instrument is used over hundreds or thousands of managers. The larger the normative database for an instrument, and the more varied the use, the more likely it is that sizable norm data are available for diverse populations. The disadvantage of an instrument customized for use by a single client is that norms may not exist, unless the customized instrument is simply a shortened version of a standard tool.

Conclusion

Taking the time to evaluate your needs as well as the features and benefits of a variety of MSF instruments certainly pays off in terms of participant acceptance of both the process and the feedback. Given the significant investment of time and money when MSF is used widely or over time in an organization, this acceptance is a critical factor in obtaining the impact that you desire from the process.

References

American Educational Research Association (AERA), American Psychological Association (APA), and National Council on Measurement in Education (NCME). *Standards for Educational and Psychological Testing.* Washington, D.C.: AERA Publications, 1999.

Brutus, S., London, M., and Martineau, J. "The Differential Impact of Interpersonal Feedback from Subordinates, Peers, Supervisors, and Self on Developmental Planning." Paper presented at the fourteenth annual conference of the Society for Industrial and Organizational Psychology, Atlanta, Ga., May 1999.

Campbell, D. *Campbell Leadership Index (CLI).* Rosemont, Ill.: National Computer Systems Workforce Development, 1998.

Chappelow, C. T. "360-Degree Feedback." In C. D. McCauley, R. S. Moxley, and E. Van Velsor (eds.), *Center for Creative Leadership Handbook of Leadership Development.* San Francisco: Jossey-Bass, 1998.

Leslie, J. B., and Fleenor, J. W. *Feedback to Managers.* Greensboro, N.C.: Center for Creative Leadership, 1998.

Leslie, J. B., Gryskiewicz, N. D., and Dalton, M. A. "Cultural Influences on the 360-Degree Feedback Process." In W. W. Tornow and M. London (eds.), *Maximizing the Value of 360-Degree Feedback: A Process for Successful Individual and Organizational Development.* San Francisco: Jossey-Bass, 1998.

Lombardo, M. M., and McCauley, C. D. *Benchmarks: Developmental Reference Points for Managers and Executives.* Greensboro, N.C.: Center for Creative Leadership, 1994.

Martineau, J. "Using 360-Degree Surveys to Assess Change." In W. W. Tornow and M. London (eds.), *Maximizing the Value of 360-Degree*

Feedback: A Process for Successful Individual and Organizational Development. San Francisco: Jossey-Bass, 1998.

Van Velsor, E. "Designing 360-Feedback to Enhance Involvement, Self-Determination, and Commitment." In W. W. Tornow and M. London (eds.), *Maximizing the Value of 360-Degree Feedback: A Process for Successful Individual and Organizational Development.* San Francisco: Jossey-Bass, 1998.

Van Velsor, E., Leslie, J. B., and Fleenor, J. W. *Choosing 360: A Guide to Selecting 360-Degree Instruments.* Greensboro, N.C.: Center for Creative Leadership, 1998.

CHAPTER 6

Instrumentation Design

Steven G. Rogelberg
Janine Waclawski

A high-quality measurement instrument is essential to any multi-source feedback (MSF) effort or intervention. Without good instrumentation, feedback providers (raters) may withhold participation. Alternatively, for those who do participate, invalid or misleading data may be collected. This chapter examines issues pertaining to designing an MSF instrument. The design issues considered are generally micro in nature, ranging from constructing the items to pilot testing your MSF instrument.

First Steps

Instrument construction is a difficult, time-consuming, and often politically charged task. As a result, the first step in creating an MSF instrument is to form an instrument construction team. The team should be composed of a small set of core members (four to six people). Team members should represent the three main MSF stakeholder groups: feedback recipients, feedback providers, and coaches. We also recommend that a human resource representative (say, a trainer or organization development specialist) be included on the team. Finally, an external consultant may bring an objective viewpoint to the team. To further foster acceptance of the instrument—which is absolutely critical to the MSF program's success—a second set of stakeholders (five to ten members) should rotate in and out of the core group as needed, for instance to critique items.

The first task of the team is to collect some background information. Given that MSF instruments come in many forms, designers are faced with a host of choices in questions, scale, and format. To facilitate the process of designing the type of instrument that is appropriate given your situation and needs, it is essential to have answers to several background questions. We suggest spending a few moments jotting down your answers to these questions before you begin your MSF instrument design work:

- What is the purpose of the MSF instrument you are planning on developing (individual development or administrative decisions such as pay and promotion)?
- What topics will be covered by your MSF instrument, and do you have a thorough description (including examples) of each?
- What type of information is needed and desired in the MSF report?
- What are the demographics (education level, language proficiency, experiences with other surveys, etc.) of those individuals being assessed and those providing the assessments?

As you read the rest of the chapter and are presented with a variety of design choices, consult your recorded answers to these questions so that you can best make informed design decisions.

Nature of Items

Items are the core elements of an instrument. Four types are typically found on MSF instruments: evaluation items, importance items, descriptive items, and demographic items.

Evaluation Items

Evaluation items ask raters to evaluate the focal individual. Evaluation items serve as the core of an MSF instrument, with each feedback topic being assessed by a small subset of evaluation items. Evaluation items can be targeted to managerial behaviors (for example, "presents monthly production reports at staff meetings"), managerial competencies ("is good at delegating"), and traits ("is motivated"). We generally do not recommend using trait-based evaluation items for three reasons:

1. Each feedback provider may define and operationalize the trait differently.
2. The feedback recipient is not able to readily identify which behaviors he or she needs to change to improve on an obtained rating.
3. It is difficult to assess change progress.

Behavioral evaluation items, and to a lesser extent competency items, are less subject to misinterpretation and are typically more actionable, which is critical when the MSF program has a developmental purpose.

Importance Items

Importance items ask raters to indicate the importance of certain managerial behaviors, competencies, or traits, for example, "How important is delegating work to others?" The importance rating is based on evaluating the job the focal individual holds rather than on the focal individual himself or herself. Importance ratings are not absolutely necessary to an MSF instrument, but they are useful for feedback and reporting purposes in that they help set developmental priorities (what is the focal individual's performance on the "most important" items?). Importance items may not be as critical when the MSF effort has an administrative purpose, in which case we recommend establishing the importance of items and topics by way of a systematic job analysis procedure. If importance items are desired, be sure that such an item corresponds to each and every evaluation item on the MSF instrument. There are two ways of pairing importance items with evaluation items: proximal and distal. In the proximal way, the feedback provider reads an item and then immediately offers two answers, one evaluation-oriented and the other importance-oriented (there are two answer columns for each item). In the distal approach, the feedback provider gives an evaluation answer and then, later in the instrument, the rater is presented with the same item and records an importance-oriented answer. Although the proximal manner takes up less physical space and is faster to complete, research supports using the distal manner (Church and Waclawski, 1997). Specifically, artificially high correlations between the importance assessments and evaluation assessments occur when a proximal method is used.

Descriptive Items

Descriptive items are designed to solicit examples and descriptions regarding the behavior and performance of focal individuals. Descriptive items can be narrow (perhaps providing three positive examples concerning the focal individual's communication ability) or broad (say, describing the focal individual's communication ability). Sometimes referred to as "write-in" questions, descriptive items usually are open-ended in nature (a response area is provided, rather than response choices). Descriptive items serve a couple of purposes: they help the focal individual better understand obtained quantitative ratings, and they help him or her identify actions that may be taken to improve problem areas and leverage strengths.

Descriptive items are typically fairly time consuming to complete and should be used judiciously. However, descriptive items should definitely be used if the MSF instrument has a developmental purpose. Descriptive questions can be inserted in a number of places. Some practitioners place them at the end of the instrument, and some practitioners intersperse them throughout the instrument. We recommend including a descriptive item following each feedback topic or set of similar feedback topics (for instance, those related to supervision).

Demographic Items

Demographic items assess the background of the feedback provider. Typical demographic questions include gender, tenure in organization, job level, race, tenure in job, work location, and job type. Demographic items are only needed if you are interested in examining managerial and leadership issues at an organizational level. If the host organization is interested in combining data across feedback recipients in an attempt to describe the "present state of leadership," it may be useful to be able to subdivide the aggregated data by meaningful demographic groupings. If this is the case, be sure to assuage the anonymity concerns of potential raters. Specifically, communicate why you are asking the demographic questions, how they are going to be used, and how they are *not* going to be used (as in confirming that individual feedback reports will not be subdivided by demographic variables). It is worth noting that response rates tend to be higher when demographic questions are placed at the end of the instrument (Roberson and Sundstrom, 1990).

Writing Items

To write a good set of instrument items, it is essential to thoroughly understand and flesh out the topics that need to be addressed. To do so, the instrument construction team should conduct interviews and focus groups with stakeholders. Literature searches on the various topics should be conducted, other surveys administered by the organization should be examined, and the organization's vision and value statements should be reviewed. The next task is to develop a set of items for each feedback topic.

A number of guidelines should be considered in creating items. First, the item should be constructed at the appropriate reading level given the background of the potential rater (the reading level of items can be readily determined by most major word processing software packages). Unless a well-known definition exists, to prevent misinterpretations across raters jargon and slang should be avoided. To minimize cognitive demand, items should be concise. They should be designed to contain one and only one thought. Those containing multiple thoughts ("provides timely feedback and is responsive to voice mail messages") are difficult to complete and interpret.

If the instrument is going to be translated into multiple languages, be sure the terms used in an item translate unambiguously. Many organizations use a double-translation process to ensure the integrity of item content across languages. This involves a two-step process in which the instrument is translated into another language by one translator and then translated back to its original language by a second translator. If the original and retranslated versions are similar in meaning, then the content integrity is intact.

We also recommend against using negatively worded items ("The manager does not provide timely feedback"). Although some researchers have argued that negatively worded items are needed along with positively worded ones to keep raters thinking carefully and to counter a potential rater tendency to just agree or disagree with items regardless of content, other researchers and practitioners suggest that negatively worded items can be confusing (especially when responding negatively to a reverse-scored item; double negatives result), can be difficult to read, and may introduce systematic measurement variance (see Edwards and Thomas, 1993). Furthermore, from our practical experience, raters do not like switching between positively and negatively worded items, as it becomes tedious. One last concern with negatively worded items is that a rater may fail to notice that some items are negatively worded and respond as if the item were positively worded.

Once individual items have been generated for a feedback topic, the set of individual items should be evaluated according to two criteria. First, as a set, is the feedback topic fully addressed? In other words, does each item examine an element of the feedback topic, and as a whole are all the major elements of the feedback topic sufficiently addressed? Second, even though the items should be highly interrelated, they should not be overly similar; this can irritate raters. Redundant items should be removed.

Response Scales

Each item has an answer response scale. Response scales can be open-ended or closed-ended. Open-ended response scales allow the rater to construct a response (that is, raters are given a response area rather than response choices). Open-ended response scales are typically associated with descriptive questions and are fairly time consuming to complete. Although the information from open-ended scales is rich in content and description, it is difficult and time-intensive to summarize and categorize the data collected (which may be problematic if the data are used for administrative purposes). Closed-ended response scales allow the rater to choose an answer or answers from a set of defined alternatives. Although these data are easy to summarize, closed-ended scales do not allow the rater to elaborate on responses. Furthermore, it is possible that the rater will not perceive the defined answer choices as acceptable. Closed-ended response scales usually accompany evaluation (behavioral), importance, and demographic items.

The response scales typically associated with evaluation items are agreement-oriented ("strongly disagree" to "strongly agree"; "not at all true" to "very true"; "no extent" to "a very great extent") and quality-oriented ("very poor" to "very good"; "low" to "very high"). Another possible evaluation response scale is frequency-oriented ("never" to "all of the time"; "never or one time" to "more than ten times"). Be informed, though, that frequency-based evaluation items can often be misleading in that more (that is, greater frequency) is not always an indicator of superior performance; some activities may naturally have low base rates. Finally, evaluation items can have a comparative-oriented answer scale ("worse than most" to "better than most"). Interestingly, comparative scales can also take the form of explicitly comparing and rank-ordering a variety of focal individuals on a set of dimensions. In our experience, comparative scales are more common when the MSF has an administrative purpose.

The response scales generally associated with importance items are importance-oriented ("unimportant" to "very important"), criticality-oriented ("not critical" to "very critical"), or necessity-oriented ("unneeded" to "needed"). The response scales associated with the demographic items are typically dependent on the demographic variable in question.

Some additional response scales that can be, but are usually not, used in MSF instruments include behaviorally anchored rating scales, semantic differentials, forced-choice scales, and mixed-standard scales. Consult a measurement or performance appraisal text for additional information.

All things being equal, the particular choice of a response scale revolves around the MSF purpose, which scale the raters are comfortable using, which scale feedback recipients and coaches are comfortable interpreting in data reports, and what type of MSF report is needed.

Closed-Ended Response Scale Details

Response alternatives should be well defined, complete, equally spaced, presented in a logical order, mutually exclusive from one another (they should not overlap), and appropriate (they should be consistent with what the item asks for). Unless each rater group—peers, subordinates, customers, and supervisors—receives a separate, relevant, and tailored instrument, we generally recommend using a "don't know" or "not applicable" answer choice. Although some instrument designers are concerned that this "bailout" option can lead to raters not thinking hard about the answer choices and being noncommittal, we believe these answer choices prevent a greater problem: having a rater rate the focal individual on a behavior, competency, or trait where he or she lacks adequate knowledge.

Closed-ended scales can contain any number of response choices. We generally recommend between five and seven scale values. This number of scale values allows distinctions that are fairly fine but not overly or artificially so. It is important to realize, however, that depending on your needs and the item itself, fewer than five or more than seven scale values could be most appropriate (for instance, a dichotomous "acceptable" versus "unacceptable" scale). Finally, because raters can possess neutral attitudes about focal individuals' behaviors, competency, or traits, we recommend using a scale midpoint, which is to say, there should be an odd number of scale values. Without a neutral midpoint, those with neutral attitudes may provide poor-quality data, become frustrated, or choose not to respond to the instrument.

Determining the Number of MSF Items: Instrument Length

In creating an MSF instrument, it is essential to consider its length. This issue is important because length has a direct impact on (1) the perceived user-friendliness of the instrument, (2) the quality of the feedback that can be provided (if content themes receive inadequate attention, then the feedback quality suffers), and (3) the cost (response costs = response time × by salary). These considerations represent a paradox between too many and too few questionnaire items—namely, you want enough items to adequately address the MSF purpose and topics, but not too many items such that individuals choose not to return the instrument or complete the instrument superficially.

Here are a few considerations to help achieve the appropriate balance.

Consideration One: Measuring a Topic

In determining the length of your instrument, you must consider how many items are needed to measure each topic or concept in an MSF instrument. The soundest approach to determining the correct number of items per topic is parsimony, or developing scales that attain the highest internal consistency with the fewest items (Van Velsor, 1998). This number may vary, but a rule of thumb suggested by practitioners is somewhere between three and five items per theme (Church and Waclawski, 1998a). We do not advise using a single item indicator (that is, one item to represent a topic) because this is not typically enough to reliably and thoroughly measure a concept.

Consideration Two: Competing Survey Efforts

Another consideration that should be taken into account in determining instrument length is the number of other organizational survey initiatives that are occurring simultaneously. Chances are that your MSF instrument is being administered at the same time as other organizational surveys, all of which are competing for people's time. If this is the case, a shorter survey is responded to more readily than a longer one.

Consideration Three: Time to Completion

We recommend designing the instrument so that it takes approximately fifteen minutes to complete. This advice is consistent with research on survey length. For example, according to Edwards and Ewen (1996), questionnaire raters become fatigued or frustrated after only fifteen minutes. The exact number of items that can be completed in this amount of time is difficult to determine because some items are more cognitively demanding than others. Furthermore, survey completion time depends on the background of your rater (such as his or her experience with surveys). Therefore, instead of an absolute rule of how many items should be included in an MSF instrument, rely on pilot testing to determine the average amount of time it takes relevant raters to complete your particular measure.

Overall, though it is common practice for MSF instruments to be quite long, we urge you to seriously consider these implications of using lengthy questionnaires; respondents most likely will not complete overly demanding surveys. If you feel that the instrument must be lengthy to address your MSF needs, we suggest redefining your needs so that they are narrower in focus. For example, instead of assessing a large number of survey topics, thoroughly assess a smaller number of topics, perhaps four to eight.

Putting the Survey Together

Now that the items and response scales have been created, it is time to begin assembling the instrument. We have already discussed placement of importance, descriptive, and demographic items. Evaluation items can be clustered together and listed by feedback topic, or they can be randomized so that no apparent pattern of items exists. Although randomization was often thought by classical testing theorists to be psychometrically appropriate and a way of preventing bias, we recommend classification by topic. Classification prevents the instrument from seeming haphazard and unfocused. We believe that it is easier for a rater to complete the instrument if classified by topic. At the same time, recent research suggests that organization by topic does not undermine (or improve) the psychometric qualities of the instrument data (see, for example, Harrison and McLaughlin, 1996).

The final step in putting together the survey involves the instructions. They are used not only for conveying important information about how to accurately complete the MSF instrument but also to set the tone for the MSF process. For example, unclear or inconsistent instructions convey a lack of professionalism and therefore reduce the perceived credibility of the MSF instrument and effort. Thus making sure that instructions are clear, relevant, and user-friendly is of critical importance (especially if MSF raters have not received training or instruction about how to complete the MSF instrument) (Church and Waclawski, 1998b).

Types of Instruction

Generally, instructions fall into several categories (items one through four are from Van Velsor, 1998):

1. How to choose raters and distribute forms
2. What to communicate to raters about the MSF process
3. How to return forms for scoring
4. How to think about and respond to the items in the questionnaire
5. How to use the rating scales themselves
6. Instructions regarding the appropriate time reference (for instance, "Please evaluate this person's behavior as you have observed it over the past six months")

Pilot-Testing Your Questionnaire

Before distributing your MSF instrument, it is advisable to conduct screening and pilot-testing procedures. A screening involves (1) analysis by a subject matter expert (SME) and (2) a verbal protocol analysis. Both of these techniques are more qualitative than quantitative in nature.

MSF Screening

Of these two techniques, SME analysis should occur first. In this process, individuals (external or internal to the organization) who possess a good deal of knowledge of the MSF topics to be covered are asked to review the instrument for content clarity and accuracy. Specifically, SMEs should offer insight into whether the instrument measures the ideas and themes it is intended to, it makes sense, and anything is missing.

This process should be followed by a verbal protocol analysis, a process in which potential MSF raters verbalize their thoughts while completing the instrument. By having potential raters speak aloud their thinking process and thoughts as they actually respond to an item (this unusual activity may require you to prompt and coach the rater), you can quickly and easily verify whether or not your instrument is being interpreted as you intended. For participation in this part of the screening process, we recommend working with HR partners to identify a representative sample of employees (across levels, divisions, gender, ethnicity, etc.) who will be completing the actual MSF instrument.

Pilot Testing

At this point, you are ready for a pilot test with a small subset of feedback recipients and raters. The pilot test serves a number of purposes. First, the data collected from a pilot test help answer several important questions regarding the psychometric properties of the MSF instrument, such as whether the content themes represent discrete factors (determined, for example, by factor analysis) and whether the items in the MSF subscales form a reliable measure of the content theme in question (determined by coefficient alpha).

In addition to testing the psychometric properties of your MSF instrument, according to Waldman, Atwater, and Antonioni (1998) the benefits of a pilot test can also be immense in terms of identifying political threats and problems associated with implementing MSF instruments. Moreover, pilot testing can be a useful means of getting feedback from participants about the instrument itself. For example, it is often useful to ask pilot-test participants to rate MSF items in terms of three criteria (Church and Waclawski, 1998a):

1. Clarity: Are the instructions and items easy to read?
2. Relevance: Are the items meaningful to you?
3. Specificity: Are the items detailed or are they too general?

By asking raters to assess items along these dimensions, the MSF practitioner can determine any wording changes that need to be made, or identify for deletion items that are unclear or that simply do not work.

Taken together, pilot testing is always a good idea, as practice makes perfect—or at least reduces the problems, inconsistencies, or bugs one can encounter in administering an MSF instrument. Additionally, the screening and pilot-testing processes (as outlined) involve a good deal of participation from would-be raters; in the end, this is helpful in creating a higher level of acceptance of the MSF process.

Implications of the Response Method

A discussion of instrument design would be incomplete with out mentioning how MSF instruments can be administered. There is no doubt that we are entering an era where communication media are changing regularly. As a result of this revolution in communication technology, organizations have a multitude of options to choose from in collecting MSF data—mail, fax, phone, intranet, Internet, just to start a list. As a result, organizations are often inclined to select the most cutting-edge or "sexiest" approach for administering the MSF process. However, each possible approach has a host of implications for the MSF process as whole, and in particular the response rates (which in turn can affect response bias; Rogelberg and Luong, 1998). Therefore, it is essential that the practitioner consider all the potential options for administration and data collection when creating an MSF instrument.

Currently, there are five primary modes for MSF administration (Church and Waclawski, 1998a):

1. Traditional paper and pencil
2. Optical scan (bubble)
3. Disk-based
4. Telephone voice-response unit
5. Electronic or online (e-mail, intranet, Internet, Web-based)

Each option varies in terms of the level of sophistication required (on the part of the rater) to employ it, as well as the level of technology required to implement the MSF system. Table 6.1, adapted from Church and Waclawski (1998a), provides a description of these methods and some advantages and disadvantages associated with each.

In the end, when considering the various methods of administration it is wise to remember the old adage that form follows function. In other words, be sure that the method you choose makes the most sense given the level of sophistication of your rater population, and that it gives you the most complete and accurate set of responses possible.

Table 6.1. Scale Overview.

Method	How It Works	Positives	Negatives
Paper and pencil	Participants mark answers on nonscannable MSF instrument	Easy to complete; moderate confidentiality; high degree of familiarity	Costly to print; costly to administer by mail; expensive hand data entry
Optical scan (bubble form): type A	Participants mark answers on a separate scannable answer sheet that corresponds to the MSF instrument (usually single page)	Easily faxed; easy data processing; high confidentiality; inexpensive data entry	Costly to change; printing time can take weeks; testlike appearance; potential loss of answer sheet; answer sheet may be completed incorrectly
Optical scan (bubble form): type B	Participants mark answers on the actual MSF instrument in defined response bubbles and the instrument itself is scanned	Easy to complete; moderate confidentiality; high degree of familiarity; inexpensive data entry	Costly to change; printing time can take weeks; costly to administer by mail
Disk response	Participants are sent a diskette containing the instrument; responses are made directly on the diskette and it is mailed back for processing	Moderate confidentiality; branching ability; novelty; no data-entry costs	Requires computer literacy; costly to produce disks; significant time for initial setup; costly to change; systems need to be compatible
Telephone voice response unit	Participants respond over the telephone by pushing buttons according to prerecorded statements	Easy to use; immediate data processing; branching ability; novelty	Reduced flexibility regarding length; comments are voice recorded; suspect confidentiality; significant time for setup
Electronic or online	Participants respond by e-mail or at a Website	Immediate data processing; easy to administer; easy to change at last minute; branching ability; novelty	Requires computer literacy; requires network access and familiarity; suspect confidentiality; significant time for setup

Source: Adapted and expanded from A. H. Church and J. Waclawski, *Designing and Using Organizational Surveys.* Copyright ©1998 Gower (Aldershot, England). Reprinted by permission.

Final Advice

Before closing this chapter, we present a list of points of advice on instrument design. We gathered them from several of the other authors included in this handbook (Stéphane Brutus, Marshall Goldsmith, John Fleenor, Lynn Summers, David Bracken, Manuel London, Mark Edwards, Wally Borman, Carol Timmreck, and Bob Jako). In order to get some additional expert advice on MSF instrument construction, we asked these coauthors this question: "In your experience, what are the top three things to consider, remember, or address when creating an MSF instrument?" Although not all of the authors were in agreement on each and every point, the list represents a brief summary of answers that were agreed on most consistently (that is, they were contributed by more than one MSF expert):

- A highly valid measure is not of much use for development if it is not clearly understood by the recipient.
- Top-management ownership is critical.
- Clear alignment with organizational mission, vision, strategy, and goals is critical.
- Use clear and simple language.
- Ensure readability. If necessary, hire an English as a second language (ESL) teacher to go over the instrument and modify difficult language.
- Keep the survey short. Use every opportunity to make each item and instrument shorter.
- Involve raters and ratees in writing the items, or give them the reason for the items—how they were chosen and why they are important to the company.
- Get the involvement of key stakeholders.
- Items should be written to describe observable behaviors that are job-relevant.
- Items should be short and straightforward; avoid the use of buzzwords, jargon, U.S.-centric words, and double-barreled items.
- Pilot-test the instrument.
- Train the raters on how to use the instrument and the scales, how to give good open-ended responses, etc.

- Include clear instructions.
- Keep in mind what you want your feedback report to look like.
- Make sure the instrument fits the purpose.

Conclusion

In conclusion, there are myriad factors to consider in creating an MSF instrument. The instrument design process requires a good deal of thoughtful planning, research, participant involvement, expert advice, constant revision, and above all patience. In the end, no matter how well planned, designing an MSF instrument is usually not a linear exercise. For example, you may decide to conduct pilot testing at various stages along the way instead of waiting until your instrument is fully completed and ready to be launched.

In any event, this chapter has attempted to outline factors that the MSF practitioner should at least take into account when creating an instrument. Remember, although factors such as organizational support, top leadership endorsement, appropriate timing, and a smooth rollout process are all critical to the success of the feedback effort, without a well-constructed instrument the value of such an MSF effort is limited.

References

Church, A. H., and Waclawski, J. "The Importance of Being Earnest: Instrumentation Effects on Multirater Assessments." Paper presented at the annual meeting of the American Psychological Society, Washington, D.C., May 1997.

Church, A. H., and Waclawski, J. *Designing and Using Organizational Surveys.* Aldershot, England: Gower, 1998a.

Church, A. H., and Waclawski, J. "Making Multirater Feedback Systems Work." *Quality Progress,* 1998b, *31*(4), 81–89.

Edwards, J. E., and Thomas, M. D. "The Organizational Survey Process: General Steps and Practical Considerations." In P. Rosenfeld, J. E. Edwards, and M. D. Thomas (eds.), *Improving Organizational Surveys: New Directions, Methods, and Applications.* Thousand Oaks, Calif.: Sage, 1993.

Edwards, M. R., and Ewen, A. J. *360-Degree Feedback: The Powerful New Model for Employee Assessment and Performance Improvement.* New York: AMACOM, 1996.

Harrison, D. A., and McLaughlin, M. E. "Structural Properties and Psychometric Qualities of Organizational Self-Reports: Field Tests of

Connections Predicted by Cognitive Theory." *Journal of Management,* 1996, *22,* 313–338.

Roberson, M. T., and Sundstrom, E. "Questionnaire Design, Return Rates, and Response Favorableness in an Employee Attitude Questionnaire." *Journal of Applied Psychology,* 1990, *75,* 354–357.

Rogelberg, S. G., and Luong, A. "Nonresponse to Mailed Surveys: A Review and Guide." *Current Directions in Psychological Science,* 1998, *7,* 60–65.

Van Velsor, E., "Designing 360-Degree Feedback to Enhance Involvement, Self-Determination, and Commitment." In W. W. Tornow and M. London (eds.), *Maximizing the Value of 360-Degree Feedback: A Process for Successful Individual and Organizational Development.* San Francisco: Jossey-Bass, 1998.

Waldman, D. A., Atwater, L. E., and Antonioni, D. "Has 360-Degree Feedback Gone Amok?" *Academy of Management Executive,* 1998, *12*(20), 86–94.

CHAPTER 7

Rater Selection
Sources of Feedback

James L. Farr
Daniel A. Newman

In this chapter, we address issues related to selecting raters for multisource feedback (MSF) systems. By definition, an MSF system has multiple raters who represent different sources of work behavior information. Each category of feedback source typically has its own role relationship to the target work performer (hereafter called the ratee). The feedback sources that are frequently mentioned within the context of MSF systems are the ratee's supervisor, higher-level managers, peers, subordinates, internal and external customers, and managers who are not hierarchically related (a task force or project leader in a matrix organization), as well as the ratee herself. Whereas some sources are usually made up of only a single rater (self, ratee's supervisor), others are made up of several raters (group of peers, group of subordinates of the ratee). As we will see, there are a number of important issues to consider when selecting sources and raters for MSF systems, but little empirical research has been conducted to guide the selection process.

Validity of Rater Selection Decisions

Selecting raters for a MSF system can be thought of as a two-step process: selecting source categories, and then selecting individual raters within each source category. For both steps of the selection process, the critical concern is the *validity* of the selection decisions. In the context of a multisource rating system, validation of the selection system focuses on whether useful rating sources have been chosen and whether raters selected to represent each rating source can provide useful ratings. Defining validity in this manner begs the question, "Useful for what?"

In their discussion of the validity of multisource ratings, Murphy, Cleveland, and Mohler (see Chapter Nine) note that there are multiple dimensions for assessing the validity or usefulness of any assessment device. The dimensions chosen to determine the validity of a multisource rater selection process should be driven by the intended uses of the rating information. Two primary possible uses for a given MSF system are development of the ratee's job skills and performance (developmental purpose), and input for a personnel decision-making process (administrative purpose). See Chapter Twenty-Three for more detail on these purposes for gathering multisource ratings.

In this chapter, we primarily contrast the sole developmental use versus the sole administrative use of multisource ratings and do not consider in detail instances where both uses occur simultaneously.

Multisource Rating Purpose and Validity Considerations

Performance ratings can be used as input for a number of human resource decisions, including promotions, terminations, lateral transfers, pay increases, and bonuses (Landy and Farr, 1983). Using multisource ratings as part of an administrative decision-making process has as primary concerns for validity the accuracy, comprehensiveness, and job relatedness of the ratings. The defensibility of the ratings and the personnel decisions they support is important both with regard to formal legal challenges to the decisions and to questions raised by affected employees. We do not address the legal issues related to multisource rating systems, although their importance cannot be overstated (see Chapter Twenty-Eight for more detail). Our focus now is on the reactions and behavior of employees affected by the MSF system. Figure 7.1 presents our current thinking on how multisource rating purpose and rater selection processes influence employee attitudes and behaviors.

**Figure 7.1. Factors Influencing Perceived
Fairness and Acceptability of Ratings.**

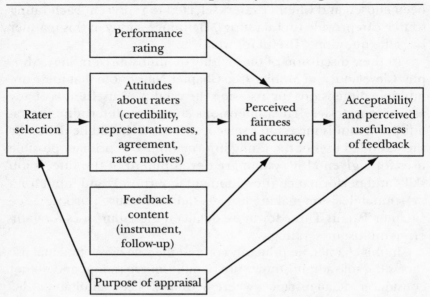

Sources: Dickinson, 1993; Secunda, 1983.

Ratees and other employees affected by administrative decisions are likely to accept decisions and their supporting ratings to the extent that the means by which rater sources and individual raters are selected enhance perception of procedural fairness and the accuracy of ratings. Research examining the characteristics of performance rating systems that affect their perceived fairness (Gilliland and Langdon, 1998) indicates that individuals perceive fairness and justice

- When they are able to participate in designing and implementing the rating process
- When there is open and detailed communication about the ratings and their uses
- When the process is administered consistently
- When the ratings have job relevance

Although the effects of rater selection on employee reactions to multisource rating systems have not been widely researched, studies on reactions to single-rater performance appraisals suggest that many of the same issues apply to *multisource* rating systems used for administrative decision making. Then, likewise, a multisource rating system for administrative purposes should be seen as fair to the extent that

- It includes ratee input to the rater selection process (including self-ratings)
- The procedures used for selecting rater sources and individual raters are well known and applied consistently
- Explicit procedures exist for maximizing the job relevance and information basis for the ratings made by each rater source
- Rater selection procedures exclude raters who have potential conflicts of interest with the target ratee (say, eliminating peers who might be in competition for a promotion)

Gilliland and Langdon (1998) also suggest that the procedural factors influencing the fairness perceptions of ratees similarly influence the fairness perceptions of other system users (including raters), and that raters' perceptions of the fairness of a rating system affect the ratings they give. Thus, valid rater selection procedures in multisource rating systems can improve the validity of the final ratings, operating through the criterion of perceived procedural fairness.

Validity considerations for selecting raters for a multisource rating system that is used primarily for developmental purposes share some common elements with those used for administrative decisions, but they are not identical. Both developmental and administrative purposes are concerned with the job relevance of the ratings and comprehensive coverage of the job domain as they affect the ratee's perception of rating accuracy and fairness. We anticipate that multisource ratings used for important administrative purposes are held to more stringent standards of job relevance and comprehensiveness by the ratee than are similar ratings used for developmental purposes. Accuracy and fairness perceptions then influence the ratee's acceptance of the feedback, perception of its usefulness, and motivation to change as suggested by the feedback (see Figure 7.1).

Choosing Sources of Feedback Ratings

As we have noted above, there are two components of rater selection for multisource rating systems: choosing the sources from which to obtain ratings, and selecting the specific individuals within each source to provide the ratings. The types of potential sources for performance ratings are generally well known and include the self, the supervisor, higher-level managers, peers, subordinates, and internal and external customers, as well as managers and other organizational members outside of the usual hierarchy (task force members, project managers in a matrix organization). The assumption of an MSF system is that each of these sources may have unique and useful information about the performance of the target ratee. However, not all sources have relevant information for every use of such ratings. Thus, useful sources must be selected *for each application* of multisource evaluation.

The central variable that has been discussed as the basis for rater selection decisions is the opportunity to be knowledgeable about the performance effectiveness of the ratee. This has often been labeled as the "opportunity to observe" the performance of the ratee (see Rothstein, 1990). However, using that term may have too narrow a connotation when the selection of rating sources is made, as it suggests that a rater must be able to directly observe the behavior of the ratee. Some potential sources, especially customers, may have knowledge of the *results* of the behavior of the ratee, without directly observing the behavior that produced those results. Also, members of work groups may increasingly be connected electronically, or individuals may be managed at a distance, such that direct observation is limited. Thus, though we recognize that direct observation of ratee job behaviors is often ideal, we prefer the term "opportunity to be knowledgeable" about performance.

Sources are likely to be knowledgeable about different dimensions of a ratee's work performance (especially if we consider both task and contextual performance; see Borman and Motowidlo, 1992), or likely to define differing behaviors as effective. The decision of which sources to include in a particular multisource rating process should be informed by the strategic purpose of the appraisal. That is, the intended uses of the rating information are related to the validity of specific performance dimensions.

One possible method for assessing each potential rating source's opportunity to be knowledgeable about each performance dimension is to build a matrix of performance dimensions and rating sources, with the judged level of knowledge opportunity entered in each cell. (Possible judgment categories might be "none or little," "indirect," and "direct"; see Table 7.1 for an example of what such a matrix might look like.)

Rating-source selection is based on the matrix of opportunity judgments. Guiding principles are as follows:

* Rating sources are to be selected such that every relevant performance dimension can be rated by at least one source with a minimum of indirect knowledge opportunity.
* Two or more knowledgeable rating sources are to be selected for as many performance dimensions as possible.
* Every rating source with direct observation of a performance dimension is to be selected to rate that dimension.

Table 7.1. "Opportunity to Be Knowledgeable" Matrix for Selecting Sources.

Rating Sources	Performance Dimensions[a]		
	Confronting Problem Employees	Work Team Orientation	Resourcefulness
Peer 1	None/Little[b]	None/Little	Indirect
Peer 2	Indirect	Indirect	Direct
Subordinate 1	Direct	Indirect	Indirect
Subordinate 2	Indirect	Indirect	None/Little
Subordinate 3	Direct	Indirect	None/Little
Self	Direct	Direct	Indirect

[a]Performance dimensions from Lombardo and McCauley, 1994.

[b]Three levels of opportunity to be knowledgeable: (1) none or little, (2) indirect, and (3) direct.

Who makes the opportunity judgments? The ideal is to solicit the participation of various organizational stakeholders in the MSF system. As part of the process of developing the multisource rating system, representative ratees and potential sources (supervisors, higher managers, peers, subordinates, internal customers, etc.) can be surveyed about their degree of knowledge regarding various job performance dimensions of an incumbent in the target position. Aggregated judgments from each source group can then be used to make the source selections for the relevant dimensions. The opportunity for external customers to be knowledgeable about various performance dimensions may need to be judged by internal organization members.

As we suggested earlier, selecting rating sources is the first of a two-step rater selection process. Once this is accomplished, attention should be directed to selecting the individual raters who compose each rating source. In cases where there is only a single possible individual within the source, this second step is obvious. It is in cases where multiple individuals make up the rating source that rater selection is an issue of importance.

Selecting Individual Raters

Selecting individual raters is readily recognized as a critical part of developing an effective MSF system. A consideration that is often overlooked, however, is that the individual raters chosen to participate in the assessment form a *rater group,* whose feedback is combined in some fashion (both formally and informally) to support the ratee's inferences about his own performance (when used for developmental purposes) and to support the organization's inferences about future performance of the ratee (when used for administrative purposes). What becomes evident when we explicitly consider the rater group for a ratee is that selecting each rater ideally takes into account the attributes of the *other raters* who have been selected.

We begin here by identifying attributes of *individual* raters and of the rater-ratee dyadic relationship that warrant consideration in making rater selection decisions, and then proceed to issues of selecting for rater *groups.*

In general, as noted previously, a greater opportunity to observe the ratee's performance is often considered to lead to greater accuracy in ratings (Furnham and Stringfield, 1998). This contention is supported by the assumption that the opportunity to observe contributes to the opportunity to be knowledgeable about ratee performance. Empirical findings lend some support to this assumption by demonstrating that agreement in supervisory ratings (a sign of rating precision) tended to improve with ratee tenure in the organization (Rothstein, 1990), and that correlations between self and supervisor judgments were higher for behaviors that were rated as more observable by supervisors (Warr and Bourne, 1999). The validity of assessment center predictors has also been shown to improve considerably once the supervisor and ratee have worked together in excess of two years (Moser, Schuler, and Funke, 1999). Greater opportunity to observe has also corresponded with lower rater bias (Conway, 1996).

In some cases, however, opportunity to observe performance may be a two-edged sword, such as when length of acquaintance with supervisor leads to overestimation of ratee performance (Sundvik and Lindeman, 1998). (Overestimated ratings by a supervisor might be mistakenly viewed as underestimated self-ratings by the target; see Chapter Thirteen.) Given that length of acquaintance can lead to overrating the ratee's level of performance, we suggest that longer is not necessarily better. It should be expected that there exists some asymptote past in which diminishing returns are realized for additional opportunities to observe. Dalessio (1998) and Yukl and Lepsinger (1995) suggest a minimum of one year of working closely together when selecting raters for a given ratee. This is not an unreasonable benchmark, but we believe that opportunity to be knowledgeable about an individual's job performance is not simply a function of the duration of exposure; it depends also on the nature of the interaction (see Table 7.1). Six months working together closely on a project team may be the equivalent of much longer exposures of a less intense nature.

Professional judgment is required to make a determination of the minimum length of rater-ratee exposure that allows the potential rater a reasonable opportunity to become knowledgeable about ratee performance in a specific application of multisource rating. In the interests of both information quality and perceived fairness of the system, input from the system stakeholders is also useful. Once this has been done, a list of eligible raters can be developed for each ratee-source combination.

Size of Rater Group

Returning to the issue of selecting raters to form a *rater group,* a commonly asked question is, "How many individuals should compose the rater group for each source?" Debates about the optimal size of a rating group often rely on psychometric arguments derived from classical notions of measurement reliability. This approach usually assumes that there exists a "true score" of performance that can be identified by examining the *agreement* in ratings between multiple raters, occasions, or instruments. The advantage of this true-score assumption is that it offers a quantitative method by which the number of raters required to achieve a given level of rating precision can be determined. For example, Greguras and Robie (1998) followed this type of approach and concluded that more raters were needed than typically used, within-source agreement among raters was generally low, and many raters did not rate consistently across ratees. The results of within-source-agreement research suggest that interrater agreement is frequently so low that acceptable levels of reliability can only be achieved by increasing the number of raters. Murphy, Cleveland, and Mohler (see Chapter Nine) offer additional discussion of this topic, but the bottom line is that some level of within-source agreement seems necessary to make the overall ratings credible, to the organization as well as to the ratee.

Pragmatically, choices of how many subordinates to use in an assessment are usually based on common practice, or best practice. A typical distribution of raters is one boss, five peers, and five subordinates (Chappelow, 1998). The number of raters selected also depends on such considerations as cost (rater time), magnitude of data to be managed, and how representative the rater group must be. We recommend that administrators of the feedback system conduct a thoughtful analysis of the trade-offs inherent in different group sizes, rather than simply adopting the habits of other organizations. However, it seems reasonable that for rating sources in which five or fewer eligible raters are available, then all should be selected.

Assuming that the number of eligible raters for a source exceeds five, how are the final raters selected? Existing practice, as represented in published articles about MSF systems, indicates that frequently the ratee is asked to select or nominate his own raters. The purpose of the ratings is likely to affect the validity of this selection approach. Ratee selection of raters has the advantage of the ratee perceiving high fairness and associated judgments of rater credibility and accuracy that enhance rating acceptance and motivation to change (Figure 7.1). Thus, ratee selection of raters may be useful for developmental purposes. However, the performance level of the ratee may moderate this usefulness. Low-performing ratees may be especially motivated to select raters whom they expect to give them biased ratings that confirm the ratee's existing self-appraisal. In this way, they avoid unexpected "bad news," but they also may have less reason to seek skill development.

For administrative uses, selecting specific raters from the eligible list should be more under organizational control. Ratee input may be desired, but the final selection should be made by management with input from human resource agents regarding issues such as how representative (in social, demographic, or functional terms) the set of raters are. Dalessio (1998) advocates random selection of raters whenever there are many eligible raters. Although we agree that random selection of raters can enhance perceptions of fairness, we suggest that stratified random sampling (say, random sampling within each social group) may be preferable when the organization has concerns about the chosen raters being representative.

We have focused so far on selecting rating sources and individual raters in dealing with the two principal purposes of obtaining multisource ratings: to provide developmental feedback to the ratee and to make administrative decisions concerning the ratee. Next, we consider some other potential uses of multisource rating information that suggest additional issues regarding selection of rating sources and individual raters.

Selecting Rater Sources to Make Planned Comparisons

In making informed professional judgments about the validity of the selection of a set of rating sources, attention must turn to *what is done with* the ratings. Whereas the importance of agreement between raters becomes evident when one recalls that measurement validity is limited by measurement reliability (see Chapter Nine), overemphasizing agreement between raters misses one of the primary purposes of MSF: to obtain *differing* perspectives concerning job performance. Furthermore, there may be occasions when such divergent performance information is useful for examining the effectiveness of groups of job incumbents, organizational units or systems, or even the total organization. Therefore, we now look at rater selection as selecting differing perspectives on performance, with the implication that rating-source disagreement can be managed according to the purpose of the appraisal system.

With regard to the differential or comparative nature of possible rating-source disagreements, we believe that—to some extent—the comparisons of ratings obtained from different sources can be planned, so that rating discrepancies can then support systemic inferences about the organization. Table 7.2 summarizes our initial propositions regarding selection of raters for "planned comparison." Rating discrepancies between sources as well as within sources are interpreted in this framework.

The first discrepancy is between external and internal rating sources—say, customers and suppliers. Recognition of the importance of this discrepancy is not new, but we see value in explaining it again here. Customer ratings are likely to reflect performance *outcomes* more than performance *behaviors* and thus are open to contaminating factors beyond the control of the target performer. They therefore sometimes speak more to the deficiencies of the system than to those of the individual being rated. One example of poor performance is late delivery. Whereas the customer may attribute the lateness to personal characteristics of the immediate contact person, these deficiencies may be alternatively attributable to company operations or to an organizational culture over which the target has little control. The external-internal distinction can apply to discrepancies between raters in different work units within

**Table 7.2. Purposes of "Planned Comparisons"
of Rating Sources.**

Rating Discrepancy	Purpose of Comparison
External (customer) vs. internal (organization)	Customer satisfaction
Self vs. other	Personal development, promotion and termination, fit and turnover, cooperation and coordination
Source vs. source	Alignment of values from different sources, redefinition of performance (dynamic, multifaceted criteria)
Rater vs. rater (within a source)	Rater perceptions of fairness

the company, as well as to discrepancies between customer and supplier organizations.

The second discrepancy—between ratings by self and other—is at the heart of most MSF programs, which are intended for individual development. Such programs usually allow the ratee to select her own raters. Aside from benchmarking personal and interpersonal development, these rating disagreements can address the issues of fit with the organization, as well as team process (cooperation, coordination, role clarity). Though much has been written on the topic of self-other agreement (see Ashford, 1989; Atwater and Yammarino, 1997; London, 1995; Johnson and Ferstl, 1999; and Yammarino and Atwater, Chapter Thirteen), we focus here on psychological research that pertains to a ratee's desire for and reactions to feedback from various others. In a study of responsiveness to feedback regarding personal attributes, college students showed a preference for partners whose feedback both verified and enhanced their own self-assessments (Swann, Pelham, and Krull, 1989). Interestingly, they also preferred a nonenhancing, verifying partner to one who enhanced them without verifying their self-appraisals (Swann, Pelham, and Krull, 1989). This indicates that a manager may choose those raters whose assessments she believes coincide with her own, even before choosing ones whose assessments potentially overrate her performance. Interestingly, a ratee may be purposefully choosing raters so as to minimize self-other discrepancy.

This type of overemphasis on rating agreement is a likely consequence if the assessment is framed under the true-score assumption, but it may undermine the main purpose of the feedback system, which is to take the perspectives of those who disagree with the self-ratings. An alternative selection technique is to choose raters who are most likely to disagree with each other, and then purposively interpret the ways in which they disagree. Yammarino and Atwater (see Chapter Thirteen) give detail on types of rater agreements and their corresponding inferences.

In the third planned comparison presented in Table 7.2, rating discrepancies between two sources reveal variation in ways of thinking about work performance at different levels in the organization. Raters from different sources are likely to differ in age, experience, and values as well as in job description. Because of this, they might bring into the assessment divergent assumptions and implicit theories about what good performance means for the target. For example, when rating a given target manager on "clearly believes that managerial success is built by having a team of strong [subordinates]" (Lombardo and McCauley, 1994), the supervisor may give high marks, while the peer gives intermediate marks, and the subordinates give low marks. The same item is *qualitatively* distinct for each source. Individuals within the same source may also have differing "folk theories" of performance (Borman, 1987). (We offer the caveat that rating discrepancies should not be compared arithmetically when it is believed that diverse performance theories underlie the ratings.)

Rather than supposing that this is an intractable measurement problem, it is believed that these differences are interpretable in themselves. (Implicit configurations of target performance can be assessed systematically—between raters and between sources—using multitrait, multimethod (MTMM) analyses. These can elucidate how various raters categorize impressions of overall performance and how they differ in these categorizations; Conway, 1999; Mount and others, 1998; and Conway, 1998.) Specifically, it should be asked how these differences may offer valuable data on the issues of organizational politics and power, or on the differential opportunities of raters to observe performance in various settings and at various frequencies.

The lack of agreement between two distinct sources can lead to improved understanding of the values and goals of the target's many constituents. For example, if supervisors and subordinates place incompatible demands on the target, attention to this discrepancy may incite systemwide understanding of *what performance means* in various contexts.

The last rating comparison to make is between raters within a given source (we deal here with multiple subordinates). Agreement between raters of a given source indicates measurement reliability and contributes to source credibility, but it may result in negative perceptions of rating-system fairness. If subordinates are deliberately selected by the ratee to enhance agreement between them, the ratee may inadvertently give off the message that only one type of rater's opinions are important to him (and to the organization). If managers distribute rating forms exclusively to subordinates from their in-group, then they may give the appearance to unselected subordinates that the MSF system is a conspiracy. Care should be taken to represent the important subordinate constituencies, despite the cost in terms of measurement reliability and group size.

Of course, trade-offs must be negotiated between reliability, cost, representativeness, and confidentiality. Although there are many pros and cons to be considered in selecting raters, one overarching recommendation is that the selected raters each have some perspective and knowledge that is relevant to the goals of organizational strategy.

General Issues and Organizational Realities of Rater Selection

When choosing several from among many subordinates or peers to participate in evaluating a manager, one should be sensitive to several organizational realities that affect how the selection is interpreted. First, selecting a subgroup of subordinates sends a message about whose opinions are valued by the company. Selecting individuals to rate a manager implies some level of rater expertise or understanding of managerial tasks. This threatens to become particularly problematic if certain informal groups are left out of the process. If the rater group comprises members who are all from the same social group, demographic category, or status level, it may appear (and rightly so) that some constituencies are being systematically excluded.

Also, in explaining rater characteristics that are likely to influence the ratings given, it is important that we reemphasize the role of rater motives for the evaluation. At the risk of stating the obvious, upward feedback is a form of vertical communication. An upward appraisal system may represent one of the most meaningful ways that a subordinate can communicate with the manager above his own manager. The importance of this consideration is that those who select raters should be wary of individual agendas for the appraisal that could possibly diverge from the good-faith reporting of observed performance.

Lastly, the selector of raters should attend to the demands that rating places on those selected. These can include lost time, heavier workload, and the cognitive and emotional demands of conscientiously judging another person's work. These demands are likely to have a serious impact on the willingness of raters to provide good information, which is central to the success of any performance feedback system. The willingness issue is specially salient if the raters are outside of the organization (say, customers), and if rater training and the feedback instrument are lengthy and difficult.

Two recommendations are offered to address rater motivation. The first is to be open and responsive to the negative effects that rating demands have on raters. Ask them (anonymously) whether they felt that the instrument and the rating circumstances were conducive to giving good information. Give raters some sort of reward or break for willingly participating (the best reward may be information about how their feedback was used to change a behavior, policy, or system). Finally, one should not underestimate the critical role of "feedback about the feedback." Like anyone else, raters are sensitive to whether their input appears to be taken seriously by the organization. Whether the raters actually see changes formally implemented, are consulted for clarification about their observations and interpretations, are asked about how rater training might be modified, or are shown some meaningful type of appreciation, the act of acknowledging the raters' efforts in some way probably predicts the seriousness with which ratings are made in the future.

Final Considerations

When considering rater selection in an MSF system, it is useful to think about each ratee having a rater group, comprising both groupings of individual raters within a source (subordinates Joe, Dawn, and Allen) and a collection of sources (supervisor, peers, subordinates, self, and customers). Each component of a rater group has its own features:

- Implicit theories of what good performance is
- Opportunities to observe the performance
- Roles in the organizational milieu
- Sets of priorities for the target's performance

Selection of individual raters and rating sources should take into account both the compensatory/complementary and the differential/comparative nature of the sources. That is, each performance rating is significant in its ability to disconfirm the ratings of other sources as well as its ability to corroborate other sources. Indeed, the underlying logic of MSF systems is that the sources are expected to provide differential information—ratings that differ. However, ratings that appear too disparate may lead to less acceptance by the ratee (especially with developmental purposes) and by organizational management (especially with administrative purposes). The successful rater selection system must manage to balance agreement and disagreement.

References

Ashford, S. "Self-Assessments in Organizations: A Literature Review and Integrative Model." In L. L. Cummings and B. M. Staw (eds.), *Research in Organizational Behavior.* Vol. 11. Greenwich, Conn.: JAI Press, 1989.

Atwater, L. E., and Yammarino, F. J. "Self and Other Rating Agreement: A Review of a Model." In G. Ferris (ed.), *Research in Personnel and Human Resources Management.* Vol. 15. Greenwich, Conn.: JAI Press, 1997.

Borman, W. C. "Personal Constructs, Performance Schemata, and 'Folk Theories' of Subordinate Effectiveness: Explorations in an Army Officer Sample." *Organizational Behavior and Human Decision Processes,* 1987, *40,* 307–322.

Borman, W. C., and Motowidlo, S. J. "Expanding the Criterion Domain to Include Elements of Contextual Performance." In N. Schmitt, W. C. Borman, and Associates, *Personnel Selection in Organizations.* San Francisco: Jossey-Bass, 1992.

Chappelow, C. T. "360-Degree Feedback." In C. D. McCauley, R. S. Moxley, and E. Van Velsor (eds.), *Center for Creative Leadership Handbook of Leadership Development.* San Francisco: Jossey-Bass, 1998.

Conway, J. M. "Additional Construct Validity Evidence for the Task/Contextual Performance Distinction." *Human Performance,* 1996, *9,* 309–329.

Conway, J. M. "Understanding Method Variance in Multitrait-Multirater Performance Appraisal Matrices: Examples Using General Impressions and Interpersonal Affect as Measured Method Factors." *Human Performance,* 1998, *11,* 29–55.

Conway, J. M. "Distinguishing Contextual Performance from Task Performance for Managerial Jobs." *Journal of Applied Psychology,* 1999, *84,* 3–13.

Dalessio, A. T. "Using Multisource Feedback for Employee Development and Personnel Decisions: Practice and Research." In J. W. Smither (ed.), *Performance Appraisal: State of the Art in Practice.* San Francisco: Jossey-Bass, 1998.

Dickinson, T. L. "Attitudes About Performance Appraisal." In H. Schuler, J. L. Farr, and M. Smith (eds.), *Personnel Selection and Assessment: Individual and Organizational Perspectives.* Mahwah, N.J.: Erlbaum, 1993.

Furnham, A., and Stringfield, P. "Congruence in Job Performance Ratings: A Study of 360-Feedback Examining Self, Manager, Peers, and Consultant Ratings." *Human Relations,* 1998, *51,* 517–530.

Gilliland, S. W., and Langdon, J. C. "Creating Performance Management Systems That Promote Perceptions of Fairness." In J. W. Smither (ed.), *Performance Appraisal: State of the Art in Practice.* San Francisco: Jossey-Bass, 1998.

Greguras, G. J., and Robie, C. "A New Look at Within-Source Interrater Reliability of 360-Degree Feedback Ratings." *Journal of Applied Psychology,* 1998, *83,* 960–968.

Johnson, J. W., and Ferstl, K. L. "The Effects of Interrater and Self-Other Agreement on Performance Improvement Following Upward Feedback." *Personnel Psychology,* 1999, *52,* 271–303.

Landy, F. J., and Farr, J. L. *The Measurement of Work Performance: Methods, Theory, and Applications.* Orlando, Fla.: Academic Press, 1983.

Lombardo, M. M., and McCauley, C. D. *Benchmarks: Developmental Reference Points for Managers and Executives.* Greensboro, N.C.: Center for Creative Leadership, 1994.

London, M. *Self and Interpersonal Insight: How People Gain Understanding of Themselves and Others in Organizations.* New York: Oxford University Press, 1995.

Moser, K., Schuler, H., and Funke, U. "The Moderating Effects of Raters' Opportunities to Observe Ratees' Job Performance on the Validity of an Assessment Centre." *International Journal of Selection and Assessment,* 1999, *7,* 133–141.

Mount, M. K., and others. "Trait, Rater and Level Effects in 360-Degree Performance Ratings." *Personnel Psychology,* 1998, *51,* 557–576.

Rothstein, H. R. "Interrater Reliability of Job Performance Ratings: Growth to Asymptote Level with Increasing Opportunity to Observe." *Journal of Applied Psychology,* 1990, *75,* 322–327.

Secunda, M. D. "Employee Perceptions of Performance Appraisal Systems: Causal Determinants of Fairness, Accuracy, and Acceptability." Unpublished doctoral dissertation, Old Dominion University, Norfolk, Va., 1983.

Sundvik, L., and Lindeman, M. "Acquaintanceship and the Discrepancy Between Supervisor and Self-Assessments." *Journal of Social Behavior and Personality,* 1998, *13,* 117–126.

Swann, W. B., Pelham, B. W., and Krull, D. S. "Agreeable Fancy or Disagreeable Truth? Reconciling Self-Enhancement and Self-Verification." *Journal of Personality and Social Psychology,* 1989, *57,* 782–791.

Warr, P., and Bourne, A. "Factors Influencing Two Types of Congruence in Multirater Judgments." *Human Performance,* 1999, *12,* 183–210.

Yukl, G. A., and Lepsinger, R. "How to Get the Most out of 360-Degree Feedback." *Training,* 1995, *32,* 45–50.

CHAPTER 8

Improving the Quality of Multisource Rater Performance

David Antonioni
David J. Woehr

Multisource feedback (MSF) provides information about on-the-job performance by eliciting responses from multiple raters, including supervisors, peers, direct reports, and, in some cases, customers or clients. The basic premise behind MSF is that observations from multiple sources result in a valid, meaningful, and useful assessment of an individual's work behaviors or competencies. However, polling multiple sources is only one part of gathering "high quality" ratings—those that mirror actual performance and minimize the impact of influences not related to performance. To produce an accurate measurement of work performance, steps must also be taken to reduce systematic attributions and biases on the part of raters.

There are two main perspectives on improving the performance of individual raters. One perspective emphasizes the rater's *ability* to rate performance; proponents of this idea hold that a rater's inability to accurately assess and evaluate performance leads to low-quality ratings. The other perspective posits that the quality of performance ratings is less a function of raters' ability and more a function of their motivation or *willingness* to provide accurate ratings (Murphy and Cleveland, 1995; Harris, 1994). Research indicates that raters are more willing to participate in the MSF process when they feel they are able to rate others effectively and when they perceive that there are benefits to rating others (Westerman and Rosse, 1997). Fortunately, the research related to rater ability and motivation presents a relatively optimistic picture. Researchers have identified specific factors that are likely to impact rater ability or motivation and consequently the value of the ratings produced.

The purpose of this chapter is to increase the awareness of practitioners who are using MSF as to the factors that influence rater ability and motivation. First, we present two main factors that influence rater behavior and hence the quality of performance ratings: rater perceptions and expectations of the MSF process, and rater training. Second, we outline a set of recommendations, based on those factors, aimed at optimizing both rater ability and motivation.

Rater Perceptions and Expectations of MSF

Much of the emerging literature on MSF indicates that rater perceptions and expectations of the MSF process directly impact raters' ability and willingness to expend effort and energy on the rating process and to provide reliable and honest performance feedback. Specifically, raters may be affected by their perceptions of the purpose of the MSF process, their perceptions of the MSF instrument, their understanding of rater selection, the extent to which raters have anonymity and accountability, their expectations of the outcomes of the rating process, and their perceptions of the time and effort required. Perceptions and expectations like these can be addressed through rater training. The next sections introduce the issues that MSF practitioners must address in setting up an MSF process and discusses these issues in terms of rater expectations.

Purposes of MSF

Organizations use MSF for employee development, for evaluation, or for a combination of both. A developmental objective means that MSF feedback is used only to inform ratees about the extent to which their work behaviors, competencies, or results are meeting, not meeting, or exceeding the raters' expectations. On the other hand, when the purpose of MSF is evaluation, the feedback may be used to make decisions about a ratee's merit raise, promotion, demotion, or even termination of employment.

Raters are more willing to participate in the MSF process when they know the feedback is used for developmental rather than evaluative purposes (Westerman and Rosse, 1997). However, they want ratees to be accountable for making needed improvements. A developmental MSF process works well provided that all ratees make significant attempts to improve in areas in which they rated low. There are a number of ways to improve ratee accountability (Antonioni, 1996; London, Smither, and Adsit, 1997). Some organizations now require that ratees share their MSF results with their immediate supervisors along with specific improvement goals and action plans. Other organizations have linked MSF results to annual performance appraisals and/or to personnel decisions (evaluation) in an attempt to hold ratees more accountable. The problem with these evaluative methods is that many raters feel they lose control of their ratings by allowing management to use their MSF feedback for evaluation. Peers in particular do not like their ratings to be used for this purpose. According to McEvoy and Butler (1987), peers were significantly more favorable in their attitudes toward developmental peer appraisals than toward evaluative peer appraisals.

As much as organizations would like to increase ratee accountability by using MSF for evaluation, rater perceptions have to be considered and addressed in order to have an MSF process that is valid, reliable, and acceptable. The best way to increase both ratee and rater accountability is to require that ratees summarize the MSF results to their raters and have a facilitator guide a dialogue between the raters and ratees (Antonioni, 1996; London, Smither, and Adsit, 1997). The objective is to gain new information about the feedback that can enhance learning. This approach, when done well, also teaches raters and the ratee how to have a caring, candid conversation, with the possibility of creating an informal MSF feedback. This approach requires three to five years to develop. Raters and ratees need to build trust and learn how to give and receive constructive feedback effectively.

Perceptions of the MSF Instrument Items

An assumption underlying developmental use of MSF is that individual development is ultimately linked to organizational development. Consequently, it is essential that feedback focus on the knowledge, skills, and abilities most relevant to job performance and organizational goals. Procedures such as job analysis that serve as the basis for identifying training needs and traditional job performance measures should also serve as the basis for developing the MSF instrument.

MSF rating instruments may take many formats, ranging from adjective or behavioral checklists, in which respondents simply check those items that apply, to dimension-based multipoint rating scales. Of concern here is the extent to which the particular format used to gather ratings might influence the performance description. Researchers have studied rating formats to determine whether any one format results in higher-quality ratings. This research is inconclusive at best, but one fact emerges: carefully developed formats that are easy to use and understand generally facilitate better-quality ratings.

To facilitate rater performance, the rating procedure must focus on items that are observable and measurable. In addition, it is crucial that the measurement focus be appropriate for the targeted position and rating source. No single set of items is likely to be universally appropriate for all positions and rating sources. For example, some MSF instruments use the same items for upward, downward, and horizontal (peer) ratings. Although questions regarding a manager's delegation behaviors are appropriate in upward appraisals, problems occur when peers are asked the same questions because they do not directly experience the manager's delegation. Rating quality is detrimentally affected if raters are asked to provide feedback on behaviors that are irrelevant to the ratee's position or that they have little opportunity to observe. Furthermore, ratees question the validity of raters' assessing work behaviors where there is limited opportunity to observe.

The best MSF instruments have some items that all raters respond to and other items that are unique to particular raters. All raters are asked to respond to items that reflect the organization's values and the work behaviors desired from all employees ("respects individual differences"). However, the MSF instrument should also include items that are unique to ratees in particular positions, as well as items that specific raters are able to observe and assess. For example, items for senior managers may include "clearly articulates strategic thinking" and "clearly communicates strategic initiatives," while items for midlevel managers may include "effectively communicates organizational goals" and "effectively uses resources to attain goals." These items signal or cue raters and ratees about desired work behaviors and competencies that are specific to each level of management.

Rater Anonymity and Accountability

An important decision in implementing an MSF system is whether raters are identified or remain anonymous. Applied research indicates that anonymous raters are more likely to provide candid, objective feedback compared to raters who are required to sign their names on the MSF form (Antonioni, 1994). Nonanonymous raters are primarily concerned that ratees might retaliate. This is particularly true when the ratees are their supervisors. Therefore, rater anonymity is a requirement in the MSF process.

To provide valid MSF feedback, raters should be held accountable for accurate and meaningful responses to items on the MSF instrument. Accountability refers to the amount of perceived or experienced social pressure to justify ratings (Tetlock, 1985). It is assumed that raters are more accountable if they know that they will discuss their ratings face-to-face with the ratees. Unfortunately, requiring direct face-to-face feedback also precludes rater anonymity. Raters can be held accountable in different ways. Supervisors generally give nonanonymous ratings and can be held accountable in this way. The best way to increase accountability for direct reports or peers, who give anonymous ratings, is to provide high-quality rater training and to strongly recommend that they provide written comments to support any low ratings that they give.

Perceptions About Rater Selection

Some raters, such as the ratee's immediate supervisor, are automatically included in the rating process because of their work relationship with the ratee. Ratees in managerial positions are also expected to include their direct reports as raters. Selecting peers as raters is not as easy, and there is some concern that ratees may select raters who only give them high ratings. To prevent this from occurring, some organizations require that peer raters must have an interdependent work relationship with the ratees. That is, peer raters must be internal customers of peer ratees. This selection policy increases rating validity and has additional organizational benefits. It raises employees' awareness of their internal customers and supports the concept of the horizontal organization, in which peers work with peers across the boundaries of their departments to get the work done. To help employees identify peer raters and to help control for validity, some organizations require that ratees and their immediate supervisors mutually agree on the selection of peer raters.

Perceptions of the Outcomes from the MSF Process

It is important to consider raters' expectations of outcomes from an MSF process because they are the customers of this process. If raters take time to complete MSF instruments, then it is reasonable for them to expect some benefit from the process. If the MSF process is effective, raters should expect a number of outcomes, including the ratee's increased awareness of the raters' expectations, greater alignment of expectations between raters and ratees, improved work behaviors or results, and improved communication about work expectations (Antonioni, 1996).

Raters often perceive that the MSF process is unidirectional: ratees get feedback on their strengths and weaknesses. One of the purposes of the MSF process is for raters to provide ratees with positive feedback about things they are doing well and constructive information about areas that need improvement. Raters need to know that this is one of the objectives because it gives them permission to discriminate between the items and thus spread their ratings to clearly indicate a ratee's areas of strength and areas for improvement.

Generally, raters want ratees to give them a brief summary report (oral or written) of the ratings produced by their rater group. This summary report identifies strengths and weakness and includes the ratee's improvement goals and an action plan. Most raters are tired of filling out surveys for the organization and then never hearing about the results or any plans based on the results. The summary report also gives raters general yet useful information about how their ratings compared to others.

Raters also expect ratees to demonstrate a desire to improve weak areas, especially if those areas affect the rater's work relationship and work outcomes. Raters, however, need to know that ratees do not change their behaviors in a vacuum. Raters need to understand their part in changing their coworkers' work behaviors by providing timely recognition of improvements. Ratees need to understand that if they have not made improvements by the second year of the MSF, then raters may lower their ratings in the second year or become disillusioned about the MSF process. To prevent this from happening, a number of organizations require that ratees receive coaching. This helps ratees receive recognition for improvement and helps raise accountability.

Time and Effort Needed in the MSF Process

It is important to be mindful of the existing demands on employees when implementing an MSF process. Many employees feel that they barely have time to complete their work on time. Therefore, if employees perceive that the MSF process requires a great deal of time, they may develop a negative attitude toward it. Instruments that require more than thirty to forty-five minutes for completion become a burden, especially if employees are expected to do a number of them. In some instances, raters have been asked to complete as many as twenty-five MSF instruments. For example, an individual in middle management may be required to provide ratings of all subordinates, a number of peers, and direct (and potentially indirect) supervisors.

Under these conditions, both rater ability and willingness to provide accurate, unbiased ratings may be adversely affected. There is no direct evidence indicating an optimal number of rating targets, but there is evidence that as the demands associated with the rating task increase, rating quality decreases. With respect to ability, Martell (1991) found that unintentional rater biases in ratings are more likely to occur under conditions of high information-processing demand. Evidence also suggests that if the rating task is demanding, raters are likely to rely on relatively superficial general impressions rather than an in-depth consideration of each aspect of performance.

Rater Training

A great deal of research indicates that rater training has tremendous potential for improving the effectiveness and utility of performance ratings (Woehr and Huffcutt, 1994). Rater training is critical because many of the individuals participating in the MSF process are rating work behaviors or competencies for the first time. The process of rating others should not be taken lightly; raters need to understand their responsibility. This means that raters must provide bias-free ratings based on actual behaviors and results, not ratings based on how much they like a ratee or on very limited observations. Organizations must offer training and support to increase rater responsibility. Rater training needs to address five areas:

1. Familiarizing raters with the each of the performance dimensions
2. Establishing standards pertaining to each of the dimensions to be rated
3. Improving behavioral observation skills
4. Preventing common rating errors
5. Writing descriptive, not evaluative, comments to support ratings

Finally, the training should include time for individuals to practice giving ratings and an opportunity to get feedback on the practice ratings.

Performance Dimension Training

A dimension is a major category of leadership behaviors or competencies. Common leadership dimensions include areas such as planning, communicating, team building, motivating, and coaching. MSF raters need to have an opportunity to review the MSF instrument before they make assessments of others. Unfortunately, some organizations distribute the MSF instruments and expect raters to complete them immediately.

One way to improve rater performance is to expose raters to the MSF instrument and review each performance dimension before asking them to respond to it. To do this training effectively, raters must receive the MSF instrument several months prior to completing it. In the training session, each of the performance dimensions should be reviewed. Raters should be trained to recognize which specific behaviors (individual MSF instrument items) constitute each of the dimensions. Performance dimension training helps raters improve their ability to assess people according to the appropriate dimensions, and it may also help them learn what behaviors to observe.

Frame-of-Reference Training

This type of training extends beyond performance dimension training by defining standards for each of the dimensions measured by the MSF instrument. Raters receive examples of behavioral incidents for each dimension and are told how the behaviors correspond to different levels of performance. Thus, if the MSF instrument item for leadership is "aligns departmental goals with organization's objectives," raters have to know what behaviors constitute poor, average, and exceptional performance. Raters may easily make discriminations among three levels of performance; however, many MSF instruments use response scales with five to ten categories. The more response categories, the more difficult it is for raters to discriminate between performance levels, unless raters receive behavioral anchors (examples) for each level of performance.

Behavioral Observation Training

The objective of this training is to improve raters' observation skills. Good observation skills are important for two reasons. First, raters learn to collect information that can help them reduce rating errors (such as leniency or halo). Halo errors occur when raters observe either a positive or negative work incident and then generalize this incident to other performance dimensions. For example, if a rater observes that a ratee is a poor listener in meetings, that rater might generalize this judgment to other areas and give low ratings to other performance dimensions such as interpersonal communication or conflict resolution. In behavioral observation training, raters learn how to record their observations on a work sample form or a journal. Keeping good records of observations may be a remedy for halo error, and it also helps raters deal with memory lapse. In addition, keeping a record of observations reduces the recency effect: basing ratings on a work incident that occurred just before the MSF instrument was filled out.

Common Rating Error Training

Raters need training to learn how to reduce common rater errors. The most common ones include leniency (giving mostly high ratings), harshness (giving mostly low ratings), central tendency (using only the middle rating category), and halo (generalizing the rating from one MSF items to all other items; Landy and Farr, 1980). In this training session, raters can be taught to recognize these errors and asked *not* to make them. It is critical that the training not specify correct rating distributions because this can lead raters to simply spread their ratings in order to have a "good looking" distribution, which simply leads to another type of inaccuracy (Latham, 1986).

One other rater error that is frequently overlooked is a rater's strong positive or negative reaction toward the ratee. Research results indicate that there is a strong correlation between rater affect and upward appraisal ratings (Antonioni, 1999). There are a number of ways in which rater affect can be handled. In training, raters need to know what rater affect is: a strong liking or disliking for a specific ratee. Next, raters should determine if any strong rater affect situation exists. If it does, then raters should meet with their immediate supervisors or personnel from human resources and discuss how they can rate more objectively, or disqualify themselves as raters of those ratees.

Writing Descriptive Comment Training

Ratings by themselves may not provide enough information for ratees to know specifically what to change about their behaviors or how to improve in a competency. Applied research indicates that ratees value written feedback more than numeric ratings (Antonioni, 1996). Perhaps this is why many MSF instruments now include a written comment section. Raters are commonly asked to respond to:

- What the ratee should do more of
- What the ratee should do less of
- What the ratee should keep doing

Raters need to be trained in how to write descriptive comments to these questions. A descriptive comment focuses on a specific desired behavior, such as "In our monthly meetings, get everyone's input on problems we are experiencing with our projects, record them on a flip chart, and then do a quick check for consensus about problems." Raters need to avoid making nonsubstantive evaluative comments ("Your meetings are bad"). They must be specific in their positive comments as well.

Rater training in behavioral observation should help raters write specific comments because they then have a record of specific work samples. Some raters are concerned about being identified if their comments are too specific, especially if it is constructive feedback. The best way to manage this concern is to let raters know that rater anonymity is more important than how specific comments are. However, raters need to know that if they rate the same individual in the future and they want the individual to improve, then the goal is to provide descriptive written feedback that contains "useful information" the ratee can apply to making improvements.

Many organizations getting into or using an MSF process question whether to put resources into rater training. It has been shown, however, that rater-error training reduces rating errors, performance dimension and frame-of-reference training increases rating accuracy, and behavioral observation training increases observational accuracy (Woehr and Huffcutt, 1994). Therefore, the return for the investment in rater training is improved rater performance.

From our experience, spending time in rater training has other benefits as well. Raters get the message that they are important in the process, and those who are also receiving feedback appreciate the fact that trained raters are evaluating them. We have also found that rater feedback about the MSF instrument items involves them in improving the design of the instrument, making them more committed to the process. Training sessions can also open up conversations between raters and ratees about work relationships, leadership, teamwork, and communication, and help them find mutual understanding of the meaning of the MSF process. The training helps make the MSF process a way of life in the organization, not just another program.

Recommendations

We strongly believe that rater training is important for enhancing rater ability and motivation to improve their rating performance. We also believe the training positively influences raters' perceptions and expectations of the MSF process, and that this may contribute to the long-term success of MSF. Although we have made some general suggestions for how to improve the quality of their ratings, Table 8.1 is a listing of seventeen more specific recommendations for practitioners to follow for planning, implementation, and rater training in multisource feedback systems.

We strongly believe that the MSF process adds value to organizations. It creates opportunities for individual and organizational development. We understand that the list of recommendations presented in Table 8.1 may seem long and require that organizations invest resources to train MSF raters; nevertheless, we believe that the return on the investment is well worth it.

References

Antonioni, D. "The Effects of Feedback Accountability on Upward-Appraisal Ratings." *Personnel Psychology,* 1994, *47*(2), 349–356.

Antonioni, D. "The Design of an Effective 360-Degree Appraisal Feedback Process." *Organizational Dynamics,* 1996, *25*(2), 24–38.

Antonioni, D. "Predictors of Upward Appraisal Ratings." *Journal of Managerial Issues,* 1999, *10*(1), 26–36.

Harris, M. M. "Rater Motivation in the Performance Appraisal Context: A Theoretical Framework." *Journal of Management,* 1994, *20,* 737–756.

Landy, F. J., and Farr, J. L. "Performance Rating." *Psychological Bulletin,* 1980, *87,* 72–107.

Latham, G. "Job Performance and Appraisals." In C. I. Cooper and I. Robertson (eds.), *International Review of Industrial and Organizational Psychology.* London: Wiley, 1986.

London, M., Smither, J. W., and Adsit, D. J. "Accountability: The Achilles' Heel of Multisource Feedback." *Group and Organization Management,* 1997, *22,* 162–184.

Table 8.1. Summary Recommendations for Enhancing Rater Ability and Motivation to Improve Rating Performance.

Planning and Development

1. Plan for a two-to-three-hour rater training session months before raters are expected to complete the MSF instrument. Prior to the session, each rater should know whom they are going to be rating.

2. Raters need a solid orientation about the entire MSF process. They need to know why the organization is using MSF, the specific desired outcomes of the MSF process, and the degree of difficulty in attaining those outcomes. In addition, raters need to know what their responsibilities and accountabilities are in the MSF process as well as what the ratees' responsibilities and accountabilities will be.

3. Raters also need to know that a goal of MSF is facilitate improved communication between raters and ratees, especially in terms of expectations in working with one another. In addition, raters need to know about the importance of complimenting ratees for improvements in performance. Many ratees report that raters are not recognizing their attempts to change their work behaviors (Antonioni, 1996); therefore, raters need to recognize raters' efforts to make improvements.

4. Start the MSF process with a developmental objective; however, indicate that the process may become evaluative in the future if individuals don't take responsibility to make needed improvements. Clarify that a developmental MSF is designed to provide feedback about how well ratees are meeting raters' expectations. The objective is to create alignment of expectations between raters and ratees. When organizations begin with a developmental objective and train raters about the MSF process, there is a higher level of acceptance of the process and raters tend to be willing to give more honest ratings.

5. Establish and communicate whether MSF data is confidential and/or anonymous. Both raters and ratees should know exactly what will be reported and to whom. *Rigorously enforce any confidentiality agreements.*

6. Design and use MSF instruments that are short; that is, list no more than twenty to thirty questions or items. It is reasonable to expect employees to spend thirty minutes to complete an instrument, which would include providing written feedback.

**Table 8.1. Summary Recommendations for
Enhancing Rater Ability and Motivation to
Improve Rating Performance, Cont'd.**

Implementation

7. Make sure there are fair, logical, and consistent criteria for selecting raters. Also, each rater should know ahead of time whom they will be rating and how many MSF instruments they are expected to complete.

8. Ideally, raters and ratees should receive the MSF instrument at least six months before they are to use it. In reality, the first time organizations use a MSF process it is not likely that they will have six months lead time. However, organizations can establish that the intent of the first year of the MSF is to feed forward information; that is, the ratees will be given an opportunity to learn about raters' expectations of their work behaviors or competencies with an eye toward the next MSF.

9. Raters need to review the MSF instruments and receive explanations of each performance dimension as well as the reasons each dimension is important to the organization. Examples of the work behaviors relevant to each of the dimensions should be clearly articulated.

10. One way to address raters' concerns about not having had enough opportunity to observe particular work behaviors is to provide a "not enough information" category in the rating responses for each item. This option prevents raters from skipping over items, which often leaves ratees wondering about the lack of response. It also helps to prevent raters from making an inaccurate rating response just for the sake of responding to every item. Some MSF instruments also include the term "not applicable" in addition to the "not enough information" response option. Some organizations let raters know that the human resource department will examine aggregate ratings from different rater groups and revise the MSF instrument after identifying the items frequently checked as "not enough information" or "not applicable."

11. Generally, people can do a good job of completing seven to ten short instruments. Some organizations have established that raters may turn down requests to complete more than ten instruments; however, there may be some raters who, because of their position in the organization, need to complete more than ten instruments. In those cases, raters appreciate receiving instruments ahead of the scheduled time.

**Table 8.1. Summary Recommendations for
Enhancing Rater Ability and Motivation to
Improve Rating Performance, Cont'd.**

Rater Training

12. Rater training pertaining to the specific rating instrument used is essential. In the training, raters should be given some examples of work behaviors and then asked to identify the corresponding rating dimension. An exercise can help raters learn to associate work behaviors and items with each dimension. Trainers can then check to determine how accurately this association was done.

13. In another training exercise, raters learn how to write descriptive comments about ratees' work behaviors. Raters should be asked to work with a few of the items on the MSF instrument by recalling actual work examples from ratees and then to write about the work example they had in mind. Trainers should provide raters with good examples of descriptive written comments and contrast them to poor examples. This teaches them how to write descriptive comments. In addition, they should be encouraged to begin keeping work sample logs of their behavioral observations for each of their ratees.

14. Next, using the response scale alternatives on the MSF instrument, raters need to learn how to assign ratings to work behavior samples at different performance levels. This should be done in three steps. Trainers demonstrate how to assign ratings using poor, good, and excellent performance levels. Raters are then given an opportunity to practice assigning ratings using case examples. Finally, trainers assess how well raters assigned accurate ratings to the different performance levels, followed by coaching feedback on how to improve the quality of the ratings.

15. Rater training should help raters identify common rating errors, such as leniency, harshness, central tendency, and halo error. Again, raters should be given examples and asked to identify the type of rating error, followed by an assessment of how well they were able to identify errors, as well as recognition and or feedback to help them improve.

16. Six months after the initial MSF, raters should be asked to provide feedback by responding to those MSF items that were rated low. This process allows raters and ratees to become familiar with the items on the MFS instrument, helps reduce a rater's memory lapse, and better prepares raters for completing the full instrument in subsequent years.

**Table 8.1. Summary Recommendations for
Enhancing Rater Ability and Motivation to
Improve Rating Performance, Cont'd.**

17. Finally, the MSF process should be seen as an ongoing process, not a one-time event. Rater training should occur annually and cover many of the same topics each year. Usually raters need training on writing descriptive comments and improving their behavioral observation skills. In addition, raters should receive recognition for things they have done well and constructive feedback regarding areas that they need to improve. Recognizing raters for what they have done well may be the most important step for an effective, ongoing MSF process, because it encourages high-quality rater performance, conveys respect for rater feedback, and motivates raters to continue devoting time and effort to the rating process.

Martell, R. F. "Sex Bias at Work: The Effects of Attentional and Memory Demands on Performance Ratings of Men and Women." *Journal of Applied Social Psychology,* 1991, *21,* 1939–1960.

McEvoy, G., and Butler, P. "User Acceptance of Peer Appraisals in an Industrial Setting." *Personnel Psychology,* 1987, *37,* 687–702.

Murphy, K. R., and Cleveland, J. N. *Understanding Performance Appraisal: Social, Organizational, and Goal-Based Perspectives.* Thousand Oaks, Calif.: Sage, 1995.

Tetlock, P. E. "Accountability: The Neglected Social Context of Judgment and Choice." *Research in Organizational Behavior,* 1985, *7,* 297–332.

Westerman, J. W., and Rosse, J. G. "Reducing the Threat of Rater Non-Participation in 360-Degree Feedback Systems: An Exploratory Examination of Antecedents to Participation in Upward Ratings." *Group and Organization Management,* 1997, *22,* 288–309.

Woehr, D. J., and Huffcutt, A. I. "Rater Training for Performance Appraisal: A Quantitative Review." *Journal of Occupational and Organizational Psychology,* 1994, *67,* 189–206.

CHAPTER 9

Reliability, Validity, and Meaningfulness of Multisource Ratings

Kevin R. Murphy
Jeanette N. Cleveland
Carolyn J. Mohler

Multisource rating systems are increasingly popular (Church and Bracken, 1997), especially as a tool for employee development. These systems often include input from one or more supervisors, several peers, and several subordinates, and they may also include self-assessments or evaluations from others within or outside the organization (for instance, customer feedback).

A key assumption of a multisource rating system is that these ratings contain information that is useful and relevant to the individuals being evaluated, and that the ratings are the basis for assessment, training and development, career planning, and other similar activities. The psychometric characteristics of multisource ratings are therefore an important consideration.

Research on the reliability, validity, and other characteristics of ratings can help us understand whether, and under what conditions, multisource ratings are likely to produce information that is potentially useful to the recipient and the organization.

This chapter focuses on three questions. First, do multisource ratings contain consistent and stable information about ratees' performance and behavior in organizations (reliability)? Second, what do these ratings tell us about the individuals being evaluated—for example, do they give information about people's performance and effectiveness on the job (validity)? Third, is this information useful and meaningful to the recipient (meaningfulness)?

Reliability of Multisource Ratings

There is an extensive literature discussing the reliability of performance ratings, much of which focuses on supervisory ratings. For the most part, research on the reliability of supervisory ratings has focused on the stability of overall scores obtained from a single supervisor, who uses a multi-item performance appraisal form (Murphy and Cleveland, 1995). Early meta-analytic studies (for example, Schmidt, Hunter, and Caplan, 1981) used a test-retest approach to estimate the reliability of ratings, but more recent research has focused on interrater reliability estimates. This research has produced findings that are remarkably consistent, and generally discouraging. First, if two raters are asked to evaluate an individual's job performance, their ratings are not likely to be highly correlated. Second, interrater agreement or disagreement does not seem to depend much on organizational level (supervisors, peers, subordinates, etc.). No matter who is asked to evaluate job performance, it is likely that they will disagree.

Agreement Within Sources

Conway and Huffcutt's meta-analysis (1997) reveals that subordinates showed the lowest level of interrater reliability. On average, subordinate ratings of job performance show correlations in the low .30s; average interrater correlations are slightly higher for peers (.37). Supervisors show slightly higher levels of agreement (.50), but again, similarly situated raters tend to provide evaluations that are only moderately consistent. Viswesvaran, Ones, and Schmidt (1996) report similar estimates. In their review, average interrater correlations were .52 for supervisors and .42 for peers.

Peer ratings are sometimes viewed as superior to ratings from other sources, in part because of their supposedly higher reliability. One reason that peer ratings *seem* more reliable than supervisory ratings is that peer ratings are often averaged over several individuals, whereas supervisory ratings are usually obtained from a single individual (Scullen, 1997). In fact, if you adjust for the effects of this aggregation, peer ratings are probably *less* reliable than ratings obtained from other sources (Viswesvaran, Ones, and Schmidt, 1996). For the most part, the enhanced reliability and validity of peer ratings is a by-product of the fact that they are often presented in aggregated form rather than an indication of peers' enhanced abilities or the shortcomings of supervisors as raters.

Agreement Between Sources

A number of studies have examined agreement in ratings obtained from different sources (say, agreement between supervisory and peer ratings). For example, Harris and Schaubroeck's meta-analysis (1988) reported that an average correlation between peer and supervisor ratings was .53 (this figure is very similar to Viswesvaran and colleagues' estimate of the average correlation between supervisory ratings, namely, .52), the average self-supervisory correlation was .31, and the average self-peer correlation was also .31. They note that there are many reasons why different sources should *not* agree, including the effects of egocentric biases (self-evaluations often differ from evaluations received from others; Thornton, 1980), differences in opportunities to observe (Murphy and Cleveland, 1995), and differences in organizational level.

A more recent meta-analysis (Conway and Huffcutt, 1997) suggested that correlations between ratings obtained from different sources (supervisors, peers, subordinates) are even lower than this. This analysis suggests that the mean correlation between ratings obtained from a supervisor and a single peer is .34, and all other correlations between ratings obtained from different sources are in the .20s or lower. Recent studies of multisource rating systems (Scullen, Mount, and Goff, forthcoming; Greguras and Robie, 1998) confirm this general pattern. Raters typically do not agree, and it does not matter much whether they are at the same level (as with agreement between two supervisors) or different levels in the organization (supervisor-peer correlations).

What Do Interrater Correlations Tell Us?

A number of researchers have suggested that interrater correlations provide an estimate of the reliability of ratings (Schmidt and

Hunter, 1996; Viswesvaran, Ones, and Schmidt, 1996). Correlations between ratings from similarly situated raters are rarely much greater than .50, and correlations between ratings from different sources are sometimes even lower. If interrater correlations are interpreted as reliability estimates, this means that 50 percent or more of the variance in performance ratings is probably due to measurement error.

The argument that interrater correlations can be interpreted as reliability coefficients is based on a model that treats raters as passive measurement instruments. For example, Schmidt and Hunter claim that each "rater is analogous to a different form of the rating instrument" (1996, p. 209). In another paper, Viswesvaran, Ones, and Schmidt (1996) argue that the question of interest in evaluating the reliability of performance ratings is whether "the same ratings will be obtained if a different but equally knowledgeable judge rated the same employee" (p. 565). If raters are viewed as alternate forms of a measurement instrument, the correlation between these alternate forms should constitute an estimate of reliability.

There are several reasons to believe that raters in organizations cannot be treated as interchangeable forms of a rating instrument. First, in most organizations, raters observe different behaviors and have differing responsibilities when completing performance ratings (Borman, 1974; Murphy and Cleveland, 1995). Indeed, one explanation for disagreements between raters is that they are not equally knowledgeable (Borman, 1974) but rather observe fundamentally different aspects of a ratee's behavior.

Second, and more important, treating raters as interchangeable measurement instruments implies that measurement is a primary— or at least an important—aspect of performance rating in organizations. Most reviews of performance rating research (Cleveland and Murphy, 1992; Landy and Farr, 1980; Long, 1986; Longenecker, Sims, and Gioia, 1987; Milkovich and Wigdor, 1991; Murphy and Cleveland, 1995) suggest that raters pursue a number of goals when completing performance appraisals (for example, motivating subordinates, maintaining smooth interpersonal relationships), and that accurately evaluating their subordinates is often a relatively minor concern of raters. In contrast to a model in which raters function as alternate forms of a single measurement instrument, this research suggests that performance rating is a complexly motivated activity, sometimes driven by variables that have little to do with ratees' performance.

Low interrater correlations are usually taken as evidence of random measurement error in ratings, but there is a much simpler explanation for raters' failure to agree. Performance ratings are normally collected in settings where range restriction is ubiquitous, especially when ratings are used to make administrative decisions about ratees (such as salary and promotion; Murphy and Cleveland, 1995). For example, Bretz, Milkovich, and Read (1992, p. 333) conclude that "the norm in U.S. industry is to rate employees at the top end of the scale." Range restriction of the sort that is absolutely routine in performance appraisal can substantially limit interrater agreement. For example, if the .52 correlation cited by Viswesvaran, Ones, and Schmidt (1996) as an estimate of reliability is corrected for the level of range restriction typically found in real-world performance appraisals, reliability estimates are more likely to be in the .70s and .80s than in the .50s.

Even if low interrater correlations are not an indication of low reliability, they do represent a serious problem for multisource rating systems. As we noted earlier, any system that features multiple ratings is likely to produce substantial disagreements between raters. Disagreements might be more pronounced when comparing evaluations from different sources, but even if all ratings are collected from the same source, disagreement is likely to be the norm, not the exception.

One potential solution to the problems of low agreement among raters is to pool data from several raters and provide feedback in the form of aggregated ratings. Aggregation is widely recommended as a potential solution to limited reliability (Scullen, Mount, and Goff, forthcoming; see, however, Greguras and Robie, 1998). This technique might be even more valuable as a means of reducing the inconsistency in ratings and performance feedback that is virtually guaranteed if individual ratings from multiple sources are fed back to employees.

Is Aggregation a Solution or a Problem?

There are two reasons one might want to present multisource ratings in aggregated form (for example, if there are four peer ratings, the average over peers can be presented to the recipient rather than four separate ratings). First, aggregating ratings increases their reliability (Scullen, 1997). In the preceding section, we noted that low interrater agreement was a chronic problem in multisource feedback (MSF) systems, and aggregation can certainly help here. Greguras and Robie (1998) note that MSF programs rarely include sufficient numbers of raters at any level, especially supervisors, to achieve high reliability, so aggregation must be thought of as a partial rather than a full solution to the reliability problem; still, it can help.

A more compelling reason for aggregating is that it may reduce the potentially disruptive influence of interrater disagreements. As noted earlier, multisource rating systems are almost certain to produce inconsistent evaluations, and they might produce more confusion than clarity. The low levels of interrater agreement reviewed earlier mean that many ratees are likely to receive favorable evaluations from some raters and unfavorable ones from others. This may diminish the credibility of ratings and lead to "selective listening," in which unfavorable feedback is dismissed. Aggregated ratings may give a better picture of how an individual's performance is viewed by peers, supervisors, etc., as a group than can be obtained from individual ratings.

One potential downside of the strategy of aggregating ratings is that aggregation may have undesirable effects on the ratings themselves. London, Smither, and Adsit (1997) suggest that accountability may be the Achilles heel of multisource rating systems. They correctly note that raters often have even less accountability under multisource systems (ratings may be anonymous, or averaged over raters) than under traditional systems. Cleveland and Murphy (1992) note that raters are only rarely held accountable by organizations, and the accountability pressures that do exist (for instance, the need to give subordinates disappointing feedback) often serve to inflate ratings. Thus, there may be relatively little accountability to lose in moving from single-rater to multiple-rater scenarios. Nevertheless, the concerns expressed by London, Smither, and Adsit (1997) are important ones. Multisource rating systems may undercut what little accountability exists in rating systems, and this is likely to detract from the quality and usefulness of rating data.

Should Ratings Be Aggregated by Source?

The idea of aggregating ratings by source—for example, averaging peer ratings together—makes intuitive sense, and it is common practice in multisource rating systems (Bozeman, 1997). However, there is little clear evidence that different sources provide truly distinct information, or that aggregating by source really makes sense. For example, Mount and others (1998) suggest that source effects in multisource rating systems are small, and that what are often taken for source differences (disagreements between, for example, peers and supervisors) are probably due to the generally low levels of agreement between raters, regardless of their position in the organization (similar results have been reported by Conway and Huffcutt, 1997; and Scullen, Mount, and Goff, forthcoming). That is, grouping ratings by peers, supervisors, subordinates, etc., may not make much psychometric sense. On the other hand, it makes obvious psychological sense, and it is likely to enhance the acceptability and impact of ratings. It is important to keep in mind that pooling ratings by source may lead to unwarranted conclusions about differences in how your performance is viewed by superiors, peers, subordinates, and so on; nevertheless, aggregating by source is likely to provide more benefits than drawbacks.

Validity of Multisource Ratings

Several methods have been used to estimate the validity of performance ratings. The most obvious approach is to correlate ratings with objective measures of performance and effectiveness. For example, Heneman (1986) reviewed correlations between supervisory ratings and results-oriented measures of performance. The corrected mean correlation between the two was .27, but there was substantial variability in the r values. Higher correlations were found for some rating methods (composite ratings and relative ratings produced higher correlations), but these two classes of measures cannot be treated as interchangeable. A subsequent meta-analysis (Bommer and others, 1995), which focused solely on objective measures of countable behaviors or outcomes, suggested that the correlation between supervisory ratings and objective performance indices was substantially higher (a corrected correlation of .39 was reported). Conway, Lowe, and Langley (1999) report a similar meta-analysis involving peer and subordinate ratings; they report corrected correlations between ratings and objective measures of .34 and .30 for peers and subordinates, respectively. These reviews suggest that performance ratings and objective measures do overlap but are not interchangeable.

Correlations between objective measures and ratings produce useful information, but they are not by themselves a comprehensive index of the validity of ratings. Objective measures of performance and effectiveness rarely capture all of the facets of the performance domain (Murphy and Cleveland, 1995), and it is not clear that objective measures are any better than subjective judgments as an indication of how well or poorly individuals perform. An alternative to relying on correlations with objective measures to evaluate validity is to adopt a construct validation approach. A review of performance ratings conducted by the National Research Council (Milkovich and Wigdor, 1991) concluded that supervisory ratings of performance do indeed show evidence of construct validity. This review did not explicitly consider the validity of peer, subordinate, or self-ratings, but the patterns of evidence that led to the conclusion that supervisory ratings are valid also appears to apply to peer and subordinate ratings.

Woehr, Sheehan, and Bennett's analysis (1999) suggests that supervisors, peers, and other sources agree substantially in terms of the constructs that underlie their ratings, and further that interrater disagreements cannot be dismissed as measurement error. Raters observe different behaviors and apply various standards when evaluating behaviors (see also Murphy and Cleveland, 1995), and their disagreements may in part reflect systematic differences in what they are evaluating. In any case, multisource ratings do appear to show evidence of construct validity.

Validity for What?

Murphy and Cleveland (1995) note that performance ratings cannot be thought of as tests or measurement instruments designed simply to give a numerical estimate of someone's performance. Rather, performance ratings reflect a complex interaction between what the ratee is doing, the goals of the rater (see also Cleveland

and Murphy, 1992), the context in which ratings occur, etc. If we define *validity* in terms of the question "Do these ratings reflect the person's true performance level?" we are likely to come to different conclusions about validity than if we ask another set of questions ("Do these ratings reflect other people's *perceptions* of performance and effectiveness?"). That is, multisource ratings may or may not yield information about "true performance"; though there is evidence for the construct validity of performance ratings, there is also clear evidence that factors other than performance influence ratings, regardless of the source (Murphy and Cleveland, 1995).

Multisource ratings are more likely to provide valid information about how one's performance is perceived at various levels of the organization, and regardless of whether these perceptions are accurate, it should be useful information to find out that your subordinates, peers, and so on believe that you are effective or ineffective in various aspects of your job.

Perceptions of Validity and Users' Acceptance of Rating Information

Validity can be assessed statistically, correlating between ratings with indicators of individual and organizational success (including promotion, salary, and so forth), but in evaluating the validity and utility of multisource ratings it is important to go beyond simple statistical procedures. In particular, it is important to determine whether the participants themselves believe that multisource ratings provide valid and useful information about performance. Ratings are unlikely to be useful or to lead to meaningful change unless raters and ratees accept them as valid indicators of performance and effectiveness (see Chapter Thirty).

There is evidence that perceived validity of MSF depends not only on who is being evaluated but also on which performance areas or competencies are assessed and on the purpose or use of ratings. For example, supervisors are likely to believe that subordinates can evaluate some dimensions of their job but not others (McEvoy, 1990). Dimensions or competencies that managers believe can be reasonably assessed by subordinates include leadership, oral communication, delegation, coordination, interest in subordinates, performance feedback that offers work guidance, composure and self-control, and interpersonal skills. By contrast, managers are less likely to believe subordinates can evaluate such dimensions as planning and organizing, budgeting, goal setting, decision making, creativity, quantity of work, quality of work, analytical ability, and technical ability.

There are a number of beliefs that limit supervisors' willingness to accept subordinate ratings of their performance (Bernardin, 1986). Supervisors often report that subordinates:

• Lack the information or skills needed to make valid ratings
• Are inexperienced as raters
• Have not been trained to make accurate ratings
• Harshly rate managers who are demanding
• Inflate ratings to avoid retaliation from managers
• Use ratings to undermine the authority of managers

Additionally, managers avoid organizations that use subordinate ratings, causing difficulties recruiting and retaining managers. Lastly, supervisors report subordinate ratings being nothing more than a popularity contest.

Peer ratings are often cited as a valuable source of performance feedback (Cardy and Dobbins, 1994; Wexley and Klimoski, 1984). Peers are often in a better position to evaluate job performance than supervisors, they may be more sensitive to the system factors that influence performance and how a person is able to respond to them, and they may have better understanding of the behaviors that are critical for successful job performance (Cardy and Dobbins, 1994). There is evidence that peer evaluations can be used to predict future performance, forecast final grades, and predict job advancement (Reilly and Chao, 1982; Shore, Shore, and Thornton, 1992). However, relatively little is known about the perceived validity of peer ratings.

One potential barrier to using peer ratings is the fact that employees often do not like evaluating each other; widespread dislike of rating one's peers may also interfere with the acceptance of such evaluations (Cederblom and Lounsbury, 1980; Love, 1981). Employees are more likely to accept peer ratings if appraisals are used for only developmental purposes rather than administrative (Farh, Cannella, and Bedeian, 1991). Managers are often skeptical of peer ratings because they are thought to be biased by friendship and similarity between the rater and ratee (Love, 1981) and may give less weight to evaluations from an individual's peers than to ratings from superiors.

It is often argued that employees are more familiar with their own performance than other sources and thus are in a position to make accurate self-evaluations. Further, comparing self-ratings and supervisory ratings constitutes a method for identifying system factors that restrict performance, and for clarifying subordinate expectations about job and role requirements (Cardy and Dobbins, 1994). Although self-ratings do not show strong agreement with supervisory or peer ratings, there is evidence for the empirical validity of self-ratings in predicting objective performance. Self-ratings of performance are relatively easy to obtain and may yield at least two benefits in the feedback process: contributing to positive employee perceptions about due process and participation in important organizational decisions, and offering valuable information about system or nonindividual performance factors that have generally enhanced or inhibited effective and ineffective employee performance.

Although hardly free from bias, supervisory ratings are often accepted as valid simply because of their source. That is, the job of a manager or supervisor revolves around planning, organizing, directing, controlling, and being held accountable for accomplishing organizational objectives through his or her subordinates. Managers and supervisors are assumed to have information about the behavior and performance of their subordinates, and the task of evaluating their performance is a natural part of the supervisor's job. Multisource rating systems require out-of-role behaviors from many participants (as when subordinates are asked to evaluate their superiors); the fact that performance rating is an in-role behavior for managers and supervisors is likely to enhance the perceived validity and legitimacy of supervisory ratings.

Supervisors, peers, subordinates, and others are likely to have access to different sorts of information about an individual's performance. For example, self-raters rely more on their actual behaviors when rating, while supervisor have access to both ratee behavior and outcomes. There is evidence that supervisors rely more heavily on work outcomes than employee behaviors in making evaluations (Carson, Cardy, and Dobbins, 1991), which may help to explain why there is low agreement between supervisory and self-ratings.

Cardy and Dobbins (1994) suggest that peer raters consider both work outcomes and work behaviors when assessing performance, whereas subordinate ratings are likely be affected more by employee behavior than by outcomes. Subordinates often do not have access to the work outcomes of their supervisors and rely on direct observation of supervisory behaviors on which to based their evaluations. In general, ratings are more likely to be viewed as valid and useful by recipients if they can be confident that raters have access to the information needed to assess performance, and if they believe that raters are motivated to provide accurate evaluations. As we note below, the structure of multisource rating systems may make it easier to obtain ratings that are both accurate and credible to recipients, in comparison to ratings obtained in traditional top-down rating systems.

Is MSF Useful and Meaningful to Recipients?

The ultimate criterion for evaluating multisource feedback is probably the extent to which this information is useful and meaningful to recipients. There is an extensive literature dealing with performance feedback and its effects on individual behavior, and it is beyond the scope of this chapter to review the literature in detail. However, we can present some broad principles that are likely to affect the usefulness and meaningfulness of multisource ratings.

First, recipients' interpretation of MSF is likely to be affected by its consistency, by a comparison of information obtained from multiple perspectives with that obtained from traditional top-down evaluation systems, and by individual difference variables. Second, changes in behavior following feedback may depend on motivational factors more than on the feedback itself. Finally, perceptions of the fairness of feedback may substantially affect the success of MSF systems.

Interpreting MSF: Consistency, Value-Added, and Individual Differences

Information that is not consistent can affect interpretation of feedback, and it may also affect the degree to which behavior changes result. We have noted earlier that disagreement is common in multisource feedback. There is evidence that some individuals pay attention to consistent information only and disregard feedback when raters disagree (Korman, 1976). These individuals may find MSF to be limited in value. However, inconsistency is not always a barrier to useful feedback. The degree of consistency can itself be a useful piece of information, because it helps determine the amount of change needed by providing comparative information to the recipient (London and Smither, 1995).

The information from MSF is likely to be evaluated in comparison to that from traditional top-down approaches, and the utility of multisource information is likely to be enhanced if recipients see added value to obtaining feedback from multiple perspectives. There is relatively little empirical research on the factors that lead recipients to perceive MSF as relatively valuable, or as redundant with traditional forms of feedback, and more work is clearly needed in this area.

From the rater's perspective, one important advantage of multisource rating is that information is often presented in an anonymous or aggregated form, whereas in traditional top-down approaches the source of ratings is known. This may give raters the ability to make more accurate ratings, and it may reduce pressures to provide the overly favorable evaluations usually encountered in top-down rating systems (Cleveland and Murphy, 1992). Enhancing the accuracy of ratings may also enhance the acceptability and perceived value of these ratings. Many of the raters in a multisource system are also ratees, and if raters believe that the structure of the rating system enhances their own ability to rate accurately, they are more likely to believe that ratings they obtain are also more accurate than would be expected under traditional top-down systems.

London and Smither (1995) identified several individual difference variables that can affect interpretation of feedback, including self-image, feedback-seeking behaviors, and self-monitoring. For example, low self-image can lead to lower self-ratings, producing an inaccurate comparison between self and other ratings. A person's propensity to concentrate on positive or negative aspects of feedback can affect his or her perceptions of the validity of the ratings received. McFarland and Miller (1994) suggest that individuals who focus on positive aspects of feedback are more likely to accept and value the feedback and are more likely to believe that they can use it to improve their own performance.

Change in Performance Following Feedback

The simple act of receiving feedback does not always change behavior. Kluger and De Nisi's 1996 meta-analysis of feedback interventions concluded that the majority of feedback recipients demonstrated a positive change in performance. However, approximately one-third of those who receive feedback showed decreases in performance. Those researchers suggest that feedback directed to the self instead of tasks is relatively ineffective in producing beneficial behavior change.

Other studies have demonstrated similar positive results in behavior and performance change following performance feedback. For example, Hazucha, Hezlett, and Schneider (1993) reported increases in managerial skill two years after receiving 360-degree feedback. Similarly, ratings of leader behaviors generally improved after feedback, (Atwater, Roush, and Fischthal, 1995). Managers whose inflated self-ratings were inconsistent with others' ratings tend to improve performance (Johnson and Ferstl, 1999). Clearly, individual perceptions of performance and behavior can change following feedback. However, change following feedback may depend on a number of factors, notably the recipient's motivation to change.

Perceptions of Fairness

Multisource assessments are thought to be more procedurally fair than traditional top-down ratings because they involve voice from each level of organization. For example, Edwards and Ewen's study (1996) of organizations that adopted MSF systems reported a 50 percent increase in perceived fairness as compared to traditional top-down systems. Multisource rating systems not only extend more opportunities for members of the organization to have some voice in evaluation but also present information in ways that reduce pressures to distort ratings. Murphy and Cleveland (1995) note that raters in a traditional system are strongly motivated to provide lenient ratings. In multisource systems, ratees often receive feedback that is anonymous or aggregated, and raters have less to fear if they give frank and accurate ratings.

Perceptions of fairness may substantially affect motivation to change behavior as a result of ratings. Raters who believe that the performance feedback they receive is unfair or biased are unlikely to expend a great deal of effort in changing their behavior; nor are they likely to accept their ratings as useful information for improving their performance in the future. Indeed, one might argue that the largest benefit of multisource rating systems is that they have the potential to deliver information in a form that is viewed as relatively fair, accurate, and unbiased. That is, the true value of these systems may lie more in the credibility of the information than in the fact that they produce more information than what is usually obtained from top-down rating systems.

Conclusions

Raters, ratees, and organizations are likely to emphasize different criteria in evaluating multisource ratings. From the perspective of the ratee, the most important issue is probably the extent to which ratings yield valid and meaningful information that helps them improve their performance and effectiveness. Reliability and validity are both important facets of this evaluation (meaning, if ratings are unreliable, they are unlikely to be useful), but the credibility and perceived fairness of ratings is also important.

From the rater's perspective, the most important criteria may be those that are tied to how ratings are collected and used (are ratings aggregated?). Organizations are likely to be concerned with a wide range of criteria, including cost, effectiveness of feedback, legal defensibility, etc. The standard psychometric criteria (reliability, validity, and so on) are likely to be important considerations to many of the participants in multisource rating systems, but these criteria are rarely sufficient for evaluating this method of collecting and disseminating performance information.

Low levels of interrater agreement provide a real challenge to the integrity and usefulness of multisource rating systems, but the effects of disagreement between raters may have various implications depending on how the system is administered (again as an example, are ratings aggregated?) and, more important, how multisource ratings are used. Performance ratings are used for a wide range of purposes in organizations (Cleveland, Murphy, and

Williams, 1989), and it is likely that multisource ratings may also serve a number of purposes. Disagreements between raters may give useful information when providing developmental feedback, but they may undermine the credibility and defensibility of the same ratings if they are used for administrative purposes (salary, promotion). The relative emphasis given to different criteria (reliability, validity, perceived validity, fairness perceptions, etc.) in evaluating multisource rating systems is likely to depend on the purposes and goals of the system.

References

Atwater, L. E., Roush, P., and Fischthal, A. "The Influence of Upward Feedback on Self and Follower Ratings of Leadership." *Personnel Psychology*, 1995, *48*, 35–59.

Bernardin, H. J. "Subordinate Appraisal: A Valuable Source of Information About Managers." *Human Resource Management*, 1986, *25*, 421–439.

Bommer, W. H., and others. "On the Interchangeability of Objective and Subjective Measures of Employee Performance: A Meta-Analysis." *Personnel Psychology*, 1995, *48*, 587–605.

Borman, W. C. "The Rating of Individuals in Organizations: An Alternative Approach." *Organizational Behavior and Human Performance*, 1974, *12*, 105–124.

Bozeman, D. P. "Interrater Agreement in Multisource Performance Appraisal: A Commentary." *Journal of Organizational Behavior*, 1997, *18*, 313–316.

Bretz, R. D., Milkovich, G. T., and Read, W. "The Current State of Performance Research and Practice: Concerns, Directions, and Implications." *Journal of Management*, 1992, *18*, 321–352.

Cardy, R. L., and Dobbins, G. H. *Performance Appraisal: Alternative Perspectives*. Cincinnati, Ohio: South-Western, 1994.

Carson, K. P., Cardy, R. L., and Dobbins, G. H. "Performance Appraisal as Effective Management or Deadly Management Disease: Two Initial Empirical Investigations." *Group and Organization Studies*, 1991, *16*, 143–159.

Cederblom, D., and Lounsbury, J. W. "An Investigation of User Acceptance of Peer Evaluations." *Personnel Psychology*, 1980, *33*, 567–579.

Church, A. H., and Bracken, D. W. "Advancing the State of the Art of 360-Degree Feedback: Guest Editors' Comments on the Research and Practice of Multirater Assessment Methods." *Group and Organization Management*, 1997, *22*, 149–161.

Cleveland, J. N., and Murphy, K. R. "Analyzing Performance Appraisal as Goal-Directed Behavior." In G. Ferris and K. Rowland (eds.), *Research in Personnel and Human Resources Management*. Vol. 10. Greenwich, Conn.: JAI Press, 1992.

Cleveland, J. N., Murphy, K. R., and Williams, R. "Multiple Uses of Performance Appraisal: Prevalence and Correlates." *Journal of Applied Psychology*, 1989, *74*, 130–135.

Conway, J. M., and Huffcutt, A. I. "Psychometric Properties of Multisource Performance Ratings: A Meta-Analysis of Subordinate, Supervisor, Peer, and Self-Ratings." *Human Performance*, 1997, *10*, 331–360.

Conway, J. M., Lowe, K. L., and Langley, K. C. "Peer and Subordinate Ratings and Objective Performance, Ability, and Personality: A Meta-Analysis." Unpublished manuscript, 1999.

Edwards, M. R., and Ewen, A. J. *360-Degree Feedback: The Powerful New Model for Employee Assessment and Performance Improvement.* New York: AMACOM, 1996.

Farh, J. L., Cannella, A. A., and Bedeian, A. G. "Peer Ratings: The Impact of Purpose on Rating Quality and User Acceptance." *Group and Organization Studies*, 1991, *16*, 367–386.

Greguras, G. J., and Robie, C. "A New Look at Within-Source Interrater Reliability of 360-Degree Feedback Ratings." *Journal of Applied Psychology*, 1998, *83*, 960–968.

Harris, M. H., and Schaubroeck, J. "A Meta-Analysis of Self-Supervisory, Self-Peer, and Peer-Supervisory Ratings." *Personnel Psychology*, 1988, *41*, 43–62.

Hazucha, J. F., Hezlett, S. A., and Schneider, R. J. "The Impact of 360-Degree Feedback on Management Skills Development." *Human Resource Management*, 1993, *32*, 325–351.

Heneman, R. L. "The Relationship Between Supervisory Ratings and Results-Oriented Measures of Performance: A Meta-Analysis." *Personnel Psychology*, 1986, *39*, 811–826.

Johnson, J. W., and Ferstl, K. L. "The Effects of Interrater and Self-Other Agreement on Performance Improvement Following Upward Feedback." *Personnel Psychology*, 1999, *52*, 272–303.

Kluger, A. N., and De Nisi, A. "The Effects of Feedback Interventions on Performance: A Historical Review, a Meta-Analysis, and a Preliminary Feedback Intervention Theory." *Psychological Bulletin*, 1996, *119*, 254–284.

Korman, A. K. "Hypothesis of Work Behavior Revisited and an Extension." *Academy of Management Review*, 1976, *1*, 50–63.

Landy, F. J., and Farr, J. L. "Performance Rating." *Psychological Bulletin*, 1980, *87*, 72–107.

London, M., and Smither, J. W. "Can Multisource Feedback Change Perceptions of Goal Accomplishment, Self-Evaluations, and Performance-Related Outcomes? Theory-Based Applications and Directions for Research." *Personnel Psychology*, 1995, *48*, 803–839.

London, M., Smither, J. W., and Adsit, D. J. "Accountability: The Achilles' Heel of Multisource Feedback." *Group and Organization Management*, 1997, *22*, 162–184.

Long, P. *Performance Appraisal Revisited*. London: Institute of Personnel Management, 1986.

Longenecker, C. O., Sims, H. P., and Gioia, D. A. "Behind the Mask: The Politics of Employee Appraisal." *Academy of Management Executive*, 1987, *1*, 183–193.

Love, K. G. "Comparison of Peer Assessment Methods: Reliability, Validity, Friendship Bias, and User Reaction." *Journal of Applied Psychology*, 1981, *66*, 451–457.

McEvoy, G. M. "Public Sector Managers' Reactions to Appraisals by Subordinates." *Public Personnel Management*, 1990, *19*, 201–212.

McFarland, C., and Miller, D. T. "The Framing of Relative Performance Feedback: Seeing the Glass as Half Empty or Half Full." *Journal of Personality and Social Psychology*, 1994, *66*, 1061–1073.

Milkovich, G. T., and Wigdor, A. K. *Pay for Performance*. Washington, D.C.: National Academy Press, 1991.

Mount, M. K., and others. "Trait, Rater and Level Effects in 360-Degree Performance Ratings." *Personnel Psychology*, 1998, *51*, 557–576.

Murphy, K., and Cleveland, J. *Understanding Performance Appraisal: Social, Organizational, and Goal-Oriented Perspectives*. Thousand Oaks, Calif.: Sage, 1995.

Reilly, R. R., and Chao, G. T. "Validity and Fairness of Some Alternate Employee Selection Procedures." *Personnel Psychology*, 1982, *35*, 1–67.

Schmidt, F. L., and Hunter, J. E. "Measurement Error in Psychological Research: Lessons from 26 Research Scenarios." *Psychological Methods*, 1996, *1*, 199–223.

Schmidt, F. L, Hunter, J. E., and Caplan, R. "Validity Generalization Results for Two Jobs in the Petroleum Industry." *Journal of Applied Psychology*, 1981, *66*, 261–273.

Scullen, S. E. "When Ratings from One Source Have Been Averaged, But Ratings from Another Source Have Not: Problems and Solutions." *Journal of Applied Psychology*, 1997, *82*, 880–888.

Scullen, S. E., Mount, M. K., and Goff, M. "Understanding the Latent Structure of Job Performance Ratings." *Journal of Applied Psychology*, forthcoming.

Shore, T. H., Shore, L. M., and Thornton, G. C. "Construct Validity of

Self- and Peer Evaluations of Performance Dimensions in an Assessment Center." *Journal of Applied Psychology*, 1992, *77*, 42–54.

Thornton, G. C., III. "Psychometric Properties of Self-Appraisals of Job Performance." *Personnel Psychology*, 1980, *33*, 263–271.

Viswesvaran, C., Ones, D. S., and Schmidt, F. L. "Comparative Analysis of the Reliability of Job Performance Ratings." *Journal of Applied Psychology*, 1996, *81*, 557–574.

Wexley, K. N., and Klimoski, R. J. "Performance Appraisal: An Update." In G. R. Ferris and K. M. Rowland (eds.), *Research in Personnel and Human Resources Management*. Vol. 2. Greenwich, Conn.: JAI Press, 1984.

Woehr, D. J., Sheehan, M. K., and Bennett, W. "Understanding Disagreement Across Rating Sources: An Assessment of the Measurement Equivalence of Raters in 360-Degree Feedback Systems." Paper presented at the fourteenth annual conference of the Society for Industrial and Organizational Psychology, Atlanta, Ga., May 1999.

CHAPTER 10

Working with a Vendor for a Successful Project

Carol W. Timmreck
Tom Wentworth

Much of this handbook is devoted to design or follow-through aspects of multisource feedback (MSF). In this chapter, we explore a very important aspect of implementing the project aspects of MSF with an external vendor. Whereas some organizations handle the technical aspects of data capture and processing internally, others seek outside help for numerous reasons, among them desiring to outsource these aspects to someone whose core business it is to process MSF; or wanting to reinforce the objectivity, anonymity, and confidentiality of the process by having it handled by a third party. It is for these situations that it becomes very important to work with a "vendor" for a successful project.

Our working definition of *vendor* is an external manager of the technical aspects of project enrollment, data collection, and data processing (rather than a consultant who offers a broader range of consulting services such as content development, or follow-up training and coaching). We address this topic from our perspectives and professional experience as an internal consultant and a processing vendor. Many views expressed in this chapter reflect a bias to outsource this process to a competent, experienced vendor; the bias comes from the experience and perspective of the internal consultant accountable to management for the quality of the outcome.

There are several themes evident throughout this chapter. Two related themes are those of *trusting partnership* and *managing relationships*. An important element in a successful project is regarding your vendor as a partner, with each of you having a stake in the other's success, and approaching the project with a win-win attitude of mutual benefit and mutual satisfaction (Covey, 1989). There are many occasions throughout a project when time spent building and maintaining relationships proves to be a good investment. These relationships are internal to the company, internal to the vendor's company, and company to vendor.

A third theme is the importance of at least one partner in the relationship having *MSF project experience,* and preferably both. A vendor should have significant experience with a wide variety of implementations to offer solid analysis of the impact of the client's preferred methods of implementation. An experienced client understands implications of various decisions, recognizes potential problem areas, and can coach a less experienced vendor on desirable applications.

A fourth theme is that of the *impact of vendor technology,* the vendor's ability to manage mixed-media processes, and the selected media's dual potential of being either an enabler or a driver of the process.

The Client-Vendor Relationship: Aligning Expectations

If any single thing most contributes to the success of a project, it is clear understanding of who's doing what, when, how, and at what cost. "Contracting," in the informal more than the formal and legal sense, is extremely important at the beginning and throughout the life of a project. Here is a checklist of some critical areas on which to reach understanding. The intent here, consistent with maintaining relationships, is not to establish rigid, fine-print rules that can lead to "gotcha's," but to have some clearly articulated expectations on both sides.

Contracting Checklist

☐ Scope (divisions of the company included; job level or type of employee participants; scope of vendor services requested; and enrollment, assessment, and reporting media)

☐ Realistic time line and deadlines
☐ Roles (vendor as processing department or adviser; client as either active designer of every aspect of project or passive acceptor of all vendor turnkey processing design features)
☐ Responsibilities: vendor and client (survey design, language translations, participant enrollment aspects, communication design and delivery, report format design)
☐ Stakeholders identified and considered (including participants and raters)
☐ Resources required, accessed, and applied
☐ Costs
☐ Contingency planning
☐ Disposition, handling, and use of data during and after project
☐ Confidentiality agreements
  Contacts:
  ☐ Primary client contact for overall direction
  ☐ Secondary client contacts, to organize and coordinate selected client populations
  ☐ Primary vendor contact, responsible for production deliverables and client interaction
  ☐ Secondary vendor contact, for client interaction in absence of primary vendor contact
☐ Ownership of data and copyrights
☐ Billing and payment schedules
☐ Boundaries (including inappropriate requests or uses of data)

These defined expectations help each party plan, allocate resources, support, and implement so as to maximize both parties' satisfaction with the process. Approaching the task in the mentality of trusting partners with a common goal of a successful outcome gets the project off to an optimal start. MSF processes are dynamic and require a certain amount of flexibility. Contracts that attempt to define all aspects and don't allow for adjustments limit the project potential; they can have a negative impact on delivery times if changes need to go through formal recontracting before they can be delivered.

An obvious area of misunderstanding is that of project costs, but frustrations and project delays can occur just as often from lack of clear up-front agreement on such things as project scope, responsibilities, realistic time lines and deadlines, and a plan to accommodate scheduling issues that typically arise. Less obvious areas include confidentiality agreements, ownership of content, data or norms, use or disposition of data after the project, payment schedules, client and vendor contacts, and internal roles.

The principle of seeking first to understand and then to be understood (Covey, 1989) greatly enables the contracting process and enhances relationship building. The two perspectives—those of client and vendor—can have areas of overlap as well as areas of difference, each complementing the other and affording a rounded view for project design and implementation. These perspectives are best leveraged if both parties are open to listening and understanding the other's point of view at least as much as advocating their own.

Whether or not to have a formal contract depends on your company policy, personal style, and experience, and those of your vendor. The less you know of the vendor from references, referrals, or operating experience, the more valuable a formal contract is. The main components of a typical formal contract are confidentiality, ownership, and price.

Managing relationships does not mean schmoozing or engaging in manipulative behavior, but instead genuine interest in the other party's personnel, their perspective as process stakeholder with business needs and objectives, the other's capabilities and experience, and respect for the other as a person. When problems occur, each party needs to be supportive of timely, accurate problem solving instead of placing blame. Define a process to address issues as they come up, rather than letting them build and affect both parties' satisfaction.

Managing relationships begins early and continues both throughout and between projects. Most interactions are likely with the vendor's project manager (coordinator), who, along with the client representative, has a pivotal role in the success of the project. Simply knowing each other on a personal level—being aware of interests, work style, and family, for example—can be a foundation on which to build the frequent contacts necessary in MSF projects; it is also especially helpful to draw on such familiarity at stressful, high-activity project stages.

Checking in regularly maintains contact, keeps one another aware of project status from the other's viewpoint, and makes it easier to tackle problems together if they arise. (A vendor with systems for responsive, accurate status reporting orally, on paper, or by electronic media helps to enhance this relationship.) Building trust through regular positive interactions encourages candor and early alert should problems occur. Other things also enable relationship building, notably celebrating successes—don't overlook positives or hesitate to compliment and thank each other for them.

Just as there are enablers, there are also some identified *roadblocks* to maintaining relationships:

Unrealistic Expectations

Unrealistic expectations on the part of the client, fueled by lack of knowledge of or experience with sound MSF design and implementation, can lead to misunderstanding and friction. An example where this typically occurs is when a client predetermines an administration medium (say, electronic) for the project based on misguided assumptions about access and acceptance of the medium or its impact on price or speed.

Bait and Switch

Several things can interfere with building or maintaining a relationship, but few can be so damaging as a violation of trust by either party. Vendors may overstate their capabilities relating to various media or capacity, or bill for services they deem beyond the original project scope. For various reasons—including overenthusiastic or uninformed sales representatives or overly optimistic evaluation of capabilities or capacity—vendors may propose services they cannot deliver. The best prevention is clear contracting (enhanced by MSF project experience), thorough descriptions of the vendor's material and service deliverables, and careful checking of multiple vendor references.

Scope Creep

The client counterpart of bait and switch is "scope creep," where the client requirements expand during the project, with the unrealistic expectation that there is no impact on cost or deadlines.

Examples include increasing the number of raters per participant and changing media or distribution methods. All too frequently, clients also ignore or push back interim deadlines, while keeping the final deadline fixed. Both client and vendor should realize that it is in their best interest to be accurate and honest as to the realistic time it takes to deliver on a process component once its scheduled time has been changed.

Project Cancellation

Vendors occasionally also have to deal with the consequences of projects being delayed or even canceled. Assuming that they planned and dedicated resources to the project's requirements and time line, this results in lost revenue and a need to reassign resources from the project. In the event the project is delayed substantially, then the vendor is in the potential position of having resources idle during the delay, and possibly already allocated to another project during the new time line. Of course, a formal contract clause could protect the vendor, but the loss of goodwill from the client under these circumstances might discourage a vendor from exercising the clause.

MSF Project Management

Having clear agreements, a defined problem-resolution process, and a partnering mind-set constitute a foundation to deal with the typical situations that arise during the various stages of MSF projects. It helps to approach the project as a whole (and each of its stages) with a picture of what "success" would look like and an examination of who the "customer" is for each decision made. Also important is considering the implications of various decisions on other project aspects, on the total project, or on other systems of which MSF is a part. The answers may be unique to your situation, but being aware of and paying attention to the question keeps you focused on optimizing for a successful project. Being accessible so that issues can be addressed as they surface avoids time delays and potential compounding of problems caused by "default decisions" being made without full consideration of client circumstances.

Preimplementation Planning

The planning phase of the project offers an early opportunity to reap the benefits of a good vendor-client fit. Here is a place where the knowledge and experience of client and vendor greatly enable the success of the project. An experienced vendor can accurately predict time frames and potential roadblocks given the client's situation. This is especially helpful if the client is inexperienced. An experienced client can better evaluate vendor suggestions in light of knowledge of their situation and experience with implications of various decisions. There are many technical aspects of MSF that are transparent to even the most experienced client; vendor experience optimizes the likelihood that these aspects are implemented error-free.

The primary client contact serves as an intermediary between the vendor and internal clients. As such, the primary contact needs to manage expectations, agreements, and relationships internally as well as with the vendor. Secondary contacts should be identified early on and involved appropriately according to their roles, whether it be getting their input on project decisions, keeping them informed of all relevant project information, or enlisting their help in providing necessary information for the vendor. This phase is also a good time to begin securing other internal resource people who are required, scheduling their time for project stages, and informing them of relevant project information. Here you are essentially building at least a virtual project team.

Project success can be enhanced by such basic team-building aspects as setting clear goals, having clear roles and responsibilities, sharing expectations, aligning activities with goals, conducting periodic status and process checks, and outlining a process for addressing concerns (Dyer, 1995).

MSF processing using paper typically spans six to eight weeks; using electronic means typically takes three to five weeks. Whereas electronic processes have the potential of considerably shorter times, many client-driven factors can lengthen the times required. Clients should understand that promises of shorter time may not take user-driven and client-driven delays into consideration, that is, shorter time quotes may be only under ideal circumstances.

Clients should plan for changes in the process to accommodate situations within their company that they did not expect. Many clients overestimate the access, viability, and acceptance of technical (mainly Internet, intranet, e-mail, and interactive voice-response) media. Our experience is that even in technically savvy companies a significant number of employees are unable or disinclined to use the medium initially specified. This is the time to study the feasibility of the preferred technology for your company.

The main driver of media selection should be whether they enhance the administration and feedback experience. Participants and raters should be given enrollments and assessments in a medium that is efficient and easy for them to use. The feedback reporting should complement and enhance the development, action planning, and training processes instead of being their driver. Decisions to use a particular medium or multiple media should take into account realistically corporationwide access to and acceptance of the planned media (Bracken, Summers, and Fleenor, 1998). Finally, technical preferences should include mixed-media solutions for situations that cannot accommodate a totally technical solution.

Materials Design and Production

A successful design and production phase is marked by having accurate, aesthetically pleasing MSF materials available on schedule. This phase assumes the instrument content development has already taken place (see Chapter Six). Language translations are part of this phase and can pose unique challenges (see Chapter Twenty-Seven). An experienced vendor has qualified resources to draw on for translations as required. Once the content has been developed, it is a good idea to involve the vendor in form layout design. An experienced vendor can be very helpful with suggestions drawn from experience relevant to the medium chosen.

This phase presents an early opportunity for client contribution to maintaining the schedule required to meet project deadlines. It is crucial that the client be accessible to review and approve drafts, proofs, or screens; this keeps the project on schedule and prevents compressing time required for production of paper materials. Another enabler of this process is the client's ability and willingness to do thorough, detailed review of proofs or screens, asking questions and checking assumptions along the way.

Participant Enrollment

Enrollment here refers to the stage in an MSF project when employees who will be receiving feedback are identified and registered in the vendor's system. This is a critical stage for the success of the project, since for many participants it represents their first actual contact with the MSF process. A successful enrollment results in all eligible and willing participants being correctly listed in the vendor's database only once and with accurate identifying information and activity level (at least the number of survey forms needed for their feedback process). Enrollment can also be expanded to include *approved raters* for each participant. Enrollment can be initiated by the company, by the individuals, or by a combination of the two. The company coordinators can prepare a list of participants from their data system and forward it to the vendor, individuals can register themselves by paper or electronic means, or the company can identify eligible individuals who then complete the registration process themselves.

Typical issues that arise during enrollment design and implementation frequently depend on the number and types of rating sources (as described in Chapter Seven), distribution (to participant or rater), approval of rater nomination, and the processing technology used. A vendor having knowledge and experience with several methods can be valuable in helping the client evaluate the various options and their implications. As indicated earlier, the client contact or internal consultant's being experienced also enables sound decisions for the circumstances. A vendor's proven track record optimizes the smooth flow and accuracy of this part of the process. One pitfall at this stage is in proceeding with a technology that the company is not fully capable of supporting, forcing compromises that affect the quality of the outcome. Another pitfall is vendor inexperience, particularly for large-scale enrollments, in accommodating changes to an enrollment process in progress and in the overall impact of such changes.

Forms Distribution

This stage of an MSF project concerns getting the forms, whether paper or electronic, into the possession of the correct feedback providers. In paper processes, this can be accomplished by the participants or directly by the vendor. In electronic processes, this is usually accomplished by the vendor's software application, which should not preclude hands-on monitoring, manual changes, or system adjustments by the vendor.

Among the typical issues arising during forms distribution are shipping method and schedule, particularly for international projects. Multilingual projects can place additional demands on the vendor's capability through needing to deliver multiple translations to individual participants (if, for example, a manager has direct reports in several countries). For electronic processes, access to the client company database enables efficient form distribution. Effective communication in the client company prepares participants for receiving forms and providing feedback and thus minimizes the demand placed on the client and the vendor by calls from uninformed participants.

Data Capture

This is another critical stage of the process; the vendor needs to capture all the feedback—quantitative ratings and qualitative comments—for each participant and correctly assign the feedback to the participant. All data received must be positively identified and tracked. Whereas large report groups (a common situation with employee opinion survey projects) can tolerate some instances of error without major impact on overall results, in MSF the numbers for each individual recipient are usually small enough that error can have great impact. Accuracy of feedback, beginning with data capture, is essential (Bracken, Timmreck, Fleenor, and Summers, forthcoming).

Some enablers for this stage of the processing are vendor competence and proven track record, evidenced by such things as tracking systems, documented quality assurance, and scheduled backups; for electronic processes the list goes on to include response audit trails, point-in-time restores, and security measures for rater anonymity. If the vendor does not have such experience, many things may be omitted from the process that would have ensured integrity of the data, given the variety of ways that respondents can interfere with the process (Lepsinger and Lucia, 1997). Paper forms that are not precoded to a participant can result in lost or misreported data. Data can be captured inaccurately or lost altogether if there are no checks and balances in coding. Electronic procedures, especially intranet and Internet applications, are particularly vulnerable to losing data if proper procedures are not in place. The vendor must also be able to meet the peak capacity needs of a project, whether it is paper-based or electronic. A test phase to ensure the system is working as intended is a very useful step. (See the Appendix for further guidelines on ensuring accuracy of MSF data.)

Data Processing

Next in the process comes running the analyses that result in summary statistics of the feedback data. Successful data processing results in having the data analyzed accurately and correct summary statistics generated; this can be simple or difficult to achieve depending on the competence of the vendor. This phase implies a cutoff time for including data in analyses and reports. A typical policy is to have a cutoff that is one week after the published deadline. Rules for extending the cutoff (for individuals or the project) should be defined up front as to what accommodations are acceptable. Calculating internal norms (averages of a comparison group, usually the whole organization or divisions) for batch processes requires a cutoff date beyond which no data can be accepted. Planning for deadlines and cutoffs within the standard communicated procedures should minimize questions from individual participants. Planning ahead by coding the data for any custom analyses that are not included in the vendor's standard package avoids delays in generating these reports later.

Obstacles to accurate data processing include program bugs and inexperience of programmers, which are minimized with an experienced, competent vendor. Historical comparison—capturing and comparing current feedback with one or more cycles of feedback for each recipient—can pose a unique programming challenge.

Historical comparison requires finding not only each individual's data in several places but also each repeating survey item in different places, if the survey instrument was modified from one administration to the next. Historical data must also accurately represent what was reported the previous time, excluding, for example, any data captured after reports were generated. Start-up processing vendors typically have not faced this challenge with new projects; they may be learning on yours.

Processing of written comments can pose challenges unique to the technology used. In paper processes, comment transcription, review, possible language translation, and category sorting can create a time-consuming, labor-intensive process, but one that is nevertheless enhanced by human handling. In electronic processes, the comments from online respondents are often merely captured into a database without human review or screening (for reasons of legal issues, deleting expletives, or eliminating references to individuals by name); this practice saves time and money, but arguably at the expense of quality control.

Reporting

MSF reporting (see Chapter Twelve) is the next stage of the project. Successful reporting results in summary statistics and comments being reported accurately according to predetermined decision rules, and then being labeled and delivered to the correct participant. Technology can again be an enabler (by creating online reporting capability, for instance) or it can be a limiting driver, if certain minimum standards are not attainable because of the design of the technology. A typical issue that occurs at this stage is the vendor's (and by implication, technology's) role in writing decision rules, which interacts with the level of knowledge and experience of both vendor and client. By *decision rules*, we mean such things as the minimum number of responses required to display an item's results, whether and how to combine data sources if minimum requirements are not met, or whether to rerun reports that include late returns. These decisions have an impact on the anonymity we consider vital to the success of an MSF process.

Conflicts can arise if decisions reflect a priority for one type of customer (the recipient, for example, who might want to see all data points or to have later returns included in a second report; or the raters, who want their anonymity protected). Other issues that occur at the reporting stage are the choice of medium—paper or electronic—for reporting, the delivery process, and identification of the report recipients, all of which can have some bearing on confidentiality of the feedback. The ability to customize reports to support development, training, and coaching processes is a desirable feature from the client's perspective, as opposed to predefined feedback report styles that require the client to modify their process. Here is another place where technology can be either an enabler or a restrictive driver of the process.

Planning ahead for this stage can greatly enhance the outcome. The client should expect and allow time for working with the vendor in defining decision rules and testing the reporting process on dummy or real data before the report deadline. In paper reporting, the vendor should be able to anticipate the demand for printing, binding, packaging, and shipping, and allocate the resources required to deliver reports promptly.

As in other stages of the MSF process, pitfalls of the reporting stage can be the vendor's lack of competence or experience, or the client's underestimating the time or resources required to manage this stage. Vendors should be expected to refer decisions on questionable or inappropriate requests to the knowledgeable client contact. (Inappropriate requests would include rerunning reports if so doing would inadvertently compromise anonymity.) Here is another place where a partnering relationship is helpful; vendor and client have a mutual interest in a successful, trustworthy, ethical outcome and support each other in the face of occasional pressure to compromise professional standards.

Follow-Up

From the perspective of working with a vendor, another opportunity occurs for the client when a vendor has the capability to link MSF to other HR systems. (Organizational integration of MSF is discussed in Chapters Four and Twenty-Six.) Another important aspect is postproject evaluation, some of which can be accomplished both by the vendor's capability to run participation or activity reports and by a face-to-face project debrief between vendor and client. Debriefing is an important aspect of the project, not only from a technical standpoint but also from that of the partnering relationship. Debriefing identifies areas of opportunity to improve on what should be a dynamic process, and it also helps both the vendor and the client improve the process in other projects.

Enabling Characteristics of Vendors and Clients

The topic of vendor selection is beyond the scope of this chapter, but we can nevertheless describe some technical, organizational, and personal characteristics of vendors and clients that align with the philosophy and practice we have described.

Vendors

Vendors should have *technical* experience with MSF and have well-documented procedures and systems for responsiveness, quality, tracking, status reporting, language translations, late enrollments, late survey submissions, and report generation (including tracking historical data). They should have a strong information technology and information systems (IT/IS) capability. Multisource processing should be a core business. For electronic processes, vendors should have systems in place that can accommodate other media, at least in small groups or as individual exceptions for the various enrollment, assessment, and reporting components. (Some of our recent experiences raise the question of when a vendor has sufficient "expertise" to advise on content versus technology; we have found some vendors who are starting to act like consultants, without sufficient background.) Vigilance for security of data and client information is essential. Highly desirable is the ability to conduct follow-up analyses or research on the database, either internally or through competent subcontractors.

Desirable organizational characteristics for vendors are organizational stability and resourcing capability to adapt to changing markets and the ups and downs of a multisource project. Particularly in the face of a growing market for MSF, vendors often face the challenges of a fast-growing business and have to frequently re-

cruit, hire, train, and assimilate staff to support the projects that
have been contracted. Even highly competent, experienced vendors can easily experience quality-control problems during such a
state. The existence of structured training and quality programs
within the vendor's company minimizes these concerns. Start-up
companies that are still in the process of designing processes and
building software applications to support them have an even
greater challenge to maintain the quality, speed, and accuracy that
is essential to MSF projects.

To support the client-vendor relationship that is so important
to the success of a project, the vendor's primary contact person
should be customer-focused, accessible, flexible, willing, and able
to engage in meaningful communication. Trustworthiness, demonstrated over time, is essential.

Client

Client contacts ideally come to the project with multisource knowledge and experience, or at least a sound grasp of relevant principles and issues that improve their ability to be active, informed
partners in the project.

Clients should have credibility in their own organizations, with
authority to make project decisions that enhance the speed and
ease with which the project can proceed. The client contact is an
intermediary between the vendor and the organization; effectively
managing relationships on both sides is essential to the smooth
progress of the project.

Ideal clients are those who can clearly articulate expectations
that are reasonable in light of their own company's capabilities and
resources, who are open to suggestions, who honor deadlines, and
who are sufficiently detail-oriented to afford the level of review required for approvals yet not lose sight of the larger picture and system implications of various decisions. Should something go wrong,
the ideal client first focuses on the problem and its solution to
move the project along with minimum interruption rather than
spending time placing blame. A comprehensive review of causes
of a problem is essential to developing preventive measures for future administrations.

Summary

MSF processing presents many unique challenges that draw on the resourcefulness of the client and the vendor. In this chapter, we have explored some of those challenges and suggested a framework for addressing them that is highly dependent on clear understanding of requirements, capabilities, and implications, along with a partnering approach to the client-vendor relationship and the competence and experience of the partners.

References

Bracken, D. W., Summers, L., and Fleenor, J. W. "High-Tech 360." *Training and Development*, 1998, *52*(8), 42–45.

Bracken, D. W., Timmreck, C. W., Fleenor, J. W., and Summers, L. "360-Degree Feedback from Another Angle." *Human Resource Management*, forthcoming.

Covey, S. R. *The Seven Habits of Highly Effective People*. New York: Simon & Schuster, 1989.

Dyer, W. G. *Team Building and Alternatives*. (3rd ed.) Reading, Mass.: Addison-Wesley, 1995.

Lepsinger, R., and Lucia, A. D. *The Art and Science of 360-Degree Feedback*. San Francisco: Pfeiffer, 1997.

CHAPTER 11

Web Technologies for Administering Multisource Feedback Programs

Lynn Summers

Since the good old days when multisource feedback (MSF) was necessarily paperbound, successive waves of technology have streamlined the administration of this inherently complex process. As personal computers became commonplace in offices, methods were developed for administering MSF by distributing and collecting diskettes. Then, as the Internet ascended, new methods were developed that involved sending raters electronic questionnaires embedded in e-mails and having them return the completed forms electronically. As of this writing, in typical Internet-facilitated MSF, e-mails are used to coordinate the program as participants perform key tasks (such as completing an evaluation questionnaire) at a secure Website.

There are two issues that significantly infuse and enliven discussions of Internet-facilitated MSF. The first has to do with whether the process should be "run" on the Internet at a Website hosted by an external service provider or whether the organization runs the process itself on its own intranet. In this chapter, the emphasis is on Internet-based MSF. This approach follows the "outsource" model, which has become increasingly prevalent. Industry analysts

I extend my appreciation to Dave Woolf, Michael Plant, Leah Groehler, and Elizabeth O'Keefe for thoughtful input during the preparation of this chapter.

anticipate that most HR departments will soon be using solutions that are housed almost entirely on the Web, representing a significant shift away from the notion that for an application to have value the organization must "own it" (Lehman, 1999; K. Moser, personal communication, Dec. 1999).

The second issue concerns the purpose, or intent, of an MSF program (the subject of Chapter Twenty-Three). To effectively implement a program that serves administrative purposes requires that the technology support substantially different features than for a development-only program. Specifically, many (if not all) employees must be evaluated on a regular schedule, supervisors must oversee the rater selection process, multiple parties access individual results, aggregated results may be mined to identify specific individuals with particular strengths or development needs, and managers use results to aid in compensation decisions. Because administrative MSF programs are inherently more complex, this chapter focuses on how Web technology can support such programs.

Example of an Online Process

An Internet-based MSF process might run something like this.

Participants access the service provider's Website, key in their password, and build the list of raters who will be asked to provide feedback to them. Then the designated raters access the Website, enter their assigned passwords, and complete questionnaires for the participants they've been invited to rate. When the assessment period ends, feedback reports are provided electronically to participants and their managers. The client organization can access electronic reports of the aggregated data.

This thumbnail description represents one of several variations on the Web-based MSF theme. This variety in implementation approaches is due to the fact that a number of service providers have worked somewhat independently of each other since the mid-1990s to build their systems. Some vendors developed their online services within the development-only tradition, while others designed their systems to accommodate clients' administrative needs. Furthermore, some providers have a fixed approach; others offer a wide variety of ways to administer the process, and still others custom-build applications to fit each client's requirements.

How Web Technology Can Facilitate the MSF Process

Here are some of the ways Web technology is being used to facilitate each of the steps in an MSF process.

Rater Selection

In a fully automated Web-based process, participants log on at the Website and build their rater lists online. In the simplest variation, they enter raters' names and e-mail addresses and indicate to which rater group each person belongs. In more sophisticated applications, participants can select their raters from a list of employees. (This list is derived from the client's human resources information system, or HRIS, and includes, in the background, all employees' e-mail addresses.) The advantages of this approach are that it is easier for participants ("Just click on the name you want added to your rater list") and it dramatically reduces the incidence of incorrect e-mail addresses (because the addresses are already in the system).

The rater list can be partially constructed before participants log on by preloading the participant's own name as well as the names of the supervisor, subordinates, and peers. (Preloading requires that reporting relationships be included in the HRIS data.) If a client's policy requires participants to be rated by their supervisor and all their direct reports, this policy may be enforced by preloading these individuals' names on their rater lists and not allowing participants to remove them.

Popular employees can be overwhelmed with requests to be a rater, leading to rater overload. Technology offers a practical way to limit the rating requirements imposed on any one employee. When participants are building their rater lists, if they select an employee who is already "booked up" to the preset limit, a message pops up informing them that their intended rater is not available and another rater should be chosen.

When MSF is used for administrative purposes, a separate review stage can be inserted immediately following the nomination stage so that supervisors can check their subordinates' lists for balance, deleting and adding raters as appropriate (of course, such a stage might be appropriate for developmental uses of MSF as well).

Throughout the nomination and review stages, the administrator who is responsible for the MSF program on the client side can keep tabs on progress. Real-time status reports at the Website can alert the administrator to potential problems (for example, which participants have nominated too few raters, or have not built their rater lists at all).

Data Collection

When raters log on to complete evaluations, they see a list of the participants they've been asked to rate. Clicking on one of the names opens the blank instrument appropriate to that ratee (management, sales, professional, etc.).

Online systems can be designed to take advantage of real-time interaction with the rater to enhance rating quality. The system can be programmed to detect certain undesirable rating tendencies and to interact with the rater when these tendencies are detected. For example, a "straight-ticket" notice can be invoked onscreen if a rater enters the same rating for most of the items on an instrument. This notice would suggest that the rater revisit the ratings, revising them to add realistic variability and to help identify the ratee's strengths and development needs.

Different approaches to designing the graphical user interface can make it easier (or more difficult) for raters to make their input. The best designs enable raters to complete their work quickly while also encouraging thoughtful and accurate feedback. It should be easy, for example, for raters to find their way around a Website to complete both numeric ratings and written comments for multiple participants without getting lost.

Conventional wisdom regarding Web questionnaire design favors radio buttons (little circles for each response option). The rater uses a mouse to click on the appropriate button to complete each rating. Although radio buttons are aesthetically pleasing, they require extensive "real estate" on screen and can be tedious to use, especially if the rater is using a laptop without a standard mouse. Typing a rating value in a box for each item may be less glamorous but more efficient and user-friendly. Mainly, however, this is a matter of taste and vendors will probably offer client organizations a choice between these two styles of completing ratings.

Participation can be boosted by sending reminder e-mails. These reminders are programmed to be sent automatically only to those raters who haven't completed their ratings. Reminders typically create a spike in online rater activity and result in higher participation rates (Summers and Groehler, 2000).

In addition to generating status reports to the administrator during this stage, it is also useful to give *ratees* real-time status information about their raters' progress. These reports tell them how many of their raters have completed their feedback, but they do not reveal names (in the interest of maintaining rater anonymity). Ratees who see that few of their raters have completed their ratings as the evaluation period is winding down are advised to contact all of their raters to encourage participation.

Rater Training

Thanks to its cost-effectiveness and the lessened administrative burden, outsourced Web-based MSF enables organizations to apply the technique to a much larger group of employees. In fact, some organizations that have adopted MSF as an input to periodic compensation decisions use the technique to evaluate *most* employees annually or even more frequently. However, a challenge created by this broader reach is that many employees who have never been asked to evaluate anyone in their lives are now asked to evaluate their supervisors and coworkers.

A tremendous opportunity exists to use Web technology to provide online rater training. Existing rater training programs can be adapted to the Web environment to permit individualized interactive training. Raters can be required to complete the online training successfully before being given access to their ratees' evaluation forms. In addition, measures of training performance can be correlated with actual rating quality after training.

London (see Chapter Twenty-Three) suggests providing raters feedback on their ratings as a means of eliminating rater distortion. We have experimented with this notion as it applies to supervisory ratings and have found that it produces largely positive outcomes (Summers, 1999). Web technology makes it relatively easy to give raters information comparing their own ratings with the aggregated ratings others have made of the same ratees. There are, however, some logistical issues associated with this idea (an additional period of time must be inserted for raters to receive and act on their feedback), and of course precautions must be taken to ensure rater anonymity and feedback confidentiality according to agreed-on policies.

Data Processing

Speed of delivering results is one of the hallmarks of Internet-based MSF. Because raters themselves do the data entry, preparing reports is a matter of the vendor processing the data.

Most vendors offer features for post-rating enhancement of data quality; however, these features are not unique to Web-based systems. One such feature involves identifying and eliminating individual outlier ratings. There is an interesting opportunity here for an Internet MSF system to notify raters who contribute an excessive number of outlier ratings and provide them feedback on the quality of their ratings. (This represents a special case of rater training, as discussed above.)

Most MSF implementations involve the supervisor as just another provider of input whose ratings may be compared and contrasted (mostly contrasted, it seems) with input from other rater groups. An innovative approach to MSF puts the supervisor in the role of feedback integrator in addition to being a source of feedback (Summers, 1999). In this approach, after all the input has been collected, preliminary results are prepared and supervisors review these results online for each of their subordinates. They can then edit their own input based on all the collected information. This has the potentially beneficial effects of decreasing supervisor rating bias, enhancing the supervisor's understanding of subordinate performance, and increasing the supervisor's involvement in and commitment to the MSF process.

Feedback Reporting

Individual feedback reports can be delivered online, sent as electronic documents, or printed and distributed in the conventional manner. In development-only programs, it is customary to print the reports and distribute them to ratees through their coaches or at workshops especially designed to facilitate feedback acceptance and assist participants with development planning. Even when

MSF is used for administrative purposes, it is still common practice to print and distribute the reports.

There is increasing use, however, of online delivery of reports, though almost always as a supplement to the conventional paper report. Preference for paper reports is probably due to both supervisors' and ratees' comfort in having a paper report to flip through, point at, make notes on, take home, and—to satisfy bureaucratic requirements—affix a signature to. As the technology becomes more sophisticated and organizations press harder toward the paper-free office, it is likely that all of these things can be more conveniently done online and that people will become more comfortable using electronic reports.

The potential advantages of electronic reports are numerous. The online report can be designed to enable the ratee to sort the results in any number of ways. An additional substantial advantage of the online report is that supervisors may easily access the evaluation history of any of their direct reports.

Using the Results

There is a tremendous opportunity for Web technology to add value by bridging the gap between feedback and development planning. Organizations are looking for ways to automate those aspects of the coaching process that can be streamlined. This quest stems from the need to enable employees to take responsibility for their own development (reducing reliance on supervisor involvement, which historically has been scant) and to spread the individual development capability to as many employees as possible (recognizing that a live coach can't be there for everyone).

An online development planning system can offer developmental suggestions keyed to certain competencies or development need themes (time management, visionary leadership, being less abrasive, and so on). Employees can continually interact with the online system to track their own developmental progress and to link to a host of learning resources relevant to their specific development needs. They can access training program schedules and electronic resources available within their companies, and training modules available on the Web through specialized content providers.

Individual development is an expected outcome of MSF whether the program's purpose is development-only or administrative. In administrative applications, however, it is universally expected that supervisors will "sit down" with their direct reports and discuss the results. Decades of experience tell us that what is universally expected at best happens only occasionally (Meyer, 1991). Internet technology can be used to "audit" the feedback discussion (Summers and Rye, 1999). In an audit, the service provider polls employees by e-mail to determine who has and has not had a discussion and then gives the organization a complete accounting of the responses. Because supervisors are aware that the audit will be conducted, the audit itself tends to stimulate an increase in discussion activity.

Reports of the aggregated results can be accessed shortly after the evaluation period ends. Such reports can show, for example, the item-by-item distribution of ratings for the entire employee population, comparisons of subgroups to the total population, and estimates of supervisory rating leniency or severity. The value of such reports for identifying training needs is clear. What is noteworthy about this organization-level reporting capability is not that technology makes it possible (such reports can be created from paper-based MSF). Rather, technology delivers the reports in almost real time, enables the reports to encompass a large percentage of the employee population, and makes it possible to take the readings frequently.

When MSF is used for administrative purposes, one of these purposes is usually to determine the amount of an employee's annual merit increase. An online tool can assist managers in making and communicating these compensation decisions. They can refer to their subordinates' MSF results, enter overall ratings into the compensation decision tool, view policy-based merit increase ranges, select specific percentage increases, view the budgetary effects of their decisions, and then communicate their decisions to HR—all online.

Administering the Process

When MSF is used for administrative purposes, typically the entire employee population is evaluated at the same time. The most practical way to handle such large-scale MSF programs and to ensure on-time completion is to establish a time line that specifies when each stage is to begin and end. Thus everyone involved is entrained to a common schedule. For example, the period for all ratees to build their rater lists might run for seven days, to be followed immediately by another period of seven days' duration for allowing supervisors to review their direct reports' rater lists for balance, and so on.

Web-based MSF programs can also be ratee-controlled: the participant decides when to initiate the process and when enough feedback has been collected to close it. This approach is sometimes used in development-only programs. However, ratee-controlled MSF can become unwieldy (imagine thousands of employees each initiating their own MSF on completely independent schedules). By imposing some structure (say, inviting ratees to sign up to participate in one of a series of monthly cycles for which time lines have been established), the potential unruliness can be tamed.

In most vendors' applications, e-mails are used to coordinate the complex administration process. During each period of online administration, e-mails impart information to and trigger action by the key players (ratees, supervisors, and raters). E-mails are programmed and sent at the beginning of each period: to ratees when building their rater lists, to supervisors when reviewing rater lists, and to raters when completing evaluations.

Other chapters in this handbook take care to point out the importance of conveying to participants how the MSF process works. Such information includes the purpose of the MSF, how the results are used, the policies regarding anonymity of rater input and confidentiality of ratees' results, etc. Vendors have their own approaches as to how this information is conveyed. Some attempt to put the bulk of the client-specific information into e-mails (making for ponderously long e-mail messages), others try to place most of this information on the Website, and still other vendors leave communication of this critical information to the client to convey offline. Posting at the Website seems to be the most effective approach; the information is always available at the click of a mouse when the user is online and a question arises.

What About Security?

There are at least three main security issues surrounding Web-based MSF:

1. Making sure feedback is provided by the designated people
2. Protecting the data during transmission over the Internet
3. Safeguarding the results once they are in the vendor's hands

The first concern—making sure the feedback is provided by the designated people—is a matter of controlling access. Virtually all professionally developed Web-based MSF processes are designed on the principle of controlled access. After participants' roles are defined, they are assigned unique user IDs and passwords. When they log on, the system recognizes them and permits them to do only those things specified by the role (if the user's role is as a rater of Joe Smith and Betty Jones, then the user can complete only one evaluation of each ratee). In some systems, raters can return to an evaluation they've already completed and revise it within the designated time period, but they cannot complete a *second* evaluation of the same ratee.

Considerable care needs to be taken in designing systems so that the controlled-access requirement cannot be circumvented. In one system, ratees listed their raters and the raters' e-mail addresses, and then the e-mail invitations were sent to the raters directly from the ratees' computer. If the e-mails did not go through, they were returned to the ratee, exposing the assigned IDs and passwords. Unscrupulous ratees could easily log on using these codes and provide glowing feedback to themselves.

The second security concern—transmission of sensitive information over the Internet—is addressed by using industry-standard encryption and security technologies. The same methods used in safeguarding online credit card or banking transactions and trading of securities can be employed to protect MSF data. Even without encryption, what gets transmitted is usually a string of numbers—the ratings—divorced from any context (that is, the items, ratee, or company to which the ratings apply). Contrast this to completing an e-mail questionnaire in which your responses are transmitted as part of an intact document in a message that is clearly from you.

The third concern—safeguarding the results—is usually addressed by establishing industry-standard firewall protection on the vendor's side and by allowing access to online feedback reports only to authorized users. Raters who have been assured anonymity might worry that someone will be able to dig into the raw data and discover what they said about the people they rated. Granted, there seems to be a tiny (but vocal) minority of employees who believe their company's executives are actively trying to uncover this kind of information, and no amount of assurances will allay their suspicions. For most, however, clear explanations of the anonymity policy and of where the raw data reside are sufficient to gain their confidence. Incidentally, the security issue of where the data reside is one of the main reasons it is preferable to use a third party, Web-based system for conducting MSF, as opposed to the company hosting its own intranet MSF process and storing the raw data in house.

One other issue related to safeguarding the results has to do with who has access to the processed results (the individual feedback reports). Electronic access to online reports must be limited to authorized individuals. For development-only MSF, ratees and their coaches are usually the only persons given authorized access. For administrative MSF, there is usually a wider circle of individuals with access (HR staff and the chain of command above the ratees). After the client administrator prints hard copies of reports, however, the responsibility for safeguarding results rests with the client.

Often not mentioned in discussions of security is the role the user plays in maintaining it. Consider these examples. Employees typically complete ratings from their offices (more often, from their cubicles). As others walk by, it isn't difficult to notice that an evaluation form is on the cube dweller's monitor. Some vendors, anticipating that the evaluations are done in semipublic places, do not put ratees' names on the questionnaire screen. Another example involving a particular case: employees who had requested paper surveys (they didn't trust the security of the Internet) left their completed forms on the counter in the mailroom. Thus, no matter what medium is used to collect and store the feedback data, careless behavior constitutes the most likely cause of a security breach.

Organizational Readiness for Web-Enabled MSF

There are at least three dimensions along which an organization's readiness to adopt a Web-based MSF process can be assessed: technical, administrative, and cultural (see also Bracken, Summers, and Fleenor, 1998). Here are checklists highlighting some of the key concerns within the three dimensions.

Technical Readiness

Does the organization have the technical infrastructure required to fully support an Internet MSF?

☐ All participants have Internet access. (Most vendors have procedures to accommodate people who are not connected, but this can dramatically diminish the speed and efficiency of administration.)
☐ Participants use standard Web browsers (Netscape, Internet Explorer) with settings compatible with the vendor's system (usually a very simple matter to check and, if necessary, correct).
☐ All participants have e-mail addresses.
☐ The company's Internet connection has sufficient bandwidth.

Administrative Readiness

Does the organization have the administrative resources necessary to support Web-based MSF?

☐ The organization can readily create an electronic file containing accurate employee information.
☐ There is a capable administrator within the organization who can coordinate the MSF program with the vendor.
☐ A process is in place within the organization to ensure that feedback is effectively distributed (*if* paper reports are required) and used.

Cultural Readiness

Are the contextual factors existing within the organization congruent with conducting Web-facilitated MSF?

☐ Employees are familiar with and comfortable using technology.
☐ The company supports employees' use of the Internet as part of their work.
☐ The organization embraces (or at least has begun to embrace) the outsourcing model for important HR functions.
☐ Employees are prepared for MSF per se. (See Chapter Three and Bracken, Summers, and Fleenor, 1998, for complete coverage of this element of readiness.)

Other Considerations on Readiness

When an organization introduces Web-based MSF, it is usually into an environment in which occasional development-only MSF programs have been conducted with limited segments of the employee population, usually senior management and selected professional groups. Because of the administrative ease of conducting vendor-facilitated, Web-based MSF, the process quickly spreads to the majority of employees and is eventually conducted for administrative purposes.

Important cultural considerations, therefore, are the preparedness of employee groups who have not previously been involved in MSF to participate both as raters and ratees, and their readiness to be evaluated based (at least in part) on MSF results. Technology can itself contribute to this preparation through on-line rater training.

Conclusions: Advantages of Web Technology

With technology as its enabler, MSF has clearly advanced far beyond its modest, paper-based beginnings as a stimulant for individual development. Internet technology creates a host of capabilities that simply are not possible with paper or other varieties of technology. Feedback can be collected and delivered quickly. The process can be conducted with a widely dispersed population. The technology can interact with users, thereby driving high participation rates and enhancing the quality of data.

Because of the ease with which it can be conducted, MSF can be applied not just to management but to all employees (assuming the company is "ready"). With the ability to roll up MSF data and produce organization-level reports, technology can permit unprecedented visibility of the strengths and weaknesses of employees, and of the organization. Especially if MSF is facilitated by a vendor, the administrative burden on the organization is vastly eased and minimal demands are placed on the company's IT resources.

Cautionary Notes

Lest we hurtle headfirst down the Web technology path, there are some precautions to be noted.

One issue is connectivity. The reality is that most companies do not yet provide every employee a PC, e-mail address, and Internet access. In some industries, total connectivity is not likely to happen anytime soon, although in many others total connectivity will soon be a reality. Consider the problems associated with conducting Internet-based MSF in companies where not everyone is connected. If the pool of raters is limited to people who are connected, feedback accuracy is adversely affected.

A second issue is the matter of how easy it is for users to actually take advantage of an online system. Some companies have limited bandwidths in their Internet connections, causing users to experience delays as they wait for Web pages to open. Sometimes older versions of a Web browser are not able to take advantage of all the features of a vendor's Website. These and other technological glitches can produce user aggravation. However, as the technology matures and companies continue to upgrade and standardize their internal systems, this type of problem diminishes.

A third issue relates to the need to rely on a vendor, an inescapable feature of outsourced, Internet-based MSF. There are good reasons to go this route: to ease the administrative burden, reduce up-front investment, not tie up internal IT resources, allow the process to be managed by specialists in doing just that, and ensure rater anonymity. But some companies prefer to run their own MSF, use extensive (and expensive) internal resources to build and run it, and keep the information derived through this process close to the vest.

A fourth issue has to do with the risk of becoming overly dependent on technology. For example, sophisticated automation introduced to minimize the likelihood of error in aircraft flight crews can have the effects of reducing communication among the crew and actually increasing the likelihood of error (Guzzo and Dickson, 1996). So too might technology-enhanced MSF lead users to rely on the technology as a substitute for those aspects of the MSF process that require human touch. Offline management support and face-to-face discussions are still required, no matter how sophisticated technology-facilitated MSF becomes.

Technology should be used as an enabler, as a way to take care of the grunt work of gathering and delivering high-quality feedback. If technology is properly used, people's energies may be diverted from the tasks ordinarily involved in administering an MSF program and directed instead at using the data collected to guide organizationally relevant behavior change.

The Future

Some predictions can be made as logical extensions of current trends. With increased connectivity, the need for more and more employees to have Internet access to do their jobs, the growing sophistication of vendors' MSF solutions, the increasing user-friendliness of these solutions, and people's increasing comfort with technology, we should see an increase in vendor-administered, Web-based MSF.

With the trend toward using MSF for administrative purposes, it is likely that technology will increasingly be employed to give organizations better ways to do *total performance management.* MSF, with its focus on competencies, is excellent at affording a measure of one side of the performance coin: the behavioral "how" of employee performance. To capture the other side—the specific results employees achieve, or the "what" of performance—a job-specific, goal-setting process is needed. Using Web technology as an integrated and efficient way to handle this total performance management package is likely to spark a great deal of interest.

We should also anticipate that technology will take the lead in deconstructing how we currently think about MSF and stimulating thought about new ways to achieve MSF's purposes. Consider a system that enables employees to get ongoing feedback from selected feedback givers, furnished via a Web-based performance management system that continuously interacts with them. Comments can be keyed to competencies, goals, projects, or specific questions posed by the employee. With appropriate anonymity measures built in, feedback could be given and received at any time. Rather than just-in-time feedback, we would have *all-the-time feedback.*

There are perhaps two ultimate questions for those of us involved in the MSF enterprise. How can the goals of MSF be advanced using technology? And how can we resist the temptation to use technology to take us where technology can go (rather than where sound professional judgment suggests we should go)?

References

Bracken, D. W., Summers, L., and Fleenor, J. W. "High-Tech 360." *Training and Development,* 1998, *52*(8), 42–45.

Guzzo, R. A., and Dickson, M. W. "Teams in Organizations: Recent Research on Performance and Effectiveness." *Annual Review of Psychology,* 1996, *47,* 307–338.

Lehman, J. *HR Midmarket Magic Quadrant for North America in 4Q99.* Stamford, Conn.: Gartner Group, 1999.

Meyer, H. H. "A Solution to the Performance Appraisal Feedback Enigma." *Academy of Management Executive,* 1991, *5*(1), 68–76.

Summers, L. "Online 360 Integration: A Novel Approach to Improving Supervisory Ratings." Performaworks Performance Management Library, [http://www.performaworks.com/pmlibraryf.html], 1999.

Summers, L., and Groehler, L. "High-Tech Adventures in Boosting Response Rates." Paper presented at the fifteenth annual conference of the Society for Industrial and Organizational Psychology, New Orleans, La., Apr. 2000.

Summers, L., and Rye, C. "Making the Elusive Appraisal Discussion Less Elusive." Performaworks Performance Management Library, [http://www.performaworks.com/pmlibraryf.html], 1999.

CHAPTER 12

Multisource Feedback Reports
Content, Formats, and Levels of Analysis

Anthony T. Dalessio
Nicholas L. Vasilopoulos

A multisource feedback (MSF) report acts like a mirror in that it reflects evaluations of the participant on a set of job-relevant behaviors and competencies assessed through a questionnaire. Like a recently cleaned mirror, an effective feedback report presents a reflection of the feedback data that is clear. This chapter outlines some of the practical issues involved in deciding on the content and format of an MSF report to present the clearest possible reflection of the data.

The information presented in this chapter is based primarily on a review of sample feedback reports used in organizations, and on insights from interviews with practitioners who have extensive experience developing MSF processes. The chapter discusses the relative value of various types of MSF report sections and presents examples of sections to be considered for inclusion in feedback reports.

Variations on a Theme: Feedback Report Sections and Construction

The purpose of the feedback report is to summarize the MSF questionnaire data in a format that focuses the participant on the key information for action planning (Bracken, 1996). The action planning should include not only identifying developmental needs but also identifying strengths that can be leveraged to further improve performance. An effective feedback report strikes a balance between the quantity and quality of the information presented. For example, a feedback report that overwhelms the participant with too much information quickly finds its way to the bottom of the in-basket. On the other hand, a feedback report that presents a simple overview of the survey results has little practical value. In many ways, the feedback report should act as a sieve that passes only the most relevant information.

Feedback reports can be considered as having six basic parts, with each containing several subsections. Depending on the purpose of the MSF and the organizational culture, only some of these parts may be appropriate to include in the report, but consideration should be given to all of them.

The first of these six parts should include sections that give the participant introductory information about the purpose of the MSF process, general information about competencies and respondents, and instruction on how to interpret the information in the report.

The second part should contain sections that include high-level data summaries that can be used to begin to identify key areas of strengths and developmental needs.

A third part includes a section with a detailed presentation of the MSF data, which can be used to identify specific behavioral items that are strengths and developmental needs. The participant can use parts two and three in combination first to quickly identify strengths and developmental needs at a high level, and then to target more specific behaviors through use of the detailed information.

A fourth part should contain sections presenting gap analysis data, showing where large differences exist between ratings and benchmarks, or among sources.

The fifth part includes verbatim comments, and the final part offers developmental suggestions based on the competencies assessed.

Part One: Introductory Information

The first section of part one of the basic feedback report is recommended for an overview of the organization's purpose for implementing the MSF process, a description of the information summarized in the report, and advice on how to interpret and use the report data. For example, this section may have a brief discussion of whether the feedback process is a purely developmental process or is to be used currently or in the future as input to performance appraisal. Participants can also be informed here about who receives a copy of their report, and guidelines on how to read it. The rating scale and anchors used on the questionnaire are also presented. This section can set the number of respondents required to present information for a given source, as well as relate how missing data and rounding are handled. The method for aggregating data within and across sources is also presented here, as well as suggested benchmark values for interpreting ratings. Finally, this section can also briefly summarize the type of information in each of the major sections of the report. See Exhibit 12.1 for an example of a report introduction and guidelines for reading the report.

The second section in part one can present brief definitions of the competencies on which the participant receives feedback. The third section in part one may include a table of the number of individuals who have been sent the multisource questionnaire, and the number responding to the questionnaire, broken down by source (direct reports, peers, customers, supervisor, and so on). See Exhibit 12.2 for an example.

This third type of section helps the participant understand at the beginning of the report whether any particular groups of respondents are overrepresented or underrepresented in the report. Also, this information helps participants understand the relative weight that respondent groups may have in determining overall averages. Finally, this information shows the number of raters on which the average ratings by source are based.

Part Two: High-Level Data Summary

High-level data summaries that begin the presentation of the actual feedback data are the focus of part two of the report, followed by a more detailed presentation of the data in part three. One of the first issues that must be considered when analyzing and presenting feedback data is how to aggregate the data from the MSF questionnaires. Addressing this issue requires choosing an index of central tendency for summarizing the data. By far the most common

Exhibit 12.1. Introduction and Guidelines for Reading the Feedback Report.

Introduction

The purpose of this report is to assist in your effort to continuously improve as a leader and manager. This report provides your ratings of your own performance and summarizes the ratings by your employees, peers, and immediate supervisor. It also includes suggestions for your development.

The 360° Feedback Questionnaire was custom designed for XYZ Corporation's ABC Division with a focus on the corporate goal of communicating and fostering organizational change. The behavioral statements in the questionnaire were based on input from employees at all levels.

Because the purpose of this report is to guide *your* growth and development as a leader and manager, *only you have received a copy.* The investment you make in self-development based on the information in this report will increase both your personal effectiveness and the overall effectiveness of our organization.

Guidelines for Reading Your Report

This report includes ratings by your respondents on the 360° Feedback Survey. All of the ratings are based on the 5-point scale used in the survey. As you recall, the questionnaire asked, "To what extent did the person you are rating demonstrate the following behaviors during the past six months?" The scale used in the 360° Feedback Questionnaire was:

5	To a very great extent
4	To a great extent
3	To a moderate extent
2	To a small extent
1	Not at all
N/A	Not applicable

Missing Data

With the exception of your self and manager ratings, at least three responses were required to calculate average behavioral statement ratings from any source (peers and direct reports). If you received fewer than three responses from a source, you will see an "X" in place of the average for that statement.

Rounding

Results are based upon all available data and have been rounded to one decimal place. As a result, the ratings for a single competency may not always equal the average score for the statements within that competency.

Source: Copyright © 2000, adapted from Assessment Alternatives, Inc., Florham Park, N.J., Sample Report.

Exhibit 12.2. Summary of the Number of Survey Respondents.

	Survey Respondents *Betsy Sample*	
Respondent Category	Number of Individuals from Whom You Requested Feedback	Number of Individuals Who Responded
Supervisor	1	1
Direct reports	6	4
External customers	5	5
Peers	8	5
Self	1	1

Source: Copyright © 2000, adapted from Applied Psychological Techniques, Darien, Conn., Sample Report.

index used is the *mean* (Dalessio, 1998; Timmreck and Bracken, 1995). Mean ratings for each source are often calculated for competencies and items. Overall mean ratings on competencies that include data from all sources (except self-ratings) are also commonly calculated.

Other indices of central tendency, such as the *mode* or *median,* are virtually never used, because they typically are not so easily understood. An argument can be made, however, that the median in particular is a better representation of the ratings because it is not as easily distorted by extreme ratings. The mode can also be a useful index to present; however, there are often not enough data, particularly within a source, to make the mode meaningful. Since the mean is easily understood, it is a sound choice as the measure of central tendency; still, consideration can also be given to the median.

A major decision to be made in aggregating MSF data is how to weight raters and rating sources when calculating overall average ratings on items. Two options exist. One approach is to weight all the individual raters equally when calculating an average rating for an item. The philosophy here is that the participant has individual dyadic professional relationships with many people, and the mean for the item should reflect the average feedback evaluation of all these relationships.

The other approach is to first calculate an average rating on the item for each source, and then average the mean ratings for the sources. This approach results in equally weighting the sources. So, for example, a single supervisor rating would have equal weight in determining the overall average rating compared to an average of several peer ratings. The philosophy here is that the supervisor and other sources with fewer numbers of participants need to be equally represented in the overall rating. The argument could be made that the supervisor does not need to be equally weighted in calculating the overall average, since the supervisor is presented as a separate source in the feedback report, and thus the participant has an opportunity to understand the supervisor's perspective. The supervisor also provides the candidate feedback in annual performance reviews.

Both the weighted and unweighted approaches are used in practice. Whichever approach is chosen, the participant needs to clearly understand how the data were combined, the philosophy behind combining the data, and how to interpret the data.

Based on the data aggregation method that is chosen, a reasonable initial set of data to present in a first section in part two of the report is the overall average ratings (excluding self-ratings) for the competencies. A suggestion for this section is to list the competencies for each participant from the highest-average-rated competency to the lowest-rated competency. This presentation may involve additional programming, as compared to listing the competencies in the same order for each participant. However, presenting average competency ratings from the highest rated to the lowest rated allows the participant to quickly identify competency-level strengths and developmental needs. These data can be presented numerically, or in a bar chart. If a bar chart is used, numbers representing the average ratings may need to be associated with each bar so that participants have a detailed understanding of their data. Comparison norm data can also be presented in this section for each competency.

The next section in part two can begin introducing specific information. For example, a section can be included at this point that lists the five to ten items on which the participant was rated highest, and the five to ten items on which the participant was rated lowest. The ratings used to identify these items should be based on the overall average rating for the item (excluding the self-rating). For comparison purposes, the participant's self-rating on each item or a comparison norm for each item can also be presented. See Exhibit 12.3 for one example of this section.

In addition, the competency or category for the item can also be listed next to each item in this section. This information can be helpful in determining whether the participant's behavioral

Exhibit 12.3. Ranking of the Five Highest-Rated and Five Lowest-Rated Items.

Behavioral Statement Ranking   Jan Sample

This section lists the five behavioral statements on which you were ranked highest and the five on which you were ranked lowest. Both lists are in descending order. The rankings are based upon combined averages across all rating sources except your self-rating. Your self-ratings for each item are shown separately. The purpose of the ranking is to assist you in determining specific opportunities for personal development.

Top Five Behaviors	*Self*	*Others*
Practiced teamwork by helping others meet their goals when possible.	4.0	4.7
Actively participated in team projects and goals to ensure success.	5.0	4.5
Was willing to change roles, directions, and work processes.	3.0	4.3
Willingly altered personal schedule when necessary.	3.0	4.2
Provided positive/constructive feedback to others for specific incidents at the time of occurrence.	4.0	4.2

Lowest Five Behaviors	*Self*	*Others*
Influenced customers to take action that will benefit them and the corporation.	3.0	2.7
Was well informed about the corporation's products, services, and programs.	3.0	2.8
Responded quickly to customer problems.	3.0	2.9
Listened actively to determine customer wants, needs, and expectations.	4.0	2.9
Effectively used diplomacy and/or negotiating skills to resolve contractor/customer problems.	4.0	2.9

Source: Copyright © 2000, adapted from Assessment Alternatives, Florham Park, N.J., Sample Report.

strengths and developmental needs are focused primarily in one or two competency categories or spread out across the competencies.

A third type of section that very often is included in part two is a comparison of the average competency ratings by source (London and Smither, 1995). This comparison can be presented in a table format, where the competencies are presented as rows and the sources as columns. The entries in this matrix are average competency ratings for each source. These data can be used by the participant to begin determining where sources agree, and where differences in ratings occur among the sources. The data are also helpful in determining where self-perceptions differ from ratings by other sources. One useful variation for highlighting differences in self-ratings is to shade or outline the average competency ratings for the sources that are one scale point above or below the self-rating. See Exhibit 12.4 for an example of this type of data presentation.

Line graphs are another effective format for displaying the data for each source. These displays can be used to quickly identify where sources disagree or agree, or show clearly where the sources perceive the same pattern of strengths and developmental needs but at different levels of effectiveness. Although line graphs give an effective visual picture, this presentation typically cannot provide the more detailed numerical information shown using a matrix of average ratings by source.

Whether presented as a matrix of ratings or as a line graph, this report section can be very useful for developmental action planning. For example, if all sources agree and the rating is low, this is an important area to consider for development. If all sources agree and the rating is high, this is a strength that should be considered to be built on. If some sources rate the participant high while others are low, this may be a competency that is displayed in some situations but not others. This pattern of ratings may indicate that the competency is a set of behaviors that the participant has in his or her repertoire but needs to develop further so that the behaviors are displayed consistently across situations. If all sources agree and rate the candidate low but the self-rating is high, the participant may consider this as an area for development. In considering this pattern of ratings, the participant should be aware that self-ratings tend on the average to be lenient (Harris and Schaubroeck, 1988); however, some raters do make accurate self-ratings (Atwater, 1998; see also Chapter Thirteen).

Exhibit 12.4. Average Competency Ratings by Source.

Average Competency Ratings   Jan Sample

This section lists your average ratings by source for each competency in the Survey. Each average rating is a roll-up of the ratings for all of the behavioral statements making up the competency.

Competency	Self	Direct Reports	Peers	Manager
Is customer-focused	3.5	3.5	3.0	3.8
Communication	4.0	3.4	3.4	3.0
Demonstrates adaptability and flexibility	3.6	4.1	4.2	4.0
Develops oneself and others	3.0	4.2	4.0	3.8
Functional expertise	4.5	3.5	3.9	3.5

1.0 or more *above* self-rating

1.0 or more *below* self-rating

Source: Copyright © 2000, adapted from Assessment Alternatives, Florham Park, N.J., and Compendium Corp., Bloomington, Minn., Sample Report.

Part Three: Detailed Presentation of MSF Data

This part of the report typically contains a section that displays detailed average item and competency ratings, for each source and overall (excluding the self-rating). This type of section is included in most MSF reports (London and Smither, 1995) and is usually presented in a table format with numerical average ratings for each source (and overall) on each competency and item. Relevant items are listed under each competency with average ratings by source (and overall) presented in columns to the right of the competency heading and items.

This section is particularly useful for identifying key behavioral items to target for development within competencies that are rated on the average as low. Similarly, this section can be used to target specific behaviors for leveraging that are aspects of competencies rated as strengths.

When calculating average item ratings for each source, a decision needs to be made regarding the minimum number of raters required to present the average rating in the feedback report. To protect rater anonymity, a minimum of three raters for the source is usually required to present the average (London and Smither, 1995; see also the Appendix of this handbook). If fewer raters are available, the cell for this source is left blank. If one or two raters from the source do rate the participant on this item, these data can still be included in the overall average rating for the item.

As shown in Exhibit 12.5, presentation of the data in this type of section is enhanced by adding various "flags" to item and average ratings. For example, if the MSF process is an ongoing program administered yearly, participants can be asked to identify the behavioral items that are the major focus of their developmental plans. These items can be noted with an asterisk. Also the behavioral items for which a particular source has provided an improved (or a lower) rating since the last survey administration can be flagged. The amount of change required to produce a flag should be determined—for example, a half-point change. Items showing improvement can be marked with an up arrow, and those showing a lower rating with a down arrow (as in Exhibit 12.5).

Flags of this type can be useful, for example, for tracking changes in specific behavioral ratings over a time period. However, adding these flags needs to be balanced with presenting too much information to the participant, such that the feedback page becomes too busy to the point where it is difficult for the participant to focus on the salient information.

Another variation for this type of section includes presenting not only average ratings but also frequency data at the item level. Figure 12.1 is an example of this type of presentation. The figure displays the number of responses for each source on each item, and the number of respondents choosing each point on the rating scale broken out by source. It also illustrates the use of bar graphs and associated mean ratings for each source.

Exhibit 12.5. Sample Comparison of Self, Direct Report, Peer, Manager, and Overall Ratings on Competencies and Items.

Competency and Behavioral Statement Ratings   Jan Sample

For each behavioral statement, review your self-ratings and compare them to the average ratings for other sources. The numbers represent the extent to which others in each source felt you demonstrated the behavior.
(1 = Not at all; 3 = To an average extent; 5 = To a very great extent)

	Self	Direct Reports	Peers	Manager	Overall
Is customer-focused	3.5	3.5	3.0	3.8↑	3.4
Solicited feedback from customers to determine their needs and satisfaction with services and products.	4.0	4.2↑	3.3	4.0↑	3.6↑
Responded quickly to customer problems.*	3.0	2.8	2.7	3.0↑	2.9
Displayed a dedicated focus on customers, internal and external.	4.0	3.8	3.0↓	4.0	3.5
Managed multiple customer expectations to ensure their satisfaction.*	3.0	3.2	2.9	4.0↑	3.2
Communication	4.0↑	3.4	3.4	3.0	3.4
Listened actively to determine customer wants, needs, and expectations.*	4.0↑	3.0↑	2.9	3.0	2.9
Kept others informed of activities and results (verbally or in writing).	4.0↑	3.4↑	4.0↑	4.0↑	3.7↑
Communicated technical or nontechnical information with customers in a clear and concise manner.	4.0	3.9	3.5	3.0↓	3.6
Effectively used diplomacy and/or negotiating skills to resolve contractor or customer problems.	4.0↑	2.9↓	2.9↓	2.0↓	2.9↓

↑ Improved since previous administration (your score increased by .50 or greater)

↓ Gotten worse since previous administration (your score decreased by .50 or greater)

* Areas you indicated you focused upon since receiving your last feedback report

Source: Copyright © 2000, adapted from Assessment Alternatives, Florham Park, N.J., and Questar, Minneapolis, Sample Report.

Figure 12.1. Sample Comparison of Self, Boss, Peers, Direct Reports, and Others Using Average Rating and Frequency Data.

Behaviors
16. Displays confidence in his or her abilities to get the job done
43. Finds opportunities for self-improvement
55. Will say "I was wrong" when a decision clearly backfires
79. Makes use of resources within the organization for areas in which he or she is weak

Source: Copyright © 2000, adapted from Compendium Corp., Bloomington, Minn., Sample Report.

Figure 12.1. Sample Comparison of Self, Boss, Peers, Direct Reports, and Others Using Average Rating and Frequency Data, Cont'd.

Chris Datason

Item Profile

	Valid N	Mean Graph w/Res. Rates					Group Mean	Company Mean
		1	2	3	4	5		
Boss	1	5.00					4.50	4.24
Peer	4	4.50					4.24	4.36
		0	0	0	2	2		
Direct report	6	4.67					4.37	4.48
		0	0	0	2	4		
Other	4	4.25					4.33	4.46
		0	0	1	1	2		
Boss	1	4.00					4.25	3.91
Peer	4	3.25					4.07	3.94
		0	1	2	0	1		
Direct report	5	4.20					4.07	4.03
		0	0	1	2	2		
Other	4	3.75					4.23	4.07
		0	0	1	3	0		
Boss	1	4.00					4.63	4.17
Peer	3	3.00					4.31	3.99
		0	2	0	0	1		
Direct report	5	4.40					4.18	3.96
		0	0	1	1	3		
Other	3	4.00					4.47	4.05
		0	0	1	1	1		
Boss	1	4.00					4.25	3.86
Peer	4	3.50					4.14	3.96
		0	0	2	2	0		
Direct report	5	4.20					4.20	4.02
		0	0	0	4	1		
Other	4	3.50					4.00	4.04
		0	0	2	2	0		

Another type of section for inclusion in part three of the report is strategic improvement analysis. This type can be included only if ratings of the criticality of the items for successful performance of the participant's job have been gathered in addition to the typical item ratings of the participant's skill level. These criticality or importance ratings can help the participant decide which behaviors are the most pertinent to focus on for development. A useful method for helping participants conduct a strategic improvement analysis is to plot the criticality and skill level ratings for the items on a grid, where the Y axis represents criticality and the X axis represents skill or effectiveness. Dividing the grid into quadrants allows the participant to begin identifying both opportunities for development (for example, highly critical items where low skill ratings were received) and strengths (highly critical items where high effectiveness ratings were achieved). See Figure 12.2 for an example of this type of presentation.

Figure 12.2. Sample Strategic Improvement Grid.

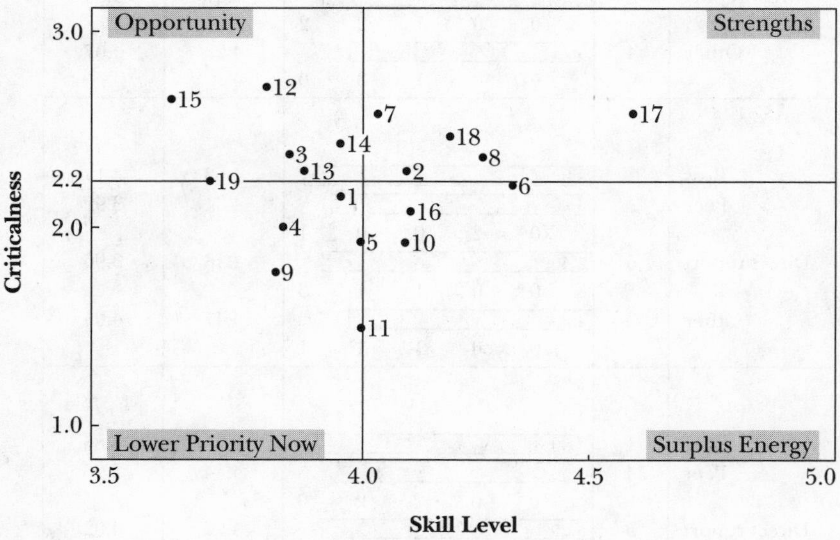

Source: Copyright © 2000, adapted from Compendium Corp., Bloomington, Minn., Sample Report.

Part Four: Gap Analysis

The fourth part of the feedback report can be for sections that present gap-analysis data. These sections present comparisons among various participant ratings in earlier sections of the feedback report. In addition, ratings may be compared to benchmarks. For example, they may display comparisons between overall average ratings (excluding the self-rating) and a predetermined target rating that the participant ideally may be expected to achieve, or alternatively a norm based on a relevant comparison group. The sections may also show where large differences in ratings occur between the self-rating and each source, or among all sources excluding self-ratings.

These sections typically present data at the competency level rather than the item level. An example of a gap-analysis presentation is shown in Figure 12.3, for a comparison between overall average ratings (excluding the self-rating) and predetermined target ratings assigned to the participant by the supervisor. Sections of this type can help further identify key differences in ratings among sources that may have been initially discovered in sections

Figure 12.3. Sample Gap Analysis Between Overall Ratings and a Target Rating on Competencies.

	0	1	2	3	4	5	
Customer focus							
Supervisor's Target							4.0
All Respondent's Rating							3.0
Accountability							
Supervisor's Target							5.0
All Respondent's Rating							3.9
Teamwork							
Supervisor's Target							3.0
All Respondent's Rating							3.1

Source: Copyright © 2000, adapted from Applied Psychological Techniques, Darien, Conn., Sample Report.

in part two, where comparisons in average competency ratings among sources were provided.

One caution about gap-analysis sections is that participants may ignore or gloss over them in practice, particularly if the section summarizes only gaps in data that have already been uncovered through perusal of previous parts of the report. This may be particularly true if the section is simply identifying gaps among sources, rather than presenting gaps between an overall rating and a standard that has not been presented previously. Practitioners need to consider what length of report is most effective for presenting data when deciding on whether to include this type of section.

Part Five: Presentation of Verbatim Comments

Verbatim comments typically are collected on the MSF questionnaire and presented in the feedback report (Timmreck and Bracken, 1995). They give the participant information that can be helpful in understanding the ratings, as well as additional information about behaviors not directly assessed through the MSF process. Verbatim comments usually appear as bulleted items in a section of the feedback report. Frequently some editing of verbatim comments is done: correcting spelling, removing identifying terms and names, as well as deleting expletive language. This editing is done so as not to change the meaning of the comments. A less often chosen option is to do no editing at all of the verbatims. One advantage of this approach is that the participant is presented with the evaluator's full content and meaning. However, if names are not removed, the evaluator's anonymity can be compromised.

Verbatim comments can be organized for presentation in a variety of ways. The most common approach is to group them for presentation into two categories: strengths and developmental needs. Two other approaches are to group comments by competency or rating source. Presenting verbatims by rating source gives the candidate additional information on similarities and differences that may exist among the sources, and it may be useful information to consider in conjunction with rating data from the various sources. Still, one major drawback of this approach is that the participant may be able to easily identify which raters provided which comments. The benefits of presenting comments by rating source may not outweigh these potential risks.

A final option is to use a summary of the themes reflected in the comments through a content analysis. The benefit of this approach is that it minimizes the risk to rater anonymity. The drawback is that the specific meaning of some of the comments may be altered.

Part Six: Developmental Suggestions

Suggestions for development are often presented to participants either as a final part of the feedback report or as a separate reference guide. The developmental suggestions can be very useful in designing action plans to enhance performance on competencies and behaviors identified as developmental needs.

Typically, developmental suggestions are organized by competency. For each competency, the definition should first be restated. Then, three possible types of developmental suggestions may be presented: on-the-job activities or behaviors that can be undertaken, references for reading, and training courses to improve on the competencies. An example of a page presenting developmental suggestions from a sample feedback report is shown in Exhibit 12.6.

Other Considerations for Presenting Feedback Report Data

Several additional issues should be considered when designing feedback reports.

Norms

Feedback reports often include sections comparing the scores obtained by the participant and those obtained by a relevant norm group. As previously discussed, norms can be presented in sections that appear in any of parts two, three, or four of the report. Norms can enhance interpretation of feedback data by constituting a useful benchmark for interpreting ratings (Yukl and Lepsinger, 1995; see also the Appendix in this handbook).

Exhibit 12.6. Example of Developmental Suggestions for a Competency.

Suggestions for Development

You now have a better understanding of how your employees, peers, and manager perceive your effectiveness as a leader and manager. Your next step is to begin creating your own development plan.

This section provides several recommendations for strengthening your skills in each competency. Development suggestions and recommended readings are provided alphabetically for each competency.

It is recommended that you work on only one competency at a time. Keep in mind that a low rating in a particular category does not imply that you have no skill in that area, just as a high rating does not imply that you should not focus on maintaining or improving your skills in that area. You may want to focus first on competencies related to the lowest-rated behaviors.

As you read through the suggestions, highlight or place a checkmark beside those that seem the most relevant. These are only suggestions to guide your efforts, and our organization is providing additional resources to assist with your ongoing self-development.

Keep this report as a reference to update your progress on the development plan you will be designing. You may also want to consider using this report as a guide for future feedback sessions with your employees, peers, or manager.

Is Customer-Focused

Gives top priority to customer needs and desires. Consistently works to uncover their needs, respond to them, and build relationships with customers.

Developmental Suggestions

Examine everything you do against the criterion, "Does this contribute to meeting customer needs?"

List the needs you believe your customers have. Then ask your customers what their needs are. Note the differences.

Within one week of resolving a customer complaint, follow up with phone call to ensure their satisfaction.

Stay in touch with your customers' businesses and industries. If possible, keep general information files on events relevant to your key customers.

**Exhibit 12.6. Example of Developmental
Suggestions for a Competency, Cont'd.**

Treat your internal customers with same care you'd give to external customers. As a manager, consider your staff to be your customers.

Take time every day to ask customers, "How are we doing?" and actively listen to what they say.

Identify others in your organization who have a reputation for focusing on customers. Ask them what makes their efforts so successful.

Recommended Reading

Barrow, J., & Maller, C. (1996). *A Complaint Is a Gift*. San Francisco: Berrett-Koehler.

Davidow, W. H., & Uttal, B. (1990). *Total Customer Service*. New York: Harper Perennial.

Sewell, C., & Brown, P. B. (1991).*Customers for Life: How to Turn That One-Time Buyer into a Lifetime Customer*. New York: Doubleday Currency.

Toschohl, J. (1991). *Achieving Excellence Through Customer Service*. Upper Saddle River, NJ: Prentice Hall.

Zemke, R. (1991).*The Service Edge: 101 Companies That Profit from Customer Care*. New York: Penguin Books.

Source: Copyright © 2000, adapted from Assessment Alternatives, Inc., Florham Park, N.J., Sample Report.

The most common approach to presenting normative data is to compare participants with average ratings of other individuals in their work group, department, or company. The last two columns of Figure 12.1 give an example of presenting norm data for the participant's workgroup and company. Norm groups can also be defined by organizational level, and by national norms based on either functional or organizational level. Generally, presenting more than one norm group in the feedback report should be avoided so that the participant can focus on the most relevant comparison group when interpreting the feedback data, and so that the participant is not overwhelmed with feedback data.

One factor that can affect the decision about which norm group to present is the size of the organization. Small organizations may find it necessary to use national norms because of the lack of available internal data. Availability of data is less likely to be an issue for larger organizations where norm groups can be more easily constructed at the functional unit, department, or organizational level.

One caution regarding presentation of norms is that participants may not feel motivated to address a behavior where they are rated low and the normative rating for the behavior is also low. Participants may recognize that they are not performing well on this behavior but dismiss it as an important area for developmental planning since others in the comparison group are also generally evaluated low on the behavior. Participants need to understand not only that these are behaviors they need to address individually but also that larger scale group interventions have to be introduced so that the entire norm group can address the behavior as a developmental need. Despite this caution, norms are still a useful benchmark for comparison of participant ratings.

Other Benchmarks for Interpreting Feedback Results

Besides using norms, there are several other methods for establishing benchmarks to aid in interpreting feedback ratings. One approach is to define a scale value above the midpoint as a benchmark for average performance—say, 3.5 or 4.0 on a 5-point scale. The scale midpoint typically is not an adequate benchmark for average performance, since average MSF ratings on items and competencies tend to be above the scale midpoint for most participants. If normative data are not available, care must be taken in suggesting a single scale point for benchmarking on all competencies, since participants as a group may generally be rated higher on some types of competencies (perhaps problem-solving skills) and lower on other types of competencies (perhaps interpersonal skills).

Another approach to this issue is to establish benchmarks for each competency through a consensus of subject matter experts. A final approach is to have each participant establish benchmarks with his or her supervisor or coach. In addition to using these benchmarks, participants should also be instructed to consider their overall pattern of results on the competencies and thus focus on their relative top strengths and developmental needs for action planning. For example, even if the participant exceeds the benchmark value on all the competencies (or falls short on all competencies), his or her pattern of results still suggests areas of relative strength and developmental needs for action planning.

Inclusion of Variance Estimates

Information about distribution of ratings can be given to the participant by presenting either an index of item variance (such as the standard deviation or range) or a frequency distribution of the ratings on the items. Another option is to use an index of rater agreement for sources that include multiple raters. An example of such an index is r_{wg} offered by James, Demaree, and Wolf (1984). This type of information probably best fits part three of the report, where detailed data analyses are presented, or perhaps some sections of part two, where item data are found.

The extent to which an index of item variance or rater agreement is actually included in feedback reports in practice is not completely clear. For example, London and Smither (1995) reported that 70 percent of the organizations they surveyed had an index of within-source agreement in the feedback report, while only 17 percent of the MSF processes reviewed by Timmreck and Bracken (1995) used an index of item variance.

Although the range or other indices of item variance yield somewhat less specific information compared to frequency data, an index of item variance does help protect rater anonymity better than frequency data. The effect of using the range versus frequency can be seen in an example. Two individuals, each with eight direct reports, receive a mean item rating of 3 on a 5-point scale. In both cases, the ratings range from 1 to 5. On the basis of this information, one would conclude that the ratings suggest identical developmental needs. However, examining the frequency of ratings suggests otherwise. The first individual received one rating of 1, six ratings of 3, and one rating of 5. This frequency distribution suggests strong agreement on the part of direct subordinates. The second individual received four ratings of 1 and four ratings of 5. This frequency distribution suggests a polarization in how direct reports view the individual. Clearly, the differences in the frequency distributions suggest that the individuals have contrasting developmental needs.

An important factor to consider when choosing between the range and frequency of ratings is whether the organizational culture promotes sharing of information. If individuals are very comfortable giving feedback to others, then presenting variance data can enhance the quality of the data. On the other hand, if individuals are uncomfortable giving feedback, the potential loss of rater anonymity may sabotage the MSF process.

Another consideration in presenting frequency data or an index of item variance is whether it is simply too much information for the candidate to process efficiently and use effectively. Too much information may inhibit the participant's ability to wade through the feedback report and identify the key strengths and developmental needs. If frequencies or an index of item variance are included in the report, perhaps consideration should be given to streamlining other aspects of the report so that the participant is not overwhelmed with data (Dalessio, 1998).

Conclusions

The purpose of the feedback report is to summarize the MSF data, so that the participant can easily and clearly identify strengths and developmental needs at competency, behavioral, and source levels. This information can then be used as a basis for leveraging strengths and addressing developmental needs.

Designers of feedback reports should keep in mind that no matter how well the report is designed, any two participants may interpret the same feedback report data differently, because reactions to the feedback data are influenced to some extent by the participant's own preconceptions and biases. The Broadway play *Art* provides some interesting food for thought on this topic. It is about three friends' reactions when one of them purchases a piece of art that is simply a white canvas with white diagonal lines. During the play, the friends display strongly positive or negative emotional reactions to the piece of art. The amazing reality is that in fact all three friends are viewing a virtually blank canvas.

The designers of feedback reports can take a lesson from the play. Before any participant views the printed information on the feedback report, he or she brings to the viewing of the report preconceptions, biases, and previous experiences. Although participants are reacting to the numbers and graphs on the pages of the feedback report, like the three friends in the play they are probably also reacting to the blank background behind the numbers. Designers of feedback reports need to keep this in mind, because no matter how much information is displayed, graphed, or presented with black or colored ink, to some extent participants are looking past that information and responding to the white background colored by past experience.

References

Atwater, L. E. "The Advantages and Pitfalls of Self-Assessment in Organizations." In J. W. Smither (ed.), *Performance Appraisal: State of the Art in Practice*. San Francisco: Jossey-Bass, 1998.

Bracken, D. W. "Multisource (360-Degree) Feedback: Surveys for Individual and Organizational Development." In A. I. Kraut (ed.), *Organizational Surveys: Tools for Assessment and Change*. San Francisco: Jossey-Bass, 1996.

Dalessio, A. T. "Using Multisource Feedback for Employee Development and Personnel Decisions: Practice and Research." In J. W. Smither (ed.), *Performance Appraisal: State of the Art in Practice*. San Francisco: Jossey-Bass, 1998.

Harris, M. M., and Schaubroeck, J. "A Meta-Analysis of Self-Supervisor, Self-Peer, and Peer-Supervisor Ratings." *Personnel Psychology*, 1988, *41*, 43–62.

James, L. R., Demaree, R. G., and Wolf, G. "Estimating Within-Group Interrater Reliability with and Without Response Bias." *Journal of Applied Psychology*, 1984, *69*, 85–98.

London, M., and Smither, J. W. "Can Multisource Feedback Change Perceptions of Goal Accomplishment, Self-Evaluations, and Performance-Related Outcomes? Theory-Based Applications and Directions for Research." *Personnel Psychology*, 1995, *48*, 803–839.

Timmreck, C. W., and Bracken, D. W. "Upward Feedback in the Trenches: Challenges and Realities." Paper presented at the tenth annual conference of the Society for Industrial and Organizational Psychology, Orlando, Fla., May 1995.

Yukl, G., and Lepsinger, R. "How to Get the Most out of 360-Degree Feedback." *Training*, 1995, *32*, 45–50.

CHAPTER 13

Understanding Agreement in Multisource Feedback

Francis J. Yammarino
Leanne E. Atwater

Understanding self-other agreement has key implications for leadership development, especially when the extent of agreement is reflected in a multisource feedback (MSF) report. Assessing self-other agreement has a long history, evolving about eighty years ago when problems with relying on only self-estimates were demonstrated. As such, there are numerous approaches available for assessing self-other agreement in general and MSF ratings in particular.

The work of Edwards (1993, 1994), Atwater and Yammarino (1997), and Atwater, Ostroff, Yammarino, and Fleenor (1998) provide extensive reviews and discussion of these approaches, including evaluation of the relative strengths and weaknesses of each approach. Yammarino and Atwater (1997), in particular, draw out the implications of these approaches for feedback and human resource management practices. Although difference scores (including algebraic, absolute, and squared differences), profile similarity indices, agreement indices, categories of agreement (overestimators, underestimators, and in-agreement raters; Atwater and Yammarino, 1992, 1997; Yammarino and Atwater, 1997), and polynomial regression analyses (Edwards, 1993, 1994) have been explored quite extensively in prior work, using within and between analysis (WABA) in this area of research has been suggested but not fully developed (see Atwater and Yammarino, 1997).

As such, the purpose of this chapter is to develop an approach for assessing the type and degree of agreement among different-source ratings based on the "varient" approach and its analytic component, WABA (see Dansereau, Alutto, and Yammarino, 1984; Yammarino, 1998; Yammarino and Markham, 1992). *Varient* is a new term formed from two words: *vari*ables (in this case, the *dimensions* of multisource feedback) and *ent*ities (or levels of analysis, in this case, the *source* of those ratings). In particular, we are interested in (1) a focal leader or manager who provides *self*-ratings on dimensions of interest; (2) a boss or superior, peers or coworkers, and customers or clients who provide *other* ratings on the same relevant dimensions; and (3) the degree and type of *agreement* among these rating sources.

We focus on this approach because we believe that the degree and type of self-other agreement are relevant to human resource management practices, including individual and organizational performance and effectiveness, as well as to leadership development, especially through training and feedback (Yammarino and Atwater, 1997). In other words, it is critical to understand the implications of self-other agreement or disagreement for leadership development. In particular, whether focal leaders are overraters, underraters, or have ratings in agreement with other sources produces varying information and perspectives on how people handle feedback and on which dimensions necessitate training and development. This information can appear in a feedback report for use in leader development.

Moreover, agreement inherently deals with issues of level of analysis (for instance, can a group of raters be considered a "group," or is there dyadic agreement between a leader and his or her boss?); WABA, a multiple-level data-analytic technique, is ideally suited to address these concerns in the realm of self-other agreement (see Dansereau, Alutto, and Yammarino, 1984; Yammarino, 1998; Yammarino and Markham, 1992). Specifically, WABA can be used to assess the level of analysis of agreement or disagreement in multisource feedback, and this information can then be used to formulate leadership development strategies and programs.

Key Questions and Levels of Analysis

Varient/WABA Approach

From a varient/WABA perspective (see Dansereau, Alutto, and Yammarino, 1984; Yammarino, 1998; Yammarino and Markham, 1992), each self-other and other-other comparison in the MSF process can be viewed in terms of the type of agreement shown between raters. Specifically, agreement or disagreement can take the form of (1) patterned agreement (self and other scores are similar),(2) patterned disagreement (self and other scores are opposite), or (3) lacking agreement (self and other scores are not related). These conceptual and theoretical conditions of agreement and their alignment with the varient/WABA conditions are shown in Table 13.1 and are explained in detail below.

The general varient/WABA framework can then be applied to these specific assessments of agreement: (1) *between* self-other rating sources (for example, self-subordinates comparison), (2) *within* rating sources (for example, among all the subordinates of a focal manager), and (3) *between* other-other ratings sources (for example, subordinates-customers comparison) to determine the level of analysis of the agreement in the multisource ratings. For example, do subordinates generally agree when rating their leader? If so, the group level is an appropriate level for analysis, and in a

Table 13.1. Varient/WABA Approach for Agreement in Multisource Feedback.

Theoretical Condition	Varient Condition	WABA Condition
Patterned agreement	Wholes	Between
Patterned disagreement ("agreeing to disagree")	Parts	Within
Lack of agreement (nonpatterned disagreement)	Equivocal; inexplicable	Between and within; neither between nor within

Note: Conditions apply to *within*-source comparisons as well as *between*-source comparisons for self-other and other-other assessments (also see Figures 13.1 and 13.2).

feedback report it may be appropriate to give an average rating by the subordinates to the focal manager. If not, perhaps the dyad level is operating, and in the feedback report it may be appropriate to give individual break-out scores from each subordinate to the focal manager.

Specifically, for all thirteen comparisons shown in Table 13.2, it is possible to determine, using WABA, (1) the level of analysis that is relevant (for example, group or dyad), (2) the agreement pattern for each level of analysis (for example, patterned agreement or disagreement), and (3) the strength of the agreement in each case (for example, strongly positive or negative). These assessments can be made for each dimension of interest (such as leadership), for bivariate relationships between focal dimensions (the relationship between leadership and performance), and for

**Table 13.2. WABA Assessments for Agreement
in Multisource Feedback.**

Key Question	WABA Level
Is there agreement *within* a rating source?	
For subordinates (G1)?	Group
For coworkers/peers (G2)?	Group
For customers/clients (G3)?	Group
Is there agreement *between* self-other ratings?	
For self-subordinates (D1)?	Dyad
For self-coworkers (D2)?	Dyad
For self-customers (D3)?	Dyad
For self-superior (D4)?	Dyad
Is there agreement *between* other-other ratings?	
For subordinates-superior (OD1)?	Dyad
For subordinates-coworkers (OD2)?	Dyad
For subordinates-customers (OD3)?	Dyad
For coworkers-superior (OD4)?	Dyad
For coworkers-customers (OD5)?	Dyad
For customers-superior (OD6)?	Dyad

Note: G1 to G3, D1 to D4, and OD1 to OD6 are also shown in Figures 13.1 and 13.2.

multivariate relationships among multiple dimensions (the multiple prediction of performance by leadership and effort); see Yammarino (1998). Each type of agreement as it pertains to each rating comparison is discussed below.

Between Self-Other Ratings

Is there agreement *between* self-other ratings? This question is relevant to MSF in that the degree of agreement may signal a self-rater's degree of self-awareness. Acute self-awareness, in turn, is often predictive of many positive individual and organizational outcomes (Atwater and Yammarino, 1997; Yammarino and Atwater, 1997). Four self-other comparisons can be made in multisource feedback: self-subordinates, self-coworkers, self-customers, and self-superior ratings. Three types of agreement—patterned agreement, lack of agreement, and patterned disagreement—may be observed that have implications for feedback providers, as well as for individual and organizational performance.

Patterned Agreement

Patterned agreement is the case where self-other scores are similar. In the work of Atwater and Yammarino (1997) and Yammarino and Atwater (1997), two cases of patterned agreement are "in-agreement/good," where high self-ratings are similar to high other ratings; and "in-agreement/poor," where low self-ratings are similar to low other ratings. In the varient/WABA approach, these cases represent a *wholes* condition, that is, agreement among ratings sources about a focal manager but differences between the ratings of various focal managers. As such, $S1 \approx O1$ and $S2 \approx O2$, and there are differences *between* $S1/O1$ and $S2/O2$ (where S is a self-score and O is an other score; 1 and 2 are different raters).

Patterned Disagreement

Patterned disagreement is "agreeing to disagree," the case where self-other scores are differentially positioned. Two cases of patterned disagreement are overestimators, where self-ratings are significantly greater than other ratings; and underestimators, where self-ratings are significantly less than other ratings (see Atwater and Yammarino, 1997; Yammarino and Atwater, 1997). In the varient/WABA approach, these cases represent a *parts* condition, that is, disagreement among ratings sources about a focal manager, with this disagreement evident across several focal managers. As such, *within* each self-other comparison, S1 ≠ O1 and S2 ≠ O2, and there is a relative positioning of the scores (for example, as S1 and S2 increase by 1, O1 and O2 decrease by 1).

Lack of Agreement

Lack of agreement is a case where there is no discernible patterned agreement or disagreement across the self-other scores. Across the set of comparisons, all kinds of things are happening: agreement, disagreement, relative positioning, nonrelative positioning, or perhaps even no variability in scores whatsoever. These are *equivocal* or *inexplicable* cases in the varient/WABA approach; S and O scores vary both between and within *or* neither between nor within the set of self-other comparisons. This case is simply nonpatterned disagreement.

As an illustration, suppose we obtain self-ratings of leadership from two focal sales managers to go along with the various other (say, subordinate) ratings. For the sake of simplicity, let's assume we have the case of patterned agreement for the other scores. That is, all of manager 1's subordinates rated her high; all of manager 2's subordinates rated him low. As such, the average of the subordinates' scores for each manager reliably represents their views of the managers. This meaningful average score could be used in a feedback report. Manager 1's self-score can be assessed for agreement with her subordinates' average score, and likewise for manager 2.

Again, the three potential patterns of agreement or disagreement noted in Table 13.1 can result when we examine ratings within and between the managers and the average scores from their subordinates, that is, within and between the manager-subordinate dyads. Thus for patterned agreement (wholes), we might find that manager 1's self-rating and her average subordinate rating are both high (in agreement and good), while for manager 2 the self-rating and average subordinate rating are both low (in agreement and poor). In the patterned disagreement (parts) case, we might find these results: manager 1's self-rating is low and her subordinate average rating is high (an underestimator); manager

2's self-rating is high and his average subordinate rating is low (an overestimator). Likewise, we can envision various types of equivocal or inexplicable results for these dyads.

These dyadic comparisons also can be conducted for self-coworkers, self-customers, and self-superior ratings. An inference can be drawn in each case regarding the nature of agreement or disagreement. Moreover, we can relax our simplification of the "reliable average rating" by subordinates, coworkers, and customers. In other words, if there is patterned disagreement or nonpatterned disagreement (lack of agreement) within a rating source (for instance, among all subordinates of a manager; see below), then dyadic analyses should proceed with a self-rating compared to *each unique* other rating, and not the average other rating. In this case, the average rating across all subordinates may not be meaningful, as each subordinate rating is different. So each unique rating from each subordinate could be used in a feedback report. Although more complicated, the same three overall conclusions about agreement noted in Table 13.1 are plausible.

Within a Rating Source

Is there agreement *within* a rating source? This question is relevant for the *group* of subordinates, coworkers or peers, and customers or clients rating a focal leader or manager. It is particularly relevant given the preceding example in that it helps us decide whether or not it is appropriate to average other ratings. If we discover that there is no within-rating source agreement, the averaged or group score has little meaning. For example, suppose three subordinates, three coworkers, and three customers all provided leadership ratings about a sales manager, and we obtained similar leadership ratings for an additional sales manager. We have six subordinate ratings (three for each of two managers), six coworker ratings, and six customer ratings; we can now determine the nature of agreement within each rating source.

As an illustration, each of manager 1's subordinates may rate her high and each of manager 2's subordinates may rate him low. There is agreement within each group of ratings for each manager, but there is a difference between the ratings for manager 1 and manager 2. This is patterned agreement, or a wholes condition. If instead manager 1's scores (on a scale from 1 = low to 5 = high) from her three subordinates were 5, 3, and 1, respectively, and this was also the case for manager 2, then we have a case of patterned disagreement or parts within each rating group—no difference between the average ratings for manager 1 and manager 2, but patterned differences among the ratings for each manager. In each case, the manager would receive an average score of 3, but this score would not be very representative of his or her actual scores, and so not very useful in a feedback report.

Another possibility is that the scores (on a scale from 1 = low to 6 = high) from manager 1's subordinates are 1, 2, and 3, respectively, while those for manager 2 are 4, 5, and 6, respectively. In this case, there is nonpatterned disagreement, or lack of agreement, as the scores vary within and between the rating groups of subordinates, an equivocal condition. Multisource feedback in this case is meaningfully provided from each rater individually in a feedback report.

A final possibility is that all ratings about manager 1 and manager 2 from all their subordinates are the same. In this case, there is no variability within nor between the rating groups of subordinates, an inexplicable condition. All managers were rated the same by all subordinates; say, everyone got a 2 from all raters. These ratings are not very useful or helpful for individual feedback because every manager received the same or an identical score, and one cannot assess relative standing or whether improvement is necessary. On the other hand, if these scores are accurate and the same for each manager, it may be indicative of an organizationwide issue (we may be in a company of "2-level performers").

These same scenarios also can be examined for the coworker and customer groups that provide ratings about a focal manager. For each of the three groups of ratings from subordinates, coworkers, and customers (see Table 13.2), an inference about the nature of agreement can be drawn (see Table 13.1). Unless the patterned-agreement condition holds, aggregation or averaging of raters in a group is not very meaningful. Presentation of individual scores from each rater (without identifying who gave what rating) provides more useful information.

Between Other-Other Ratings

Although a typical focus in multisource ratings is on self-other agreement, there are times when other-other comparisons are appropriate. "Other" sources have unique perspectives on focal leaders, which can provide valuable developmental information. Continuing the preceding examples for feedback and developmental purposes, we may wish to know whether different "internals"—say, subordinates and coworkers—see the focal manager's leadership similarly. This may be particularly important if the organization intends to use the multisource ratings for goal setting or evaluation. For example, how does a supervisor set goals if there is no agreement among sources as to the supervisor's development needs? Perhaps differential goals are required. Similarly, feedback to managers comparing internal-external perspectives—say, superior and customers—may yield useful developmental information. If your boss thinks you are doing a great job but the customer does not, there are potential problems to address.

In these cases, is there agreement *between* other-other ratings? This question is relevant for certain comparison ratings in multisource feedback:

- Subordinates-superior
- Subordinates-coworkers
- Subordinates-customers
- Coworkers-superior
- Coworkers-customers
- Customers-superior

Note that three of these comparisons involve different *internal* perspectives on the focal manager, while three involve *internal-external* perspectives on the person. Analogous to the discussion in the preceding section on agreement between self-other ratings, a series of *dyadic* analyses and comparisons can be made and a conclusion drawn regarding the nature of agreement for each of the six other-other assessments. The dyads in all these cases are made up of two different other sources, as shown in Table 13.2. Again, whether the average rating for a rating group is reliable or not determines whether an average score is meaningful to use in these analyses and feedback, or whether individual scores should be provided and analyzed.

Integration of Agreement Results

The self-other and other-other agreement assessments from the previous sections are summarized in Figures 13.1 and 13.2. Essentially, the entire varient/WABA framework is applied to the assessment process in four steps:

1. Examine *within-source* rating agreement via group-level analyses G1, G2, and G3. Based on these results, determine whether to use simplified (that is, average ratings) or more complete (unique, nonaverage ratings) dyadic analyses.
2. Examine *between-source self-other* rating agreement via dyad-level analyses D1, D2, D3, and D4.
3. Examine *between-source other-other* rating agreement via dyad-level analyses OD1, OD2, OD3, OD4, OD5, and OD6.

Figure 13.1. WABA Assessments for Self-Other Agreement.

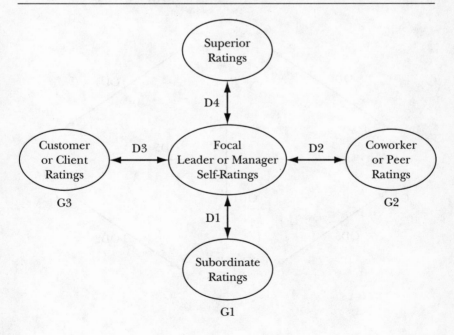

4. Summarize and integrate the results of Steps 1, 2, and 3 to draw an overall conclusion.

In particular, for a set of managers or an entire organization, the comparisons and empirical results at multiple levels of analysis form the basis for inferences about the nature (degree and type) of agreement or disagreement among rating sources. This information can be fed back globally to the entire organization, and in specific fashion to each manager individually. Further examination of results for each manager within the patterned agreement, patterned disagreement (agreeing to disagree), and lack of agreement (nonpatterned disagreement) conditions then permits a judgment to be made about the differential approaches to development required for those managers who are overestimators, underestimators, in agreement and good, or in agreement and poor relative to other rating sources.

**Figure 13.2. WABA Assessments for
Other-Other Agreement.**

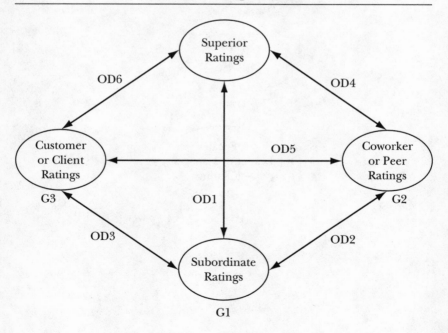

Implications for Leadership Development

Ultimately, all analyses and comparisons at multiple levels assist identifying the appropriate level of analysis and the degree and type of agreement. First, whether aggregation of scores is appropriate can be determined. If aggregation is appropriate (there is within-group agreement), averaged scores for a rater group are reliably used in analyses and should be provided as feedback. If aggregation is not appropriate, analyses should proceed and feedback should be provided in terms of individual ratings. For example, an individual may receive information about how many raters gave him or her a 5, 4, 3, 2, or 1, rather than the average of the scores from each of the rater groups.

In addition, the results and inferences regarding patterned agreement, patterned disagreement, or lack of agreement from the varient/WABA approach allow identification of four self-other agreement categories (see Atwater and Yammarino, 1997; Yammarino and Atwater, 1997):

1. *Overestimator,* where self-ratings are significantly greater than other ratings
2. *Underestimator,* where self-ratings are significantly less than other ratings
3. *In-agreement and good,* where high self-ratings are similar to high other ratings
4. *In-agreement and poor,* where low self-ratings are similar to low other ratings

For each of these categories, the implications for feedback and leadership development differ and are discussed next.

Overestimator

Self-ratings are often inflated because of an individual's ignorance of how he or she is seen by others, aided by raters' tendencies to withhold negative feedback (see Atwater and Yammarino, 1997). It is well documented that most individuals do not enjoy giving negative feedback face-to face and thus avoid it. As a consequence, most of us receive less negative feedback than is realistic, and the little that we do receive is often sugarcoated. This shortcoming contributes to a tendency for individuals to see themselves in an unrealistically positive light.

These self-raters are "inaccurate" in that they "think" they are good performers, but others see them as performing less favorably. Inaccurate self-perception also can result because individuals tend to discount or rationalize negative feedback, while generally accepting positive feedback as more accurate and informational. This tendency may occur because positive information is more consistent with our self-perception. As such, in the case of the overestimator, there is considerable evidence that outcomes, for both the focal individual and the organization, are *very negative* (see Yammarino and Atwater, 1997).

In general, overestimators tend to misdiagnose their strengths and weaknesses; make less effective job-relevant decisions; have negative attitudes, including hostility and resentment; suffer from career derailment; fail to see the need for training and development; and have high absenteeism, low commitment, high turnover, and frequent conflicts with supervisors and coworkers. However, overestimators often improve their performance and lower their self-evaluations when feedback from others is provided (see Atwater and Yammarino, 1997; Johnson and Ferstl, 1999).

Underestimator

In this case, the self-rater either does not recognize his or her strengths or is being overly modest (see Atwater and Yammarino, 1997). Regardless, these self-raters are inaccurate in that they think they are poor or average performers, but others see them as performing more favorably. The good news is that with continued positive feedback from others, there is potential for improvement. Here, the evidence suggests that the individual and organizational outcomes are *mixed*, some being positive, others negative (see Yammarino and Atwater, 1997).

Generally, underestimators tend to be somewhat successful and effective, misdiagnose their strengths and weaknesses, make ineffective job-relevant decisions, set low aspiration levels and underachieve, have emotional highs and lows, display low self-worth yet are pleasant to be around, and not pursue leadership positions or realize their full potential. Moreover, underestimators generally maintain their performance and raise their self-evaluations when feedback from others is provided (see Atwater and Yammarino, 1997; Johnson and Ferstl, 1999).

In-Agreement and Good

Self-raters in this category are the "ideal employees," "good managers," and "effective leaders" we encounter all too rarely in organizations (see Atwater and Yammarino, 1997). They are also "accurate" raters in that the self and others ratings are "high" and in agreement. In this case, the evidence is that individual and organizational outcomes are *very positive* (see Yammarino and Atwater, 1997).

In general, in-agreement and good individuals tend to be successful and the best performers; make effective job-relevant decisions; develop favorable efficacy expectations and commensurate achievement; have the most promotability; have very positive job attitudes; be more successful and effective leaders; have low absenteeism, high commitment, low turnover, and few conflicts with others; and use feedback from others constructively to alter their behavior as needed.

In-Agreement and Poor

This self-rater recognizes personal weaknesses or acknowledges being perceived negatively by others (see Atwater and Yammarino, 1997). Even though the self-perception may be accurate, the behaviors and performance are not those labeled ideal or desirable. These self-raters are accurate as self and other ratings are in-agreement, but they are low. In this case, there is evidence that outcomes, for both the focal individual and the organization, are *negative*, but perhaps not as negative as in the case of the overestimator (see Yammarino and Atwater, 1997).

Generally, individuals in the in-agreement and poor category tend to be unsuccessful, poor performers; make ineffective job-relevant decisions; have low KSAs (knowledge, skills, and abilities), negative attitude, or both; have low self-worth and self-esteem; demonstrate either high or low motivation to improve, depending on the cause of poor performance (such as ability versus attitude); have high absenteeism, low commitment, and high turnover; and accurately diagnose weaknesses but take few actions to improve their performance.

Overall Implications

These self-other rating types and their differential individual and organizational outcomes suggest several implications for leadership training and development. First, most of the issues we have noted can be addressed by training and education programs. Consequently, a comprehensive, organizationwide training needs assessment and evaluation effort is critical. All individuals, regardless of job positions, should be monitored, evaluated, and assessed from a variety of sources, on various job-relevant dimensions. Line managers and human resource staff can use the results of these efforts to determine the nature of training and development programs for each individual.

Second, using feedback in leadership training and development programs to enhance self-perception accuracy and self-other agreement is likewise critical. Individuals need information about their knowledge, skills, and abilities, as well as about their individual characteristics, performance, and leadership, and they should have this information from several sources. They must understand how this information is similar to or different from their own perceptions of themselves. More important, they require constructive feedback to help them change or maintain appropriate on-the-job behaviors and attitudes. Essentially, constructive feedback, as part of a leadership training program, tends to bring subsequent self-ratings in line with the ratings focal individuals and managers receive from others.

Third, high self-other rating agreement should be a goal of all leadership training programs that use feedback as a developmental tool. High self-other rating agreement is generally indicative of high self-awareness. In turn, individuals who are acutely self-aware tend to be the more successful, effective, and promotable individuals in organizations. As such, reducing self-other rating discrepancies and enhancing other ratings and commensurate self-ratings pulls more individuals into the in-agreement and good category—

people who tend to be the best performers, managers, and leaders. It seems critical for organizational success and effectiveness to develop as many of these ideal employees as resources permit.

Fourth, over time, in both leadership training programs and tracking of employee career paths, a declining self-other rating discrepancy can be used as an indicator of improved self-perception accuracy. Acute self-awareness, or seeing ourselves as others see us, creates an opportunity for accurate self-assessment and substantial self-development. Through such a process, a reasonable though difficult goal is to develop an organization of "in-agreement and goods." In this way, individual and organizational outcomes tend toward the very positive, and organizational resources are well spent with a resulting high benefit-to-cost ratio.

Fifth, using MSF with the intention of changing self-ratings and behaviors must be approached cautiously. Researchers and professionals who have used MSF emphasize the importance of rater training. Simply cautioning people about common rating errors (leniency bias, central tendency bias, and so forth) can be very helpful. The training should also address people's insecurities about the rating process, its purpose and goals, and how anonymity and confidentiality are maintained. (See Chapter Eight.)

Sixth, individuals receiving feedback that is more negative than expected (overestimators) may need some special attention. These managers and individuals may suffer from reduced self-esteem, temporary depression, or feelings of inadequacy. In some cases, one-to-one discussions with a counselor or facilitator ease some of these ill feelings. Also, overestimators may benefit by receiving feedback as part of a group, rather than individually. They may find comfort in seeing that others also have received ratings that are more negative than they expected.

In conclusion, by conducting a multilevel analysis of self-other agreement in multisource feedback by way of the varient/WABA approach, one can gain additional insight about self-rater categorization. Appropriate analysis and feedback of multisource ratings is critical for both rater categorization and leader development. Fuller knowledge of rater categorization (that is, overestimator, underestimator, in-agreement and good estimators, and in-agreement and poor estimators) can result in better understanding of individuals *and* the design of leadership development programs that help employees and managers become more effective and successful organizational contributors. As such, MSF is the key to leadership development.

References

Atwater, L. E., Ostroff, C., Yammarino, F. J., and Fleenor, J. W. "Self-Other Agreement: Does It Really Matter?" *Personnel Psychology*, 1998, *51*, 577–598.

Atwater, L. E., and Yammarino, F. J. "Does Self-Other Agreement on Leadership Perceptions Moderate the Validity of Leadership and Performance Predictions?" *Personnel Psychology*, 1992, *45*, 141–164.

Atwater, L. E., and Yammarino, F. J. "Self-Other Rating Agreement: A Review and Model." *Research in Personnel and Human Resources Management*, 1997, *15*, 121–174.

Dansereau, F., Alutto, J. A., and Yammarino, F. J. *Theory Testing in Organizational Behavior: The Varient Approach.* Upper Saddle River, N.J.: Prentice Hall, 1984.

Edwards, J. R. "Problem with Use of Profile Similarity Indices in the Study of Congruence in Organizational Research." *Personnel Psychology*, 1993, *46*, 641–665.

Edwards, J. R. "The Study of Congruence in Organizational Behavior Research: Critique and a Proposed Alternative." *Organizational Behavior and Human Decisions Processes*, 1994, *58*, 51–100; erratum, *58*, 323–325.

Johnson, J. W., and Ferstl, K. L. "The Effects of Interrater and Self-Other Agreement on Performance Improvement Following Upward Feedback." *Personnel Psychology*, 1999, *52*, 271–303.

Yammarino, F. J. "Multivariate Aspects of the Varient/WABA Approach: A Discussion and Leadership Illustration." *Leadership Quarterly*, 1998, *9*, 203–227.

Yammarino, F. J., and Atwater, L. E. "Do Managers See Themselves as Others See Them? Implications of Self-Other Rating Agreement for Human Resource Management." *Organizational Dynamics*, 1997, *25*(4), 35–44.

Yammarino, F. J., and Markham, S. E. "On the Application of Within and Between Analysis: Are Absence and Affect Really Group-Based Phenomena?" *Journal of Applied Psychology*, 1992, *77*, 168–176.

CHAPTER 14

Tools and Resources for Helping People Move Forward Following Multisource Feedback

David B. Peterson
Mary Dee Hicks
Jeffrey D. Stoner

From the moment of consciousness, we enter a world where every action we take has an effect. A baby's cry elicits the response of a caring parent, a toddler's touching a sharp object results in a clear signal of pain, and a second grader's outburst receives the cool glare of the teacher. What is experienced in each of these situations varies, but the constant reality is that our actions generate feedback. This feedback plays an indispensable role in our lives, for without feedback it would be virtually impossible for us to learn, grow, or even survive. Whether we perceive or respond to the feedback is another question.

If feedback is constantly available and is so essential to learning, why don't more people learn from it? For one thing, today's fast-paced, rapidly changing work culture does not lend itself to patient listening, reflection, and contemplation. There is probably more feedback available in today's work environment than at any point in history, but most people have a hard time sorting through the overwhelming volume of information. In the process, they may tune out some of the data that are most important to their learning. Our job as practitioners is to help people hear and interpret meaningful feedback and use it to guide their development.

These are the conditions necessary for feedback to drive learning:

- The feedback is relevant to the person's own goals and values.
- The feedback is clear.
- The feedback is credible.
- The person is ready to hear the feedback.

Multisource feedback (MSF) tools can often provide clear, credible feedback, but they are only part of the development equation. There is a dramatic difference in the degree of learning between people who use MSF simply to understand what others think of them and those who use it to sharpen their development priorities and spur development action. People who put learning and development in the forefront can take the best of what their MSF experience has to offer and put it to use in a concerted effort to improve.

It is your job to help the person maximize her learning from the feedback experience by engaging her in hearing the most important messages, examining where the information is most relevant, and then helping her pursue the kinds of action that result in real learning. When the feedback leads to sustained changes in behavior, people experience an increased sense of awareness and control over their lives at work, a benefit that goes far beyond the immediate payback from a particular feedback conversation. This chapter outlines a process for making that happen, beginning with the feedback conversation itself and then focusing on how you can help the person continue to move forward after feedback.

Getting the Most Value from the Feedback Discussion

Approach every feedback conversation as a change intervention. Keep in mind that the purpose is not to "give feedback" but to cultivate insight and foster action that results in meaningful changes for people and their organizations.

Before the Feedback

Encourage people to prepare for the feedback discussion by reflecting on these questions:

- From whom and in what areas do I most need feedback?
- How important is honest, accurate feedback to my success?
- What specific questions do I hope to answer through my multisource feedback?
- If I look at my style and behavior from other people's perspective, what do I honestly expect them to say about me?

During the Feedback

Because so many people are familiar with the MSF process, it pays to find out what their experience has been and what their expectations are for this session. Give the person an overview of the process you typically use for the conversation, addressing issues such as confidentiality of the data and any follow-up involvement you will have with him or his organization.

Next, help him understand the larger context of the feedback. Too often, the feedback or the instrument itself becomes the center of attention. In order to learn and improve his performance, the person needs to understand much more than just the feedback. The GAPS grid is a simple but powerful tool for highlighting where feedback fits in the development process (Peterson and Hicks, 1995, 1996). GAPS is an acronym for the four types of information that people require in identifying meaningful development priorities (see Table 14.1):

1. Goals and values: what matters to the person
2. Abilities: how the person sees himself or herself
3. Perceptions: how others see the person
4. Success factors: what matters to others

Feedback (perception information) is most valuable when it helps people determine how they can be more effective relative to what matters to them (goals and values) and to their organization

Table 14.1. GAPS: Critical Information for Development.

	Where the Person Is	*Where the Person Is Going*
The Person's View	**A**bilities How the person sees himself or herself The person's view of his or her capabilities, style, and performance, especially in relation to important goals, values, and success factors	**G**oals and values What matters to the person The motivators that energize and drive the person's behavior, including interests, values, desires, work objectives, and career aspirations
Others' Views	**P**erceptions How others see the person How others perceive the person's capabilities, style, performance, motives, priorities, and values	**S**uccess factors What matters to others What other people, such as the boss, senior management, peers, and direct reports, expect or desire from the person; success factors are based on formal roles and responsibilities, the organization's cultural norms, and the competitive environment

(success factors). Therefore, clarifying the information in the right-hand column of the GAPS grid is crucial to identifying which feedback is most important.

Begin the feedback discussion with a short exploration of the person's goals and values. This can include a range of values, interests, and priorities, such as money, family, learning, making a contribution, autonomy, status, helping others, and feeling like part of a team. If she is able to articulate and clarify what matters most to her, she can identify which feedback is most relevant to those priorities. The connection between feedback and important goals and values is the source of the most powerful motivation for development.

Next, discuss the success factors that are most important to others. This answers the question, "What does it take to be successful around here?" Success factors include formal elements of the job as well as the organization's informal norms and cultural values.

Third, get a snapshot of how the person views her own abilities. Each of these might take five to ten minutes, depending on how much time and information are available. If you discover gaping holes in her understanding of what is expected, help her devise a plan for filling in this critical information.

With the context established, examine the multisource feedback, connecting it to other GAPS information. As you work through the information, you can enhance insight by identifying, exploring, and validating themes or patterns in the data.

Even when the connection between perceptions and success factors is clear, people may not see its personal relevance. At such times it is crucial that you explicitly clarify the relationships between their behavior, its impact, and the personal consequences. Feedback often focuses just on behavior and its impact, such as "When you don't listen to people [behavior], they feel like you don't value their opinions [impact]." The personal *consequences* of that often need to be spelled out for people: "As a result, your colleagues are less likely to bring you important information, and they will be less motivated to help you. You will be cut off from valuable information, and you'll have a much harder time getting buy-in."

Not surprisingly, when people achieve new levels of insight and personal awareness as a result of the MSF experience, all parties may feel satisfied that the task has been completed. However, insight alone is never enough. What is required next is for the person to begin to transfer that insight back into his real-world work and life circumstances. This can be accomplished by having the person

- Describe what he learned in the session
- Capture the most important insights and themes
- State what implications those lessons have for his behavior at work
- Define a few small, simple steps he can take to begin doing things differently
- Make a commitment to thank everyone who provided feedback

- Plan to follow-up with people as needed to clarify the feedback and answer any questions
- Prepare to embark on the development process

After the Feedback

Since multisource feedback is just the beginning of the development process, take a few minutes to help people outline their plan for continuous learning and self-development. They may not yet know exactly what their development objectives will be, but you can offer them a roadmap for gathering additional GAPS information, defining high-priority objectives, and staying on the development path. The remainder of this chapter focuses on a practical approach to self-development and some of the tools that people can use along the way.

Helping People Embark on the Development Process

Jack Welch, CEO of General Electric during one of the most revolutionary organizational changes in contemporary business, anticipated the need for change and did something about it—before the need was apparent to others. His advice? "Change before you have to."

His perspective on business transformation is just as essential to personal transformation: look ahead and prepare yourself now, while you have the time. Don't wait for a crisis, because you won't have nearly enough time or bandwidth to learn then.

Helping people see the need for change now—while their world is stable and before the need is apparent to others—is a difficult element of being a practitioner. One place to start is by helping people look outside their organization: Where are customers or competitors raising the bar? Where are new competitive threats likely to come from? What new competencies might be important in responding to those changes? Help the person change before he has to.

Development Need Not Be a Solo Climb

Assistance and support can come from many sources: a coach, boss, colleague, human resource professional, or mentor, as well as various Websites on the Internet. Development partners may include anyone (or even a network of people, in any location) who cares about the person and is willing to contribute to her success. Help the person actively search for development partners who

- Have access to resources she can use
- Know other people who can help
- Are good at something the person wants to learn
- Can help her stay on track
- Can extend support and encouragement

As a practitioner you may fill many of these roles some of the time. It is important, however, to help the person broaden her network of development partners. Encourage her to enlist a manager or another sponsor inside their organization as well as colleagues outside the company. The emergence of the Internet has made geographic proximity less important than it used to be, so guide her in thinking broadly about who might offer assistance. She should also search for ways to connect to learning and development communities on the Web. Throughout the rest of this chapter, we present suggestions on how development partners can support the development process and be successfully leveraged by the person you are working with.

Development FIRST

A user-friendly roadmap is helpful on any journey into new territory. If you are already familiar with a well-established self-development process, share it with the people you are working with. Otherwise, consider the strategies outlined in *Development FIRST* (Peterson and Hicks, 1995) as a simple way to guide development and establish a cycle of continuous learning:

1. *Focus* on priorities: identify the critical issues and development objectives.
2. *Implement* something every day: stretch the comfort zone.
3. *Reflect* on what happens: extract maximum learning from experience.
4. *Seek* feedback and support: learn from others' ideas and perspectives.

5. *Transfer* learning to the next level: adapt and plan for continued learning.

Other books that address self-development include *Deep Change*
(Quinn, 1996), *High Flyers* (McCall, 1998), *Learning as a Way of
Being* (Vaill, 1996), and *The Learning Edge* (Wick and Leon, 1993).

Focus on Priorities: Identify Critical Issues and Development Objectives

Development is most powerful when it fulfills two objectives:
enhancing the person's performance and making work more
meaningful and fulfilling. The development process starts with
identifying high-priority development targets that actually make a
difference in both of those objectives. Unfortunately, this first step
is often shortchanged. It is far too easy to choose the most self-
evident learning objectives, those aimed at acquiring new skills or
shoring up a distinct weakness. But such goals rarely afford a person the best leverage in achieving the results that matter most; thus
they often inspire little energy and commitment from either the
person or the organization.

The process of determining which development objectives
make the most difference requires information gathering, reflection, and analysis. MSF is only one piece of this process.

Contrary to conventional wisdom, people should not automatically choose to work on weaknesses. A person may improve a weakness that is not critical to job performance, thus guaranteeing a
negligible (or even negative) outcome. Sometimes the prospect of
working, once again, on perennial weaknesses leaves the person
frustrated and discouraged. There may be excellent reasons for
not cultivating these skills in the first place.

Instead of targeting their weaknesses, you can direct people to
start with these questions: "Where will development add the greatest value? What am I most willing to work on now?" Good answers
to these questions lead to development objectives and results that
people care about.

GAPS Analysis

The MSF process begins a GAPS analysis. To help people continue
to update their GAPS information, give them a GAPS grid and a

copy of the worksheets in *Development FIRST* (Peterson and Hicks, 1995). These tools can help them structure their GAPS exploration through regular self-reflection, discussions, and additional data and feedback, including multisource feedback.

Once they are given good information, have them examine it to find the greatest leverage for their development priorities. The first question is identifying development areas that can generate both personal and organizational payback. A second filter for choosing what to work on is a return on investment (ROI) analysis, which takes into account how much effort is required before one commits to a specific objective. For example, an *easy* development objective that generates a moderate payback has a decent ROI and may well be worth the effort, while a *difficult* objective with moderate payback may not.

A Plan for Development

With carefully chosen development priorities, the person is now in position to prepare a plan for development. Encourage him to prepare this plan as he would any other important project plan, leveraging his experience writing business or project plans. Many of the same elements are required: goals, time frames, action steps. Find a format that works for the person and that he will actually use to overcome obstacles and stay focused on development.

Once he has chosen specific objectives to work on, these questions can help him put the plan in action:

- What is the personal and organizational rationale that will keep me *motivated* to achieve each objective?
- What are the *new behaviors* that I plan to implement?
- What situations, people, or events will I use to *signal* that right now is the time to put my new behaviors into action? What cues will remind me to take small steps on my plan every day?
- How will I *reflect* on my learning experiences and consolidate what I've learned each day? How will I take stock at major milestones to reevaluate my goals and priorities?
- How will I *seek information* to measure my progress? How can I get ongoing feedback as well as at major milestones?
- What other *resources and opportunities* do I need in order to learn and apply my new behaviors (for example, mentors, advocates, training, books, and support)?

Helping Individuals Find Organizational Developmental Resources

At no time in history has access to information been as easy as it is today. By way of the Internet, anyone with a computer and a phone line has easy access to a wealth of pertinent information and resources. Chat rooms, virtual coaches, online training, subject matter experts, and myriad courses and books have become accessible, far beyond even the resources of the typical person's own manager and training department. What a relief! What power! Every person with access to the Internet can connect to the world of development opportunities and resources in just a few clicks of a mouse. Here are a few resources we recommend:

- Brainbench—http://brainbench.com
- Development Dimensions International (DDI), Opal— http://www.ddiworld.com/products/opal.asp
- Forum, Performance Compass—http://wwwforum.com/ perfcomp/index.htm
- McGraw-Hill, Harvard Managementor—http://www.hbsp. harvard.edu/hmmdemo/hmm/index.htm
- Personnel Decisions International (PDI), eAdvisor— http://developmentor.pdi-corp.com/eAdvisor/Lcdemo
- Strategic Management Group, CareerPoint—http://www. concepsys.com/careerpt/cpthome.html

In addition to Internet-based resources, most organizations offer a range of supports and tools:

- Training catalogs of workshops and classes
- Mentoring programs
- Enterprisewide online systems (such as PDI's DevelopMentor and eAdvisor, the Saba Systems Group dynamic learning software, and DDI's Opal software) that put the employee in touch with development advice, resources, and opportunities
- The organization's resource library, easily found through the human resource department or corporate university
- Resource and development guides, such as the *Successful Manager's Handbook* (Davis and others, 1996) and the *Successful Ex-*

ecutive's Handbook (Gebelein, Lee, Nelson-Neuhaus, and Sloan, 2000)
- Organizational leaders willing to meet with and share information, experiences, and stories
- Tuition reimbursement policies and continuing education programs

Because many people have been conditioned to equate development support with course offerings and books, few have taken a careful inventory of the range of development resources that are available to them. They are often pleasantly surprised when they look beyond traditional sources.

Implement Something Every Day: Stretch Your Comfort Zone

In Search of Excellence (1982), by Peters and Waterman, identified "a bias for action" as a prime characteristic of excellent organizations. There is a striking parallel in personal development. Even extensive feedback, planning, and information gathering does not enhance performance if people don't *do* something with it. In fact, most knowledge is useless until it is acted on. People often need new information and ideas as they develop, but lack of knowledge is rarely the most significant barrier to development; lack of action is.

You can instill a sense of urgency and build a bias for action by having the person search for ways to spend *five minutes a day on development*. In this regard, development is similar to physical exercise; short periods of regular exercise—twenty minutes of aerobic exercise every other day—quickly get you into shape. That's just five hours a month. If you waited until the last weekend of the month and spent those five hours in a concentrated burst of strenuous activity, you wouldn't grow fit. In fact, your body would probably suffer more than benefit. Similarly, one intensive training program each year, with no practice, reflection, or support back on the job rarely yields true developmental fitness. The easiest *and* most effective way to develop is to chip away at it in small, bite-sized pieces. Just five minutes a day, used wisely, makes a tremendous difference.

To help the person make development activity a regular part of his daily routine, guide him in focusing on situations with high-voltage change potential, where particular elements are present:

- High stakes, where he is directly responsible for the outcome and where success or failure make a visible difference
- Novelty, where the person is forced to think and act in new ways because he can't draw on what has worked in the past
- Challenge, where he must do more with less, or do it faster and better than ever before
- Interaction, where a person must work with or through people, particularly when he is working with others more skilled than he is, on a new team, or with a larger group than before

Help the person seize the opportunity of high-stakes situations. The next time he finds himself in a situation that is challenging, novel, and interactive, have him remind himself that this is his greatest opportunity to learn important lessons quickly!

Create an Opportunity

Since their time is in such short supply, work with people to link their learning with what they are already doing. A person probably faces a dozen opportunities each day to act more decisively, build better relationships, perform more effectively in meetings, or influence peers. Encourage the person to find time each morning to examine the development opportunities that are right in front of her, and identify one specific task that stretches the comfort zone that day. Here are some common situations and opportunities that emerge every day:

Leveraging a Strength

- Try a new angle: she can leverage solid writing skills by writing the first draft of work for her boss or someone else as part of a joint project.
- Add a new element: build on strong strategic abilities by paying attention to strategic issues in every decision, even those that appear to be very tactical ones.

Balance the Talent Portfolio

- Face the challenge that exists now: coach a difficult employee directly instead of passing the task to someone else.
- Address unresolved problems: work on planning and organizing skills by volunteering to spearhead a process improvement project.
- Find a need and fill it: strengthen leadership skills by championing a new idea or initiative.

Invest in the Future

- Do old things in new ways: take a new approach to something just for the sake of cultivating a sense of exploration, such as attempting a new way to run department meetings to see what can be done to make them more effective.
- Look for openings: scan the environment for events that can stimulate learning that goes beyond the scope of the present job. For example, she could volunteer to make a presentation on behalf of her boss or department, or simply ask to attend meetings where new topics are discussed.
- Walk a mile in someone's shoes: step back from the routine of work to determine how the issues look from other perspectives. Consider the perspective of a customer, someone from another department or function, or someone who is two levels higher in the organization. Have her ask herself what she would do if she were in the other person's place.

Take Intelligent Risks

Growth occurs when people are willing to venture into the unknown. If someone knows how he will fare before he starts, he isn't experimenting and is unlikely to learn much. The best way to learn is through taking intelligent risks—new behaviors with a reasonable chance for success, as well as a reasonable measure of doubt. This entails moving ahead in small steps that push a person into the unknown without taking him over the edge where the consequences of failure are too great.

When Thomas Edison reported, "I found five thousand ways not to make a light bulb," he exemplified the process of intelligent risk taking: systematically trying new things that have a reasonable but not certain chance of success. He wasn't foolhardy, but he persisted until he found what worked. Push those you work with to new solutions and learning by having them pursue unfamiliar paths.

Resources for Action: Helping People Act Now

As a practitioner, you can help people find resources that reinforce the notion of implementing something every day in small doses. Resource and reference guides that are designed for quick access and have a bias toward implementing new behavior now and within the context of the job appear to have the most appeal to people. These resources also seem to be a key ingredient in facilitating change. Here are examples of this type of resource:

- Clear, concise, action-oriented development suggestions as part of the MSF report
- Easily accessible handbooks and guides such as the *Successful Manager's Handbook* and *Successful Executive's Handbook*
- Online libraries of development content, such as DevelopMentor, eAdvisor, and the Saba Software System
- Online or real-time coaching support

Finally, an often overlooked yet potentially powerful resource for development is the performance appraisal and performance management system. In many organizations, development plan creation and implementation are an integral part of the performance appraisal and management system. If these systemwide expectations are not in place, you can enhance personal accountability and commitment by encouraging people to voluntarily make their development goals a measurable and tangible part of their performance plan.

Reflect on What Happens: Extract Maximum Learning from Experience

Development requires action, but action requires analysis and reflection if improvement is to be sustained. Reflection is focused, purposeful analysis of specific actions, not vague contemplation of fuzzy ideas. The purpose of reflection is threefold:

- To solidify insights and remember the lessons just learned.
- To identify the themes and patterns in what a person does over time. Only over time can someone see her progress, habits, and limits. Without identifying her own behavior patterns and examining what she can do differently, a person may end up with one year of experience ten times instead of ten years of experience.
- To question and challenge assumptions to make sure the person learns the right lessons and remains open to new learning.

Here are several questions that can help a person reflect in ways that solidify her lessons and guide her continued learning:

The Short View

- What can I learn from my developmental experience today?
- What worked, and why?
- What didn't work, and why?
- What do I want to do differently the next time I'm in a similar situation?

The Long View

- What are the patterns and trends over time?
- How does my current skill level compare with what it was when I started my development?
- How does my current skill level compare with my goal?
- What progress can I feel good about?

Seek Feedback and Support: Learn from Others' Ideas and Perspectives

Feedback from a variety of sources is critical not only when development is launched but throughout the course of the development process as well. After reflection, for example, people may need to gather more feedback to test their own perceptions, calibrate the effectiveness of their new behaviors, and discover new ways to continue building capabilities.

Encourage people to seek ongoing feedback in two ways. First, in the spirit of working on development in small steps, encourage people to ask short, focused questions of a wide range of people.

Walking out of a meeting, he might say, "I was really trying to keep the meeting on track. How did I do? What could I have done better?" This type of feedback and idea gathering should be done frequently, and handled in a casual, everyday tone.

Second, encourage people to involve one or two trusted colleagues who can help them periodically step back and gauge their progress. They might explain their developmental objectives and ask a colleague to watch for specific behaviors and signs of progress. For example, "Susan, I'd really appreciate your support on one of my development objectives. I'm trying to do a better job of keeping meetings on track. I tend to let people go off on tangents, and I want to rein them in quicker. I'd like to structure the meeting better, use a clearer agenda, and make sure that we bring issues to closure so that we don't have to rework the same topics in later meetings. I'm hoping you'll be willing to watch me and give me your thoughts."

Publicly sharing a goal is another powerful way to boost social support and motivation. For example, one of the authors decided to train to run a marathon even though his past workouts had never exceeded two miles. Knowing this goal was a stretch, and to prevent himself from backing out, he began sharing it with others. Soon, those he told began asking about the training and how it was going. To avoid embarrassment, the author had little choice but to pursue the goal—and he happily completed the marathon in a very respectable time.

Deep commitment to a challenging goal requires significant support. Encourage people to write down when and with whom they will share their goal and the kinds of support they would like from each. If a person receives feedback and support only through the MSF survey, or if others decide to offer it, the development process will probably fail. Long-term success and continuous learning require that people take the initiative to get the feedback and support they need regularly.

Transfer Learning to the Next Level: Adapt and Plan for Continued Learning

Periodically, as the person gathers feedback and reviews her progress, she will find that she has accomplished her current objectives. But there is little room for resting on laurels, of course, because learning is never complete. Each time objectives are met, the FIRST process is renewed, beginning with another GAPS analysis to identify the next development priority. Only through believing in the necessity of continuous learning, and the ongoing practice of sound development strategies, can people hope to satisfy the requirements of ever-changing goals and expectations.

Conclusion

Development has become a critical success factor in today's world. Feedback plays three powerful roles in development. New, surprising input from others can highlight a development need or convey the urgency of changing one's style, thus serving as a potent force in motivating development. Feedback from others also serves to focus a person's development efforts where they can bring the greatest value. As a guide and checkpoint for development progress, feedback is essential throughout the process.

Because feedback is such a powerful tool, it can often overload or demotivate people. To keep this dynamic in check, people should be encouraged to seek clearer and more accurate feedback on those things that matter most to them, and to keep the focus on learning and improvement, and on the ultimate goals of greater performance and more rewarding lives.

References

Davis, B. L., and others (eds.). *Successful Manager's Handbook.* Minneapolis: Personnel Decisions International, 1996.

Gebelein, S. H., Lee, D. G., Nelson-Neuhaus, K. J., and Sloan, E. B. (eds.). *Successful Executive's Handbook.* Minneapolis: Personnel Decisions International, 2000.

McCall, M. W., Jr. *High Flyers: Developing the Next Generation of Leaders.* Boston: Harvard Business School Press, 1998.

Peters, T. J., and Waterman, R. H. *In Search of Excellence.* New York: Harper-Collins, 1982.

Peterson, D. B., and Hicks, M. D. *Development FIRST: Strategies for Self-Development.* Minneapolis: Personnel Decisions International, 1995.

Peterson, D. B., and Hicks, M. D. *Leader as Coach: Strategies for Coaching and Developing Others.* Minneapolis: Personnel Decisions International, 1996.

Quinn, R. E. *Deep Change: Discovering the Leader Within.* San Francisco: Jossey-Bass, 1996.

Vaill, P. B. *Learning as a Way of Being: Strategies for Survival in a World of Permanent White Water.* San Francisco: Jossey-Bass, 1996.

Wick, C. W., and Leon, L. S. *The Learning Edge: How Smart Managers and Smart Companies Stay Ahead.* New York: McGraw-Hill, 1993.

CHAPTER 15

How Do Users React to Multisource Feedback?

Mark R. Edwards
Ann J. Ewen
Kiran Vendantam

User reaction examines how users respond to the multisource feedback (MSF) process, including how they

- Perceive the process
- Feel about cultural issues such as receiving feedback from direct reports
- Believe the MSF process met its stated objectives
- Feel about such structural issues as the associated technology, respondent anonymity, safeguards, and appropriate confidentiality of the MSF results

The assessment of user satisfaction reported here examines aggregate satisfaction across user groups in many companies. It does not examine how individuals reacted to their MSF data. London offers an excellent summary of individual reactions to feedback (1997). Yammarino and Atwater have summarized self-other perceptions and reactions (1997).

Measuring user reactions offers the key to the acceptance and future viability of the MSF process. Our research indicates many

The authors wish to thank Karen Bruggeman for her excellent work in extracting and analyzing the data.

organizations expend all their energy on MSF process development, including development of the competency model, and have nothing left over for process evaluation. For example, the TEAMS 1998 MSF industry survey indicated that fewer than 16 percent of organizations using MSF employed a structured process to collect data on process effectiveness.

Criticality of User Reactions

User reactions serve a critical purpose because they

- Answer the most important question: How did users (leaders and individual contributors) react to the MSF process?
- Provide intelligence that supports successful rollout of the MSF process to a broader segment of the organization
- Identify which process elements need to be improved
- Identify remaining obstacles to organizational acceptance of the MSF process
- Share important communication about process success in meeting MSF objectives
- Set the stage for wider use of the MSF data, such as for performance management
- Build organizational justification to continue the MSF process
- Create documentation for legal defensibility associated with fairness, accuracy, and credibility

Without a systematic user evaluation of the MSF process, the organization must rely on anecdotal information or insight from a few people who come forward with observations. Such information naturally represents the two extremes: people who adore the process and people who think it stinks. Failing a structured process assessment, organizations get confused in determining what is noise and what is signal. Noise comes from one or a few highly vocal or powerful people. A signal comes from the consensus of those who use the MSF process.

The critical questions have less to do with liking, and more to do with the degree to which the MSF process met organizational objectives. Probably the most important information collected from the postproject evaluation is what concerns people have and how to make the process more effective.

Three Metrics of User Reactions

Three effective approaches to creating metrics of user reactions are (1) a simply open-ended question to users, (2) a targeted survey of users, and (3) analysis based on project objections. Let us look at each method in turn.

Method One: Litmus Test

Some organizations conduct an MSF pilot and then ask users—those who provided and received feedback—their feelings about MSF. User reactions are defined by asking, "How do users, those who provided feedback and who received feedback, perceive the MSF process?"

This global open-ended question elicits "top of mind" insight into user feelings about the process. The basic question may be presented to users through a quick survey or simply through interviews, staff meetings, or focus groups.

Method Two: User Survey

Other organizations use a structured MSF process evaluation survey that may include the following sample constructs (Edwards and Ewen, 1996a).

Evaluating the MSF Process

1. It provides useful information ("The MSF process produces useful information I can use to develop myself in my job").
2. It motivates ("The MSF process motivates me to increase my effectiveness").
3. The process is fair ("The MSF process provides fair behavior feedback").
4. The results can be trusted ("The results are credible to me").
5. The results are accurate ("This process reflects an accurate assessment of important behaviors that affect my performance on the job").
6. It provides safeguards ("I believe the MSF process provides safeguards that lessen the effects of politics, biases, and favoritism in determining my rating").

7. Evaluation forms are simple to complete ("The evaluation forms are simple and easy to complete").
8. The reports are understandable ("The behavior feedback reports are clear to me").
9. Reports are confidential ("I believe my reports were kept confidential").
10. Ratings are anonymous ("I believe my ratings of others were anonymous").
11. The feedback receiver should select the evaluation team ("I think each participant should select his or her own evaluation team").
12. Pretraining helps ("The training helped me understand how to provide accurate feedback for others and what was expected of me during the MSF process").
13. Posttraining helps ("This training helped me understand how I might react to the reports, how to read my reports, and how to develop an action plan").
14. Time is used efficiently ("Overall, this process was an efficient use of my time").
15. The process improves communications ("I believe this process will improve communication with my coworkers, manager, and customers").
16. Continued use is recommended ("With some modifications, I recommend continued use of this process").

A series of open-ended constructs such as those that follow are designed to elicit user reactions on a broader set of issues.

17. What would you like to *change* most in the MSF process?
_____
_____

18. What are the *strongest* aspects of the MSF process?
_____
_____

19. What are the *weakest* aspects of the MSF process?
_____
_____

20. Overall, I prefer to receive feedback from:
___ My supervisor only
___ My coworkers only
___ Both my supervisor and my coworkers

Why?

_____

_____

21. In the future, how should the MSF data be used?
    ___ Only for individual development
    ___ For development and as an input to performance
    management
    Why?

    _____

    _____

Method Three: Process Objectives

A strong method for process evaluation is to turn the MSF process objectives into questions. Assume process objectives included fairness, accuracy, simplicity, trustworthiness, and speed. For example, question fifteen in the preceding list inquires about whether the MSF process meets the objective of improving communications.

Process Evaluation Historical Findings

TEAMS International has conducted several hundred MSF process evaluations with clients because process evaluation is built into the process design. The results give valuable insight into MSF systems. However, they may not generalize to less sophisticated MSF processes because the projects reported in this research all followed a standard protocol. This scientific approach included user pretraining and posttraining, a formal communications plan, strong user participation in process design and policies, and extensive process and technology safeguards (Edwards and Ewen, 1996b).

A composite from sixteen MSF projects from 1987 to 1989, representing some 1,477 individuals who both received feedback and returned a process evaluation, indicated generally positive perceptions of MSF, as shown in Figure 15.1.

These data include MSF projects from the 1980s with user response rates over 40 percent for four regulated, four public sector, and eight industrial companies. Note that question number two in Figure 15.1 is reverse scored.

These user evaluations showed no difference in satisfaction for subjects who received higher MSF ratings, which was contrary to

**Figure 15.1. MSF Process Assessment
Across Sixteen Projects.**

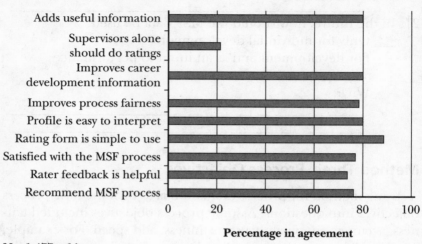

Percentage in agreement

N = 1,477 subjects

Source: M. R. Edwards, "Sustaining Culture Change with Multiple-Rater Systems for Career Development and Performance Appraisal Systems." In R. Bellingham, B. Cohen, M. R. Edwards, and J. Allen (eds.), *The Corporate Culture Sourcebook.* Amherst, Mass.: Human Resource Development Press, 1990, p. 201. Used with permission.

expectation. Younger participants tended to be more positive than older ones, which helps explain why many organizations have trouble convincing their executive staff that MSF offers value. Other researchers in the 1980s reported user support for a single project as being over 90 percent (McEvoy, Butler, and Roghaar, 1989). Unfortunately, the MSF project at Schneier Foods, the subject of the case discussion, ended after two years.

Process Evaluation Recent Findings

Postproject evaluations in the 1990s, although slightly more positive, correspond fairly closely to project evaluations in the 1980s. The standard set of process-evaluation questions used by TEAMS changed in 1993, but the basic constructs associated with fairness, accuracy, simplicity, trustworthiness, and process speed have been retained. Project evaluation results across fifty-nine MSF projects during 1996 and 1997 follow and represent more than twenty thousand individuals or feedback receivers. The data set initially contained ninety-nine sequential project evaluations, but forty projects were eliminated because in each case the project met one or more disqualifying criteria:

- Trivial (fewer than thirty subjects in a pilot project)
- Executive only (executives may not be representative of their organizations)
- Small process-assessment sample (low response rate for overall population—less than 25 percent)
- Confidentiality requirements (absolute data confidentiality must be ensured for the client, even for aggregated research purposes)

The forty projects were eliminated from the data set because these factors may cause the projects to underrepresent the larger organizations in which the projects occurred. Analysis of the forty eliminated projects indicated similar results, although overall agreement was about 6 percent lower.

It is critical to note that these MSF projects followed a standard protocol that included user pretraining and posttraining, a communications plan, absolute respondent anonymity, and process and technology safeguards (Edwards and Ewen, 1996a). These data do not generalize to informal or nonscientific MSF projects. The projects followed the guidelines suggested in the Appendix of this handbook.

This analysis selected the eight process-evaluation dimensions reported below from a set of about sixteen used in a majority of the user-satisfaction surveys. These dimensions were discussed in the prior section of postprocess analysis headed "Method Two: User Surveys."

Analysis found that the first item, "The MSF process provides useful results" is a surrogate measure for the other dimensions. Hence, this question was used to explore MSF project differences. The other evaluation dimensions were proportional and yielded essentially similar results.

Strongest Aspects: Anonymous, Motivational, and Fair

Across all fifty-nine projects, highest user satisfaction occurred for "Ratings are anonymous," "Motivates me," and "Process is fair." The lowest user satisfaction occurred for "Efficient use of time." There was modest variation across industries; for example, "Efficient use of time" showed more than 90 percent agreement in pharmaceuticals and about 74 percent agreement in manufacturing. However, on a relative basis, items such as "Motivates me," "The process is fair," "Trust the results," and "Simple to use" were toward the middle of the satisfaction distribution for nearly all industries (see Figure 15.2).

The positive user perception that "Ratings are anonymous" is contrary to expectation because a large number of these projects, about half, used software installed on site to run their MSF data. Several vendors sell MSF service bureau business with the argument that only off-site scoring and reporting creates the perception of respondent anonymity. These data indicate that respondent

**Figure 15.2. MSF Process Assessments Results
for Fifty-Nine Projects, 1997 to 1998.**

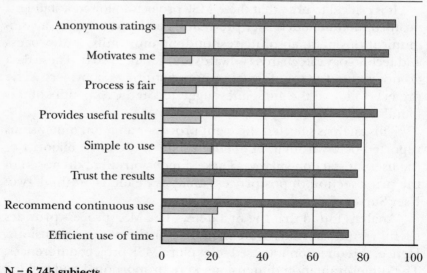

N = 6,745 subjects

■ Agree   □ Disagree

anonymity can be sustained when the organization runs its own data on site with secure software.

Even though these results are generally positive, the average project reported here shows slightly less than 80 percent user support for "Recommend continued use." However, if the public sector projects are removed, as shown in the results by industry section, overall user satisfaction increases substantially (see Figure 15.3).

Figure 15.3. MSF Project Assessments Recommended Continued Use by Industry, 1996 to 1997.

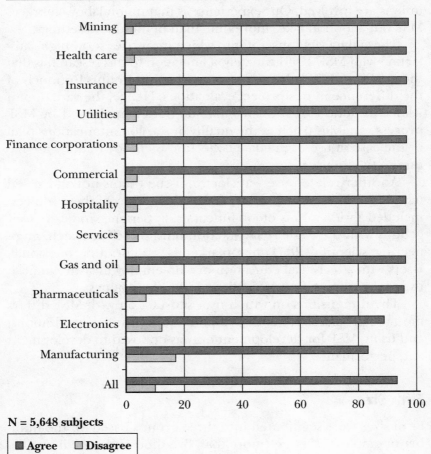

N = 5,648 subjects

■ Agree □ Disagree

Note: Each industry included at least three MSF projects. Public sector projects were not included as an industry.

Results by Industry

The results by industry indicate that MSF seems to be best received in mining, health care, and insurance. Results by industry show user satisfaction above 90 percent for all industries except electronics and manufacturing. This finding may be influenced by the fact that several electronics and manufacturing projects included a large segment of hourly labor in the MSF projects. Although these data did not break out hourly versus salaried groups, other project analysis has shown that the hourly labor force may be slower to adopt MSF. The hourly labor effect becomes magnified where unions are involved. Our experience is that union labor embraces MSF but adoption takes more time than in nonunion settings.

These data yield insight into which industries show high satisfaction with MSF. Unfortunately, a limitation to this research is that the quality in MSF administration probably accounts for much of the difference in postproject evaluations. Hence, the variation of user-satisfaction by industry may be better explained by MSF process variables (such as the quality of the communications plan or the ease of use of the data-collection method) than by the nature of the industry.

Another related user-satisfaction issue that is not addressed here is user demographics by job function. Many of these projects included a wide variety of job functions. Experience indicates user groups with the highest satisfaction tend to be high-tech, engineering, scientific, R&D units, marketing, and health professional. Users with a technical education or who employ measurement in their jobs seem to find MSF aligned with their values.

The dimensions on which user satisfaction with MSF differs most are project size, public compared with private organizations, and using MSF for development only as opposed to development and performance.

Firm Size

Firm sizes were segmented into three groups based on the number of employees: large (more than five thousand), medium (between two hundred and five thousand), and small (less than two hundred). The data (see Figure 15.4) indicate a modest inverse relationship between firm size and user satisfaction. Covariance, such as more large organizations from public sector organizations, does not seem to account for this variation. It may be that smaller firms have better communications and user training than larger ones. However, we have no theory to explain an effect based on firm size.

Firm size does not correspond to project size because several large organizations completed relatively small MSF projects.

Public and Private

The lower user-satisfaction rates for public MSF processes may be due to several reasons (see Figure 15.5).

Figure 15.4. "MSF Provides Useful Results" by Firm Size.

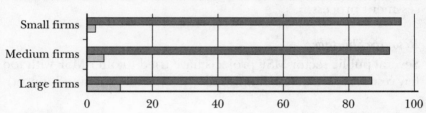

N = 5,648 Subjects

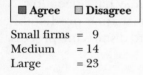

Small firms = 9
Medium = 14
Large = 23

**Figure 15.5. "MSF Provides Useful Results"
by Public or Private Sector.**

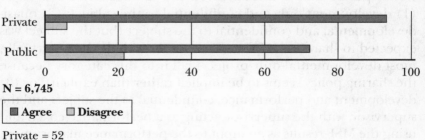

N = 6,745

Private = 52
Public = 7

Prior Satisfaction

Premeasures of satisfaction with performance feedback and appraisal processes in public sector organizations tend to be lower than private, often by 20 to 40 percent. Hence, MSF processes in public sector organizations need larger change scores to create the same levels of MSF user satisfaction as the private sector. The change score that compares the old single-source process with the new MSF process may be a better metric for public organizations than simply a postmeasure of user satisfaction.

History

Some public sector organizations have a history of either no appraisal or a very weak feedback process. Even when MSF is used as a developmental tool, it represents a substantial change in the assessment process.

Resource Shortage

Several public sector MSF projects have tried to offer MSF with too few resources (such as administrative people and training support).

Accountability

Accountability in some public organizations may have been low. A MSF process that acts to identify nonperformance predictably causes some organizational members to want to dismiss the process.

Use of Data

The most interesting finding in this data set was how the MSF data were used (see Figure 15.6).

The classifications in Figure 15.6 were based on the organizational policy that communicated the data as intended to be (1) development only and confidential to the subject; (2) quasi-developmental and confidential to the subject (but the subject was expected to share some form of the results with the boss—actually, most developmental-only projects fall into this category because the sharing policy seems to be implicit rather than explicit); or (3) development and performance, confidential to the subject and the supervisor, with the supervisor acting as a performance coach and using the MSF results as an input to the performance management process.

**Figure 15.6. "MSF Provides Useful Results"
by How the Data Were Used.**

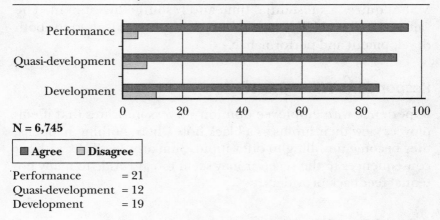

N = 6,745

☑ **Agree** ☐ **Disagree**

Performance   = 21
Quasi-development = 12
Development   = 19

Insights

The slightly higher MSF user satisfaction for performance projects, compared with those purely for development, may have occurred by chance. For example, if several public sector developmental-only projects were excluded, there was no difference. However, the data are reported here because the results were unexpected. If other research supports these counterintuitive findings, it may be that the effect occurs because of insights gained from focus groups, interviews, and staff meetings from various types of projects.

Integration

MSF used as an input to performance allows organizations to enhance procedural justice in processes that were dominated by single-source or exclusive sets of decision makers (such as selection, opportunities for training and development, placement, appraisals, and promotions).

No Accountability

If feedback rests entirely with the feedback receiver, no accountability exists for behavioral change.

Value-Added

MSF requires a substantial time and resource investment. The value-added for MSF is maximized if the process is used for both development and performance.

Respondent Willingness

Experience with employee opinion surveys indicates that if employees view their inputs as a black hole where nothing happens, they become unwilling to offer input. Similarly, feedback without consequences to the receiver may seem too altruistic to many potential feedback providers.

Sustain Two Processes

Many organizational members are annoyed at the requirement to sustain two assessment processes, one purely for development and one for development and performance. Few organizations find two systems to be sustainable beyond a few years.

Waste Avoidance or Greed

Even if some people in the organization want purely developmental MSF, many others do not want to waste what they view as high-value measures of human capital. In some organizations, MSF offers the highest-credibility data available on performance and potential. Organizational members, especially leaders, are reluctant to waste the best available information about people.

Artifacts

Data artifacts may also play a role in the slightly higher satisfaction scores for MSF performance projects. Many organizations first pilot MSF with a developmental-only theme. By the time the organization migrates to performance applications, the bugs should have been worked out of the MSF process. These data across the projects *exclude* small initial pilots because they underrepresent an organizational consensus and are too easily influenced by the Hawthorne effect.

This data set included only one organization that migrated from development to performance and then back to development. User satisfaction improved nearly 10 percent when they migrated from development to performance. Not only did the user satisfaction drop 13 percent when MSF was repositioned as development only but response rates fell from 94 percent to about 73 percent. Predictably, the MSF process was dropped the following year for lack of support.

Observations

The experience of collecting and analyzing these data offers a few underlying summary observations (see Table 15.1).

Most of these data were not coded for demographics. However, general observations about users who tended to be highly satisfied with MSF revealed them to be younger, better educated, and newer to the organization, but not necessarily better performers. Anticipated differences in user satisfaction that we have not seen include differences by gender, ethnicity, organization level, and leader status.

Table 15.1. Summary of MSF User Reactions.

Tend to Be Higher When Users . . .	Tend to Be Lower When Users . . .
Are trained before and after process	Are in a low-trust culture
Are clear about process objectives, especially data confidentiality and use	Are not given clear communications about why the organization is using MSF
Are involved in creating the MSF process and the associated policies	Are pushed into MSF as a quick fix
Understand the process and technology safeguards such as anonymity	Are worried about other people "gaming the system" and gaining unfair advantage
Have a stated need for better career development or performance information	Are required to complete long instruments
Are experienced in the MSF process	Are not aware of "what's in it for them"

Future Research

What we know about user reaction represents a fraction of what is needed to sustain development and implementation of MSF. The practical action of measuring MSF readiness and even user satisfaction exceeds the energy and resource levels of many organizations. We see a need for critical inquiry in each area, including investigation of these questions:

1. Why do so few organizations evaluate their MSF process?
2. What other leverage factors are critical for successful MSF process, beyond fairness, accuracy, simplicity, credibility, and process speed?
3. What other factors, beyond those addressed here, associate with user satisfaction?
4. Do user evaluations predict the shelf life or longevity of MSF systems?

These and many other questions need answers.

Summary

Measuring user reactions is not only hard but sometimes dangerous. We have never seen a pilot MSF system where users did not identify some needed change. These recommendations often scare MSF project managers and executives. Yet user reactions are the key to future success and to sustaining the process. Unfortunately, fewer than one out of five organizations currently include a structured process-evaluation segment as part of developing and implementing their MSF process.

For organizations to consistently gauge user reactions, it will be necessary to build project evaluation into the MSF process. Advanced, automated MSF software systems offer this feature and make it easy and fast. However, organizational leaders still need the courage to query user satisfaction. Measuring the value-added from the MSF process by creating these metrics will move MSF systems from a "nice to do" process to a "mission critical" one.

References

Edwards, M. R., and Ewen, A. J. *Providing 360-Degree Feedback: An Approach to Enhancing Individual and Organizational Performance.* Scottsdale, Ariz.: American Compensation Association, 1996a.

Edwards, M. R., and Ewen, A. J. *360-Degree Feedback: The Powerful New Model for Employee Assessment and Performance Management.* New York: AMACOM, 1996b.

London, M. *Job Feedback: Giving, Seeking, and Using Feedback for Performance Improvement.* Mahwah, N.J.: LEA, 1997.

McEvoy, G. M., Butler, P. F., and Roghaar, S. R. "A Jury of One's Peers." *Personnel Administrator,* 1988, *33*(5), 94–101.

Yammarino, F. J., and Atwater, L. E. "Do Managers See Themselves as Others See Them? Implications of Self-Other Rating Agreement for Human Resource Management." *Organizational Dynamics,* 1997, *25*(4), 35–44.

CHAPTER 16

Measuring the Impact of Multisource Feedback

James W. Smither
Alan G. Walker

In this chapter, we focus on the impact of multisource feedback (MSF). Specifically, how can practitioners evaluate whether the introduction of an MSF program has achieved the intended impact for the participants and organization?

It is worth noting that MSF programs may sometimes be used to determine whether a developmental intervention (for a manager or an organization) is needed (and, if so, to direct attention to the precise skills and behaviors that need to be developed). Multisource feedback can also be used to evaluate the impact of other developmental interventions (such as developmental assignments, a mentoring relationship, or off-site education or training courses). But our focus in this chapter is more limited; we ask whether MSF programs achieve their intended impact.

We have observed many reasons for introducing an MSF program. At one company, results from the employee opinion survey and employee focus groups revealed that employees felt managers did not seek or listen to their input. The company introduced an upward feedback program as one of several approaches to addressing this concern.

Another company identified key characteristics of its high-performing competitors. The company realized that it lagged competitors on several of these characteristics. Numerous efforts were undertaken to focus everyone's attention on characteristics where the company needed to improve performance (for example, having a pervasive growth mind-set, global focus, and improved cycle time). The company also implemented an MSF program that assessed managers on these key characteristics.

A third company sought to change its culture—to become less hierarchical and more team-based. The company introduced MSF to emphasize the importance of upward and peer feedback in the new culture they hoped to create.

Although different goals led each of these companies to introduce an MSF program, they all have one thing in common. In each case, individual behavior change was a prerequisite for improved organizational performance.

One framework that can be used to consider the impact of MSF is Kirkpatrick's well-known description (1983) of four types of criteria: reactions, learning, behavior, and organizational results. Edwards and Ewen (see Chapter Fifteen) offer an excellent discussion of participant reactions to MSF. Our primary focus is therefore on whether individuals who receive MSF change their behavior in desired ways (that is, behavior criteria). We also discuss linkage research (results criteria) and describe some of the difficulties that organizations face in attempting to determine whether MSF or development interventions cause changes in such key metrics as customer retention or organizational productivity and profitability.

The Problems of Measuring Change

At first glance, measuring change seems relatively straightforward. For example, why not simply compare the feedback a manager received at time 1 (the first administration of an MSF program) with the feedback the manager receives at time 2 (the second administration of the program, perhaps six or twelve months later)? If the manager's scores go up, then the manager's performance has improved. If the manager's scores go down, then the manager's performance has declined. If there is no change in the manager's scores, then the manager's performance has not changed.

Although much has been written about measuring change (it is far beyond the scope of this chapter to include a how-to recipe for practitioners concerning the numerous research and statistical approaches that are available), there are several potential problems with such a (deceptively) simple approach. The first has been called response-shift bias. A second problem is regression to the mean. A third problem is created by ceiling effects. A fourth problem involves using difference scores. Let us discuss each of these briefly.

Response-Shift Bias

Our summary of response-shift bias is taken from an excellent and practitioner-friendly discussion by Martineau (1998). Consider a manager who completes an MSF process before starting an off-site executive development program. One item asks the manager to rate her own "empowerment" skills. The manager knows that she often delegates work and encourages people to make their own decisions, so she gives herself a rating of 6 (on a scale of 1 = low to 7 = high). During the executive development program, she learns that empowerment is much more than simply delegating and encouraging people to make their own decisions. For example, she learns that empowerment also involves concepts such as self-efficacy, self-determination, personal control, and trust. It includes fostering personal mastery by giving people the opportunity to accomplish successively more difficult tasks, helping them work with others who can serve as coaches or mentors, extending support and resources, organizing teams, sharing information widely, etc. After the program, the manager sets some goals and makes some clear, noticeable progress in this area. When it is time to rate herself again, she does so based on what she has learned about empowerment. She gives herself a rating of 5 on the same 1-to-7 scale.

In this example, the manager actually improves her behavior as a result of the executive development program, but her self-rating declines. To understand response-shift bias, we need to consider three types of change: alpha, beta, and gamma.

Alpha change refers to real or true change. It's what we hope to capture when we evaluate the impact of MSF programs. In our example, the manager improves her empowerment skills after participating in the executive development program.

Beta change occurs when the respondent subjectively recalibrates the rating scale between time 1 and time 2. For example, I may initially rate a colleague's conflict management skills as 4 (average on our 1-to-7 scale) before I participate in a company-sponsored workshop on conflict management. After the workshop, I might rate my colleague's conflict management skills as 3 on the same scale. My colleague's conflict management skills have not changed, but my expectations have changed. Behaviors that I would have rated as 4 before attending the workshop, I now rate as only a 3.

Gamma change occurs when the rater reconceptualizes the construct we are measuring. For example, our manager changes her understanding of what it means to create an empowered work-team. Before the executive development program, she thought empowerment was about delegation and encouraging people to make their own decisions. She thought she was pretty good in these two areas and gave herself a rating of 6. After the executive development program, she realizes that empowerment is a much more complex skill than she previously thought. Although she makes some real improvements in this area, she now recognizes several aspects of empowerment-related behaviors where she needs to improve, so she gives herself a rating of 5.

Response-shift bias is most commonly observed with self-report data (for example, self-ratings on an MSF instrument). Less is known about the extent to which response-shift bias affects ratings from others, but there is no reason to assume that ratings from others are immune to it. Response-shift bias is also a feature of research designs where time 1 ratings (pretest) are compared with time 2 ratings (posttest).

Several approaches to dealing with response-shift bias have been suggested. One approach is to use retrospective pretests. For example, raters are asked to make two ratings at time 2. The first rating asks the rater to evaluate retrospectively the effectiveness of the person's behavior at time 1. The second rating asks the rater to evaluate the effectiveness of the person's behavior now (at time 2). The same rating scale and anchors are used to guide both ratings. Because both ratings are made at the same time, beta and gamma change are minimized.

Another approach to deal with response-shift bias involves using a retrospective degree-of-change rating. In this approach, change is assessed directly rather than being inferred from a comparison of pretest and posttest (time 1 versus time 2) scores. For example, at time 2, raters can be asked to rate the person's current level of effectiveness (from 1 = low to 4 = average to 7 = high) and rate the degree of change that has taken place (from 1 = no change to 4 = moderate change to 7 = great change).

Figure 16.1 presents a simple rating scale that the first author has used to gather retrospective degree-of-change ratings.

Goldsmith and Underhill (see Chapter Seventeen) present a similar questionnaire that directly assesses whether managers have become more or less effective since receiving MSF. Martineau describes several studies that found retrospective pretests or retrospective degree-of-change ratings yielded more accurate representations of change than did traditional pretests (such as comparing time 1 and time 2 ratings).

Regression to the Mean

Consider a company that implements an MSF program. The company selects the 10 percent of its managers who received the least-favorable feedback and sends them to a special development program. Six months later, the company readministers the MSF only for these managers and discovers that their ratings have, on average, improved noticeably. The company declares its special development program to be a success.

In this example, the improved ratings among these managers (who initially scored very poorly) could be due to regression to the mean rather than to real behavior change and improvement. Regression to the mean is observed on any measure that is less than perfectly reliable (that is, as determined by test-retest reliability, not internal consistency). If a measure is perfectly reliable, there will be no regression to the mean. The less reliable a measure is, the more regression to the mean occurs.

Figure 16.1. Sample Scale for Measuring Retrospective Change.

Circle the number that best reflects the extent to which this individual's behavior has changed with respect to this skill.

Declined Substantially	Declined Moderately	Declined Slightly	No Change	Improved Slightly	Improved Moderately	Improved Substantially
1	2	3	4	5	6	7

One consequence of regression to the mean is that those who score very high on the first administration of a somewhat unreliable measure are likely to score somewhat lower on a second administration of the measure. Similarly, those who score very low on the first administration of a somewhat unreliable measure are likely to score somewhat higher on a second administration of the measure.

Because MSF instruments are less than perfectly reliable, the "scores" that managers receive when rated by their coworkers are subject to regression to the mean.

Several studies, described later in this chapter, have addressed this issue by first estimating the test-retest reliability of the MSF instrument. The reliability of the instrument was then used to estimate how much low scores will increase (or high scores will decrease) solely because of regression to the mean. In these studies, only improvements beyond what could be expected because of regression to the mean are considered worthy of attention. (See Smither and others, 1995, for technical details.)

Ceiling Effect

Consider a manager who receives an average rating from coworkers of 4.7 on a rating scale of 1 (low) to 5 (high). A second manager receives an average rating from coworkers of 3.0. On a second administration of the MSF instrument, the first manager again receives an average rating of 4.7, while the second manager receives an average rating of 3.5. Apparently, the first manager has not improved, while the second manager has done so.

This is an example of where the ceiling effect may mask real improvement. Stated differently, the first manager has very little room to improve on the 5-point rating scale (most raters are already giving the manager a rating of 5), whereas the second manager has much more room to improve. It is possible that the first manager improves but it is not detected due to the ceiling effect. Dalessio (1998) indicates that MSF applications tend to use rating scales ranging from four to seven points. But we do not know whether using more rating points (say, 7 rather than 5) allows us to better detect modest changes in behavior (or lessen the impact of the ceiling effect) or whether doing so merely creates more noise (unreliability) in the ratings.

Retrospective degree-of-change ratings (described earlier) offer a simple way to detect improvement, even among managers who initially receive ratings near the top of the rating scale. One final caveat: it has been our experience that some companies are reluctant to use retrospective pretests or retrospective degree-of-change ratings (despite what we thought were compelling arguments to do so). For example, a company may be legitimately concerned that retrospective pretests require raters to rate each item twice at time 2. This may explain why virtually all of the published research we describe later compares time 1 and time 2 ratings to assess the impact of MSF programs.

Difference Scores

Some people have proposed that the difference between self-ratings and ratings from others should be related to subsequent performance change. For example, a manager who overrates himself (relative to ratings provided by coworkers) may be more motivated to improve than a manager who underrates herself. The use of difference scores as predictors (as in the previous example) or as criteria (for example, the difference between year 2 and year 1 ratings as a measure of improvement over time) has been widely criticized, for a host of reasons. Edwards (1995) offers more detail and describes using polynomial regression analysis as an approach to avoid the statistical difficulties created by using difference scores (see also Johnson and Ferstl, 1999).

What We Know So Far

Next, we review studies that have examined the impact of MSF. Nearly all research to date has examined the impact of upward feedback (from subordinates).

Hegarty (1974) looked at fifty-six supervisors of staff employees at the University of North Carolina. Supervisors were rated by subordinates and assigned at random to one of two groups, one group receiving subordinate feedback and the other not. The researchers held a sixty-to-ninety-minute session with each supervisor who received feedback to go over the supervisor's feedback report. Hegarty found that subordinates perceived performance improvement (ten weeks later) among supervisors who received upward feedback, whereas subordinates did not perceive any improvement among supervisors who did not receive upward feedback.

Another study (Hazucha, Hezlett, and Schneider, 1993) found skill increases and higher self-coworker agreement among managers at a large Midwestern utility company two years after receiving multisource feedback. However, only 48 of the original 198 managers who initially received feedback volunteered to participate in the follow-up two years later, thus raising the question of whether changes among the 48 managers were representative of changes in the larger sample that initially received feedback.

In a study of MSF for 48 assistant store managers in a retail clothing chain, Bernardin, Hagan, Ross, and Kane (1995) found that subordinate ratings (upward feedback) increased over time.

Smither and others (1995) examined upward feedback given to 238 managers in the international operations division of a large organization at two points in time about six months apart. The managers represented all parts of the organization (including finance, human resources, international marketing support, and regional operations); 71 percent were based in the United States while the remainder were in Europe, Asia, or Central and South America. Most (81 percent) were U.S. citizens. Feedback was collected using a thirty-three-item survey developed with input from internal subject matter experts. Results indicated that managers whose initial feedback scores were moderate or low improved over the six-month period, and the improvement could not be attributed solely to regression to the mean. Reilly, Smither, and Vasilopoulos (1996) extended the study by Smither and colleagues (1995) by following 171 of the original 238 managers for a third administration of the upward feedback questionnaire, and 92 of the managers for a fourth administration two and a half years later. They found that managers whose initial feedback scores were low sustained their performance improvements over the later administrations.

Atwater, Roush, and Fischthal (1995) looked at follower ratings of 978 student leaders at the U.S. Naval Academy (for example, juniors modeling leadership to freshmen regarding military protocol, assisting with academics, and setting an example of appropriate military leadership). They found that follower ratings improved after upward feedback was given to leaders. They also found that leaders receiving "negative" feedback (defined as those for whom follower ratings were substantially below self-ratings) improved the most.

A study by Johnson and Ferstl (1999) collected self-ratings and subordinate ratings from 1,888 managers of a large accounting firm at two points in time one year apart. These authors found that managers who overrated themselves relative to how others rated them tended to improve their performance from one year to the next (this effect was observed over the entire range of initial scores), and underraters tended to decline.

Atwater, Waldman, Atwater, and Cartier (2000) collected upward feedback ratings for supervisors from a state police agency. Supervisors were randomly assigned to one of three conditions. In the first (the feedback condition, $n = 53$), supervisors rated themselves and were rated by their subordinates at two time periods (time 1 and time 2) separated by ten months. These supervisors received feedback (self-ratings and averaged subordinate ratings on each item) at time 1 and time 2. In a second condition (survey only, $n = 43$), supervisors rated themselves and were rated by their subordinates at two time periods (time 1 and time 2). These supervisors only received feedback at time 2. In a third condition (control, $n = 61$), supervisors rated themselves and were rated by their subordinates only at time 2. These supervisors received feedback at time 2.

There was improvement from time 1 to time 2 for supervisors in the feedback condition, but none for supervisors in the survey-only condition. Also, among supervisors who received feedback at time 1, those who were cynical about organizational change at time 1 were less likely to improve from time 1 to time 2 than those less cynical. Supervisors' acceptance of the feedback (as shown, for example, by belief that feedback was honest and valuable and led to goal setting) was positively related to improvement over time. Finally, receiving relatively favorable feedback from subordinates at time 1 increased supervisors' level of commitment to their subordinates at time 2; and receiving relatively unfavorable feedback from subordinates at time 1 decreased supervisors' level of commitment to their subordinates at time 2.

A Case Study of Reactions, Behavior, and Results

Walker and Smither (1999) followed 252 managers from a regional bank over five annual administrations of an upward feedback program. Here we describe their findings along with other results from analyses conducted by Walker and colleagues.

The organization implemented a development-focused upward feedback program in 1991 as part of a major organizational development effort. In this setting, favorable feedback was associated with the lower end of the 5-point rating scale (1 was the most favorable rating and 5 the least favorable). The organization looked at reactions, behavior, and results criteria.

Participant Reactions

Reactions from participants were quite positive. For example, 78 percent of employees believed their manager's feedback meeting (the manager meeting with his or her employees as a group to discuss and clarify the manager's feedback) was successful, and 62 percent noticed positive changes in the manager's behavior as a direct result of the survey process. Among managers, 81 percent indicated the survey was an effective tool in helping develop their leadership skills; 62 percent indicated the survey helped to increase productivity in their work unit.

Behavior Change

Managers' average total scores (mean across the items) did not improve significantly from 1991 to 1992. The organization remained patient, and upon the third administration significant differences in scores were found over first-year baseline results (from 2.13 to 2.02 for the 359 managers involved in all three years). Over the next seven years, managers' scores remained significantly better than initial first-year baseline results, and scores improved incrementally from year to year (2.12 in 1991, 2.11 in 1992, 1.99 in 1993, 1.94 in 1994, 1.94 in 1995, 1.89 in 1996, 1.84 in 1997) for the 182 managers involved in all seven years.

The organization included this item in each year's survey: "My manager has held a feedback session concerning last year's Leadership Survey with our work unit." It found that (1) managers who met with direct reports to discuss their upward feedback improved more than other managers, and (2) managers improved more in years when they discussed the previous year's feedback with direct reports than in years when they did not do so. This finding is important because it is the first published research evidence demonstrating that what managers do with upward feedback is related to its benefits. (See Chapter Seventeen in this handbook for additional evidence concerning the value of manager follow-up after multisource feedback.)

Also, managers initially rated poor or moderate showed significant improvements in upward feedback ratings. These improvements were beyond what would be expected due to regression to the mean. This offered evidence that the program was successful with the very group of managers that may need help the most.

Other analyses (Walker and Walker, 1998) revealed that males and females had similar scores and were improving at the same rate. Results also revealed that all levels of managers, from first-line supervisors to executives, were able to improve their scores (Walker and Frietze, 1999).

Organizational Results

The organization identified key organizational outcome metrics that were measured at the retail branch level so they could be correlated with branch managers' upward feedback scores. Branch managers' total upward feedback scores correlated significantly ($-.18$; $p < .05$) with branch measures of customer loyalty (for instance, a customer's stated intentions to remain a customer). Previous research conducted by the organization's marketing department found that loyal customers were, on average, $100 per year more profitable than nonloyal customers. Given that the organization has 500,000 customers, increasing the number of loyal customers by only 1 percent (5,000) would result in a $500,000 revenue enhancement.

Additionally, the marketing department determined that, on average, 89 percent of loyal customers would be retained the following year, while only 80 percent of nonloyal customers would be retained. Given that the average customer revenue is $750 per year, this results in an additional $337,500 revenue enhancement per year (5,000 customers times .09, which represents the nine-point differential in customer retention—the additional 450 customers that will be retained—times $750). Thus, by increasing customer loyalty 1 percent, the present organization could expect a revenue enhancement of $837,500 in just one year.

Although these analyses do not establish a causal direction for the observed relationships (see our discussion later concerning causal issues in linkage research), they did represent a step forward in suggesting the potential bottom-line impact of the program.

Taken together, these longitudinal studies indicate that managers generally improve their performance (at least as reflected by subsequent feedback from their subordinates) after receiving upward feedback; score improvement is greatest among managers who initially receive the most negative feedback or who initially overrate themselves. Unfortunately, only two of these studies (Hegarty, 1974; Atwater, Waldman, Atwater, and Cartier, 2000) included a control group (where managers did not receive feedback), but the results from these studies were promising. It is also encouraging that these findings have been observed across a number of settings, including an accounting firm, an international operations division of a global company, a utility company, staff supervisors at a university, a regional bank, a state police agency, and the Naval Academy. Furthermore, several of these studies (Atwater, Roush, and Fischthal, 1995; Johnson and Ferstl, 1999; Reilly, Smither, and Vasilopoulos, 1996; Smither and others, 1995, Walker and Smither, 1999) demonstrated that performance improvements were not merely due to the effects of regression to the mean. Finally, research is now starting to explore the circumstances under which managers are most likely to benefit from such feedback (see Walker and Smither's findings described above).

It is also clear that much more research is needed. Especially desirable would be true experimental designs (where managers are randomly assigned to receive or not receive feedback), studies that use alternatives to time 1 versus time 2 comparisons (for example, by using retrospective degree-of-change ratings), and studies that focus on feedback from multiple sources (peers, subordinates, and customers). For example, it is important to learn whether managers who receive MSF are perceived as improving by all rating sources (peers, subordinates, customers, and the supervisor all agree the person is improving) or only by one rating source (say, subordinates). More studies examining the validity of retrospective ratings will be helpful.

Other Approaches to Measuring the Impact of Multisource Feedback

It is noteworthy that MSF instruments routinely contain thirty, forty, or more items. Of course, it is unrealistic for managers to improve on all these items between two administrations of an MSF instrument. Instead, managers are generally advised to select a small number of areas (two or three) where they want to focus their development efforts. At one packaging company, managers were asked to set two personal-improvement goals after they received MSF. Six months later, coworkers were asked to rate the extent to which each manager's performance or behavior had improved (or declined) with respect to each of the manager's two goals. These ratings were collected using a retrospective degree-of-change rating scale. Goldsmith and Underhill, in Chapter Seventeen of this handbook, advocate a similar approach. Such an approach illustrates the importance of tracking change at the level of each manager's goals (rather than merely comparing time 1 and time 2 ratings across the entire MSF instrument).

A growing number of companies are asking increasingly sophisticated questions to assess the impact of their MSF programs. For example, the first author is working with one company that, like many others, offers external executive coaching to senior-level managers when they receive MSF. This company is assessing the impact of the coaching by asking senior-level managers to rate the behavior of their executive coaches. The company will then determine whether improvement over time (as measured by changes in MSF) is related to the frequency or quality of executive coaching.

These approaches move beyond merely comparing time 1 and time 2 ratings. In doing so, they illustrate how impact studies need to focus first on the personal or organizational factors that facilitate (or detract from) changes following MSF, and second on the specific goals set by individual managers after receiving MSF. These approaches to measuring impact are especially useful because they can help practitioners refine how specific aspects of an MSF program are handled, thereby enhancing the overall impact of the program.

The impact of MSF on organizational results also deserves attention. For example, linkage research suggests that leadership values and practices (presumably reflected in MSF) shape employee attitudes and behaviors, which in turn directly affect customer satisfaction and loyalty, which in turn affect business performance (sales, profitability, and the like). For example, Schneider, White, and Paul (1998) developed a causal model that identified reciprocal relationships between service climate (as shaped by a host of management practices) and customer perceptions of service quality in banks. Sears (Rucci, Kirn, and Quinn, 1998) has also developed a model of an employee-customer-profit chain that shows the links among employee attitudes and behavior, customer impressions and retention, and financial indicators such as return on assets and operating margin.

It is important to note that establishing causal links requires the availability of longitudinal data. Cross-sectional data that examine correlations among data collected at the same time from employees, customers, and business performance (see Gross and Levy, 1998, and also this chapter's earlier discussion of a case study of a regional bank) can be ambiguous and easily misinterpreted. For example, a recent report (Watson Wyatt, 2000) gathered financial performance data on more than four hundred companies and asked about each organization's human resource practices. The language of the report repeatedly hints at causal relationships ("a significant improvement in thirty key HR practices is associated with a 30 percent increase in market value"), and only in a note on the final page is the reader told that "our research does not show a direct cause and effect between good human capital management and high economic value creation. It is even quite possible that the relationship runs in the opposite direction."

We would add that any observed relationships might also be affected by a third, perhaps unmeasured factor: variables such as other changes in operations that affect HR practices and business performance. Some organizations may be reluctant to grapple with the challenges posed by linkage research (despite its considerable promise). Still, research concerning other organizational outcomes would be valuable; for instance, is improvement over time in multisource ratings associated with a decline in turnover?

Conclusion

Measuring change can be complicated by a host of problems: response-shift bias, regression to the mean, the ceiling effect, and difficulties associated with difference scores. The use of alternative methods, such as retrospective degree-of-change ratings and polynomial regression analysis, can help overcome some of these problems. To date, longitudinal studies indicate that managers generally improve their performance after receiving upward feedback; score improvement is greatest among managers who initially receive the most negative feedback or who initially overrate themselves, and among managers who follow up with raters to discuss and clarify the feedback. Still, we need additional research that focuses on the personal or organizational factors that facilitate (or detract from) changes following multisource feedback, the specific goals set by individual managers after receiving it, and the causal linkages between MSF interventions and key measures of organizational results.

References

Atwater, L., Roush, P., and Fischthal, A. "The Influence of Upward Feedback on Self- and Follower Ratings of Leadership." *Personnel Psychology*, 1995, *48*, 34–59.

Atwater, L., Waldman, D., Atwater, D., and Cartier, P. "An Upward Feedback Field Experiment: Supervisors' Cynicism, Reactions, and Commitment to Subordinates." Working paper, Arizona State University West, 2000.

Bernardin, H. J., Hagan, C., Ross, S., and Kane, J. S. "The Effects of a 360-Degree Appraisal System on Managerial Performance." Paper presented at the tenth annual conference of the Society for Industrial and Organizational Psychology, Orlando, Fla., May 1995.

Dalessio, A. T. "Using Multisource Feedback for Employee Development and Personnel Decisions: Practice and Research." In J. W. Smither (ed.), *Performance Appraisal: State of the Art in Practice*. San Francisco: Jossey-Bass, 1998.

Edwards, J. R. "Alternatives to Difference Scores as Dependent Variables in the Study of Congruence in Organizational Research." *Organizational Behavior and Human Decision Processes*, 1995, *64*, 307–324.

Gross, F. A., and Levy, P. E. "Do 360-Degree Feedback Appraisals Predict Managerial Effectiveness?" Paper presented at the thirteenth annual conference of the Society for Industrial and Organizational Psychology, Dallas, Tex., Apr. 1998.

Hazucha, J. F., Hezlett, S. A., and Schneider, R. J. "The Impact of 360-Degree Feedback on Management Skills Development." *Human Resource Management*, 1993, *32*, 325–351.

Hegarty, W. H. "Using Subordinate Ratings to Elicit Behavioral Changes in Managers." *Journal of Applied Psychology*, 1974, *59*, 764–766.

Johnson, J. W., and Ferstl, K. L. "The Effects of Interrater and Self-Other Agreement on Performance Improvement Following Upward Feedback." *Personnel Psychology*, 1999, *52*, 271–303.

Kirkpatrick, D. "Four Steps to Measuring Training Effectiveness." *Personnel Administrator*, 1983, *28*(11), 19–25.

Martineau, J. "Using 360-Degree Surveys to Assess Change." In W. W. Tornow and M. London (eds.), *Maximizing the Value of 360-Degree Feedback: A Process for Successful Individual and Organizational Development*. San Francisco: Jossey-Bass, 1998.

Reilly, R. R., Smither, J. W., and Vasilopoulos, N. L. "A Longitudinal Study of Upward Feedback." *Personnel Psychology*, 1996, *49*, 599–612.

Rucci, A. J., Kirn, S. P., and Quinn, R. T. "The Employee-Customer-Profit Chain at Sears." *Harvard Business Review*, Jan.–Feb. 1998, pp. 82–97.

Schneider, B., White, S. S., and Paul, M. C. "Linking Service Climate and Customer Perceptions of Service Quality: Test of a Causal Model." *Journal of Applied Psychology*, 1998, *83*, 150–163.

Smither, J. W., and others. "An Examination of the Effects of an Upward Feedback Program over Time." *Personnel Psychology*, 1995, *48*, 1–34.

Walker, A. G., and Frietze, J. D. "Upward Feedback: Effects of Managerial Level over Seven Years." Paper presented at the fourteenth annual conference of the Society for Industrial and Organizational Psychology, Atlanta, Ga., May 1999.

Walker, A. G., and Smither, J. W. "A Five-Year Study of Upward Feedback: What Managers Do with Their Results Matters." *Personnel Psychology*, 1999, *52*, 393–423.

Walker, A. G., and Walker, S. A. "Gender Differences in Upward Feedback Program Scores over Six Years." Paper presented at the thirteenth annual conference of the Society for Industrial and Organizational Psychology, Dallas, Tex., Apr. 1998.

Watson Wyatt. *The Human Capital Index: Linking Human Capital and Shareholder Value*. Bethesda, Md.: Watson Wyatt, Inc., 2000.

PART 2

Applications of Multisource Feedback

CHAPTER 17

Multisource Feedback for Executive Development

Marshall Goldsmith
Brian O. Underhill

Today's executives are increasingly seeking relevant, focused, and time-efficient development experiences. Multisource feedback (MSF) is fast becoming a preferred "tool" for delivering this type of executive learning. When done correctly, it can be the highest-impact development experience an executive encounters throughout the course of a career.

Peter Drucker has noted, "The leader of the past was someone who knew how to tell. The leader of the future will be someone who knows how to ask" (personal communication, Jan. 1998). The rise of the knowledge worker, interdependent partnerships, shared leadership, and continuous technological improvement (among many other challenges) require leaders to be continuously in tune with feedback from multiple sources in order to maximize individual and organizational effectiveness. MSF is one effective way to deliver this information in a timely and confidential manner.

The ultimate goal of an effective MSF process should be to help individuals achieve *positive, measurable, long-term change in leadership behavior*. We have found that using an "executive-owned" leadership profile, engaging executives in the *process* (rather than creating a one-time event), encouraging follow-up, and providing ongoing coaching are the most critical variables in successfully using MSF as an executive development tool. These key success factors are covered in more detail in this chapter, along with new research findings

275

on the "global leader of the future" (as reported by Andersen Consulting Institute for Strategic Change, 1999; and Keilty, Goldsmith & Company, 1992).

Developing a Custom Profile for Executives

More and more organizations are choosing to develop custom leadership profiles for their executives. In our experience (through developing more than seventy such profiles and reviewing countless others), we've found that no one profile is the ultimate. What is really important in a custom profile is that the executives and their organizations *take ownership* for them.

With ownership, executives sense that the profile speaks the language of the organization. They find it intrinsically comfortable, not foreign or irrelevant. Although they may not agree with every item on the inventory, they are likely to find that the majority of items are relevant to the leadership challenges their specific organizations face.

A successful profile involves executives heavily in the development and editing process. Executives should be interviewed regarding their views on successful leadership behavior for the organization. They should then have multiple opportunities to offer input on the various drafts of the inventory. The most critical reason for this approach is that executives have to take ownership for the inventory.

In larger organizations, it is often beneficial to develop multiple (but closely related) profiles. Executives, middle managers, and individual contributors may each develop their own inventories. (Johnson and Johnson employs three inventories: executive inventory, advanced manager, and individual contributor.) This approach distinguishes the executive profile from those employed in the rest of the organization. Executives will better appreciate the profile's relevance to their unique challenges.

The Profile Development Process

Custom profiles are not difficult to develop. Assuming relatively unobstructed access to executives' schedules and other materials, one can develop a profile in about a month. Here are the recommended steps to develop a custom inventory (see Chapter Six for more on this subject):

1. *Ask.* Conduct interviews with executives, customers, suppliers, and any other key stakeholders. Ask them: "What do you want out of your leaders for the future?" "What specific behaviors would you like to see leaders demonstrate?" "What specific behaviors would you like to see leaders avoid?" Also consider the vision, values, culture, and strategy of the organization in the data-collection process.

2. *Create.* Organize the data into key themes, and draft the profile based on those themes. Create inventory items that closely match the feel of what was expressed in the data. Use as many "native" words as possible. Create items that are easy to comprehend, avoiding complex phrasing or compound sentences.

3. *Revise.* Gather as much feedback on the profile from as many individuals as possible. It is very important to allow every executive the opportunity to offer input. Their ownership is critical.

4. *Refine.* Refine the inventory to reflect the input received. It may be necessary to gather input several times to get it "just right." The important part is that, in the end, executives feel that it is *their* inventory.

5. *Gain final sign-off.* The CEO of the organization should review and approve the final inventory. In the best-case scenario, the CEO personally endorses the inventory with a signed cover letter.

You may find that one inventory is not significantly better than another; what is really important is that the inventory be designed specifically to capture the language and feel of the organization.

Key Competencies for the Future: The Andersen Global Leader of the Future Inventory

With all the talk about customization, many executives still prefer a standardized, credible, best-in-class leadership profile. Recent comprehensive research with more than two hundred high-potential leaders from more than a hundred of the top organizations around the world (jointly conducted by Andersen Consulting and Keilty, Goldsmith & Company) has led to development of the Andersen

Global Leader of the Future Inventory (Andersen Consulting Institute for Strategic Change, 1999).

The inventory anticipates the necessary competencies required to lead the global organization of the future. The research pool was purposely restricted to those identified as "high-potentials" in their organizations. These individuals were handpicked as potential future leaders of their organizations. The data collected from interviews, surveys, and focus groups of these individuals resulted in the Global Leader of the Future Inventory.

Some of the inventory's competencies may initially appear familiar, but research indicates that future executives need to continuously elevate their leadership skills in these and new competencies in order to successfully compete in tomorrow's global marketplace, as this list details.

The Global Leader of the Future . . .

Thinks globally

Anticipates opportunity

Creates a shared vision

Develops and empowers people

Appreciates cultural diversity

Builds teamwork and partnerships

Embraces change

Shows technological savvy

Encourages constructive challenge

Ensures customer satisfaction

Achieves a competitive advantage

Demonstrates personal mastery

Shares leadership

Lives values

A few of these key competencies are worth highlighting.

• *Shows technological savvy* (Goldsmith and Walt, 1999). Awareness of how technology can influence the organization and its environment is a necessity and can no longer be delegated to the technical people. Executives must know how to make and manage strategic investments in technology.

- *Thinks globally.* Today's organizations are already competing in a global marketplace. Tomorrow's executives will not only need to understand globalization but also have to continuously make skilled decisions with a global mind-set and regularly help others understand the impact of globalization.
- *Shares leadership.* Future executives need to rely more on influence than authority. The concept of a shared vision becomes an even more critical component in motivating people across boundaries.

The Global Leader of the Future Inventory is one example of a standardized profile. Like others in the field, it represents well-researched findings on the future of global leadership. This adds credibility to the profile, encouraging executives to adopt it for use in their own organizations.

Using MSF to Develop Leaders and Executives: A Process, Not an Event

Regardless of the customized or standardized approach selected, an MSF process is only as good as its *process*. Multisource feedback should not be viewed as a one-time event to be checked off an executive's to-do list. It is a process that must continue long after the feedback report is delivered.

After consulting to countless executives and their organizations, we've identified six steps to represent the best practice in an effective MSF process:

1. *Solicit feedback.* Begin by distributing assessments. Direct reports, peers, customers, suppliers, "matrixed" direct reports, and others may be asked to give feedback to the executive participant.
2. *Review results.* Participants receive coaching from an outside expert, highlighting the themes of the feedback and assisting the leader in selecting one or two (maximum) areas of development.

3. *Develop an action plan.* A written action plan consisting of specific, measurable goals is necessary. This can be easy to compile. Most people already know what to do; often they just need the discipline to do it.

4. *Respond.* Participants need to follow up with their respondents, thank them for their feedback, share what they're working on, and ask for future-focused suggestions relating to their areas of development.

5. *Follow up.* Every two months, participants check in with respondents to gauge their improvement over time.

6. *Do a minisurvey.* Carry out a brief multisource minisurvey of two to four items, targeted directly at the executive's selected areas of development, to measure improvement over time. Several rounds of minisurveys are suggested. Repeat the full assessment in two years.

Most multisource feedback processes tend to fade away after the initial coaching session or action planning. This is an incomplete approach and does very little to promise long-term behavioral change (and it may even invite cynicism). Leaders need to execute a sustained follow-up strategy to ensure success. Compelling evidence demonstrates that executives can achieve successful behavioral change through regular follow-up with others.

The Impact of Follow-Up on Leadership Effectiveness

Over the past several years, we have compiled follow-up data on executives from a number of industries. The same finding constantly reappears: follow-up works.

The graphs in this chapter represent composite follow-up data of executive groups from five major organizations. (Because each organization had a different number of executives in our database, we reweighted the data so that each organization accounted for an equal amount.) In each organization, executives received multisource feedback, selected areas for development, created action plans, and were strongly encouraged to respond and follow up with their respondents regularly.

Approximately three to six months after the original feedback session, the executives participated in a follow-up minisurvey (see

Exhibit 17.1 for a sample). Minisurveys are very short, targeted multisource assessments aimed at measuring change in leadership effectiveness over time. Each minisurvey contains questions relating to the executive's perceived change in overall leadership effectiveness, follow-up behavior, and several specific self-selected items relating to their own personal areas of development.

The key survey question asks, "Do you feel this person has become more or less effective as a leader in the past six months?" Respondents rated the executives on a scale from –3 (less effective) to +3 (more effective).

The results are quite impressive (see Figure 17.1). Overall, 42 percent of the executives improved at the +2 or +3 level. An impressive 76 percent improved at a +1, +2, or +3 level. Only 4 percent got worse.

However, a striking difference appears when the results are separated between those who followed up with others and those who did not (see Figure 17.2). Respondents were asked to indicate if the executive had followed up with them regarding what he or she learned from their leadership feedback.

The differences are compelling. Forty-nine percent of leaders who followed up improved at a +2 or +3 level, compared to 35 percent of leaders who did not follow up. Eighty-four percent of leaders who followed up improved at a +1, +2, or +3 level, compared with 67 percent of those who did not. Sixteen percent of leaders who did follow up stayed the same or got worse. For leaders who did not follow up, the figure more than doubles: 33 percent of those leaders stayed the same or got worse.

Clearly, following up with others is a key success factor in positively altering people's perceptions of leadership effectiveness. We've also discovered that the *amount* of follow-up is positively correlated with perceived change in leadership effectiveness (Keilty, Goldsmith & Company, 1992). Similar research with leadership groups around the world reveals surprisingly similar results. Additionally, findings from nonexecutive leaders are also very similar to the data presented here.

This degree of success at the executive level has far-reaching benefits for the organization. Executives receiving positive minisurvey results are more likely to continue practicing their new behaviors, follow up regularly, and enthusiastically support the multisource assessment process as it proceeds further into the

Exhibit 17.1. Sample Minisurvey Questionnaire.

Manager: _Demonstration Manager_

Answer each question.

1. Your relationship to this manager is as: (check one)

    _____ Direct report _____ Peer

2. In the past six months, did this manager follow up with you on what he or she learned from the Leadership Effectiveness Inventory feedback? (check one)

    _____ Yes _____ No

3. Do you feel this person has become more or less effective as a leader in the past six months? (circle one)

$$-3 \quad -2 \quad -1 \quad 0 \quad 1 \quad 2 \quad 3$$

$$\longleftarrow \text{less} \qquad \text{more} \longrightarrow$$
$$\text{effective} \quad \text{effective}$$

Please rate the extent to which this manager has increased or decreased in effectiveness in the following areas of development within the past six months: (circle one response for each item)

Self-selected items

1. Takes responsibility for her or his decisions $-3 \quad -2 \quad -1 \quad 0 \quad 1 \quad 2 \quad 3$

2. Follows up to help ensure customer satisfaction $-3 \quad -2 \quad -1 \quad 0 \quad 1 \quad 2 \quad 3$

Additional comments:

What has this manager done in the past few months that you have found to be particularly effective?

What can he or she do to become more effective as a manager in the areas of development noted above?

Figure 17.1. Change in Overall Leadership Effectiveness.

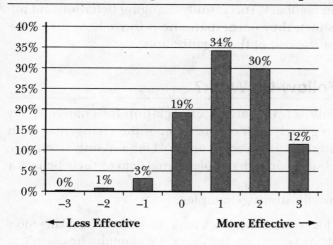

Note: N = 3,838 respondents.

Figure 17.2. Change in Overall Leadership Effectiveness (Follow-Up).

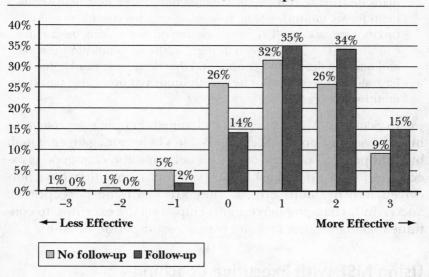

Note: N = 3,655 respondents.

organization. Additionally, the executives are seen as role models for encouraging feedback, successfully changing behavior, and following-up; in short, they perpetuate the positive benefits of the MSF process for the rest of the organization.

Why Does Follow-Up Work?

Leaders who follow up create an expectation for change. They then check in regularly with others to see if the change has been noticed. In doing this, the leaders are working not only to change their behavior but to change people's *perceptions* of their behavior as well.

Consider two illustrative examples.

Scenario A: "Joe" receives feedback indicating that he's making too many destructive comments. For the next six months, he doesn't make a single discouraging remark. In the sixth month, Joe slips and makes a destructive comment. What do people around him think? "That Joe, he never changes!"

Scenario B: Joe receives feedback indicating that he's making too many destructive comments. He does not make a destructive comment for six months, *and* he follows up with his coworkers every two months, asking, "I've been working on not making destructive comments. How have I been doing?" In the sixth month, Joe slips and makes a destructive comment. What do people think? "Joe may have slipped recently. But he's really improved over these past few months."

In Scenario A, Joe's behavior changed. People's *perceptions* of his behavior did not. In Scenario B, Joe's behavior again changed, but now people's perceptions of his behavior also changed. As executives follow up and ask others whether or not they have perceived improvement efforts, they are changing perceptions. Successfully changing perceptions empowers the executive to continue making positive changes over a longer period of time.

Using MSF with Executive Coaching

In recent years, MSF has been more frequently used with long-term executive coaching engagements. This business is growing rapidly;

requests for ongoing, behavioral coaching are increasing swiftly among multisource feedback clients. Assigning credible, external executive coaches to work with executives is an effective strategy for maximizing the value of feedback and driving behavioral change. The coach works as an objective third party, extending unbiased analysis, suggestions, and observations on the executive's behavior.

The coach is also there for the long run. He or she serves as the leader's conscience, providing on-the-job tips, observations, and instructions. In many ways, a coach serves as a "behavioral personal trainer," reminding the leader to continuously work toward his or her developmental goals and to follow up with others. Through coaching, organizations ensure they are creating the greatest amount of behavioral change from the multisource process.

Coaching should be frequent but brief. It should not waste time. Executives want to improve, but they don't want to spend an inordinate amount of time trying to do so. After a few up-front visits, coaching should continue mostly by phone, e-mail, or video-conferencing, with the primary purpose of monitoring follow-up activities. Executive coaching should be specific, targeted, and just-in-time. The behavioral-change coaching process should be followed, as we highlight next.

The Behavioral-Change Coaching Process

The steps in the behavioral-change coaching process are not unlike those presented for the multisource feedback process; they're just more in depth (see also Goldsmith, 1996).

First, identify raters. Prior to feedback collection, the coach and the executive work together to determine who should provide feedback (direct reports, peers, customers, suppliers, members of the management team, and so on). It is important to select a good mix of individuals.

Second, gather feedback. The MSF inventory is used for this purpose, however some coaches may choose a qualitative multisource data-gathering process as well (say, interviewing key stakeholders confidentially to gain insight on the participant's positive and negative behaviors).

Third, analyze results, and get buy-in. Review the feedback report. Look for themes. The individual must accept that he or she needs improvement in a few areas. Select one or two areas of development that represent both the largest gap and the greatest potential for success.

Fourth, create an action plan. The most appreciated outcome of any executive coaching program is specific advice. Coaches should work with executives in offering specific tips and suggestions. SMART goals (specific, measurable, actionable, relevant, and time-bounded) should be outlined.

Fifth, respond. The executive should speak with each respondent, indicate her or his selected areas of development, and collect additional suggestions for improvement. The coach needs to monitor and ensure that the executive conducts these conversations with every member of the key stakeholder groups.

Sixth, follow up. The executive should regularly follow up with everyone regarding his or her development action plans. At this point, the coach serves more as a personal trainer, reminding the leader to continuously work the action plan goals and follow up regularly with others.

Seventh, use minisurvey measurements. Ongoing, follow-up minisurveys constitute a measurement of improvement. Success is defined not necessarily by the individual being coached but by key "customers" of the coaching process: direct reports, peers, boss, internal customers, and others.

Although it is not difficult to understand change in behavior, it's difficult to *do*. Nonetheless, leaders who want to improve, create action plans, and develop a disciplined follow-up plan almost always improve. The good news is that as they improve, their self-confidence increases. They keep practicing the new behaviors, and they keep improving.

When Feedback and Coaching Do *Not* Lead to Behavioral Change

Feedback and coaching do not always lead to behavioral change. We've found four roadblocks that interfere with successful behavioral change efforts (see also Goldsmith, 1996).

The first roadblock occurs if the leader is not willing to make a sincere effort to change. Consider the old adage "You can lead a horse to water, but you can't make it drink." If people do not truly want to change, they won't. This point is exactly similar to the critical first step in Alcoholics Anonymous: participants must admit, "I'm an alcoholic." If this step is missing (or faked), behavioral change will not occur.

The second is if the person isn't given the opportunity to succeed. If the rest of the organization has written off or otherwise given up on the individual, behavioral change is unlikely. Others won't be willing to give the person a fair chance to make changes and experience success.

In the third situation, the individual lacks the intelligence or functional skills to do the job. Behavioral coaching cannot fix gaps in intelligence or in requisite functional skills.

The fourth roadblock occurs when the individual lacks integrity. These individuals are not worth employing in your organization. Behavioral coaching does not help them. Most people will not give them a chance to change.

Conclusion: Living Up to the Promise of MSF

A danger with any popular organizational improvement tool is the risk that it could be labeled a fad. Multisource feedback at this point may very well be a fad, in the sense that the increasing frequency with which it is being used can produce careless administration, underqualified practitioners, and executive cynicism (or even disdain) for the process. The summarizing points here are well worth keeping in mind in undertaking such an effort.

- *Creating ownership.* An inventory that is not relevant to executives and their organization is likely to fail. As soon as executives complete the process, they may likely tell others, "Yes, I took it. It wasn't really relevant." It is critical to develop an inventory that the organization owns. If this is not possible, select a well-established standardized inventory with a positive reputation.
- *Attention to the process.* If executives go through the process in a half-committed way, the process may likely stall thanks to ambivalence. Participating executives should be made aware of the entire process before embarking on a feedback experience. They need to understand all the expectations; they can't just receive the report and check it off their to-do list. Coaching, action planning,

288 THE HANDBOOK OF MULTISOURCE FEEDBACK

and follow-up are all critical and required components of the process.

• *The oversurveyed problem.* Increased MSF administrations result in more surveys for people to complete. Many organizations also regularly conduct an employee opinion survey, a culture survey, a values survey, customer satisfaction surveys, etc. Each survey process then repeats itself every year! Regarding multisource feedback, we strongly suggest using more frequent minisurveys and less frequent full multisource administrations. Leaders can only keep a few key developmental areas in mind at any given moment; targeted minisurveys help keep them focused. Minisurveys also generate motivation. People are more likely to work harder at something if they know it is going to be measured.

• *Coaching.* Behavioral change requires ongoing support. Without the support, participants are likely to falter and blame the process (rather than their own failings) as the culprit. Behavioral coaching is a highly effective approach to providing ongoing support.

When done correctly, the promise of multisource feedback is extremely obtainable and well worth the effort. Executives regularly solicit the input of others to increase their effectiveness. Organizational members are more actively in tune with their strengths and areas of development. Participants regularly follow up with each other to support their developmental goals. And leaders successfully achieve positive, measurable, long-term change in leadership behavior.

References

Andersen Consulting Institute for Strategic Change. *The Evolving Role of Executive Leadership.* New York: Andersen Consulting, 1999. (Contact Terry Corby, terrycorby@ac.com)

Goldsmith, M. "Coaching for Behavioral Change." *Leader to Leader,* no. 2. San Francisco: Jossey-Bass, 1996.

Goldsmith, M., and Walt, C. *Developing Technological Savvy: Leader to Leader.* San Francisco: Jossey-Bass, 1999.

Keilty, Goldsmith & Company. *The Impact of Direct Report Feedback and Follow-Up on Leadership Effectiveness.* San Diego: Keilty, Goldsmith & Company, 1992.

CHAPTER 18

Multisource Feedback for Teams

Glenn Hallam

Other chapters of this book have addressed multisource feedback (MSF) designed to help individuals. In contrast, this chapter discusses feedback for groups of people: feedback on a team's performance, its strengths, and its developmental needs. I address a number of basic questions about multisource feedback for teams:

- How does MSF fit into team development?
- What MSF instruments are available for teams?
- What do team MSF tools measure?
- Who is the object of evaluation?
- Who does the evaluating?
- How is the feedback collected, scored, and displayed?
- Who sees the feedback?
- What types of teams can benefit from multisource feedback?
- How is the feedback used?

The premise of this chapter is that MSF can be a powerful component in a team development process. Also, many of the principles of individual feedback apply to team feedback, but there is an added dimension of complexity both in collecting and providing feedback to teams.

Multisource Feedback in Team Development

Multisource feedback is generally used in the context of team development. Like individual development, team development is a process of creating awareness and breaking down obstacles to effective performance. There are many paths to such awareness: reading books or hearing lectures on teamwork, team diagnosis (by an outside expert or by the team itself), and team experiential activities such as outdoor team challenges. Perhaps the most common form of team development, experiential training, helps team members grasp the requirements of effective teamwork by experiencing effective or ineffective teamwork.

The goal of team development generally is to help team members and their leaders learn about their strengths and weaknesses as a team and the strategies and mind-set they need to perform effectively as a team. Any activity that serves to open lines of communication, force the team to acknowledge its problems, and teach team members about effective teamwork is team development.

The process of team development is often done without multisource feedback. For example, most experiential training is conducted without any prior assessment. However, MSF can help group facilitators identify team needs so that they can tailor the program to meet these needs. (I say more about this later.) It also can be powerful in creating awareness of team problems and strengths.

What MSF Instruments Are Available for Teams?

Numerous human resource consulting and publishing firms offer MSF tools for teams (although they usually are not called multisource feedback tools). Examples include Team Excellence (Larson and La Fasto, 1989), the Parker Team Player Survey (Parker, 1991), and TeamView/360 (Brousseau and Perrault, 1993). A number of large organizations have even developed their own customized assessment tool for teams.

I have had the opportunity to work extensively with a tool published by National Computer Systems, the Campbell-Hallam Team

Development Survey, or TDS (Campbell and Hallam, 1994). Thousands of teams have completed the TDS and received feedback. Thus many of the examples used in this chapter are drawn from our work with this instrument.

What Do Team MSF Tools Measure?

Multisource instruments for teams usually measure a hodgepodge of constructs related to team effectiveness, including individual characteristics (for example, perceptions of whether the team possesses the skills and knowledge they need), team process variables (for example, team coordination and communication), team leadership (perhaps whether the leader clarifies the goals of the team or keeps the team informed), and team success measures (for example, customer satisfaction, team productivity). Some tools, including the TDS, allow teams to add items to augment standard scales.

Here are examples of team MSF items:

- We have the right mix of skills.
- Team members manage conflict well.
- Our leader imparts a clear vision and direction.
- I am happy to be a part of this team.
- Our meetings are productive.
- We are meeting our objectives.

As you can see, the domain of evaluation can be much broader than the domain for evaluating individuals. For example, Larson and La Fasto (1989) measure areas with these scale titles:

Clear, elevating goal

Results-driven structure

Competent team members

Unified commitment

Collaborative climate

Standards of excellence

External support and recognition

Principled leadership

The TDS measures these dimensions:

Information
Time and staffing
Material resources
Organizational support
Skills
Commitment
Mission clarity
Team coordination
Team unity
Individual goals
Empowerment
Team assessment
Feedback
Rewards
Leadership
Satisfaction
Performance

Who Is the Object of Valuation?

Team feedback can best be described as multisource and multi-object. Typically, the observers evaluate (1) the team members in general, (2) the team leader, (3) the specific members of the team, and (4) the organization (if, for example, observers evaluate the climate for teamwork).

The most common object of rating, however, is the team in general. Raters assess how well the team resolves problems, shares information, coordinates its activities, and so on. Raters may also assess how well the team leader motivates the team, keeps members informed, solicits information from outside the team, and the like.

One challenge is to adequately define the team. In reality, the composition of most teams frequently changes as members leave and others join. Thus most teams are a kind of moving target. The best time to provide multisource feedback to teams is when its membership has been relatively stable for some time. Also, when raters assess the team, they benefit from a clear definition of the team that includes the names of members.

Even if the composition of the team is stable, there still may be vast differences among the contributions of the individual members, which can make it difficult to rate the team overall. For example, suppose nine team members are extremely hard working and one is constantly loafing; how does one assess the *team's* level of effort? Although these problems are surmountable, being forced to make assessments of this kind can contribute to measurement error.

Who Does the Evaluation?

There are three types of raters in most team MSF systems: team members, team leaders, and outside observers such as customers or managers at a higher level in the organization. In selecting which type of rater to survey, two questions are critical: Who has the opportunity to evaluate the team in the areas measured by the assessment? And whose perceptions really count?

These two questions do not always lead to the same observers. For example, leaders may want to learn how new members feel about the team, but these members usually have not had an opportunity to observe the team. For this reason, new members often do not provide feedback.

Similarly, the perceptions of the team's customers clearly are important, at least in evaluating the success of the team, but they do not necessarily have the opportunity to observe the team working together. This often leads to rating forms that vary with the type of rater. On the TDS, for example, a much shorter assessment is completed by outside observers. This form solicits feedback primarily about the success of the team in meeting customers' needs. It also collects information about the extent to which team members appear to make decisions without having to ask for permission (an aspect of empowerment). Outside observers typically have sufficient information to give meaningful feedback in these areas, but not in other areas, such as how well the team handles conflict.

As one might expect, the members themselves can have widely divergent views of the team. Just as observers often disagree about the effectiveness of an individual, each team member experiences the team in his or her own way. Each member brings to the team unique expectations. For example, a member who has recently left a team that was working eighty hours a week may be critical of another team that works only forty hours. Also, members are exposed to different experiences while they are on the team. A person who works most frequently with the most energetic members is likely to rate the team's energy level higher than the member who works more frequently with relatively lazy members. Thus, the spread of ratings can be quite high, perhaps higher than that of multisource ratings received by individuals.

In addition, members may be inaccurate judges of their strengths and weaknesses as a team. Members sometimes engage in a kind of groupthink, whereby they converge on an glowing but erroneous impression of the team and shield themselves from information that is critical of the team. Also, in certain cultures, criticizing the team is not allowed, so ratings become inflated and meaningless.

How Is the Feedback Collected, Scored, and Displayed?

Team MSF tools vary widely in level of sophistication. At one end of the spectrum are, say, thirty-item surveys that are hand-scored. Their advantage is that they are inexpensive and easy to use. At the other end of the spectrum are tools such as the TDS, which has seventy-two items and two forms, one completed by team members and leaders, the other by outside observers; the surveys are then sent in for computer scoring.

The advantages of the more lengthy kind of tool are that it is comprehensive and has known psychometric properties (scale scores are derived from responses to clusters of items), it allows teams to compare themselves to other teams (scores are normed), and the results are presented in great depth to allow analysis and diagnosis. The disadvantages are that it is more expensive, takes longer to complete and process, and can sometimes overwhelm teams with a wealth of data, thus requiring the support of a group facilitator who is trained in using and interpreting the assessment.

A sample profile from the TDS—just one element of a larger report—appears in Figure 18.1. The scores on this assessment are *T* scores, whereby the mean is 50 and the standard deviation is 10. The norms are based on the responses of nearly two hundred teams working in a variety of industries. Each team member receives a report that compares his or her responses to the responses of the team in general and an aggregation of outside observers. In addition to this overall profile, team members also receive a detailed analysis of each of the items on the survey. (The full report is ten or eleven pages long, depending on whether custom items have been added.)

One instrument that seems to combine the comprehensiveness of computer-scored surveys and the ease of use of hand-scored surveys is a tool recently developed at the Center for Creative Leadership in Colorado Springs. This tool uses a checklist in combination with scale ratings to allow team members to rate a large array of areas in a short period of time. The tool, which measures the constructs of the Team Effectiveness Leadership Model (Ginnett, 1993), takes only about ten minutes to complete yet covers more than twenty dimensions, including several aspects of the organizational context for teamwork. The results are calculated and graphed as part of a team exercise that reveals team problems and the potential origins of these problems in the organization at large (for example, absence of information systems to support the team in its work).

Who Sees the Feedback?

Team MSF is usually viewed by the team leader, members of the team, a consultant who is working with the team, and in some cases other people in the team's organization. Whether or not the results are viewed by outside observers should depend on what team raters (including team members) are told when their feedback is solicited. Generally, if people outside the team are shown the feedback, it should be in aggregate form (that is, an average of ratings).

What Types of Teams Can Benefit from MSF?

There are two questions to ask in assessing whether a team should receive multisource feedback. First, can observers offer meaningful

Figure 18.1. TDS Sample Profile.

CAMPELL-HALLAM TEAM DEVELOPMENT SURVEY
CHRIS SAMPLE and His Team: ABC Team
(January 15, 1997; eight respondents)

See the next
page for help
in reading
this profile.

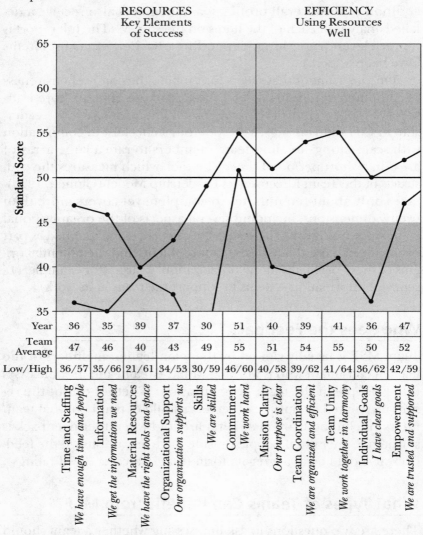

	RESOURCES Key Elements of Success						EFFICIENCY Using Resources Well				
Year	36	35	39	37	30	51	40	39	41	36	47
Team Average	47	46	40	43	49	55	51	54	55	50	52
Low/High	36/57	35/66	21/61	34/53	30/59	46/60	40/58	39/62	41/64	36/62	42/59

Categories (left to right):
- Time and Staffing — *We have enough time and people*
- Information — *We get the information we need*
- Material Resources — *We have the right tools and space*
- Organizational Support — *Our organization supports us*
- Skills — *We are skilled*
- Commitment — *We work hard*
- Mission Clarity — *Our purpose is clear*
- Team Coordination — *We are organized and efficient*
- Team Unity — *We work together in harmony*
- Individual Goals — *I have clear goals*
- Empowerment — *We are trusted and supported*

Figure 18.1. TDS Sample Profile, Cont'd.

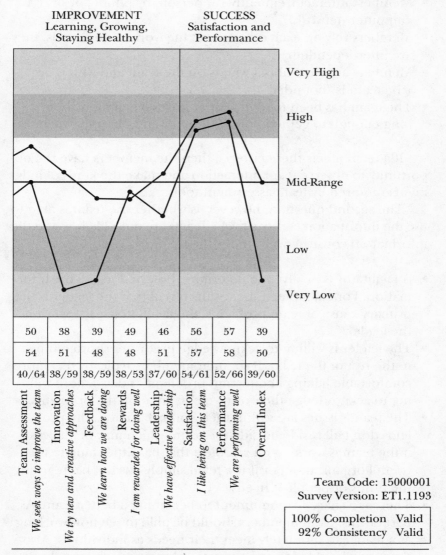

Responces	SA	A	sa	sd	D	SD	Valid
Percent	06	25	31	28	07	04	Pattern

——— CHRIS SAMPLE
- - - Team Average

IMPROVEMENT
Learning, Growing,
Staying Healthy

SUCCESS
Satisfaction and
Performance

Very High

High

Mid-Range

Low

Very Low

50	38	39	49	46	56	57	39
54	51	48	48	51	57	58	50
40/64	38/59	38/59	38/53	37/60	54/61	52/66	39/60

Team Assessment
We seek ways to improve the team

Innovation
We try new and creative approaches

Feedback
We learn how we are doing

Rewards
I am rewarded for doing well

Leadership
We have effective leadership

Satisfaction
I like being on this team

Performance
We are performing well

Overall Index

Team Code: 15000001
Survey Version: ET1.1193

| 100% Completion | Valid |
| 92% Consistency | Valid |

Campbell-Hallam Team Development Survey instrument is one of the
Campbell Development Surveys by David Campbell, Ph.D. "Campbell-Hallam
Team Development Survey," "TDS," and "Campbell Development Surveys" are
trademarks owned by David Campbell, Ph.D.

feedback on the team? Second, is the team capable of using the results constructively?

Observers (including the team members themselves) generally are able to provide meaningful feedback if the team meets these criteria:

- Members interact frequently (in person, by phone, or over a computer network).
- Members rely on each other to get the work done (that is, they are interdependent).
- Members are clear about who is on the team and who is not (the team is "bounded").
- The team has been together for at least several months, or long enough to get to know each other and observe dynamics.

If a team meets these criteria, then the members have the opportunity to observe team interaction and make the kinds of judgments required by team assessment tools.

The second question, however, is whether the team is able to use the information constructively. Teams are most likely to use the information constructively under the following conditions:

- A facilitator is involved to determine how best to use the information. For example, if the results reveal that the leader is the primary cause of team problems, the facilitator may focus on the leader.
- The leader is willing to acknowledge his or her shortcomings to the rest of the team. If so, then members typically feel more comfortable talking about team problems and are more willing to acknowledge their own role in creating the problems.
- The team's issues are within their control. That is, the problems don't all reside outside the team, which may be the case if the team is working on a project that has little value to the overall organization, or if the team simply has not been given the funds or people it needs.
- There is a shared commitment to becoming a better team. As part of this, team members should be able to see how working as a team can ultimately meet their needs as individuals. Also, the team should plan to be together long enough to make needed changes.

How Is the Feedback Used?

The first application of team feedback should be in conducting a needs analysis to determine how best to help the team. For example, if the results show that the team is in great conflict, then the intervention should include activities designed to help members address the conflict constructively (and perhaps build trust). If the leader receives low marks, then the intervention should focus on helping the leader to address his or her developmental needs (which may or may not require involving the other team members).

A second use of the feedback is in helping the organization identify teams in need of help. If training budgets are limited, organizations can focus investment on those teams that an assessment indicates need the most help (as reflected by low scores on a team multisource assessment).

The most common application, however, is to use the feedback to stimulate discussion among members about the strengths and developmental needs of the team. The typical process in providing teams with feedback on the TDS is to first present the feedback to the leader so that she or he is not surprised or embarrassed in the presence of the other team members. Then the team is gathered and presented with the results.

Typically, the team members are given an opportunity to study the results and then asked to select two or three areas for further analysis. For example, members may vote to examine team coordination, team conflict, and material resources as areas for further analysis and discussion. Next, the team is divided into subteams, each asked to focus on one of the areas. In working with the TDS results, the subteams address questions such as why the area is important to team performance; what may be causing low scores in the area; and what specific, practical steps the team can take to improve in the area.

One way team feedback differs from individual feedback is that responsibility for team problems can be more difficult to assign. If an executive scores low on "developing business strategy," then it is reasonable to attribute the low score to that person's skills or behavior. But if a team scores low in "team coordination," who is to blame? The leader? The other team members? The organization (perhaps for not being clear about the purpose of the team)? Identifying the cause of a problem is complex work. Does the team fight because the members come from different backgrounds? Because the leader does not adequately reward collaboration? Because members have personality differences? Because they misunderstand each other? The theories can go on and on.

Conclusion

In general, teams benefit from the process of examining, analyzing, and discussing their problems. Team MSF serves to focus the team's attention on its strengths as well as the obstacles to effective teamwork. It acts to surface issues that may be undermining team performance. It stimulates sharing ideas about how to improve the team and engages the team members in the process of working together to solve problems.

References
Brousseau, K., and Perrault, M. *TeamView/360*. Agoura Hills, Calif.: Advanced Teamware, 1993.
Campbell, D., and Hallam, G. *Manual for the Campbell-Hallam Team Development Survey*. Minneapolis, Minn.: National Computer Systems, 1994.
Ginnett, R. *The Team Effectiveness Leadership Model*. Colorado Springs, Colo.: Center for Creative Leadership, 1993.
Larson, C. E., and La Fasto, F. M. *Teamwork: What Must Go Right/What Can Go Wrong*. Thousand Oaks, Calif.: Sage, 1989.
Parker, G. M. *Parker Team Player Survey*. Palo Alto, Calif.: Consulting Psychologists Press, 1991.

CHAPTER 19

Multisource Feedback for Organization Development and Change

Allan H. Church
Janine Waclawski
W. Warner Burke

Although there are arguably as many definitions of organization development (OD) as there are OD practitioners, at its core it is a planned process of change in an organization's culture through the use of behavioral science technology, research, and theory (Burke, 1994). This definition is important because it specifies first the purpose and scale to which OD efforts should be directed, and second the source of the interventions.

One such core method—indeed, a value inherent in OD work, which is grounded both in the behavioral sciences and in the varied fields from which OD emerged—is the use of feedback. Although the content and method of collection may range from large-scale surveys to focus groups, interviews, and multisource feedback (MSF) applications, the principles and assumptions behind the OD approach represent a significant and yet often overlooked contribution to developing and practicing MSF in organizations.

Thus the purpose of this chapter is to discuss the relationship between MSF technology and organization development and change efforts. Specifically, following a brief overview of the history, theory, and assumptions of OD as they relate to using behavioral ratings data, we describe two case examples, drawn from consulting experience, of successful large-scale applications of MSF data for organization change and development.

Theoretical Underpinning and Assumptions of OD

In general, there are two major assumptions underlying an OD approach to doing MSF initiatives: action research and a systems perspective.

Action Research

When done correctly, OD is conducted through a process known as action research. Although the action research approach has recently experienced a resurgence of interest in the applied literature, it has long been an essential method and fundamental tenet of OD. It is directly attributable to Lewin's seminal work with groups (1946, 1958) and was later expanded by many others, among them French (1969); Frohman, Sashkin, and Kavanagh (1976); Beckhard and Harris (1987); and Burke (1994). In general, it is a process of systematically gathering data on the nature of a given problem or situation, analyzing the data to find patterns, feeding back a summary and analysis of the data in some form, and then taking action according to what the analysis and diagnosis of the data suggest. Thus, at its very core OD is truly a data-driven process. Here in more detail is how data are used to drive individual and organizational change.

From the OD-action research perspective, change is conceived as a three-stage process. In Lewin's model, the first step requires *unfreezing* the present level of behavior. In other words, to help an individual or organization initiate change, the specific *need* for change must be recognized; that is, a compelling case must be made for the change. This requires understanding and acknowledging that the current approach is not the best way, and that there is another, better way to behave or to be. This phase is critical in determining the goals for change; a given MSF process or system can serve as a method for unfreezing old behavior. A key question is whether there is a perceived need for MSF, and then to what ends the data will be directed.

The second stage in the approach, *movement*, consists of taking actions that represent a new direction or set of behaviors. Quite simply, once the need for change has been realized, steps toward achieving a new and better state must be taken. The content of the instruments used in MSF applications, for example, are of specific relevance here with respect to which behaviors are important to the organization and where strengths and weaknesses individually and collectively exist. Coaching individuals regarding action to take as a result of the feedback is a critical process for moving the change toward the desired goals.

The third stage, *refreezing*, requires taking deliberate steps to establish a system or process that "locks in" the new, desired behaviors or state. Typically, in MSF applications refreezing is accomplished by (1) corporate commitment to regular and repeated administrations of the feedback, (2) meaningful linkages to existing internal systems and objectives, and (3) rewards that are clearly related to the new behaviors.

Since change is rarely initiated without the occurrence of some specific event and in fact frequently meets resistance throughout an organization, MSF data are a very effective way to contribute to large-scale organizational change efforts. Feedback can be used to catalyze the unfreezing process, specify the desired behaviors and culture of an organization, and (if implemented successfully) provide a means for refreezing the changes in place as well.

Systems Perspective

Aside from its action research orientation, it is important to understand that OD is also grounded in a social systems approach (Katz and Kahn, 1978). This means that, fundamentally, organizations are conceptualized in terms of inputs-throughputs-outputs, set in an environmental context, and comprising people and technology. It also means that large-scale change efforts are seen as occurring within an organizational system and its external environment. The result is that many OD practitioners concern themselves with developing, managing, and maintaining critical linkages between OD initiatives and the strategic objectives, senior leadership, culture, reward systems, information technology, middle management behaviors, and other aspects of the existing system in order to maximize the effectiveness of the change effort.

The Burke-Litwin model (1992) of organizational performance and change—a framework for data collection, diagnosis, and change implementation—reflects these assumptions and relationships at the systemic level (see Figure 19.1).

This model has been applied extensively to a variety of private and public settings to help frame various large-scale change initiatives (Burke, 1994; Burke and Jackson, 1991) and is particularly useful in guiding and integrating data-based assessments via feedback and survey efforts (see, for example, Burke, Coruzzi, and Church, 1996; Church and Waclawski, 1998; Waclawski, 1996). When OD efforts incorporate MSF tools and approaches, it is very helpful to use a model that facilitates understanding the systemic linkages and interdependencies involved. Such a perspective, of course, is entirely consistent with the notion of MSF as a systemic process, outlined in the Preface to this handbook, which in many ways also reflects an OD orientation (see Chapters One, Four, Twenty-Six, and Thirty for more detailed discussions of some of these issues).

In addition to the impact that a systems perspective has on the OD approach to change and MSF, two other points should be made. First, OD is somewhat divergent in mind-set from many other consulting approaches in that the interventions used are aimed at changing the entire social system, not simply the individual himself or herself. Although feedback is the catalyst, only through widespread use of data-based methods and well-integrated, reinforcing initiatives can lasting organizational change be achieved. Second, and equally important, the OD approach promotes application of data at the individual level, such as the kind collected in MSF applications, to the levels of the workgroup, department, function, and ultimately the entire organization.

In general, there are at least three types of large-scale applications in which individual-level data can be used (Church, 1999):

1. Organizational assessment
2. Validation of performance models
3. Measurement of culture change

Figure 19.1. The Burke-Litwin Model of Organizational Performance and Change.

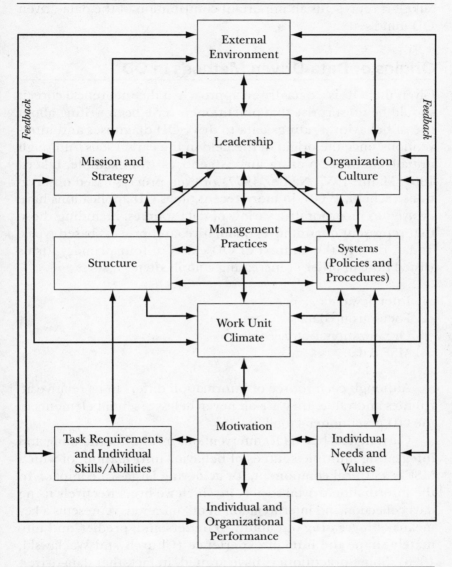

Source: From the Burke-Litwin Model of Organizational Performance and Change. Copyright ©1987, 1992 by W. Warner Burke Associates, Inc. Reprinted by permission.

Although using individual MSF results in this way might seem counterintuitive to some practitioners (consultants and academics alike), it represents an important contribution of the data-driven OD mind-set.

Origins of Data-Driven Methods in OD

Given that OD is a data-driven approach at the theoretical core, it should be no surprise that practitioners have been writing about use of behavioral-ratings data to drive OD diagnoses and interventions since the origin of the field in the early 1960s. Although initially focused on using survey feedback (for example, Likert, 1967; Mann, 1957; Nadler, 1977) or even process-based observations (Schein, 1969), in more recent times OD applications have evolved to incorporate a variety of data sources, including those that represent quantitative, qualitative, and process-based types. Today, data in the context of OD exists in four primary forms (listed here in order of increasing complexity):

1. Interview data
2. Focus group data
3. Organizational survey data
4. MSF data

Although each source of information differs in its relative attributes and value, they are all nevertheless essential elements in the OD practitioner's toolkit.

Current data-based OD interventions involve coordinating and integrating multiple sources of behavior information, of which MSF is a critical component, for achieving large-scale impact. In the information-driven society in which we live, effectively using data collection and interpretation in organizations represents a key means of increasing our ability to understand, predict, and ultimately shape the human experience (Church and Waclawski, 1998). Some practitioners have argued, in fact, that data-driven methods are one of the few skills that serve to differentiate OD, industrial-organizational psychology, and human resource development practitioners from other types of consulting professionals. In sum, although the nature and complexity of what is characterized as data have changed greatly in the past forty years, its use remains at the core of OD work.

Seven-Phase Consulting Model

Another important aspect of OD in which data serve as a key element is the consulting model that drives practice. Based again on the action research framework, it consists of seven clear phases— *phases,* not steps, since there is overlap throughout the process. We strongly advocate using all seven phases, as we believe this permits attention to the complete process from beginning to end in *any* consulting relationship (OD, industrial-organizational, human resource development, or whatever). The seven phases are as follows:

1. Entry
2. Contracting
3. Data gathering
4. Data analysis
5. Data feedback
6. Intervention
7. Evaluation

Although the consulting model (see Figure 19.2) has a broad range of application in a variety of consulting situations, it is especially important for the OD practitioner because it reinforces the importance of data in the change process. In particular, phases three through five of this model pertain exclusively to using data to create change.

The entry and contracting phases consist respectively of initial contact between the consultant and client and detailed discussion and agreement on mutual expectations and deliverables. For example, the client may contact the consultant (or several consultants) out of a desire to initiate an MSF system for the purpose of improving the climate of his or her workgroup or team. During the entry and contracting phases, the consultant and client not only discuss the client's needs and the consultant's experience but also explore such interpersonal issues as their ability to work together effectively and what they can and will accomplish.

Phases three through five of the consulting model concern collection, analysis, and feedback of data. To elaborate on the previous

Figure 19.2. The Seven-Phase Consulting Model.

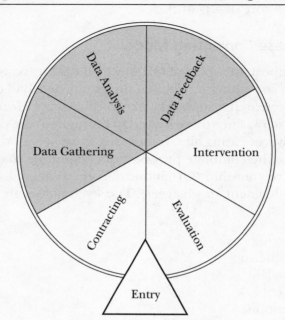

example, the MSF data collected about the workgroup climate are used to help team members understand the behaviors being exhibited as well as determine areas for improvement and change. Thus, MSF offers a means for comparing and contrasting the present with the ideal state, which is one of the basic methods by which energy for change is created.

Intervention based on the MSF results can then be planned to help realize the desired outcomes. In the context of MSF for OD, the range of interventions is varied and quite broad. The important point to remember is that subsequent interventions should be based on the MSF data (be data-driven) and that the consultant and client decide together on the action to be taken. This leads to enhanced commitment for the client and ultimately contributes to the success of the entire process.

Finally, evaluation of the success of the OD effort, including the MSF components, should be undertaken. This often involves collecting additional data regarding the impact of the intervention in light of the deliverables that were agreed on in the contracting phase.

A Normative Approach to OD

Before moving on to some concrete examples of OD-related MSF implementations, a few final points regarding OD work need to be addressed. First and foremost, OD is a normative approach to organization change. Just as industrial-organizational psychology is grounded in improving the conditions of people's lives and promoting human welfare in organizational settings, so too is the field of OD. Although not all OD practitioners act according to such ideals, there is a strong bias (and perhaps on the part of some, an ethical imperative) in OD work toward promoting human development and positive growth (Church, Burke, and Van Eynde, 1994; Waclawski, Church, and Burke, 1995). This emphasis has, in many ways, contributed significantly to the increasing popularity and widespread usage of MSF and related data-based applications (for example, surveys) for *solely developmental* purposes. Although the origins of MSF for performance assessment reside largely with industrial-organizational psychology (Landy and Farr, 1980), OD has been a driving force behind multisource application in organizations in the last twenty years.

Another important assumption of OD work, which oddly enough is also an underlying assumption of MSF and justification for its widespread application, is the notion that behavioral feedback from multiple sources leads to enhanced self-awareness on the part of the individual receiving it, which then leads to greater effectiveness, which in turn improves the performance of the organization as a whole (Church, 1994; Church and Bracken, 1997; London and Smither, 1995; Tornow, 1993). OD practitioners have been advocating data-based intervention on such beliefs since the 1970s, but empirical support for the linkage from self-awareness to performance has only appeared in the past ten years (see Atwater and Yammarino, 1992; Church, 1994, 1997; Furnham and Stringfield, 1994; Van Velsor, Taylor, and Leslie, 1993). Although recent reviews and research (for example, Kluger and De Nisi 1996; Walker and Smither, 1999) have indicated that the implementation process can significantly affect the outcome of feedback efforts, this is something that OD practitioners have been aware of for some time as well.

In sum, as a systemic process MSF fits quite well within the context of organization development and change. In fact, in many ways one could argue that OD has played a major role in shaping the state of MSF in industry today. OD has links to data feedback in general and MSF in particular, and both share many of the same underlying assumptions. In the next section, we present some applied examples of MSF systems embedded in an OD context.

Applications of MSF in Organization Development and Change

Given that OD represents a total systems approach to change, there are two primary ways in which to use MSF for organization development and change: first, as a means for enhancing and developing leadership, management, and team effectiveness across a given population; and second, as a tool for initiating, guiding, and reinforcing organizational culture change. The exact content and process by which an MSF system is designed and implemented can vary somewhat, depending on which method one is pursuing. Moreover, in some situations, both objectives may represent equally desired (and often highly integrated) outcomes.

Regardless of which approach takes priority, however, it is essential that when conducting MSF for OD purposes each client's MSF system be specifically developed, or at the very least highly customized, in conjunction with an in-depth competency analysis or needs assessment. This process affords the OD practitioner the opportunity to identify specific leadership behaviors and competencies critical to achieving the organization's strategic objectives or communicating and reinforcing the new culture that is to move the organization toward future success.

Although developing a customized assessment measure can be a time-consuming and costly process in comparison to using an off-the-shelf instrument, it is critical for the use of MSF for the purpose of organizational change. If done correctly, the instrument that is ultimately used should be a reflection of (1) the organization's culture (values, norms, beliefs, and attitudes), (2) systemic idiosyncrasies of the organization itself, and, importantly, (3) the intended purpose of the MSF initiative.

Only by using custom-designed, organization-specific competencies that align individual behaviors with corporate strategy can these two ends be accomplished. It is critical, however, when developing a customized measure or adapting an existing MSF measure to rely on good item design and measurement principles to ensure the reliability and validity of the tools involved (see Chapter Six for more on instrument design, and Chapter Nine for more on validity and reliability).

MSF for Culture Change

For anyone who has been through a culture change process, it is an understatement to say that a great deal of time and effort is required to successfully achieve it. Although MSF cannot accomplish such a change itself, it can significantly contribute to the success or failure of such a large-scale OD initiative. As noted earlier in the description of the Lewinian model, behavioral feedback, if implemented effectively, can contribute to all three major stages:

1. It serves as a catalyst for change by creating energy, thereby helping to unfreeze the present state.
2. It helps move the process forward by communicating behavioral guidelines while simultaneously offering individuals and organizations an assessment of their strengths and weakness.
3. If institutionalized as a truly successful MSF process, it serves the refreezing process by reinforcing the continued importance (vis-à-vis a continued measurement process) of the new way of doing business.

In short, MSF is a quantitative way to approach the often-overlooked people side of culture change. Here is a case example of an OD application of MSF in a culture change scenario.

A "Simply Better" Merger

About ten years ago, two large pharmaceutical companies—one headquartered in the United States and one in the United Kingdom—planned and subsequently initiated a "friendly" merger of the two organizations. At the time, the highly competitive and fractured state of the pharmaceutical industry was rampant with acquisitions, often of a less than amicable nature, which has continued to the present. Both organizations felt that a planned cooperative consolidation represented a better solution to forces facing both of them from the external environment than would a hostile takeover by some larger entity. Although the solution of "a merger of equals" may seem simple, the actual process of integrating two companies with distinct cultures (both organizationally and nationally) required a large-scale OD change approach. Thus, behavioral feedback as well as a culture survey was an integral part of this process.

Although we were already involved for some time in the organization at the senior management level, when the need to develop a new culture and a new set of leadership behaviors was articulated, additional resources were brought in to implement the data-driven aspects of the change effort. Specifically, in conjunction with designing and implementing an organizationwide culture survey based on the Burke-Litwin model (1992) and the organization's core values, a customized MSF system was also developed.

The purpose of this MSF process was to *communicate* and *assess* the newly defined set of corporate values and associated leadership principles to the entire management population. The organization embarked on a blitzkrieg of training, communication, and structural and system changes, all of which converged on a new way of doing business termed "simply better." Within two years, almost all senior and middle management had been assessed on the leadership principles, two administrations of the corporate opinion survey had occurred and were used for subsequent OD interventions at the functional and department levels, and many of the old systems and processes (rewards, performance management systems, training and development, and so on) had been either realigned or replaced entirely with a supportive set of systems that were in alignment with the new culture.

The organization has long since involved itself in other change initiatives (and consultants), but the data-driven change efforts contributed, at least in part, to the significant move in its ranking to fifth in its industry only a few short years after the merger. Moreover, the internal OD and HR functions, through shadow coaching, have developed the internal capacity to effectively administer and manage the use of their own survey and MSF efforts.

MSF for Executive and Leadership Development

In addition to its usefulness in culture change efforts, MSF can also be an effective tool in developing an organization's senior leadership and middle management ranks. This application of MSF is somewhat different from traditional executive development uses (see Chapter Seventeen) in that the feedback effort is specifically directed at a collective of managers or executives and is driven by organizational change rather than individual need. Two examples of this level of MSF effort are developing store management skills among shop floor employees in a home improvement retail chain, or increasing customer service awareness and skills among middle management in a newly acquired commercial bank.

Because these efforts are all directed at changing some fundamental aspect of the management population, they do in fact fit the systemic requirements for the OD approach in general and MSF systems as defined throughout this handbook. By contrast, using self-other feedback for other types of standard management training programs would not fall under the OD rubric.

The next section describes a case study in detail. It highlights the application and importance of MSF in this type of systemic leadership and management change process.

Consultants Developing Consultants

This MSF effort began roughly six years ago as part of a systemic organizational initiative with a large professional services firm consisting primarily of accountants. The main objective of the work was to help this firm's executive population (that is, tax and audit partners) develop the specific relationship and client management skills and behaviors needed to make the transition from operating as traditional accountants to becoming broader strategic business consultants in the eyes of their clients.

Driven by increasing competition in the marketplace and a long-standing tradition of operating with a certain mind-set, the organization initiated a number of interdependent efforts to promote such a shift in the senior service provider ranks. One very important element of this fundamental change initiative was a customized MSF process designed to assess the current skill levels and aid in developing the capabilities of the client's partners in the consulting arena.

In order to identify the right consulting competencies on which to measure (and subsequently coach) these partners, a series of critical-incident interviews were conducted with high-performing consultants within the firm. These interviews were conducted to identify the specific consulting skills that differentiated the higher-performing consultants, who were seen as already modeling the new behaviors required for the future of the firm, from the merely average-performing consultants. From this initial data collection effort, it was possible to isolate, measure, develop supporting processes, and track over time those competencies that partners had to master in order to provide better consulting services to their clients.

Once the MSF instrument was fully developed and piloted, it was sent not only to the traditional MSF constituents (that is, direct reports, peers, and supervisors) but also, more important, to a number of each partner's key clients. In this way, each senior service provider was given the opportunity (although the person may not always have seen it this way) to receive individualized feedback directly from his or her own clients regarding performance on core consulting competencies. Although the individuals in this organization had little prior experience with any type of ratings-based performance evaluation and were therefore initially anxious and skeptical, strong and consistent messages and actions regarding the strictly confidential and solely developmental use of the data gradually established considerable trust in and enthusiasm for the process in a comparatively short period of time.

As is often the case in MSF applications, partners received their individual feedback during a four-day off-site residential program. During this time, they received extensive performance coaching about their MSF feedback and personality preferences as assessed by the Myers-Briggs Type Indicator. Both small-group and one-on-one sessions with professional coaches having expertise in applied psychology were used to create personal development and action plans for each individual. Also part of the program were additional discussions and exercises focused on building knowledge and skills in change management. All in all, partners were exposed to a plethora of tools and techniques designed to help them better understand themselves vis-à-vis their new, broadened consulting role and their areas in need of (and with a plan for) change.

Now, several years later, the program is one of this organization's most successful offerings (with fifteen hundred partners having attended); it has had a lasting impact on the organization itself.

As stated in the original objectives, partners have been able to successfully transition from providing traditional accounting services to engaging their clients in a broader, consultative role. Our collaboration with this organization's internal research group has made it possible to pursue and demonstrate instrument validation and predictive relationship with respect to consulting performance as well.

Final Remarks on MSF and Change

The approaches to organizational change we have described can be characterized by a favorite adage of ours: "You can't change culture by trying directly to change culture." Presenting a list of new values with an admonition to go live them so that a new culture will emerge simply does not work. Even though having clarity about the desired culture and its underlying values is critical, the action that is taken must be at the level of individual behavior, not abstract concept. What must be identified are the specific behaviors that *lead to* the desired culture. Another way of making this point is to consider the often-expressed desire on the part of the CEO: "What we need is to change mental sets around here." Implementing MSF properly, as we have attempted to demonstrate through case examples, leads to change in mental sets, beliefs, and attitudes. For theory and research underlying this approach (and our adage), see Burke (1994) and the literature related to the James-Lange theory (such as Bargh and Chartrand, 1999; and Laird and Bresler, 1990).

Conclusion

In sum, MSF is a powerful and important tool for organization development and change. Future applications will undoubtedly raise new questions and challenges for OD practitioners, such as the advent of new technologies for data collection and feedback delivery and the distinct possibility that employees will soon feel (if they do not already) oversurveyed and even "overfeedbacked," but it is clear that data-driven methods for change, including MSF and organizational surveys, remain at the core of OD theory and interventions.

References

Atwater, L. E., and Yammarino, F. J. "Does Self-Other Agreement on Leadership Perceptions Moderate the Validity of Leadership and Performance Predictions?" *Personnel Psychology*, 1992, *45*, 141–164.

Bargh, J. A., and Chartrand, T. L. "The Unbearable Automaticity of Being." *American Psychologist*, 1999, *54*(7), 462–479.

Beckhard, R., and Harris, R. T. *Organizational Transitions: Managing Complex Change.* (2nd ed.) Reading, Mass.: Addison-Wesley, 1987.

Burke, W. W. *Organization Development: A Process of Learning and Changing.* (2nd ed.) Reading, Mass.: Addison-Wesley, 1994.

Burke, W. W., Coruzzi, C. A., and Church, A. H. "The Organizational Survey as an Intervention for Change." In A. I. Kraut (ed.), *Organizational Surveys: Tools for Assessment and Change.* San Francisco: Jossey-Bass, 1996.

Burke, W. W., and Jackson, P. "Making the SmithKline Beecham Merger Work." *Human Resource Management*, 1991, *30*, 69–87.

Burke, W. W., and Litwin, G. H. "A Causal Model of Organizational Performance and Change." *Journal of Management*, 1992, *18*, 523–545.

Church, A. H. "Managerial Self-Awareness in High-Performing Individuals in Organizations." *Dissertation Abstracts International*, 1994, *55-08B*, 2028. (University Microfilms no. AAI9427924)

Church, A. H. "Managerial Self-Awareness in High-Performing Individuals in Organizations." *Journal of Applied Psychology*, 1997, *82*, 281–292.

Church, A. H. "Large-Scale Applications of Small-Scale Data." *Performance in Practice*, Spring 1999, pp. 7–8.

Church, A. H., and Bracken, D. W. "Advancing the State of the Art of 360-Degree Feedback: Guest Editors' Comments on the Research and Practice of Multirater Assessment Methods." *Group and Organization Management*, 1997, *22*(2), 149–161.

Church, A. H., Burke, W. W., and Van Eynde, D. F. "Values, Motives, and Interventions of Organization Development Practitioners." *Group and Organization Management*, 1994, *19*(1), 5–50.

Church, A. H., and Waclawski, J. *Designing and Using Organizational Surveys.* Aldershot, England: Gower, 1998.

French, W. L. "Organization Development: Objectives, Assumptions, and Strategies." *California Management Review*, 1969, *12*, 23–34.

Frohman, M. A., Sashkin, M., and Kavanagh, M. J. "Action Research as Applied to Organization Development." *Organization and Administrative Sciences*, 1976, *7*, 129–142.

Furnham, A., and Stringfield, P. "Congruence of Self and Subordinate Ratings of Managerial Practices as a Correlate of Supervisor Evaluation." *Journal of Occupational and Organizational Psychology*, 1994, *67*, 57–67.

Katz, D., and Kahn, R. L. *The Social Psychology of Organizations*. (2nd ed.) New York: Wiley, 1978.

Kluger, A. N., and De Nisi, A. "The Effects of Feedback Interventions on Performance: A Historical Review, a Meta-Analysis and a Preliminary Feedback Intervention Theory." *Psychological Bulletin*, 1996, *119*(2), 254–284.

Laird, J. D., and Bresler, C. "William James and the Mechanisms of Emotional Experience." *Personality and Social Psychology Bulletin*, 1990, *16*, 636–651.

Landy, F., and Farr, J. L. "Performance Rating." *Psychological Bulletin*, 1980, *87*, 72–107.

Lewin, K. "Action Research and Minority Problems." *Journal of Social Issues*, 1946, *2*, 34–46.

Lewin, K. "Group Decision and Social Change." In E. E. Maccoby, T. M. Newcomer, and E. L. Harley (eds.), *Readings in Social Psychology*. Austin, Tex.: Holt, Rinehart and Winston, 1958.

Likert, R. *The Human Organization: Its Management and Value*. New York: McGraw-Hill, 1967.

London, M., and Smither, J. W. "Can Multi-Source Feedback Change Self-Awareness and Behavior? Theoretical Applications and Directions for Research." *Personnel Psychology*, 1995, *48*, 803–840.

Mann, F. C. "Studying and Creating Change: A Means to Understanding Social Organization." *Research in Industrial Human Relations*, 1957, *17*, 146–167.

Nadler, D. A. *Feedback and Organization Development: Using Data-Based Methods*. Reading, Mass.: Addison-Wesley, 1977.

Schein, E. H. *Process Consultation*. Reading, Mass.: Addison-Wesley, 1969.

Tornow, W. W. "Editor's Note: Introduction to Special Issue on 360-Degree Feedback." *Human Resource Management*, 1993, *32*(2–3), 211–219.

Van Velsor, E., Taylor, S., and Leslie, J. B. "An Examination of the Relationships Among Self-Perception Accuracy, Self-Awareness, Gender, and Leader Effectiveness." *Human Resource Management*, 1993, *32*(2–3), 249–263.

Waclawski, J. "Using Organizational Survey Results to Improve Organizational Performance." *Managing Service Quality*, 1996, *6*(4), 53–56.

Waclawski, J., Church, A. H., and Burke, W. W. "Women in Organization Development: A Profile of the Intervention Styles and Values of Today's Practitioners." *Journal of Organizational Change Management*, 1995, *8*(1), 12–22.

Walker, A. G., and Smither, J. W. "A Five-Year Study of Upward Feedback: What Managers Do with Their Results Matters." *Personnel Psychology*, 1999, *52*, 393–423.

CHAPTER 20

Performance Management and Decision Making

Richard Lepsinger
Anntoinette D. Lucia

As the popularity and importance of multisource feedback (MSF) as a method for evaluating employees increase, organizations are faced with a number of critical issues regarding its design and implementation. Its overwhelming success when used for individual feedback and development has caused many companies to look to MSF for administrative purposes, such as merit pay and advancement (London and Smither, 1995). However, the transition from development to performance management presents practitioners with some significant implementation questions. From participant perception to integration with other performance data, the benefits of multisource feedback depend greatly on how it is delivered. This chapter offers guidelines and recommendations, based on research and practitioner experience, to help ensure that when used for appraisal purposes, MSF achieves its intended objectives.

What's Wrong with Traditional Appraisal Systems?

Not surprisingly, a survey of Fortune 500 companies found that all use or plan to use an MSF process (London and Smither, 1995). Movement to a more open and participative process accurately reflects the changing nature of the manager's role, as well as the employee's responsibility for personal growth and development. Rather than relying on the supervisor as the sole source of feedback, multiple perspectives allow inclusion of data regarding teamwork, customer responsiveness, and personal development needs. The increasing emphasis in organizations on issues of empowerment, participation, and customer focus have only served to heighten the perennial issue of dissatisfaction with traditional appraisal methods (Bracken, 1996; London, 1997).

A well-designed and properly implemented performance appraisal system promotes a number of critical organizational objectives. First, it ensures that employees understand their role and the specific business results for which they are held accountable. The system may also be a powerful means of communication, delineating the organizational behaviors and values that need to be demonstrated to achieve strategic objectives (London and Beatty, 1993). Most important, an appraisal system gives participants information on their progress toward achieving agreed-on objectives, as well as an opportunity to adjust these targets or change behaviors as conditions warrant.

In our experience, several shortcomings make it difficult for traditional performance appraisal systems to achieve these objectives. Rather than discourage attempts at improving methods of evaluation, the vast amount of literature devoted to these concerns is testament to the enormous potential of feedback to enhance supervisor-subordinate relationships, foster group development, and improve service quality.

Outcome-Oriented Performance Criteria

The cornerstone of traditional performance appraisal has been outcomes. Rather than focusing on the critical behaviors required for success (the "how"), appraisals have focused primarily on whether or not success has been achieved (the "what"). The feedback process has limited impact and effectiveness unless it affords an opportunity to evaluate and discuss performance within the broader context of business performance, personal and organizational development, and corporate strategy and culture (Ulrich, 1997).

Limited Opportunities to Observe

Given the complexity of most jobs, a supervisor does not have enough information or opportunity to be the sole source of performance feedback (Fried, Tiegs, and Bellamy, 1992). Managers with several direct reports, or direct reports who are geographically dispersed, cannot observe behavior consistently or within the variety of contexts necessary to give a comprehensive view of performance. This makes it difficult for the manager to capture performance data over time and to collect sufficient information from multiple constituents.

Poor Reliability

Collecting, integrating, and evaluating performance data are cognitively complex tasks (Ilgen, Barnes-Farrell, and McKellin, 1993). Coupled with differences in rater skill, personality tendencies, and motivation, there is enormous potential for variability in rating consistency and accuracy. People remember information differently and face limitations as to the amount of information they can effectively assimilate and process. Because of this, managers may focus on a particular event, or set of events, and base the entire review on this information (Beach, 1990). The performance review is biased by the inability of a single individual to remember all the relevant information. Further, research indicates that when used for personnel decisions, ratings are even more vulnerable to error and bias (Antonioni, 1994; London and Wohlers, 1991).

Authoritarian Process

Despite the benefits feedback entails in directing, motivating, and rewarding behaviors, people do not naturally like it (London, 1997). Any process of evaluation creates concern for one's self-image, making the performance appraisal discussion challenging. When given solely by a supervisor, feedback is likely to be less favorably received (Bernardin, Dahumus, and Redmon, 1993). In this situation, the lack of additional perspectives on the employee's behavior causes the discussion to become the manager's view versus the direct report's. Requiring that multisource feedback be shared with one's manager can create a stressful and threatening situation. Inclusion of feedback from as many qualified sources as possible reduces the natural tendency of individuals to feel threatened. Reducing anxiety leads to more accurate self-assessment and thereby greater acceptance of the feedback itself (Atwater, Rousch, and Fischthal, 1995).

How MSF Can Enhance Appraisal Systems

Although MSF cannot overcome all of the problems inherent in a performance management system, it can address many of the difficulties associated with traditional methods. However, simply employing multiple sources of feedback as part of the appraisal process does not fix a system that is poorly designed or underused. When used appropriately, multisource feedback can make a significant contribution to an appraisal system in several ways.

A Common Language for Performance

The foundation of a well-developed MSF process is the skills, knowledge, and personal attributes that contribute to an individual's success in a particular job or business situation. By providing a common model of effective performance, MSF can help minimize the differences between the manager's and the direct report's perspectives regarding performance. Using a feedback questionnaire that is based on a company's existing competency model ensures that items are job-specific, relevant, and representative of current performance requirements, resulting in greater acceptance of feedback by the population assessed. The model ensures that discussion between the individual and the manager is contextual and focused on actual development needs. The data collected through the multisource assessment then serves as a basis for determining the extent to which these behaviors are being demonstrated.

Comprehensive Information

The multiple views of job performance provided by an MSF instrument decrease the chance that an important element of performance is overlooked. The value of MSF is that each source provides relevant information about a performance dimension but may evaluate the participant somewhat differently because the participant actually behaves differently toward each source (Antonioni, 1994). Participants are more willing to accept feedback (especially when it is negative) if provided by multiple sources (Antonioni, 1994). Rejecting negative feedback is more difficult if it is the shared perception of several people and not just the boss's message.

Specific Feedback

Multisource feedback provides behaviorally specific descriptors of responsibilities, skills, and abilities. The feedback is concrete and can be easily discussed, enabling those being assessed to pinpoint key action steps they can take to immediately address skill gaps or other developmental areas.

Focus for Development Priorities

By clearly showing strengths and areas for development, MSF can help participants have specific, focused goal-setting discussions that lead to realistic, challenging performance and development goals. There is extensive support for the belief that feedback enhances motivation by demonstrating which behaviors are required for successful performance (Ilgen, Fisher, and Taylor, 1979; Larson, 1984; Nadler, 1979). Therefore, individual development efforts may be focused on the competencies most critical for accomplishing key performance outcomes.

Facilitated Discussion

Integrating MSF into the performance appraisal process also facilitates open discussion. Studies show that people are more likely to change their behaviors and self-perceptions if presented with the perceptions of others through multisource feedback (see, for example, Campbell and Lee, 1988). A well-planned performance review discussion, where the manager presents balanced feedback constructively, can reduce defensiveness and allow productive goal setting and development planning. In fact, managers are more likely to provide feedback if it is perceived to be important, as well as tied to organizational rewards (Ilgen, Fisher, and Taylor, 1979; Larson, 1984; Nadler, 1979).

Are You Ready to Implement a Multisource Performance Management System?

Although enthusiasm for implementing multisource performance management systems remains high, more than half of the companies intending to use the feedback for appraisal purposes eventually decide against it (Timmreck and Bracken, 1996). Ensuring that there is a business case for implementing a multisource assessment and feedback process is fundamental to a successful effort. In addition, there are several questions you should ask before implementing a multisource performance management system; this section discusses them.

Have You Identified the Competencies Required for Success?

Many organizations assume incorrectly that in addition to assessing individual strengths and development needs, a multisource feedback tool represents a translation of an organization's vision and strategic objectives into actionable behaviors. Although it is not unusual to have several models of effectiveness being used simultaneously around a company, there needs to be agreement among members of the organization that the behaviors being measured are relevant and important to on-the-job performance. This sends a consistent message about what the organization values and helps ensure that people are open to the feedback and take the results seriously.

Have You Used MSF for Development?

Time and again, we have seen organizations fail to achieve their leadership and organizational objectives because they moved too quickly to integrate MSF into their performance management systems. Multisource feedback is a high-impact event, even when used for development only; using it in the appraisal process only raises the stakes. It is essential that participants be given time to get comfortable with the idea of receiving feedback and gain confidence in the system before moving forward with formal applications.

Do People Have Confidence in Its Integrity and Confidentiality?

Because the feedback has an impact on salary and compensation decisions (if only indirectly), it is critical that there be confidence in the system and belief that it produces an accurate picture of job-relevant behavior. The feedback instrument itself should be not only competency-based but pragmatic, flexible, and user-friendly. Perhaps most important, ensure confidentiality by establishing understanding of who is to have access to the results. Communicating that feedback is anonymous and confidential increases the likelihood of accurate and honest responses.

Can MSF Address What You Have Analyzed as Current Weakness in Appraisal?

As previously discussed, MSF does not fix a performance management system that is not currently working. Before integrating it into the performance management system, be sure to clarify which aspects of the system you hope to improve, and determine if in fact MSF addresses those issues. An effective performance management system is one that links together and integrates a variety of human resource and business activities (for example, goal setting, development planning, compensation, succession planning), helping employees and managers achieve results that support company objectives.

Does Your Culture Support Open and Honest Feedback?

If people in your organization are already comfortable giving and receiving feedback, it is likely they will be receptive to using multisource feedback as part of their appraisal. If this is not the case, it is unlikely that introducing MSF will change behavior. In this situation, work needs to be done to help people understand the value of feedback, and its potential benefit for accomplishing personal and organizational development and business goals.

Do You Have the Resources and Time to Make It Work?

In general, any performance management system is a time-consuming process. Even if efficiently administered and managed, MSF increases the time and effort required by participants. Therefore, it is essential that participants at all organizational levels understand how the feedback is used and its value for meeting personal and organizational goals.

Implementation Issues

Any organization integrating multisource feedback into its performance management system needs to address a number of issues prior to implementation. The decisions made in these areas, as well as understanding their effect, have a profound impact on the overall success of the effort.

Ownership of the Data

From our experience, we conclude that the issue creating the most difficulty in transitioning from a development-only system to using MSF data for appraisal is "ownership" of the feedback data. Decisions about who sees the data, when they see them, and how they are used directly affects trust and confidence in the system. When MSF is used exclusively for development purposes, participants are the sole recipients of their feedback. They are in control of the information, deciding the extent to which the data are shared and with whom. However, data gathered from multisource feedback intended for performance management purposes are often perceived as the property of the organization. In some cases, a supervisor may receive the feedback results before the recipient does. The feedback recipient has less control over who has access to the data and how they are used because they are now part of a system whose purpose is to get performance data into the hands of managers and HR professionals charged with helping to close performance gaps.

Perception of What Is at Stake

Although any type of feedback process is powerful, when multi-source feedback becomes part of appraisal its power is significantly increased. In development-only systems, there are generally few, if any, consequences for not meeting development goals. In these situations, the feedback recipient takes responsibility for interpreting the results and using the information to guide his or her development and performance improvement. The individual may attend training programs, read relevant books, or self-monitor use of new behaviors.

When integrated into performance management, MSF measures performance results that may affect the recipient's salary, promotion, and bonus. These decisions are much more sensitive and potentially threatening from the point of view of the feedback recipient. Direct reports are especially concerned that the feedback questionnaire must gather unbiased information that serves the interests of both the individual and the organization. See Chapter Twenty-Six for a thorough treatment of organizational integration of MSF.

Relevance of the Data

If promotion and compensation are affected by multisource feedback data, participants must believe that the behaviors being measured are relevant to effective performance on the job. Performance dimensions should be derived from analysis of the current job or the top managers' beliefs regarding those behaviors most likely to help meet future business challenges. Using competencies that have a strong correlation to individual and work-unit effectiveness helps alleviate concerns.

Time Requirements

Participants are often concerned with the amount of time and energy required to participate in an MSF process. The process is perceived as a needless departure from more pressing business responsibilities. Although the time required for a rater to complete a single questionnaire may be short, the total amount of time needed to implement the entire feedback process is significant at both individual and organizational levels. It has to include time for administering the process, completing questionnaires for multiple participants, analyzing the data, preparing feedback reports, creating development plans, and conducting the performance review and discussion.

Anonymity

Anonymity is always a major concern when implementing an MSF process, especially when it (or the intended application) is new to an organization. Raters provide the most honest, candid feedback if they are assured of their anonymity (London, 1997). The promise of anonymity gives confidence that no feedback recipient will confront a rater and accuse that person of providing negative feedback. Rater anonymity helps to ensure that a working relationship is not compromised. Therefore, using an outside firm to collect, analyze, and prepare the feedback data is preferable to doing this work internally.

Rater Selection

Studies show that feedback recipients are more likely to accept multisource feedback if it comes from a reliable and credible source. In other words, the feedback recipient must believe that the rater has enough familiarity with the recipient's tasks or behaviors and his or her performance of the tasks to make an accurate assessment. Additionally, it is important that recipients believe the raters' motives for providing feedback are well intentioned, rather than personally or politically motivated (Lepsinger and Lucia, 1997). See Chapter Seven for more on rater selection.

Collusion and Competitiveness

There is a very real concern about the effect of competitiveness on the quality of the data and perceptions of fairness and honesty in the system. Seldom will people overtly collude to ensure they get good feedback ("If you don't rate me poorly, I won't rate you poorly"). However, because the stakes are so high, some people may tacitly agree not to harm each other during the process. In addition, if the feedback is used punitively rather than as a means to build competence, over time raters move toward neutral ratings rather than give feedback they do not feel will be used constructively.

Using MSF Successfully in Performance Management Systems

For successful integration of multisource feedback into performance management, we strongly suggest that the feedback be used as only one part of the evaluation. The data should inform the boss's evaluation, not replace it with a formula or calculation to produce an overall rating. Properly used, MSF presents an opportunity to increase and diversify data inputs for the appraisal process. The weighting (mathematical or conceptual) of the feedback data versus results or objectives should be determined up front and clarified to all before the process starts. Participants should be prepared for the appraisal discussion, receiving information on what results were achieved and how those results were achieved. Ideally, feedback recipients should use their data as a starting point in a conversation with the manager regarding strengths and areas for future development. Subsequent development efforts should focus on those competencies most critical for accomplishing key performance outcomes. The Appendix of this handbook presents guidelines for using MSF in decision making. This section offers some other tips for successfully implementing multisource feedback into an appraisal process.

Involve People in the Process

Obtaining buy-in for the feedback process from key stakeholders (executives, senior line managers, HR colleagues, and so on) and developing a communication strategy to "market" the process gains support from participants and raters. Involving those likely to be evaluated using the MSF process increases individual commitment, both to the process itself and to the decisions made as a result of analyzing and interpreting the feedback. Examples of opportunities for involvement include identifying and developing competencies, selecting raters, and interpreting feedback results. Identifying a pilot group for the process, willing to provide concrete input and suggestions if needed, helps to engender commitment to and trust in the process.

To facilitate acceptance of the feedback, it is important to include participants in the selection of raters. Clearly communicate the categories of raters to be sought, as well as the rationale for doing so. Typically, feedback is collected from the recipient, supervisor, peers and colleagues, direct reports, and customers (internal or external). Establishing guidelines and recommendations regarding selection of raters helps participants to choose appropriate feedback sources. When selecting raters, the recipient should use these guidelines:

- Has this person worked with you long enough to observe you in a variety of situations?
- Do you depend on this person to get work done now?
- Will you feel comfortable discussing your key learnings from the feedback with this person—will he or she be willing to engage in honest, reflective conversation about it?
- Does this person understand the nature of your work and the challenges and opportunities you face?

The feedback recipient should also be sure to select raters with whom he or she has a range of relationships—some with whom the individual gets along well and some with whom the relationship is more difficult. The recipient should also choose raters from various groups with a variety of perspectives.

Although it can be viewed as an inconvenience, we highly recommend that people have the opportunity to work with their data to identify strengths and areas for development given their business demands. A computer generated "answer," or summary results from the boss, may leave direct reports feeling set up or judged inappropriately. Offering tools and activities to facilitate and support feedback interpretation and action planning (on-the-job opportunities, external job opportunities, coaches, role models) creates alignment between the organization's vision and day-to-day behavior (see Chapter Fourteen).

Ensure That Relevant Data Are Being Collected

The feedback questionnaire should include behaviors that have been shown to contribute solidly to on-the-job effectiveness. Even in organizations where a well-developed competency model is the basis for a cross-organizational multirater assessment, we recommend taking the additional time to validate the specific behaviors that have the strongest correlation to performance across the organization, within a level of the organization, or for a specific function (such as sales). The questionnaire items should be written as observable behaviors that raters are familiar enough with to evaluate. As a result, recipients and raters have more confidence in the quality of the data. In addition, whenever people believe the data are relevant to job performance, they are likely to be open to receiving the feedback and motivated to take action to close gaps in performance. Using behaviors that are important and equated with effective performance helps manage people's concerns about the time required to participate in the process, too.

Ensure That One Rater Cannot Distort the Results

Use of "Olympic scoring," which eliminates the highest and lowest scores, can minimize the impact of a single rater (Edwards and Ewen, 1996). Some automated programs developed for the purpose of integrating MSF into performance management systems can also detect responses that are outside an expected range and eliminate them. In addition, using a large enough sample ensures that no one rater has too great an impact on the overall results. Generally, it is recommended that a minimum of three respondents be required for a particular rater category (peers, direct reports, and so on) to be reported as such.

Train Raters in What and How to Observe

Helping raters understand which behaviors to focus on, what these behaviors look like in the workplace, how to record their observations, and how to identify critical incidents to use as examples to support their ratings ensures that the quality of the information people receive is high and that the data accurately reflect how the recipient conducts himself or herself on the job.

One client organization conducts this training in small-group settings. When multisource assessment was first introduced into the organization, all likely raters participated in a one-hour workshop. The training has been continued annually for those who are new to the process. In addition to increasing the likelihood of high-quality data, top management gets to reinforce what is important to how people successfully perform their roles, and why it is important. (See Chapter Eight for more coverage of rater training.)

Ensure Anonymity and Confidentiality of Responses

Several steps can be taken to increase people's confidence that their responses are anonymous and treated confidentially. It is recommended that organizations use a third party not affiliated with the parent organization to collect and tabulate the data, to ensure that no one inside the company sees individual responses or the individual feedback report. As we have noted, feedback from a category of raters should not be provided unless there are three or more responses for each category. Rater data should always be reported as an aggregate of each category's data (direct reports, colleagues, customers). Should there be less than the required number of respondents for a particular category, it is preferable to collapse the responses into an overall or "other" category rather than isolate or eliminate the information. Finally, the feedback report should not identify individual raters by name.

Simplify and Automate the System

The simpler the process used for collecting, tabulating, and presenting the feedback, the greater the likelihood people will participate enthusiastically. Technology has greatly streamlined the MSF process, providing possibilities for Internet and intranet administration and scoring. We have found response rates to be significantly better when organizations employ electronic survey distribution and employees understand how to use these electronic systems. In one organization, the response rate went from 65 percent to 98 percent when an electronic administration process was introduced (Lepsinger and Lucia, 1997). For more complete treatment of MSF technologies, see Chapter Eleven.

Summary

There are two clear schools of thought about whether or not multisource feedback can be used effectively as part of the appraisal process. Some researchers and practitioners believe it is not appropriate because it is difficult to get high-quality, honest data if the results are tied to promotion and compensation, and if the multisource questionnaire may not be able to accurately measure the complex relationship between individual behaviors and organizational outcomes (G. Yukl, personal communication, 1999). Others believe that the obstacles to using MSF in the performance discussion (accuracy, relevance, characteristics of human nature, and others) can be overcome. We believe that although the issues and obstacles are valid and difficult to surmount, practical techniques can be used to successfully address them. We also believe that the benefits of adding MSF to the performance management process make it worth the effort.

In general, an organization can successfully integrate multisource feedback into the performance management system if it follows three key principles. First, ensure that employees understand the business objective that using MSF addresses, as well as what's in it for them personally. Second, integrate multisource feedback over a period of time to give people an opportunity to get comfortable with the idea of giving and receiving feedback, and to demonstrate the integrity of the data collection process and the accuracy of the feedback report. Third, ensure that people on both sides of the performance discussion have the necessary skills and are prepared to have a constructive, useful performance discussion.

References

Antonioni, D. "The Effects of Feedback Accountability on Upward Appraisal Ratings." *Personnel Psychology,* 1994, *48,* 35–59.

Atwater, L. E., Rousch, P., and Fischthal, A. "The Impact of Feedback on Leaders' Performance and Self-Evaluations." Working paper, School of Management, State University of New York, Binghamton, 1992.

Atwater, L. E., Rousch, P., and Fischthal, A. "The Influence of Upward Feedback on Self- and Follower Ratings of Leadership." *Personnel Psychology,* 1995, *48,* 35–59.

Beach, L. R. *Image Theory: Decision Making in Personal and Organizational Contexts.* New York: Wiley, 1990.

Bernardin, H. J., Dahumus, S. A., and Redmon, G. "Attitudes of First-Line Supervisors Toward Subordinate Appraisals." *Human Resource Management,* 1993, *32,* 315–324.

Bracken, D. W. "Multisource (360-Degree) Feedback: Surveys for Individual and Organizational Development." In A. I. Kraut (Ed.), *Organizational Surveys: Tools for Assessment and Change.* San Francisco: Jossey-Bass, 1996.

Campbell, D. J., and Lee, C. "Self-Appraisal in Performance Evaluation: Development Versus Evaluation." *Academy of Management Review,* 1988, *13,* 302–314.

Edwards, M. R., and Ewen, A. J. *360-Degree Feedback: The Powerful New Model for Employee Assessment and Performance Improvement.* New York: AMACOM, 1996.

Fried, Y., Tiegs, R. B., and Bellamy, A. R. "Personal and Interpersonal Predictors of Supervisors' Avoidance of Evaluating Subordinates." *Journal of Applied Psychology,* 1992, *77,* 462–468.

Ilgen, D. R., Barnes-Farrell, J. L., and McKellin, D. B. "Performance Appraisal Process Research in the 1980s: What Has It Contributed to Appraisals in Use?" *Organizational Behavior and Human Decision Processes,* 1993, *54,* 321–368.

Ilgen, D. R., Fisher, C. D., and Taylor, M. S. "Consequences of Individual Feedback on Behavior in Organizations." *Journal of Applied Psychology,* 1979, *64,* 349–371.

Larson, J. R., Jr. "The Performance Feedback Process: A Preliminary Model." *Organizational Behavior and Human Performance,* 1984, *33,* 42–76.

Lepsinger, R., and Lucia, A. D. *The Art and Science of 360-Degree Feedback.* San Francisco: Pfeiffer, 1997.

London, M. *Job Feedback: Giving, Seeking and Using Feedback for Performance Improvement.* Mahwah, N.J.: Erlbaum, 1997.

London, M., and Beatty, R. W. "360-Degree Feedback as a Competitive Advantage." *Human Resource Management,* 1993, *32,* 353–372.

London, M., and Smither, J. W. "Can Multisource Feedback Change Perceptions of Goal Accomplishment, Self-Evaluations, and Performance-Related Outcomes? Theory-Based Applications and Directions for Research." *Personnel Psychology,* 1995, *48,* 803–839.

London, M., and Wohlers, A. J. "Agreement Between Subordinate and

Self-Ratings in Upward Feedback." *Personnel Psychology,* 1991, *44,* 375–390.

Nadler, D. A. "The Effects of Feedback on Task Group Behavior: A Review of the Experimental Research." *Organizational Behavior and Human Performance,* 1979, *23,* 309–338.

Timmreck, C. W., and Bracken, D. W. "Multisource Assessment: Reinforcing the Preferred 'Means' to the End." Paper presented at the eleventh annual conference of the Society for Industrial and Organizational Psychology, San Diego, Calif., Apr. 1996.

Ulrich, D. "Judge Me More by My Future Than by My Past." *Human Resource Management,* 1997, *36,* 5–8.

CHAPTER 21

Multisource Feedback for Personnel Decisions

John W. Fleenor
Stéphane Brutus

The purpose of this chapter is to consider the use of multisource feedback (MSF) for succession planning, staffing, and severance. In the first section, we review the historical challenges of using these practices. In the next section, we address how MSF can be used to improve decision making in these areas; and in the final section, we discuss appropriate and inappropriate use of MSF for these purposes.

Historical Challenges of Succession Planning, Staffing, and Severance

Succession Planning

Succession planning is an initiative taken by an organization to ensure the continued effective performance of its key people by facilitating their development and replacement (Rothwell, 1994). By making sure that potential candidates for management positions are continually identified, developed, trained, and appraised, succession planning is critical to the future success of the organization. In proactively tracking staffing needs, succession planning ensures the availability of the right types of managers to meet organizational objectives. If implemented correctly, it can result in a more efficient system for making developmental assignments and promotions into executive positions (Eastman, 1995).

Many organizations have had programs in place for years for identifying high-potential employees. Historically, the programs have focused on quantifying the promotability of employees rather than on developing their potential; however, the recent trend is for succession planning programs to be more developmental in nature.

There are several problems with identifying high-potential employees, among them that measuring potential is not an exact science. There is danger that the results could turn into a self-fulfilling prophecy and employees who are not selected become alienated. Many organizations fail to follow up the assessment with developmental activity. Organizations often require key executives to identify the individuals most likely to succeed them. Appraising managerial potential, however, is best accomplished by using the collective judgment of multiple assessors, rather than a single individual. Additionally, the input of the individuals being assessed is important to determine if the organization's plans for them match their own career goals (Gutteridge, 1986).

Although succession planning has been an important issue in organizations for years, practice continues to stay ahead of theory and research. Because succession planning involves identifying the next generation of leaders, top leadership is, of course, very interested. It is a sensitive topic to organizations, however, because much of their future success depends on how well their succession planning process proceeds. It involves identifying those individuals who will eventually move into top leadership positions—with all the political implications that such early identification implies. Organizations therefore are often reluctant to give outside researchers access to their succession planning data. In most organizations, top management develops its own succession planning system, heavily influenced by the organization's culture. In practice, succession planning systems tend to be much simpler than those proposed in the research literature (Hall, 1986).

Staffing

In some respects, staffing is similar to succession planning in that it entails selecting an individual, usually from a group of several candidates, to fill a vacant position. The primary difference is that succession planning typically involves early identification and grooming of candidates for upper-level positions, while staffing occurs at all levels of the organization.

Staffing is one area of human resource management that, over the years, has felt serious impact from legislation. The Civil Rights Act of 1991 makes it illegal to use age, ethnicity, gender, national origin, or religion as the basis for making employment decisions. Staffing decisions are often based on input from existing HR systems, such as performance appraisal ratings—for which there has been a long history of legal decisions. For example, the U.S. Supreme Court has ruled that performance appraisal systems should be held to the same standards of statistical validity as formal assessment procedures such as employment testing (*Watson* v. *Fort Worth Bank and Trust,* 1988).

In general, the courts have ruled that data used to make staffing and other employment decisions must have "a manifest relationship to the job in question" (that is, be valid). According to the courts, certain safeguards should be in place to protect employees, including a review-and-appeal process for employees who feel the system is unfair, and performance counseling for poor performers (McEvoy and Beck-Dudley, 1991).

Organizations may be required to demonstrate that their staffing procedures do not adversely affect protected classes of employees (such as women or minorities). Adverse impact is unintentional discrimination arising from practices that appear, on the surface, to be neutral (Malos, 1998). If a protected class claims that an organization's employment processes are biased against them, the employer must demonstrate that these procedures are valid and therefore not biased. Although in these situations some organizations choose to defend their employment systems in court, most cases are settled out of court. Because it is difficult to assess on-the-job performance accurately, reliance on flawed systems has motivated employers to settle quickly and for large amounts. (See Chapter Twenty-Eight for a detailed discussion of legal issues and MSF.)

In addition to any legal costs incurred for the reasons just discussed, an inefficient staffing system can have a negative long-term effect on the organization. Making poor staffing decisions can result in high productivity costs. Unfortunately, there are still gaps in our knowledge about the direct effects of good and poor staffing systems on organizational performance, and how certain staffing techniques work better in some organizations than in others. Effective staffing involves predicting and understanding not only the behavior of individuals but also of people in aggregate. Staffing researchers must maintain an organizational perspective and remember that such factors as compensation, leadership, and culture also influence organizational performance (Schneider and Schmitt, 1986).

Severance

Severance is and has always been a part of organizational life. That it is necessary to terminate incumbents who are either superfluous or unsuccessful is not debated here. Instead, we focus on the interaction between these necessary actions and MSF. The challenges of severance are similar to those of staffing or succession planning. Objectively, selecting in and selecting out both require valid information about individuals in order to decide who obtains (or keeps) a job. In both cases, a line is drawn as to who's in and who's out. Where the line is drawn is determined by information about the factors necessary to perform the job and individuals' performance on these factors.

The need for valid information is critical for severance decisions, as it is for staffing. In addition to validity issues, however, there is an emotional aspect to severance that is not present in staffing. The process of taking employment away from an individual carries an extra responsibility to do so accurately and fairly. As in staffing, there are legal precedents for basing these decisions on valid information and allowing a fair process. Research on downsizing has shown that the implications of laying off employees touch the parties directly involved with the process (supervisor and employee), of course, but also those beyond it (coworkers and other employees). The bottom line is that severance actions should be handled with extreme care; for the reasons outlined in the final section, we recommend that MSF *not* be used for making severance decisions.

How MSF Can Improve Decision Making in Organizations

MSF can improve both succession planning and staffing decisions in organizations.

Succession Planning

In today's leaner, flatter organization, succession planning has become more important than ever. A poor promotional decision in a key management position can be devastating to the organization. As a result, there is growing interest in assessing and developing managerial potential. Ratings gathered by an MSF process can be valuable for assessing potential, identifying managerial strengths and weaknesses, and making assignments to developmental activities.

Measuring Potential

Typically, identifying potential involves assessing all professional, managerial, and technical employees through middle management; succession planning per se is limited to senior management positions. Most organizations attempt to make their assessment programs as developmental as possible by using the assessment as a basis for a developmental discussion between manager and employee, and by integrating the assessment with activities such as on-the-job development (Gutteridge, 1986).

MSF instruments can be useful for measuring potential, which is an important piece of information for succession planning purposes. They can be used not just to identify individuals with high potential but to target them for developmental assignments as well. This process can limit the number of employees who need to be tracked, thus focusing attention on the most promising candidates, and reducing the administrative cost of the program. MSF therefore seems to be well suited to succession planning.

Although most MSF instruments are designed to measure current performance, some were developed to assess one's potential to perform in a more responsible role. Benchmarks, an instrument developed by the Center for Creative Leadership, or CCL (Lombardo and McCauley, 1994), has a section containing items that assess how well a manager would handle challenging job assignments, and a section with items for assessing a manager's potential for derailment.

Information on how well a manager would perform on one or more of these challenging job assignments or how likely he or she is to derail can be very important to use as input into a succession planning process, and the best method available for gathering this information appears to be MSF.

Identifying Strengths and Weaknesses

Probably the most common use of MSF is competency assessment. Typically, employees are assessed on a set of competencies that have been deemed important to the organization. Strengths and weaknesses on these competencies are measured by the MSF instrument and fed back to the individual employees, with suggestions for improving in areas of weakness. This information can be very useful as input into both succession planning and staffing decisions.

Staffing

In a common scenario for using MSF for staffing purposes, ratings are collected as part of a performance management system and then used as input into staffing decisions. Many managers see MSF as an appealing solution to problems with traditional performance management systems in which only the boss provides ratings. If ratings are gathered from many sources—such as peers, subordinates, and customers—the feedback may be more valid than with single-source ratings (Coates, 1998).

When used to make staffing decisions such as promotion, however, MSF can realistically be used only for selecting internal candidates. This is because the MSF process requires that raters be very familiar with the person they are assessing. In most cases, it's best if the raters have worked with the focal individual for a fairly long period of time. Although there may be a few instances where MSF ratings are available for external candidates, this is a rare occurrence. This limitation makes it difficult to compare internal and external candidates for the same position when MSF ratings are used. However, if there are several internal candidates vying for the same position, MSF ratings can be a useful piece of information to consider in making the selection decision. Other sources of information, such as how qualified the candidates are for the position in question, are of course relevant and should be weighted heavily.

Performance Management

Multisource feedback can be useful in performance management by setting performance standards and holding ratees accountable for their behavior. It can be a useful tool when no objective measures of performance are available, as is the case with most managerial positions (Dalton, 1998). MSF can be combined with management-by-objectives (MBO) measures to create a performance management system that captures most of the aspects of performance that lead to organizational success. Ratings from this system can then be used as input into staffing decisions. (See Chapter Twenty for more on using MSF for performance management.)

Development Versus Appraisal

The line that separates using MSF for development only from performance management purposes is very thin. Edwards and Ewen (1996) argue that MSF already is being used by most organizations, at least informally, for performance management, especially when an organization encourages its employees to share the feedback with their bosses. (For a detailed discussion of this issue, see Chapter Twenty-Three.)

Appropriate Uses of MSF for Administrative Purposes

There continues to be controversy over the use of MSF for administrative purposes, such as succession planning, compensation, staffing, and severance (Bracken and others, 1997). Data from the Upward Feedback Forum indicate that 93 percent of organizations use MSF for development purposes, and about half of the organizations that were originally planning to use it for administrative purposes have decided not to do so (Timmreck and Bracken, 1997).

A key issue to consider before using MSF administratively is the purpose for collecting the data. All administrative uses are not equal. They can be placed on a continuum, ranging from using the ratings as input into a succession planning system to using them to decide whom to lay off. Between these two extremes, there are a range of other uses, such as staffing and compensation.

Although organizations continue to be ambivalent about using MSF for administrative decision making, if it accurately measures job performance then failing to use the results for succession planning and staffing seems to be a waste of important information (Dalessio, 1998).

Confidentiality Issues with Using MSF

A key issue in implementing MSF systems for succession planning and staffing is the confidentiality of the data. In other words, who owns the data? In most development-only processes, the focal individual is seen as the owner of the data. In these processes, it is typical for a coach (who may not even work for the organization) to present the feedback to the individual in a one-on-one session and make developmental recommendations. No one else in the organization has access to the data.

When MSF is used for administrative purposes, however, the organization is seen as the owner, and a number of people may have access to the data (such as the focal individual's boss and certain HR staff). As can been seen, the level of confidentiality of the data differs considerably for these two types of MSF implementation.

The confidentiality issue is not a trivial one. The effects of allowing MSF ratings to be seen by the organization can be significant. For example, it's easy to see that employees might rate themselves differently if they know their bosses will see their data (Dalessio, 1998). There may also be similar effects on the ratings of others; managers may be less inclined to identify areas for development for their employees if they know their boss might see the ratings.

An issue related to confidentiality is anonymity. Because anonymous raters have been found to be more honest than nonanonymous raters, more accurate ratings are expected if anonymity can be assured (Kozlowski, Chao, and Morrison, 1998). Assuring anonymity depends on whether a climate of trust exists in the organization—that is, whether the raters believe their ratings will remain anonymous. However, many of today's computer-based MSF systems are able to identify who the raters are, something not as likely with paper-based systems. If the raters begin to believe that their anonymity is compromised, then less honesty can be expected in future administration of the process (Bracken, Timmreck, Fleenor, and Summers, forthcoming).

Trust is a key ingredient for a successful MSF process. In paper-based development-only systems, there is usually a high level of trust among the participants because confidentiality and anonymity can be assured. However, as MSF systems become more automated and common in staffing and other administrative purposes, the level of trust among participants starts to decline. To maintain the level of trust, administrators of such MSF systems must clearly inform the participants of the purpose for collecting the ratings, and what level of confidentiality and anonymity can be assured.

How the Purpose of Assessment Affects the MSF Process

An important factor to consider when implementing an administrative MSF process is the purpose of the assessment. Will the results be used for staffing, which is primarily administrative in nature, or will they be used for succession planning, which has a strong developmental component? The type of decision to be made using the results has a significant impact on how the MSF process is carried out (Bracken, 1996).

When MSF is used for staffing purposes, the competencies that are assessed are relevant to job incumbents in the target position. Because these competencies are directly related to the job in question, the assessment instrument is usually more focused and may be shorter than one used for succession planning. In a succession planning process, the content may be more developmental in nature and measure the individual's potential to perform at a higher level. When used for succession planning, the instrument may be longer and cover competencies that can be targeted for development.

When using MSF for staffing purposes, organizations should be able to readily demonstrate the job-relatedness of their assessment instrument. One way to do this is to ensure that the competencies measured are important for successful performance in the job in question. It also may be necessary to conduct a validity study to demonstrate that the ratings are statistically related to on-the-job performance, or that they have no adverse impact on protected classes of employees. This requires that the data be maintained so it is easily accessible to conduct validity and adverse-impact studies.

It is also necessary to have data that were collected fairly recently to use for decision making. Because a person's job performance may change over time, older data may no longer be an accurate reflection of that person's current level of performance. For developmental feedback, the CCL does not release MSF data more than one year old. This seems to be a reasonable rule of thumb to use for MSF data collected for any purpose, including staffing and succession planning.

An MSF process employed for staffing purposes generally uses a normative approach, where candidates are compared using internal norms and percentiles. Using this approach, the organization can directly compare employees who are being considered for promotion. A succession planning process usually focuses more on within-person ranking of competencies and identifying the relative strengths and weaknesses of the participant. Using this method, high-potential employees can be developed for executive-level positions through job assignments and training that afford experience in areas where development is needed.

When an MSF process is conducted for administrative purposes, the organization owns the data, which it uses to make decisions about the individual in question. Depending on the purpose of the assessment, however, different people in the organization have access to the data. If the purpose is for selection, the hiring manager and relevant HR staff have access to the data. If the purpose of the administration is succession planning, the executive team may be allowed to see the data. In any case, it should be made clear to participants up front exactly who will have access to their data. Additionally, it is important to maintain the confidentiality of the data; only people who have a legitimate need to see the data should have access.

The bottom line is that MSF processes must be carefully designed to suit the purpose of the assessment. Although feedback collected for decision making can be valuable for developmental purposes, systems intended for staffing purposes are usually not appropriate for use as succession planning tools, and vice versa.

Inappropriate Uses of Multisource Feedback

There are two areas where we recommend that MSF *not* be used: compensation and severance. This section presents the rationale for this recommendation.

Compensation

Using MSF for compensation has become a hotly debated topic (see Chapter Twenty). Some organizations are starting to use MSF for pay purposes because the ratings are credible and valid, HR supports its use for these purposes, and positive experience has been reported. Opponents of using MSF for pay purposes, however, cite several disadvantages, among them that it undermines the value of feedback for developmental purposes, and it encourages raters to use invalid rating strategies and inflate ratings (Edwards and Ewen, 1996).

According to Coates (1998), employers should be very careful when linking MSF to pay because it can lead to mistrust in the process and introduce undesirable rating bias, thus undermining the entire process. Edwards and Ewen (1996) believe solutions to these problems exist, although, as they note, it is important to realize that using MSF for pay purposes requires higher standards of legal and administrative preparation. According to Edwards and Ewen, using MSF for pay purposes requires, at a minimum:

- Clear communication to participants about the process and how the information is used
- Training on how to provide and receive multisource feedback
- Participant support for using MSF in pay decisions
- An assessment instrument customized specifically for the organization (standardized MSF instruments meet neither legal standards nor validity requirements for making pay decisions)
- Process safeguards to ensure validity and fairness

If MSF is used for pay purposes, Coates (1998) recommends that employers link only feedback about achievements or outcomes to the pay decision. Feedback about competence and behavior should only be used for development purposes. Employers should also ensure confidentiality by not allowing the boss to see all the multisource feedback. For example, Coates recommends allowing the boss to see only the average ratings on the competencies, but not the ratings on individual items.

According to Wimer and Nowack (1998), organizations often casually integrate MSF into existing pay systems, only to discover later that employees were engaged in a ratings game and that this produced a negative effect on the level of trust in subsequent MSF administrations. Wimer and Nowack warn that when ratings are integrated into pay-for-performance systems, they are usually inflated compared with ratings used solely for development purposes.

Using MSF ratings as direct input into compensation decisions, therefore, requires caution. As we have indicated, research suggests that raters are less honest in making their ratings if they know someone's pay is affected by their input. For example, Waldman, Atwater, and Antonioni (1998) report that up to 35 percent of raters indicate they would change their ratings if the ratings were used for these purposes. Additionally, participants may collude to give each other high ratings, ensuring that all involved receive pay increases. Using MSF to determine pay also gives raters the opportunity to retaliate against a disliked coworker by assigning that individual very low ratings. Because pay is one of the most sensitive and emotional issues in an organization, employees are likely to be motivated to collude and distort their ratings if MSF is tied to compensation. Usually, such problems are not present in development-only systems, where the motivation for raters to distort their ratings is much lower.

Scoring systems that eliminate statistical outliers (very high or low ratings relative to other raters)—one form of which is often referred to as the Olympic scoring method—do not appear to be a satisfactory solution for these problems (Bracken, Timmreck, Fleenor, and Summers, forthcoming). Because the true score of an individual's performance is unknown, making such corrections may actually be adding error to the ratings. For example, a subordinate could accurately assign her manager poor ratings but have these ratings thrown out because, when compared to the inflated ratings of the other subordinates, they appear to be outliers.

Although the problems discussed above also may occur if MSF is used for performance management, they are generally less severe because these ratings are usually only one of several sources of data used (for example, to make staffing decisions). If MSF ratings are used to make compensation decisions, there is a chance that an organization will use them inappropriately. Because pay decisions are usually made for all (or large groups of) employees on a very tight timetable, the organization may be tempted to use the ratings as the only input into the decision-making process. We've heard of organizations that base their compensation decisions solely on MSF ratings, without consideration of other important factors (such as how well the employee carried out assigned objectives during the rating period).

In most organizations, the amount of annual pay increase given to an employee is usually around 4–5 percent. Is it worth tainting an MSF system by linking it to compensation, when such a pay increase probably has a small motivational impact on performance? As indicated by Bracken, Timmreck, Fleenor, and Summers (forthcoming), factors that occur in one administration of MSF can have adverse effects on later administration.

Severance

Although organizations usually give poor performance as the reason for firing an employee, research suggests that people are more often terminated for their failure to get along with their coworkers (McCall and Lombardo, 1983). The interpersonal aspect of work, especially for a managerial job, is now widely recognized as an important part of job performance. MSF is an excellent tool for assessing the getting-along-with-others factor; there may be no better method for obtaining this information. It is easy, therefore, to understand why organizations are tempted to use MSF for making severance decisions. Although such usage may be defended, it is our opinion that this use compromises the long-term quality and success of the MSF process.

To explain our point of view, we'll start with a simple premise: for the most part, negative evaluations are involved in severance decisions. For us, this is a given. In the case of severance, we are dealing with specific situations in which raters make poor (often very poor) evaluations of the soon-to-be-fired individual. This type of evaluation (negative) is very important to the usefulness of the MSF process, because it allows distinction between individuals with varying levels of performance. However, the challenges associated with obtaining evaluations in the low range of the performance spectrum are substantial and unique; such challenges do not apply to obtaining positive ratings.

The rating process is voluntary and raters always have the option to communicate their opinions or not to communicate them. Before rating a coworker, raters ask themselves, consciously or unconsciously, a series of questions. First, *What are the implications, for myself, of being forthcoming with my negative evaluations?* Despite mechanisms put in place to protect the anonymity of raters and to reduce the fear of personal reprisal, many raters are suspicious or fearful that their evaluation will be known by the parties concerned. Of course, the perceived risk associated with negatively rating a coworker is contingent on how the negative evaluations are used. Collarelli and Beehr (1992) present four options for dealing with an employee who does not demonstrate adequate performance at work: remediation, motivation, disciplinary action, and firing. As one moves up (or shall we say, down) this ladder, the fear of reprisal also increases. The point is that, despite steps to ensure anonymity, some raters are reluctant to negatively rate others; this tendency is amplified when MSF is used for severance.

There is another question that raters ask themselves before putting their pencil to paper: *What are the implications for my coworkers of my being forthcoming with negative evaluations?* When MSF is used for development, raters can always find comfort in thinking that their negative evaluations make their coworkers aware of their shortcomings and perhaps contribute to their development. In this context, there is an altruistic side to giving negative evaluations. If used for severance, however, a coworker loses his or her job. In this situation, raters shoulder some of the responsibility for the severance, and this may affect the quality of their future evaluations. This is not to say that raters are always distraught by coworkers being severed; on the contrary, layoffs of unproductive coworkers are often a relief for organizational members. However, using MSF in termination may well exacerbate "survivor sickness," a phenomenon that pertains to feeling the guilt associated with retaining one's job while others lose theirs (Hickok, 1999).

Our argument against using MSF for severance rests on the fact that, in most cases, MSF processes are implemented with a long-term perspective. For those interested in one-time use of MSF, this prescription does not apply. Only when the feedback cycle is repeated—that is, when raters have observed how their ratings were used in previous administrations and are asked again to provide their ratings—do problematic trust issues arise. We believe that once an organization uses MSF to make severance decisions, employees may refuse to participate if they think the results will again be used for such a purpose.

Note that a "refusal to rate" can be subtle and impossible to detect, as when invalid ratings are provided. In these instances, it is the quality of the whole measurement process and the decisions based on that information that are jeopardized. We do recognize the need for collecting information from coworkers about the getting-along factor. As stated earlier, such information may be useful in making severance decisions. However, there are means other than MSF by which this information can be obtained. Formal grievance processes, for example, yield the same information without the problems raised by using MSF in severance.

Conclusion

It is our belief that a well-designed and implemented MSF process, one that meets relevant legal requirements, can be used successfully for succession planning and staffing purposes. However, because of the potential negative impact on future administrations, we do not recommend using MSF to make compensation or severance decisions.

References

Bracken, D. "Multisource (360-Degree) Feedback: Surveys for Individual and Organizational Development." In A. Kraut (ed.), *Organizational Surveys: Tools for Assessment and Change.* San Francisco: Jossey-Bass, 1996.

Bracken, D. W., Timmreck, C. W., Fleenor, J. W., and Summers, L. "360 Feedback from Another Angle." *Human Resource Management Journal,* forthcoming.

Bracken, D. W., and others. *Should 360-Degree Feedback Be Used Only for Developmental Purposes?* Greensboro, N.C.: Center for Creative Leadership, 1997.

Coates, D. "Don't Tie 360-Degree Feedback to Pay." *Training,* 1998, *35,* 68–75.

Collarelli, S. M., and Beehr, T. A. "Selection Out: Firings, Lay-Offs, and Retirements." In N. Schmitt, W. C. Borman, and Associates, *Personnel Selection in Organizations.* San Francisco: Jossey-Bass, 1992.

Dalessio, A. T. "Using Multisource Feedback for Employee Development and Personnel Decisions." In J. W. Smither (ed.), *Performance Appraisal: State of the Art in Practice.* San Francisco: Jossey-Bass, 1998.

Dalton, M. A. "Best Practices: Five Rationales for Using 360-Degree Feedback in Organizations." In W. W. Tornow and M. London (eds.), *Maximizing the Value of 360-Degree Feedback: A Process for Individual and Organizational Development.* San Francisco: Jossey-Bass, 1998.

Eastman, L. *Succession Planning: An Annotated Bibliography and Summary of Commonly Reported Organizational Practices.* Greensboro, N.C.: Center for Creative Leadership, 1995.

Edwards, M. R., and Ewen, A. J. "How to Manage Performance and Pay with 360-Degree Feedback." *Compensation and Benefits Review,* 1996, *28,* 41–47.

Gutteridge, T. "Organizational Career Development Systems: The State of the Practice." In D. T. Hall and Associates, *Career Development in Organizations.* San Francisco: Jossey Bass, 1986.

Hall, D. T. *Career Development in Organizations.* San Francisco: Jossey-Bass, 1986.

Hickok, T. *Workforce Reductions: An Annotated Bibliography.* Greensboro, N.C.: Center for Creative Leadership, 1999.

Kozlowski, S., Chao, G., and Morrison, R. "Games Raters Play: Politics, Strategies, and Impression Management in Performance Appraisal." In J. W. Smither (ed.), *Performance Appraisal: State of the Art in Practice.* San Francisco: Jossey-Bass, 1998.

Lombardo, M. M., and McCauley, C. D. *Benchmarks: Developmental Reference Points for Managers and Executives.* Greensboro, N.C.: Center for Creative Leadership, 1994.

Malos, S. "Current Legal Issues in Performance Appraisal." In J. W. Smither (ed.), *Performance Appraisal: State of the Art in Practice.* San Francisco: Jossey-Bass, 1998.

McCall, M. W., and Lombardo, M. M. *Off the Track: Why and How Successful Executives Get Derailed.* Greensboro, N.C.: Center for Creative Leadership, 1983.

McEvoy, G., and Beck-Dudley, C. "Legally Defensible Performance Appraisals." Paper presented at the sixth annual conference of the Society for Industrial and Organizational Psychology, St. Louis, Mo., Apr. 1991.

Rothwell, W. J. *Effective Succession Planning: Ensuring Leadership Continuity and Building Talent from Within.* New York: AMACOM, 1994.

Schneider, B., and Schmitt, N. *Staffing Organizations.* Glenview, Ill.: Scott, Foresman, 1986.

Timmreck, C. W., and Bracken, D. W. "Multisource Feedback: A Study of Its Use in Decision Making." *Employment Relations Today,* 1997, *24,* 21–27.

Waldman, D. A., Atwater, L. E., and Antonioni, D. "Has 360-Degree Feedback Gone Amok?" *Academy of Management Executive,* 1998, *12,* 86–94.

Watson v. Fort Worth Bank and Trust Co., 108 S.Ct. 2777 (1988).

Wimer, S., and Nowack, K. "13 Common Mistakes Using 360-Degree Feedback." *Training and Development,* 1998, *52,* 69–79.

CHAPTER 22

A Model for Behavior Change

Maxine A. Dalton
George P. Hollenbeck

The notion that people can and do change is remarkably recent in human history. Changes that took place in the old days (say, before the 1800s) were thought to come about as a result of external factors: God, nature, or fortuitous events, but not as a result of human intention. People were what they were, what they were born to be, and they stayed that way, barring any unusual happenings in the world around them (Seligman, 1994, provides an interesting description of the views then and now).

Although the world today can be divided into optimists and pessimists with regard to change, the arguments now center more on *how much* rather than *whether* people change. Optimists cite nurture and development (rather than nature and selection), believing that people change—a lot. They are, as they see it, well supported by evidence that people can and do change (see Hellervik, Hazucha, and Schneider, 1992), as well as by their own experience in seeing people change. Pessimists, more oriented to nature and selection, are not so sanguine about change and seem to be in ascendancy today. The authors of a recent management best-seller (Buckingham and Coffman, 1999), basing their management prescriptions on interviews with more than eighty thousand managers and a million employees, state in a *Fortune* interview, "One thing that we learned from our study of great managers [is] . . . that people don't change that much." (From the optimist's point of view, it is ironic that a pessimist on change should write a "how to" best-seller proposing to change how individuals manage.) But the possibility of change and improvement is so much a part of American ideology and entrepreneurial capitalism that it is almost un-American to believe that people can't change.

Focusing on *behaviors*, rather than people, resolves these contrasting points of view. Even though the optimists would admit that it can be difficult for a person to change, and the pessimists would concede that some people do change, both agree that *behavior* can change. A vice president of human resources commenting on the change in their company president as a result of a year's feedback and coaching, said, "He has changed his *behavior*, but I don't think that *he* has really changed." We both came away from a lively discussion happy; in our view we had succeeded, and in his view, the president himself had not changed—only his behavior had!

Most of us who use multisource feedback (MSF) are willing to accept changes in behavior as our criterion of success. And most of us are optimists. Our assumption is that people can change—their behaviors at least—and that they can be the agents of their own change, given appropriate conditions and support.

This chapter addresses how to facilitate behavior changes *after* MSF. Because we pick up after the MSF data have been gathered, we are building on the work of previous chapters. We presume several precedents: a clear and explicit, business-driven reason for the feedback intervention; an administrative process that is well thought out and transparent; a reliable and valid feedback tool; and trained, trustworthy, and credible feedback givers. Absent these preconditions, no meaningful development is likely to take place.

This is a practitioner's chapter. Although we cite references and research where available, many of our conclusions and recommendations are drawn from experiences (ours and others') in helping change happen. Although our focus is on behavior change in individuals rather than organizations, our theme is facilitating that change in a programmatic sense, rather than microanalysis of individual change.

Setting Realistic Expectations: What Is a Reasonable Outcome?

Most MSF activities are introduced for a target group, such as "all of the high potentials," or "all of the managers at grade 17." Despite the convenience of administering MSF to an entire group simultaneously, this method of delivery ignores the fact that individuals within the group almost certainly differ widely in their backgrounds, experiences and interests, their readiness and ability to change, and their baseline scores on the MSF dimensions. In even broader rollouts—such as an entire management population—the differences within the group are greater. Given their starting points and capabilities, what, then, is a reasonable expectation for change? Of course, it depends on the quality of the MSF program, from start to finish. Best practice is what this handbook is all about. But given best practice, what can organizations expect? What should they promise?

The research literature doesn't help a great deal in answering our question. Hellervik, Hazucha, and Schneider (1992) report on meta-analyses of research into the effectiveness of psychotherapy and of management development, finding median effect sizes of .78 for psychotherapy and .43 for managerial training (expressed in standard deviation units). Such results may give comfort to optimists for change, but they don't help much in answering our question of what a reasonable expectation is. MSF isn't psychotherapy, and MSF may or may not be followed by, or be a part of, management training. Rather than statistical effect sizes for total groups, some indication of who changes, how much, and under what conditions would be more useful.

Baird and Bolton (1999) suggest one estimate of the amount of change. They offer as guidelines for how much change is likely to occur as a result of a coaching intervention:

- Ninety percent will demonstrate increased self-awareness.
- Seventy percent will at least attempt the new behaviors while they are still the focus of attention.
- Twenty percent will actually be transformed; the new behavior will become part of a person's established repertoire.

McCauley and Hughes-James (1994) addressed the question somewhat differently in evaluating a program for school superintendents. They report that 58 percent of participants showed behavioral change following feedback, development planning, and a year of support and follow-up. Those who changed were new to their positions, were experiencing internal conflict in the transition, and had supportive back-home environments. Twenty-nine percent of participants changed very little; they were already doing well, were very experienced in their roles, and had stable environments. Thirteen percent showed almost no change; their issues were deep-seated and trait-based, and after the program they returned to difficult if not hostile work environments.

Surprisingly similar numbers are given by Conger (1992) in his follow-up of leadership development programs, all of which included some type of MSF. His estimates, based on his research:

- About 10 to 20 percent will show no change or little enhanced awareness.
- About 30 to 40 percent will show expanded awareness.
- About 25 to 30 percent will show some positive incremental behavior change.
- About 10 percent will make a significant positive behavioral change.

Conger points out that in the majority of cases, the primary effect from leadership development programs is building awareness—a result supported implicitly at least by Baird and Bolton. Conger (1992) goes on to discuss the vagaries of helping individuals develop, and he catches well the difficulties involved:

> Ultimately, the encouragement and development of leadership skills rests with the individual's own motivation and talent and with the receptiveness of their organizations to support and coach such skills. This leaves a lot to chance. Practicing . . . requires willpower, patience, and persistence . . . in the face of a busy day. In addition, subordinates and peers expect a sense of stability . . . [and] many organizations are simply not prepared for leadership. From the viewpoint of participants, there are additional difficulties. Not all adults can recognize and challenge their own assumptions. Some

are incapable of turning learning experiences into awareness because of their intellectual ability and defenses. For others, there may be intellectual awareness without action. . . . Some people may simply lack the will to change, to improve, to become leaders. And some may have profound psychological problems that prevent them from ever leading [pp. 181–182].

Since most MSF activities are considerably less intensive than a coaching intervention (much less a leadership development program), what level of change is reasonable to expect from what percentage of MSF participants? The less opportunity there is to consider individual issues of readiness, support, transition, and context, the lower the percentage of change likely from members of the group.

Most experienced feedback givers have had the disconcerting experience of standing in front of a group of twenty-five managers and telling them that they all *must* have an individual development plan, knowing full well that five of the people in the room don't need them, five will just go through the motions, five work for bad bosses, and perhaps ten of them are actually paying attention to what the trainer is saying. In an ideal world, only people interested in the feedback and motivated to change would be involved in a MSF process. In the real world, the facilitator must set his or her expectations appropriately and share those expectations with organizational sponsors.

The cited study results and our experience suggest that at least 10–20 percent of MSF participants are unlikely to change much, if at all. Perhaps 10 percent show significant change. Is that enough? Optimists that we are, we believe that given the importance of the behaviors addressed in good MSF programs, even those numbers are well worth the effort. Optimists that we are, we also propose that organizations can do significantly better through using tried-and-true techniques to facilitate change. In the next section, we present our model of change and the conditions necessary to support it.

Our Model of Change

To provide a framework for our discussion of the change process, we have adapted Prochaska, Norcross, and Di Clemente's six-stage change process (1995) to a four-step process. We have embedded this process of individual change within the context of the organization itself and the influence of the critical players in the individual's environment—his or her boss, peers, direct reports, and the facilitator of the MSF process.

Here are the four steps:

1. Becoming aware: developing within oneself an awareness of the need for change
2. Preparing for change and development planning: making the commitment to change, setting goals, and developing an action plan
3. Taking action: doing what it takes to develop new behaviors and discard old ones
4. Maintaining the gain: developing processes to maintain the gain

Each step in the change process is essential. Following Prochaska, Norcross, and Di Clemente (1995), we believe that significant change ordinarily begins with becoming aware and moving through each step. Again following Prochaska and colleagues, we posit that failure to change often results from jumping into the process at the wrong point (for example, taking action before preparing for change) or applying the right tools at the wrong time (say, role playing new behaviors without development planning). Let us now discuss each step in the change process.

Becoming Aware

Some years ago, we interviewed CEOs about firing very senior executives. The most surprising finding was that even (or especially) at these very senior levels, the executives in trouble "never knew." In talking with failed executives themselves, over and over we have heard "Nobody ever told me." The widespread use of MSF makes it increasingly difficult for individuals to plead that nobody told them how they were doing, either exceptionally well or exceptionally poorly. But even getting feedback doesn't guarantee awareness.

Seeing ourselves as others see us can be unsettling—especially when their vantage is not so favorable as our own—but discovering how they see us does not in itself make us want to change.

Practitioners make the mistake of assuming that because feedback can be emotionally charged and administratively expensive, discovering a self-other discrepancy in itself causes us to want to change. In fact, the response to MSF may be quite different. It may be denial ("They're wrong, I'm not really like that"); it may be discarding ("They may be right, but I don't care"); or it may be rationalization ("They may be right, but that's what I'm paid for around here").

Whatever the response, the individual may not own up to the need to change. Interestingly enough, these responses to MSF can occur whether the actual data show that people see us "better" than we see ourselves or worse; for example, they may deny that "I'm as good as I am" as well as that "I am that bad."

Awareness is the first step on the path to change. What conditions facilitate awareness?

One of the important conditions is an organization climate that encourages learning and change. If the organization—typified by one's boss—does not endorse the legitimacy of the process and the need for change, then denial, discarding, and rationalization are easy responses.

Given acceptance of the MSF data, for better or for worse, how does the individual become aware of the need for change? The key process is analysis of the gap between where I am and where I want to be. Examining the meaning of the MSF "personally, for me," how it affects "where I am versus where I want to be," is the essential task. (This process, the gap analysis, is equally as important in guiding the development plan as in helping the individual become aware.)

One such gap-analysis technique is described by Peterson and Hicks (1996) and is also discussed in Chapter Fourteen. They present a two-by-two matrix that can be used to raise awareness as well as inspire commitment. Examining where the person is and wants to be versus the person's view (and others'), they arrive at four cells: abilities, goals, perception of others, and expectation of others. Gaps can then be identified between one's abilities and one's goals, how others see you and what they expect of you, etc.

A trusted facilitator skilled at helping people own their data is key at this stage. Prochaska, Norcross, and Di Clemente (1995) present a number of specific suggestions for progressing through this stage to preparation; they have found that these early stages are where helping relationships are most valued by those who eventually change successfully.

Preparing for Change: Development Planning

Intentional change seldom takes place without commitment and planning, no matter how aware we may be of the need to change. A skilled facilitator is critical in obtaining the commitment and development plan that transforms intention and awareness into new behavior. In addition to helping to motivate and overcome the residue from sometimes messy and unexpected feedback, the facilitator brings the technology of behavioral change to the development planning process.

Goal setting is the first step in the development planning process. A key principle in goal setting is that participation in setting the goal produces the commitment and motivation to pursue it; the individual who is going to have to achieve the goal must choose the goal. In reviewing the MSF data, the facilitator may see scores that (to him or her) cry out for attention but that the individual may choose to ignore or avoid. So be it; our experience is that goals chosen by others have a short life expectancy. Following the tenets of adult education, we must begin where the learner is. The facilitator should bring attention to the risks of ignoring one piece of feedback or another, but only the individual can commit to change. Data denial is itself a message, however indirect, that the individual is not ready to change, and a message that should not be ignored.

Goal setting is fundamentally an analysis of gaps, between where we are and where we want to be. Two useful facilitation questions are: "In terms of your career, where do you want to be in five years?" and "What does the organization want (or need, or expect) from you now?" The answers mobilize individual motivation, gain commitment to change actions, and focus on what organizational support is needed to accomplish the plan.

A second principle is that goals must be few in number, clear and behavioral, and difficult but attainable. Having more than two or three developmental goals dilutes attention, reduces motivation, and too often results in ticking off activities completed rather than taking change action seriously. A clear behavioral goal goes beyond "Become a better group member" to specify behaviorally what that means—for example:

- Listen actively
- Restate what others have said for purposes of clarification
- Show others that I have heard their point of view
- From time to time, change my mind
- Acknowledge the contributions of others
- Listen more than I talk

Another principle is that developmental goals should be learning or mastery goals rather than performance or evaluation goals (see Button, Mathieu, and Zajac, 1996; Dweck, 1986; Vandewalle, 1997). Faced with a gap between what they want to do and what they can do, people have three choices:

1. Avoid situations where the skill is called for
2. Frame the deficit as a performance demand and focus effort on avoiding a poor evaluation
3. Set a *learning* goal, focused on mastery, recognizing that acquiring a new skill set requires practice and time

For difficult tasks, learning goals result in greater persistence, effort, and motivation to learn; success is more dependent on the person's own efforts. Part of helping individuals write achievable goals is to teach this concept of mastery rather than performance. (As we shall see later, the facilitators task is also to ensure that efforts toward mastery are recognized and rewarded by the organization.)

The second dynamic of development planning is to use varied and integrated learning strategies. Since publication of *The Lessons of Experience* (McCall, Lombardo, and Morrison, 1988), human resource development practitioners have accepted that development takes place primarily on the job, from challenging assignments. Often neglected, however, is that even with challenging assignments at the core, development is more likely to occur if a variety of learning strategies support the effort, including use of role models, coaches, ongoing feedback, reflection, and training courses. No single learning strategy is superior. It is the integration of a variety of strategies focused around the developmental goal and the work that produces results.

For example, a person working in information technology may have a development goal to become more effective at persuading and influencing her internal customers to adopt and use improvements in technology. A good learning strategy would be to find a current project that requires her to persuade her customers to adopt a new software package. Development is then not separate from the work, but an integral and meaningful part of getting results. Add a role model who performs this activity very well, a peer to provide ongoing feedback, and a training seminar on active listening and negotiation, and the individual is much more likely to develop the intended skill. All of these tools taken together produce a better outcome than adopting a single strategy, even if the strategy is a challenging assignment.

The skills of the development facilitator must include not only making feedback understandable and nonthreatening but also teaching how to learn, how to write developmental learning goals, how to unlearn that an individual development plan is solely about taking a course, and how to grasp that development and the work itself are completely integrated. A development plan that allows a person, at the end of the year, to say "I was too busy doing my job to work on this developmental goal" is a wrong-headed development plan. The development goal should be achieved through doing the work. Perhaps it is needless to say, but the boss must not be immune from this message.

Taking Action

Busy individuals make the mistake of assuming that development stops with the plan. Although awareness and preparation may result in learning taking place, taking action begins the process—both symbolically and in fact—of developing new skills. Like many journeys, the development journey often begins with great energy and enthusiasm. The trick is to keep the development process going. The coach or facilitator helps the individual turn the plan into action and also serves as motivator, nudge, cop, teacher—whatever it takes to help the person stay on track in developing and practicing new behaviors or discarding old ones.

The people around the individual are critical at this stage. It is especially important for individuals taking action to tell others what they are trying to do, which behaviors they are trying to change. Bosses, peers, and direct reports provide ongoing feedback, monitor changes, and provide rewards; additionally, communication helps to market the change. The adage "Get a reputation as an early riser and you can sleep till noon" reflects the natural tendency for others to hold on to their views of us, even after we have changed. Telling others what we are attempting to change helps them notice the changes. In addition, development inevitably does not take place on an ever-upward trajectory. Other people are a key source of support and motivation when the individual is discouraged from not meeting the new aspirations.

As it turns out, discussing one's feedback with direct reports may have an additional beneficial result. Walker and Smither (1999) report on a five-year follow-up study of managers who participated in an upward feedback program. They found that managers who met with direct reports to discuss their feedback improved more than managers who did not. Whether a marketing effect or reality, perceptions increased. The implication for the coach-facilitator is that MSF receivers need to know how to conduct a feedback session, and direct reports need to know also how to make such meetings useful. This is particularly important for managers who have received harsh or negative feedback from the direct reports. In such cases, the facilitator may serve a useful role in ensuring that the very behavior that triggered the negative evaluations does not sidetrack the meeting.

Peers make up another set of major players in the MSF program. One study (Farh, Canella, and Bedeian, 1991) reports that asking peers for negative as well as positive feedback enhances the peers' subsequent evaluation of the colleague who asked for the feedback. Apparently, sharing one's strengths and weaknesses increased accountability and commitment and—at least in the United States—is a way of bringing others over to one's side and actually improving their perception of one's skill.

Dalton and Hollenbeck (1996) discuss the critical role of the boss in helping turn the development plan into action. Hazucha, Hezlett, and Schneider (1993) found that the boss of the person receiving MSF was the most important factor in determining whether or not change took place. The person who was most likely to change shared the development plan with the boss, received a positive and encouraging response from the boss, and engaged in a greater variety of developmental activities. In another study, Ruderman, Ohlott, and McCauley (1996) found that a supportive boss could compensate for an individual's low self-esteem, which might otherwise hinder learning from a challenging assignment.

These studies indicate the critical role of the boss in MSF interventions. Bosses need to understand how learning occurs, how to hold a development discussion, and how to give (and get) feedback. At a minimum, they need to understand how a given MSF and development planning activity are tied to such business results as improving climate survey scores, retaining key employees, preparing successors, and developing managers for a changing work environment. Bosses support development efforts that get the work done; they are unlikely to support activities that are distracting, irrelevant, and without consequence. Bosses often hold the keys to development resources, and they should be held accountable for their reports' achieving development goals.

Maintaining the Gain

The bane of all change programs is that the changes frequently don't last. The individual may change in the classroom, but it may not carry over to the workplace. Or if the change succeeds in the workplace, there may be forces within both the individual and the organization acting to get things back to how they were. The key, of course, is an environment that supports the new behaviors.

There are a number of things that individuals can do themselves to maintain their gains: set up self-reward systems, avoid "tempting" situations, and so on. The coach-facilitator should be able to help them set up their own maintenance systems. But a major share of the responsibility for maintaining (as well as encouraging) new behaviors rests with the organization's systems and processes. The earlier quote from Conger (1992) highlights the problems of change when subordinates expect stability from their manager, and when companies may not want the new behaviors they profess (say, open feedback). The study of McCauley and Hughes-James (1994) found that supportive back-home environments encouraged change, while difficult and hostile environments discouraged it. Change from MSF intervention cannot be expected to continue unless the organization rewards and supports it. Those who plan MSF interventions would do well to examine the literature of organization change for insights into processes that support new behaviors. Organization change specialists (Nadler and others, 1995) have devoted a great deal of attention to maintaining planned organization change and implementing support processes.

Additional Organization-Level Issues: Evaluation and Accountability Systems

Three kinds of evaluation activity are essential. First, at the individual level, success in meeting development goals should be measured and rewarded. Somewhere between twelve and eighteen months after MSF, evaluation should occur, with appropriate follow-up actions; if development took place, it should be rewarded. "No change" also signals the need for action. Is the no-change outcome the result of lack of effort, lack of support, or a deficit in ability? If there are no consequences to failing to meet development goals, there will be little development.

A second evaluation should address the success of the total intervention. Were reasonable outcomes met? Did the intervention meet the business purpose of the program? Did grievances decline? Did turnover decrease? Were more internal hires made from the high-potential pool? Did design and development cycle time decrease?

The final evaluation piece is the process evaluation. To interpret the program outcomes, the program manager must determine whether the necessary action-and-result links were present. For example, did the individuals meet with the bosses? Did the boss respond positively? Were opportunities and resources provided? Are development plans integrated and work-related, or do they typically read something like "Take a course"? Only by reviewing the processes and links can the program manager know how to improve the process for the next go-round.

Conclusion

Facilitating change after MSF feedback requires understanding the change process and the conditions that contribute to lasting changes in behavior. We have presented a model that includes four stages of change: becoming aware, preparing for change, taking action, and maintaining the gain. This model is supported by a cast featuring coach-facilitator, bosses, peers, direct reports, the feedback itself, and the organization systems and processes that support and maintain change. For each stage, we have indicated briefly some of the key variables.

MSF interventions, we believe, consistently underestimate the amount of organization and individual resources required for lasting, meaningful change to occur. Overall, success in an MSF program depends on what goes into it. Dalton (1998) recently described five feedback programs, ranging in scope from a completely hands-off approach to an elaborate, yearlong intervention supported by coaches, training for bosses, and rewards for participation. Each design represents a unique development strategy and allocation of organizational resources. To the extent that the organization needs large numbers of people who actually learn, grow, and change as a result of an MSF process, it makes sense to design an intervention that addresses as many of the facilitation factors as possible.

How much does it take in the way of resources? As a rule of thumb, we would suggest that five to ten times as much effort and resources be spent on the after-MSF process as on selecting and delivering the MSF feedback. Individuals aware of the need for change, with well-prepared development plans incorporating multiple strategies that are linked to business results, organizational players who can and will support the effort, and ongoing evaluation of the process and the outcomes—these are, we believe, the necessary and sufficient conditions for significant change to take place.

References

Baird, J. A., and Bolton, M. "Coaching for Breakthroughs." Presentation made at the Tools/Benchmarks Users Conference, Greensboro, N.C., Mar. 22–23, 1999.

Buckingham, M., and Coffman, C. "First, Break All the Rules." *Fortune,* Oct. 25, 1999, p. 366.

Button, S. B., Mathieu, J. E., and Zajac, D. M. "Goal Orientation in Organizational Research: A Conceptual and Empirical Foundation." *Organizational Behavior and Human Decision Processes,* 1996, *67*(1), 26–48.

Conger, J. A. *Learning to Lead: The Art of Transforming Managers into Leaders.* San Francisco: Jossey-Bass, 1992.

Dalton, M. A. "Best Practices: Five Rationales for Using 360-Degree Feedback in Organizations." In W. W. Tornow and M. London (eds.), *Maximizing the Value of 360-Degree Feedback: A Process for Successful Individual and Organizational Development.* San Francisco: Jossey-Bass, 1998.

Dalton, M. A., and Hollenbeck, G. P. *How to Design an Effective System for Developing Managers and Individuals.* Greensboro, N.C.: Center for Creative Leadership, 1996.

Dweck, C. S. "Motivational Processes Affecting Learning." *American Psychologist,* 1986, *41*(10), 1040–1048.

Farh, J. L., Canella, A. A., and Bedeian, A. G. " Peer Ratings: The Impact of Purpose on Rating Quality and User Acceptance." *Group and Organizational Studies,* 1991, *16*(4), 367–386.

Hazucha, J. F., Hezlett, S. A., and Schneider, R. J. "The Impact of 360-Degree Feedback on Management Skills Development." *Human Resource Management,* 1993, *32,* 325–352.

Hellervik, L. W., Hazucha, J. F., and Schneider, R. J. "Behavior Change: Models, Methods, and a Review of Evidence." In M. D. Dunnette and L. M. Hough (eds.), *Handbook of Industrial and Organizational Psychology.* Vol. 3. Palo Alto, Calif.: Consulting Psychologists Press, 1992.

McCall, M. W., Jr., Lombardo, M. M., and Morrison, A. M. *The Lessons of Experience: How Successful Individuals Develop on the Job.* San Francisco: New Lexington Press, 1988.

McCauley, C. D., and Hughes-James, M. *An Evaluation of Outcomes of a Leadership Development Program.* Greensboro, N.C.: Center for Creative Leadership, 1994.

Nadler, D. A., Shaw, R. B., Walton, A. E., and Associates. *Discontinuous Change: Leading Organizational Transformations.* San Francisco: Jossey-Bass, 1995.

Peterson, D. H., and Hicks, M. D. *Leaders as Coaches: Strategies for Coaching and Developing Others.* Minneapolis: Personnel Decisions International, 1996.

Prochaska, J. O., Norcross, J. C., and Di Clemente, C. C. *Changing for Good.* New York: Avon, 1995.

Ruderman, M. N., Ohlott, P. J., and McCauley, C. D. "Developing from Job Experiences: The Role of Self-Esteem and Self-Efficacy." Paper presented at the eleventh annual conference of the Society for Industrial and Organizational Psychology, San Diego, Calif., Apr. 1996.

Seligman, M.E.P. *What You Can Change and What You Can't: The Complete Guide to Successful Self-Improvement.* New York: Knopf, 1994.

Vandewalle, D. "Development and Validation of a Work Domain Goal Orientation Instrument." *Educational and Psychological Measurement,* 1997, *57,* 995–1015.

Walker, A. G., and Smither, J. W. "A Five-Year Study of Upward Feedback: What Managers Do with Their Results Matters." *Personnel Psychology,* 1999, *52,* 393–423.

CHAPTER 23

The Great Debate

Should Multisource Feedback Be Used for Administration or Development Only?

Manuel London

Many organizations are ambivalent about using multisource feedback (MSF) for development or for personnel decisions (Church and Bracken, 1997; Dalessio, 1998; Timmreck and Bracken, 1995, 1996). One viewpoint is that it should be used only for development, and that using it to make human resource decisions undermines its value to managers receiving the feedback and to the organization. Another viewpoint is that although MSF is valuable for development, and if MSF survey results actually capture performance information accurately (otherwise, the results should not be useful for development), then the results should be used to make decisions about the ratees as well. Not to do so is wasteful of costly information at the expense of the individual and the organization.

This chapter explores this "great debate" by examining the pros and cons of using MSF for administration versus development only. The goal is to derive recommendations for when MSF should be used for development alone and when it can be useful for administrative purposes as well.

Arguments for and Against
Use for Administration

MSF may be used for three purposes: individual development, administrative decision making, and organizational development (Bracken, 1996). The particular use has key implications for designing the total process. Also, the purpose needs to be clearly established and communicated before the survey is administered so that the users fully understand it. However, there are a number of pros and cons for using MSF surveys for administration and development. First, I consider why multisource feedback is valuable for development. Then I review the pros and cons for using it for administration as well as development.

Why MSF Is Valuable for Development

A number of reasons have been given for MSF being useful for development:

• Multiple raters provide comprehensive and accurate information that gives direction for behavior change and performance improvement. Subordinates and peers are often in a better position than the immediate supervisor is to evaluate some aspects of performance, such as interpersonal behavior (Bracken, 1996; Murphy and Cleveland, 1995).

• MSF results enhance self-awareness through the cognitive process of self-reflection, and self-awareness contributes to behavior change (Church and Bracken, 1997).

• Managers value others' opinions and feel accountable to respond to them (London, Smither, and Adsit, 1997).

• Across multiple applications of the survey, the ratings constitute a basis for tracking one's own achievements—a way of pacing and rewarding oneself. Normative information (such as the average ratings received by managers at the same organizational level) is a basis for comparison, and it may engender motivation to improve through competition.

Individual development is the major use of MSF (Bracken, 1996). Coupled with guidance and resources, the ratee can be directed on how to interpret the results and obtain appropriate training and career planning resources. Several features of the survey process encourage ratees to treat the results seriously. First, rating is done anonymously (important because of the assumption that anonymous raters are more honest and so their ratings are more accurate than those of people who may have a vested interest in the results). Second, confidential rating creates psychological safety (only the ratee sees them, and the ratee is not obliged to share them with others). Third, including self-rating in the process allows the ratee to compare self-perception with the feedback results to identify gaps and direction for behavioral change and to increase self-awareness.

MSF data can also be used as an organization development tool. The results can be aggregated across managers to generate a skill profile for the entire organization or unit. This information can be used in team building and discussions about performance issues, ultimately creating a feedback-rich climate. Such data and related intervention can break down barriers created by authority and traditional hierarchy (Murphy and Cleveland, 1995).

Arguments in Favor of Use in Administration

Consider these arguments for why MSF should be used to make pay or promotion decisions:

- Good decisions about people require information from diverse sources.
- Multiple raters are needed to evaluate a manager; therefore, the results are better than any one or even several top managers' evaluations alone (an assumption that needs to be tested).
- MSF ratings are key points of information about an individual's performance, especially when performance cannot be easily quantified by more direct, objective measures, as with sales figures or production volume (Reilly and McGourty, 1998).
- The organization pays good money to collect the information, and employees take the time to complete the ratings, so the information should be used in every way that can benefit the organization.

- If the information yields better decisions about people, then the organization should use it. Not to do so is a disservice to the stockholders.
- Presumably, raters feel better about their participation and provide more reliable and accurate ratings if they know that the organization is using the information to evaluate and make decisions about the people they rate.
- Having to explain feedback results to one's boss or the raters, or to an objective third party such as a coach, engenders commitment to change (London, Smither, and Adsit, 1997).
- Some organizations ask supervisors to gather input from multiple sources before writing a performance evaluation. This may be an informal process—not a formalized requirement with a structured appraisal survey, but rather simply suggesting that managers contact the subordinate's key clients and direct reports. MSF makes this a more reliable process. Also, a multi-source survey process guards the sources' anonymity.
- MSF ratings produce additional input to the appraisal. They are not intended to be the sole input or replace other measures relevant to performance review, such as data on accomplishments, supervisory analysis, and self-assessment.
- MSF is especially useful in new forms of organization, such as a self-managing team, a flat organizational structure, or a customer-driven organizational culture in which employees are empowered to be integrally involved in the performance management process (Reilly and McGourty, 1998).

Dalton (1998) added some reasons MSF should be used for appraisal:

- MSF ratings provide ratees with feedback on skills they need for their current job. Ratings on a performance dimension bring everyone up to standard.
- The appraisal process should be as comprehensive as the development process, and individuals should be rewarded for having skills that the organization values, as seen from varied perspectives.
- MSF data are only useful if they are shared with the supervisor and used to formulate a development plan that is tied to rewards.

- The data put teeth into the process of organizational change and hold feedback recipients accountable for expected behaviors (Bracken, 1997; Tornow, 1998).
- MSF improves the likelihood that behavior change results from the appraisal.

Regarding this last point, using information from just the boss promotes an autocratic and rigid, "Theory X" culture—a condition that is especially inappropriate in team-based, flat organizational structures that are more "Theory Y" in nature (Pollman, 1997). Keeping results secret from the boss is contradictory to a culture in which team members and the supervisor need to know each other's strengths and weaknesses.

Bracken (1996) offered other reasons that using MSF for development alone may result in underuse of the full potential of the process. It may be hard to sustain the development process, for the following reasons:

- Ratees may not be accountable for follow-through and may not be motivated to change
- Ratees see the feedback as supplemental, nice to have but tangential to their real work
- Ratees see the feedback as an "event" happening only once or at long intervals, lacking ongoing involvement and feedback
- Raters may not see evidence that their input is used, and this may reduce their motivation to participate or offer honest feedback

Arguments Against Use for Administration

Although there are many reasons for using MSF results to make decisions about people, there are some strong arguments why this isn't a good idea.

- MSF may reduce supervisors' discretion over administration.
- Giving advice and counsel doesn't mix with evaluation and judgment. People resist advice from those who are judgmental. Ratees become defensive and don't focus on the implications of the results for their development (London and Tornow, 1998). People

experience role conflict when they are put in the position of being a coach and devaluator or decision maker. The boss may not be a skillful coach or, worse, may be a punitive individual (Dalton, 1997). Even for skilled managers, coaching for performance is best separated in time and place from performance appraisal discussions (Tornow, 1998; Meyer, Kay, and French, 1965).

• Managers are not open to seeking negative feedback about their behavior from supervisors, direct reports, and peers as part of the developmental process or administrative process (Ashford and Tsui, 1991). This questions the use of MSF even for development.

• Sharing feedback data with the supervisor can be stressful and threatening (Dalessio, 1998; Dalton, 1996, 1997). Ratees may cope by using strategies that are counter to personal development, such as trying to manage the supervisor's impression of them by attributing the results to uncontrollable factors in the environment.

• The ratings may be in question, at least in the eyes of the ratees, if the raters have a vested interest in the results. This could happen if, for instance, a manager's annual bonus depends, in whole or in part, on the opinions of their subordinates.

• Ratees may try to manage the impressions that the raters have of them, through ingratiation, bribes, or other subtle or not-so-subtle means.

• When ratees nominate raters (the organization may specify that the ratee select one or two managers, five to seven peers, and five to nine direct reports), they do not necessarily choose impartial raters.

• Rater anonymity makes sabotage possible. Even if this doesn't actually happen, ratees' belief that it could happen can undermine their confidence in the data. (Some counter this by arguing that raters' motives can be circumvented through rater training; cf. Farh, Cannella, and Bedeian, 1991.)

• Related to rater anonymity is the fact that peers and direct reports do not have to justify their ratings, as supervisors do in traditional performance appraisal. On the one hand, having to justify the ratings may cause raters to think longer and harder about their ratings. On the other, accountability in performance appraisal may cause raters to distort their ratings (perhaps make them lenient) because they are reluctant to convey unfavorable feedback (Klimoski and Inks, 1990). Indeed, raters say they would change their scores to be positive if they were told that the results were to be used for administrative purposes (London, Wohlers, and Gallagher, 1990).

Dalton (1998) added reasons for feedback not being used for appraisal:

- Receiving information that is inconsistent with one's self-image is extremely stressful, and the greater the discrepancy, the more defensive the individual is likely to be. The individual may deny the results or blame them on the raters or uncontrollable situational factors.
- Supervisors may not have the skill to help the subordinate process the feedback and use it to best advantage.
- People only change what they are ready to change. Also, development goals may be tied to evaluation of performance outcomes without causing defenses that interfere with processing the feedback.

Bracken (1996) notes that we are not freed from researching and validating a multisource system if it is used solely for developmental purposes. Threats to validity include lack of relevance and lack of consistency, and methods for collecting and using the data can create real or perceived unfairness in the ratings.

Rater Bias

One of the prime concerns about using MSF for making personnel decisions is the fear that it undermines rater accuracy. Actually, MSF is one way that organizations have tried to limit distortion in supervisor ratings. This lessens ratees' attempts to manage a single rater's impressions of them (for example, subordinates ingratiating themselves with managers by doing favors or complementing them repeatedly). However, multiple raters can still be biased or manipulative in a variety of ways. Consider why this might be the case and how it can be avoided.

Ratings as Game Playing

Kozlowski, Chao, and Morrison (1998) noted the importance of political considerations and game playing in performance ratings:

"In contrast to the focus on judgment and measurement accuracy, performance appraisal may be viewed as a discretionary, motivational, and political process that managers use to reward and punish subordinates" (p. 164). The organizational context can actually motivate raters to distort their ratings to achieve organizational or personal goals. Not necessarily negative, these may be intentional distortions that result in just outcomes because rating distortion is the common practice.

This happens in the armed forces, where ratings are highly lenient and hence appear favorable to avoid ratee defensiveness and maintain positive relationships in the team. However, the raters may use other mechanisms, such as indicating the size of the rater's comparison group (the ratee is the best of twenty, or best of two hundred, for example) to convey more salient and useful information about the ratee. In other cases, however, the purpose of raters' distorting their ratings may be for some less than altruistic motive, such as to ingratiate themselves with the ratee or to deliberately hurt the ratee.

Raters are especially motivated to distort their ratings if rating procedures arouse conflicting goals (Kozlowski, Chao, and Morrison, 1998). This occurs when raters have to defend their judgment to the ratees, as a supervisor does in feeding back performance appraisal ratings. In the case of multisource feedback, people may be rating each other (supervisors providing downward feedback, subordinates offering upward feedback, and peers rating their colleagues). The tendency in such cases, even if the raters are anonymous, may be to emphasize the favorable and limit recognition of performance problems. This maintains harmony and avoids feared retribution.

Kozlowski, Chao, and Morrison (1998) suggest that appraisal politics and rating distortion are more likely

- When there are multiple uses for performance appraisal ratings
- When there is a direct link between appraisal and desired, competitive organizational rewards
- When raters are not anonymous
- When raters face competing goals
- When the organization doesn't monitor the results
- When distorted ratings are tolerated and accepted as part of the organizational culture

- When distortion strategies are actually used in formal decision making (that is, recognizing that ratings need to be supplemented by other, more subtle information, such as indicating to how many others the rater is comparing the ratee)
- When informal socialization processes convey these political considerations and rating trends to new raters

Ways of Eliminating Rater Distortion

On way to limit distortion is to monitor the survey results and give feedback to raters on average ratings and variance. Another way is to give raters data on how their ratings compare to those of other sources or to objective criteria of performance. Still another is to have upper-level managers actually review the ratings and talk to the raters about their judgments. Such comparison shows raters how their ratings diverge from other, more objective or authoritative performance indicators and helps them calibrate their ratings. For instance, they may recognize that other raters are more or less lenient. This may have the disadvantage, however, of prompting raters to follow a pattern evident in the norm—that is, to rate the way others rate. It may have the advantage, though, of letting them know that others are tracking their ratings and are looking out for outlier data—ratings that are unusual in some way.

Villanova and Bernardin (1991, cited in Kozlowski, Chao, and Morrison, 1998) offer principles of good practice in performance appraisal for minimizing political considerations in an organization. These include being sure performance dimensions are clear and relevant to the job, training raters to avoid rating errors, and administering appraisals frequently and with sufficient time for thorough evaluation. Also, Kozlowski, Chao, and Morrison (1998) recommend limiting organizational politics by avoiding the perception that one unit is more or less lenient than another.

Effects of Accountability on Ratings and Use of Results

Lack of accountability in development-only systems, especially on behalf of ratees who don't have to use the feedback, is a principal reason human resource professionals believe that MSF does not live up to expectations (Church and Bracken, 1997; London,

Smither, and Adsit, 1997). In development-only systems, the ratee owns the results and is not obligated to share them, let alone use them. As a consequence, little change may occur, except for diligent ratees who take the feedback to heart and conscientiously study and use it to change their behavior. Ratees become accountable when the feedback results are used for performance appraisal as well as development.

Raters may be made accountable to provide honest and accurate ratings if they are involved in writing items, giving the feedback, and helping the ratee formulate development goals and track progress (London, Smither, and Adsit, 1997).

Psychological Safety and Rater Anonymity

The Center for Creative Leadership, which sponsors executive programs in leadership development, maintains that MSF should be used primarily for development. "A principal underlying value and belief at CCL is that individuals, in order to be ready to change and develop, need to 'own' their assessment. And to own it, they need to feel psychologically safe and to believe that the feedback data are credible and candid" (London and Tornow, 1998, p. 7).

Rater anonymity promotes candid feedback. Keeping the results confidential increases the ratee's feelings of safety, which are important for personal growth. According to this view, using MSF for performance appraisal takes away the trust, candor, and openness of communication that are vital to individual and organizational development. Once it has been administered three or more times in the organization and used for development alone, MSF is likely to engender an environment of trust and openness that supports continuous, self-directed development. (See Rousseau, Sitkin, Burt, and Camerer, 1998, for a description of organizational trust.) This sets the foundation for using MSF for administrative decisions.

Reframing the Debate: Using MSF Is Not an Either-Or Decision

The pros and cons of using MSF for development only or for development plus administration were recently debated in a symposium published by the CCL (Bracken and others, 1997). After reviewing both sides of the argument, McCauley (1997) concluded that it depends on several factors. If the purpose is learning, growth, and change over time, and if the emphasis is on internal motivation (feeling of accomplishment from meeting a challenge), then emphasizing development makes sense. If the purpose is changing specific behavior to promote organization effectiveness, and if the emphasis is on external motivation (external reward for accomplishing objectives), then emphasizing administration makes sense.

McCauley argues that the processes and contexts for good administrative decisions differ from those for good development. On the one hand, confidential feedback for development requires an organizational culture that values personal development and self-understanding. The process should cover a wide range of skills and behaviors, data should be sought from a broad range of people, raters should rate the ratee's opportunity to show competence as well as demonstration of competence, self-ratings should be included, and other self-assessment data (such as measures of personality, preferences, and values) should be collected. On the other hand, assessment for administration requires an organizational culture that supports widespread sharing of information throughout the organization and employee involvement in decision making. The process should provide feedback on targeted dimensions of performance (customized to the job) that turn out to be particular strengths and weaknesses of the individual, and on an overall dimension of performance, and self-ratings should be collected as another source of data for decision making, not a basis for self-other comparison.

McCauley concludes that organizations should use MSF surveys only after they consider what they are trying to achieve with the process and what this means for how they should implement the survey and feedback. Similarly, London and Tornow (1998) called for reframing the debate away from whether MSF should be used for either development or appraisal to determining the conditions under which both purposes can exist and under what conditions they cannot. The focus should be on the processes and conditions that are conducive to both development and human resource management decisions.

MSF is part of a long-term process, not a one-time, isolated event. As such, it takes time for raters and ratees to acclimate themselves to the process, analyze the results, use them to formulate development goals, act on the goals, and track changes in behaviors and outcomes. When MSF is first introduced in an organization, it should be used solely for development. Once conditions of trust and acceptance have been established and ratees have grown used to incorporating the results into a development plan after several administrations, the ratings can be used to evaluate and make decisions about the ratees. If, from the start, the environment is characterized by mutual trust and openness, and people are used to asking for feedback and talking about performance issues, MSF can be used for development and administration when it is introduced (London and Tornow, 1998).

Dalessio (1998) proposes options for introducing MSF. When first introduced in the organization, MSF survey results can be provided confidentially just to the ratees. The ratees can be encouraged to share the results with their supervisor, subordinates, or others. Alternatively, the results can be given to the ratees and to their supervisors, or indeed higher-level management as well. One option for phasing this in is to encourage sharing the results with the supervisor as input for development discussions six to twelve months before the next formal performance review. Then, at the time of the review, the supervisor can be asked to indicate degree of improvement since the development plan was established. Another option is to encourage the ratees to share the results with the raters (supervisors, direct reports, and peers) to help the ratees understand the results and use them to form development plans.

Yet another option is to give the actual MSF report just to the ratee, confidentially; require the ratee to use the report to construct a development plan; and then share and agree on the plan with the supervisor. The extent to which the plan's objectives are met is then part of the supervisor's year-end appraisal.

Another possibility is to give copies of the feedback report to the ratee and a consultant or coach. The coach helps the ratee clarify, interpret, and identify areas for development. The coach may even meet with the direct reports as a group with or without the ratee to share the results and gain further input and interpretation to help in the development plan. Many organizations use external coaches for their top executives (Graddick and Lane, 1998). The coaches give the executives their feedback results and work with them to establish a development plan based on the results.

Having an external coach in a confidential interaction is a way to avoid defensiveness and focus attention on areas for development (Dalton, 1996). Of course, this is expensive, since the coaches have to be paid at (usually high) consulting rates. Also, the HR staff needs to identify them, explain expectations and corporate strategies and philosophies, and evaluate their work. Another approach is to have internal people—executives and HR professionals—serve as coaches. This requires training for managers throughout the organization to accept and practice their role as coach and developer, recognizing the difficulty of being both coach and judge.

Some Implementation Guidelines

The question of who owns the data—the individual rated, or the organization or supervisor—has implications for the design of the process (Bracken, 1996). When the individual is the principal client, the use is for skill development and self-awareness. In this case, the content should be job-specific and skill-based. Participation is likely to be voluntary. Also, the important data comparisons are within the individual—that is, identifying the skills and abilities where the individual is strong and weak relative to other skills and abilities, not relative to other people. In such a case, raters are asked to think of only one person when making the ratings.

When the organization is the principal client, the use is for administration and organization development. In this case, the content of the items rated is organization-specific and values-based. Participation is likely to be required. That is, raters must provide ratings and managers must be rated and receive feedback. Data comparisons are normative (between people), and raters are asked to compare people in making the ratings. The survey is administered as needed by the organization (usually annually).

Clarify Purpose and Build Trust

When implementing multisource feedback, Timmreck and Bracken (1997) and Reilly and McGourty (1998) recommend that there be a clear statement of purpose and use. Also, they also strongly recommend that the data be used primarily for developmental purposes, at least initially. Dalton (1998) recommends that if MSF is to be used for appraisal, it should follow a careful series of interventions aimed at establishing trust, and not as a punitive measure that would punish raters for honest ratings and that does not give ratees a chance to improve their performance. Also, there should be visible and valuable rewards for high scores to make improvement worthwhile.

Separate the Processes

Bracken (1996) suggests that MSF systems used for development and decision making can coexist but should be kept separate. Separation helps focus the ownership and use of the information for all parties. He argues that if MSF is to be used in administration, then both performance appraisal and the MSF survey should use the same performance dimensions. Another reason for keeping the processes separate is that information for appraisal may be outcome-focused, while information for development may focus on the means to produce outcomes. Also, items may reflect organizational strategy on how the organization wants to do business, which is not the same as outcomes. Indeed, rater-specific forms can be designed so that raters can judge behavior they are likely to observe from the vantage point of their role (peers, direct reports, supervisors).

Consider High-Tech, On-Demand Feedback for Development

Internet-based computer techniques now allow managers to design their own MSF process whenever they want feedback. This is separate from the formal appraisal process and would not preclude using organizationwide formal MSF surveys for development and appraisal. This informal, just-in-time feedback can be customized by allowing managers to choose their own items, perhaps from a set of preestablished items for which there are corporate norms. The Internet-based program can use e-mail to automatically ask raters to complete the survey, return it via e-mail to a scoring system, and then return the results to the employee. As a purely developmental tool, this allows managers to get ahead of the curve by finding out what their colleagues think and respond to the results before the formal ratings.

Incorporate MSF into a Balanced Set of Performance Assessment Methods

As I have noted, multisource feedback is especially valuable if there are no objective, direct measures of performance. Even if there are, MSF can be combined with these direct measures as part of a set of balanced performance measures, all of which are important to individual and organizational success (Kaplan and Norton, 1996; Bracken, 1997; Reilly and McGourty, 1998). For instance, teams may have a strategy of increasing revenue, building long-term customer relationships, and enhancing team building within the organization. Revenue can be assessed directly, while customer and employee relationships can be assessed by MSF survey.

Introduce Newcomers to the Process Carefully

Once feedback is accepted in the organization as a vehicle for development and administration, newcomers to the organization who are not used to a feedback culture and are not initially versed in MSF may have to be introduced to the process gradually. Orientation programs should explain feedback, say by using testimonials from current employees in these workshops and on the job. Supervisors should guide newcomers in explaining feedback surveys, giving them sample results, and showing how they use the results with other subordinates. Newcomers may be rated and given feedback several times after starting the job (say after three, six, and nine months) before collecting feedback that is used administratively.

Conclusion

Introducing MSF is as much an organization change effort as it is an individual development and performance improvement initiative. Using MSF surveys for performance appraisal and personnel decisions risks engendering bias and distrust.

Feedback can be used for both development and administrative purposes, but this takes time. The organization may need to start by using MSF for development alone to establish a culture of interpersonal trust and attention to development. How much time this takes varies with the organization, and the environment needs to be monitored by management and the human resource staff. The process may be easier, and take less time, if the organization already has such a culture. However, even when it does, the culture shouldn't be taken for granted and MSF should be introduced carefully.

Once managers are able to trust and welcome feedback, it becomes the foundation for incorporating MSF into the performance management process and using it regularly for personnel decisions, perhaps in conjunction with on-demand surveys or departmental MSF surveys that are for development alone and administered off-cycle from the performance review.

References
Ashford, S. J., and Tsui, A. S. "Self-Regulation for Managerial Effectiveness: The Role of Active Feedback Seeking." *Academy of Management Journal,* 1991, *34,* 251–280.

Bracken, D. W. "Multisource (360-Degree) Feedback: Surveys for Individual and Organizational Development." In A. I. Kraut (ed.), *Organizational Surveys: Tools for Assessment and Change.* San Francisco: Jossey-Bass, 1996.

Bracken, D. W. "Maximizing the Uses of Multi-Rater Feedback." In D. W. Bracken and others, *Should 360-Degree Feedback Be Used Only for Developmental Purposes?* Greensboro, N.C.: Center for Creative Leadership, 1997.

Bracken, D. W., and others. *Should 360-Degree Feedback Be Used Only for Developmental Purposes?* Greensboro, N.C.: Center for Creative Leadership, 1997.

Church, A. H., and Bracken, D. W. "Advancing the State of the Art of 360-Degree Feedback: Guest Editors' Comments on the Research and Practice of Multirater Assessment Methods." *Group and Organization Management,* 1997, *22*(2), 149–161.

Dalessio, A. T. " Using Multisource Feedback for Employee Development and Personnel Decisions." In J. W. Smither (ed.), *Performance Appraisal: State of the Art in Practice.* San Francisco: Jossey-Bass, 1998.

Dalton, M. A. "Multirater Feedback and Conditions for Change." *Consulting Psychology Journal,* 1996, *48,* 12–16.

Dalton, M. A. "When the Purpose of Using Multi-Rater Feedback Is Behavior Change." In D. W. Bracken and others, *Should 360-Degree Feedback Be Used Only for Developmental Purposes?* Greensboro, N.C.: Center for Creative Leadership, 1997.

Dalton, M. A. "Best Practices: Five Rationales for Using 360-Degree Feedback in Organizations." In W. W. Tornow and M. London (eds.), *Maximizing the Value of 360-Degree Feedback: A Process for Individual and Organizational Development.* San Francisco: Jossey-Bass, 1998.

Farh, J. L., Cannella, A. A., Jr., and Bedeian, A. G. "Peer Ratings: The Impact of Purpose on Rating Quality and User Acceptance." *Group and Organization Studies,* 1991, *16,* 367–386.

Graddick, M. M., and Lane, P. "Evaluating Executive Performance." In J. W. Smither (ed.), *Performance Appraisal: State of the Art in Practice.* San Francisco: Jossey-Bass, 1998.

Kaplan, R. S., and Norton, D. P. *The Balanced Scorecard: Translating Strategy into Action.* Boston: Harvard Business School Press, 1996.

Klimoski, R., and Inks, L. "Accountability Forces in Performance Appraisal." *Organizational Behavior and Human Decision Processes,* 1990, *45,* 194–208.

Kozlowski, S.W.J., Chao, G. T., and Morrison, R. F. "Games Raters Play: Politics, Strategies, and Impression Management in Performance Appraisal." In J. W. Smither (ed.), *Performance Appraisal: State of the Art in Practice.* San Francisco: Jossey-Bass, 1998.

London, M., Smither, J. W., and Adsit, D. J. "Accountability: The Achilles' Heel of Multisource Feedback." *Group and Organization Management,* 1997, *22*(2), 162–184.

London, M., and Tornow, W. W. "360-Degree Feedback: More Than a Tool!" In W. W. Tornow and M. London (eds.), *Maximizing the Value of 360-Degree Feedback: A Process for Individual and Organizational Development.* San Francisco: Jossey-Bass, 1998.

London, M., Wohlers, A. J., and Gallagher, P. "360-Degree Feedback Surveys: A Source of Feedback to Guide Management Development." *Journal of Management Development,* 1990, *9,* 17–31.

McCauley, C. D. "On Choosing Sides: Seeing the Good in Both." In D. W. Bracken and others, *Should 360-Degree Feedback Be Used Only for Developmental Purposes?* Greensboro, N.C.: Center for Creative Leadership, 1997.

Meyer, H. H., Kay, E., and French, J. "Split Roles in Performance Appraisal." *Harvard Business Review,* 1965, *43,* 123–129.

Murphy, K. R., and Cleveland, J. N. *Understanding Performance Appraisal: Social, Organizational, and Goal-Based Perspectives.* Thousand Oaks, Calif.: Sage, 1995.

Pollman, V. A. "Some Faulty Assumptions That Support Using Multi-Rater Feedback for Performance Appraisal." In D. W. Bracken and others, *Should 360-Degree Feedback Be Used Only for Developmental Purposes?* Greensboro, N.C.: Center for Creative Leadership, 1997.

Reilly, R. R., and McGourty, J. "Performance Appraisal in Team Settings." In J. W. Smither (ed.), *Performance Appraisal: State of the Art in Practice.* San Francisco: Jossey-Bass, 1998.

Rousseau, D. M., Sitkin, S. B., Burt, R. S., and Camerer, C. "Not So Different After All: A Cross-Discipline View of Trust." *Academy of Management Review,* 1998, *23,* 393–404.

Timmreck, C. W., and Bracken, D. W. "Upward Feedback in the Trenches: Challenges and Realities." Paper presented at the tenth annual conference of the Society for Industrial and Organizational Psychology, Orlando, Fla., May 1995.

Timmreck, C. W., and Bracken, D. W. "Multisource Assessment: Reinforcing the Preferred 'Means' to the End." Paper presented at the eleventh annual conference of the Society for Industrial and Organizational Psychology, San Diego, Calif., Apr. 1996.

Timmreck, C. W., and Bracken, D. W. "Multisource Feedback: A Study of Its Use in Decision Making." *Employment Relations Today,* 1997, *24*(1), 21–27.

Tornow, W. W. "Forces That Affect the 360-Degree Feedback Process." In W. W. Tornow and M. London (eds.), *Maximizing the Value of 360-Degree Feedback: A Process for Individual and Organizational Development.* San Francisco: Jossey-Bass, 1998.

PART 3

Systems Forces in Multisource Feedback

CHAPTER 24

Introducing and Sustaining Multisource Feedback at Sears

Victoria B. Crawshaw
Sally F. Hartmann
Alicia J. Winckler

In December 1990, the senior executive responsible for operating more than eight hundred Sears stores asked a simple question: "How can I do a better job of evaluating the performance of my ten region managers?" His dilemma was a classic one in large companies with many geographically dispersed locations: genuinely understanding the performance of people he saw in person relatively few times each year. He had daily access to their sales, margin, and profit results, and he spoke fairly often with them by telephone. He correctly felt, however, that computer printouts and phone calls did not tell the whole story. What was missing was an assessment of their skill in leading, coaching, motivating, and developing people.

The solution suggested to him was to ask for performance feedback from associates who personally interacted with the region managers frequently. Simply put, the idea was to ask direct reports and region office peers to rate their region manager's leadership skills. The executive endorsed the idea, and so began Sears's ten-year involvement in multisource feedback (or "multiperspective ratings," as we initially called it).

The process seemed simple enough to plan and execute. After all, only ten people were receiving ratings. Key tasks included defining content of the rating form, writing communications, identifying all "qualified" raters, mailing and receiving forms, and analyzing data. What could not be known in 1990 was that the overall approach used and decisions made then would continue to define a process that became huge in volume and enormously complex over the years to come.

Our Initial Approach

Here is a summary of six key design elements or decisions, substantially influenced by the fact that the process was introduced to support performance review:

1. *Communication.* The senior executive began by clearly communicating the rationale and time line for the process to the region managers. He also invited the region managers to rate his performance (beginning the practice of "rating reciprocity").
2. *Rating form.* The items and the rating scale mirrored the company's performance review form.
3. *Matching process.* To ensure that all qualified raters in fact had the opportunity to provide ratings, forms were mailed directly to raters, with no involvement by the region managers.
4. *Anonymity.* Ratings were done anonymously.
5. *Professional analysis.* Completed rating forms were mailed to us for data analysis and reporting. Average ratings by item and by source were calculated; comments were paraphrased.
6. *Results to manager.* Reports were sent only to the senior executive, with the understanding that he would cover results in detail with his region managers.

Regarding this last point, with reports in hand the senior executive then discussed results one-on-one as promised, but he went one step further by presenting his own results to a gathering of his region managers. He was pleased with the process and staunchly supported its expansion. The region managers were particularly eager to use the process to help them rate their own direct reports.

Lessons Learned

There are six lessons to be learned from Sears's initial implementation of multisource feedback (MSF).

1. Never underestimate the importance of having a champion at a very senior level. (It's even better when the champion articulates the very problem that MSF solves.)

2. Be very clear about why you are initiating it. Is it to support performance review, or individual development? How you answer that question drives your approach, communications, and virtually everything else.

3. Once you have decided why you are doing it, be certain that all communications and steps in the process are entirely consistent with your purpose. For example, if results are *not* used to support performance review but rating forms are sent out just before the review process, eyebrows may be raised.

4. To build a process that is viewed as credible, make sure that, first of all, item content centers on behaviors valued by the organization, and that raters are appropriately identified.

5. Write communications that address raters' and ratees' concerns and questions. Tell the truth. Use plain English.

6. Be reasonably confident that your organization is ready, which means that a consensus or high-level support is emerging around the need for candid developmental or performance-related feedback.

Looking back across a decade of multisource feedback at Sears, we were reminded of the most important lesson of all: early decisions can have a long-lasting impact, so they had better be sound.

Growing Pains: Dealing with a Quickly Expanding Process

The Sears MSF process caught on and expanded very quickly. In 1999, nine years after the inception of the process, we distributed seventy thousand rating forms to gather data for thirty-four hundred feedback recipients. Early expansion of our process was driven by customer satisfaction and by word of mouth. Senior leaders who had used the process to improve the quality of performance review asked to have more individuals added as ratees. Other senior leaders learned of the process and wanted review managers in their groups to have the same benefits. This growth, though gratifying, was neither smooth nor easy. Challenges centered on customization, communication, policies regarding report distribution, and movement to an automated process.

Since our multisource process grew piecemeal, we (naively) catered to each new user's needs or preferences. For example, some business groups asked us to develop customized forms. Others wanted their ratees to have the opportunity to review their own rater lists and add names. Still others developed complex and confusing rules about combining rating sources when certain conditions were met. The process grew bit by bit, and in our goal to be customer-focused we created an inordinate number of special handlings. At its worst, we were managing fifty projects simultaneously in the fall of 1998.

Given the multitude of projects, we learned the hard way how vitally important it is to create effective communication. Many raters were asked to provide feedback for people in different projects, which caused confusion about deadlines for returning rating forms. Raters involved in multiple projects received multiple packets of information with rating forms, sometimes within days of each other—another source of confusion. Further, managers and ratees were sometimes unclear about when they could expect reports and how the data would be presented. Ultimately, we recognized the need to create a single message (and consistent process) to make providing and using feedback easier for participants. More on this development is presented in the next section of this chapter.

Another growing pain centered on the need for additional policies for using and distributing feedback data. As the process expanded, we received strong counsel from senior management to help new groups of ratees get used to the process by receiving one "free" year. This meant that data collected would be given only to the ratee and not to the reviewing manager as input into performance review. (In subsequent years, reports would also go to the reviewing manager.) Ultimately, the free year for report distribution proved administratively very difficult, and, in fact, it became almost impossible to search for all those participants who "deserved" this special processing. Interestingly, this marked a major shift, given that our initial approach had been to offer reports *only* to the review manager.

We also found that expanding the process required considering who else—besides the ratees and their managers—should receive the report. At Sears, many managers report to both a solid-line manager (the boss) and to a dotted-line manager who has input into performance review, as is typical of many matrix organizations today. We had to develop a protocol for who receives what report when (although we seemed to have to reexplain the protocol every year, and in so doing smooth ruffled feathers).

Five years after the inception of our MSF process, we finally acknowledged that it had become too large for us to efficiently manage internally. We turned to an outside vendor for assistance in mailing surveys and processing data. (See Chapter Ten for issues to consider in working with a vendor.) With the help of our vendor, we eventually moved to an automated process, using barcoded, scannable answer sheets. We also began to report raters' comments verbatim rather than paraphrasing them. This raised a new set of problems when raters wrote unconstructive or even hurtful comments.

Automating the process wherever possible was a simple decision from an administrative perspective, but it bumped up against a culture in which giving candid feedback was difficult. Scannable answer sheets were readily accepted by Sears raters. Barcodes, however, were not. The first time we used barcodes, our description of their purpose—to improve data integrity—was met with skepticism. In our second year, we disclosed more information—that the barcodes have embedded within them the vendor's confidential coding to identify rater, ratee, and their organizational relationship (for example, "immediate manager"). This led to many anonymous calls with questions about the "real" reason for the barcode. Also, some rating forms arrived with the barcodes torn off, making the forms unusable. Over time, however, the number of these instances has decreased significantly as raters become more comfortable with the process.

As the relationship with our outside vendor has evolved, Sears remains accountable for survey content, communication, educational materials, and "who rates whom" lists for the vendor in our defined-matching strategy. The vendor's accountabilities include packaging and distributing all materials for raters, receiving and processing completed rating forms, and generating and shipping feedback reports. The success of this balance of accountability hinged on detailing every required step of the process, precisely documenting decisions made throughout the process, and assigning clear responsibilities.

Although moving to an automated, vendor-driven process did not eliminate the headaches or fully ease the growing pains, it helped. We've also reduced the pain simply by persisting in figuring out what to do—and then by documenting what works.

Lessons Learned

Over the period of rapid expansion of multisource feedback at Sears, we have become wiser about consistency, seeking help, and the values to which we hold.

7. Avoid too much flexibility (and inconsistency) in the process. Our piecemeal growth created a process that was time-consuming; expensive; and a source of complexity, headaches, and potential errors.

8. Keep communications to participants clear and concise. Minimize the number of packages of information you send to raters. Multiple mailings can create the perception that your process is disorganized and decrease the likelihood that raters read the content (whether it is unique or duplicate information).

9. Understand your limits and where you need help. If you use an outside vendor, clearly define both parties' roles.

10. When considering use of an automated process, assess the trust and readiness of the organization. Ratees and raters need full disclosure on the purpose and safeguards. Mostly, they need reassurance that their anonymity will be preserved.

11. Be certain that you are spending money in the right places. Sears's defined-matching approach to our MSF process (in which rating forms are sent from the vendor directly to predefined raters) is expensive and complex, even with automation. It drives the need for increased administration of the process, frequent and clear communication about policies and uses, and strong awareness of the political realities in a large corporation. Although our matching strategy is expensive, we are willing to pay these costs to maintain the integrity of a system designed specifically to support performance review. (A less expensive approach is to ask ratees to

distribute rating forms; we endorse this approach when the purpose of the feedback is for development only.)

12. Coach raters to write constructive rather than blatantly hurtful comments.

13. Do *not* mail results right before the December holidays, even if that meets your business partner's time line. (This was another lesson learned the hard way when a few managers protested that "devastating feedback" arrived in the mail on Christmas Eve.)

Institutionalizing and Standardizing the Process

Despite—or because of—the intensity of interest in this process over the last decade, MSF is now ingrained in Sears's culture. It has been used each and every year since its inception, and in 1998 and 1999 our chairman mandated that the most senior tier of executives (approximately two hundred) would receive feedback. Multisource feedback is considered so important that our survey distribution is the *only* exception to a fourth-quarter mandate that all work drivers not focused on sales be eliminated in our retail stores. In fact, many managers contact us in December requesting reports prior to our January shipping date; they want the data as soon as possible to start their annual performance reviews.

The content of Sears's MSF survey is well integrated with other human resource processes, including selection, training, performance review, and succession planning. All incorporate Sears's global competency model, the Leadership Model. We measure in all these processes not just *what* people accomplish in terms of bottom-line results, but *how* they do so, vis-à-vis the Leadership Model. (See Chapters Four and Nineteen for discussions on selecting and linking MSF survey content.)

As Sears's MSF process has expanded throughout the company, our human resource partners have begun to share and capitalize on best practices in implementation and education. We had always shared information with our human resource partners, but having them share ideas directly with one another generated far more powerful lessons. A cross-functional team now meets regularly to discuss a variety of issues. Getting all stakeholders in a single room has been a win for everyone: for them, as they learn from each other; for the company, as we increase consistency in processes and decrease costs; and for our internal consulting group, as HR partners take more ownership of the process and our own administrative role becomes more manageable.

Lessons Learned

14. Capitalize on the opportunity to integrate human resource measures wherever possible. Managers value the feedback more when they see how it links to other important outcomes.

15. Identify an appropriate length for the rating form so the feedback meets its intended purpose while addressing business conditions or requirements. Our form is short (twenty-four items) to minimize the amount of time raters must spend completing it. This is particularly important since our forms are distributed during our busy fourth quarter and some raters may be asked to complete as many as thirty forms. Anything longer would most likely decrease our response rates.

16. Determine the negotiables and nonnegotiables with and for your business partners. Be clear regarding how consistency in applying your processes pays off, and drive consistency by bringing together (in a forum for candid discussion) those who make it happen. Consistency increases the comparability of the data, eases administrative difficulties, simplifies communication to participants, and lowers bottom-line costs.

Overarching Issue: Effectiveness of the Process

The effectiveness of Sears's MSF process may be analyzed in at least three ways: degree of utilization, integration with other HR processes, and extent to which development occurs.

First, our company leaders frequently tell us how difficult performance review would be without MSF. This is the precise issue faced by our first senior executive champion: how to accurately evaluate performance of individuals in geographically dispersed locations. Although managers may not see their direct reports daily, they need to understand their leadership style, environment, and events that take place within the stores. Managers at Sears consistently use the multisource feedback as one piece of data, in addition to other performance measures, to complete well-balanced performance reviews of their direct reports. As discussed previously, the rapid growth we've experienced suggests that the process is viewed as effective.

Second, our multisource feedback fully reinforces the Sears Leadership Model, which is integrated throughout all human resource systems. Since our process currently touches approximately twenty thousand employees (as raters, feedback recipients, or managers of feedback recipients), it is an excellent opportunity for a wide audience to gain intimate knowledge of the behaviors expected of Sears associates through a common language, the Leadership Model. To further foster understanding, behaviorally anchored rating scales are given to all raters and ratees to assist in evaluating strengths and development opportunities. Our process is thus viewed as being highly effective at fitting into a bigger picture.

Third, we can consider how effective Sears's MSF process is in aiding individual development. Indeed, it offers feedback recipients (ratees) and their managers valuable input on development opportunities from individuals who are in a position to observe consistent behaviors. Because it is anonymous, raters may offer much more candid feedback through this process than they would ever do in person.

Although the MSF process is designed to support development, how well it meets that goal varies tremendously throughout the organization. The burden of proper use and interpretation of the data is placed on the manager and feedback recipient, with some support from their human resource manager. Due to the dispersion of the thirty-four hundred feedback recipients across the country, we are unable to conduct training sessions and instead rely on educational brochures to help managers use the data well. The best users of this information review it to (1) find the right balance between numerical data and verbatim comments; (2) look at common themes, relative strengths, and opportunities; and (3) think through what it means when rater groups send differing messages. Another group of users grab on to one or two key findings. Still others ignore or discount the results. There is simply wide variability in managers' ability to interpret the data, which clearly determines the overall effectiveness of the process.

Lessons Learned

17. Educate all participants to maximize the effectiveness of the entire MSF process. Education is relevant for raters, ratees (feedback recipients), immediate managers, and the organization as a whole. Raters need to be educated about how the information is used, how their anonymity is maintained, the benefits of their participation, and how to provide constructive feedback. Ratees need education on how to analyze the feedback report, create a development plan, and act on the plan. Managers need information on how to analyze the feedback report, how to coach and facilitate use of this information, and how to employ this information in a productive and well-balanced performance review. For the organization, it is critical to communicate who was selected to participate in this process, why, and how this information is to be used. Poor communication about the how's and why's only allows people to create their own truths about the process.

18. Do not hesitate to communicate repeatedly and widely about the value of the process for the organization. Multisource feedback is not an end; it is a means to conducting well-rounded performance reviews and determining developmental priorities. Linking the process to results (decreased turnover, increased productivity) is one way of communicating to the organization the full value of the process. Linking the process (and content) to other human resource processes is another way of helping the organization understand its value and continuity with the belief systems of the organization.

19. To help maximize effectiveness, make the process of giving feedback administratively simple for the raters, especially if participation is not mandatory. This may necessitate fewer items, items differing by rater groups, or various methods to submit ratings (paper-and-pencil and electronic filing via e-mail or Internet, to name a couple). Even the simplest issue—prepaying postage on return envelopes—can increase response rates, thus improving the value of the feedback process.

20. Engage both human resource and business partners in the process. Champions and partnerships with key strategic leaders within the business can make or break the process. Champions may act as spokespersons and role models. These partnerships are

particularly critical with Sears's process. Our strategy of defined matching of raters and ratees absolutely requires the input of senior line managers, since organizational charts do not always tell the full story of who should be designated as "legitimate" raters. If feedback from the most appropriate raters is not included, the value and effectiveness of the process can be substantially diminished.

21. Build trust in the process from the start, through clear, truthful communication and demonstration of a consistent track record of doing the right thing. Participants' negative perceptions of a process that broke promises in the past (for example, about confidentiality of raters' responses, utilization of results, and who has access to results) may take years to mend, or they may simply never be overcome. Our steady and consistent approach to all aspects of the process has paid off in the organization's trust in the process.

Political Realities

Multisource feedback has high visibility at all levels in Sears, up to and including our chairman. This means that the process is fair game for elimination or drastic revision when expense reduction, changes in leadership, or changes in organizational priorities occur. So far at Sears, high visibility has been a plus. That said, nearly every year someone questions the timing and value of our MSF process or makes clear that they just don't like the process, and we are put in a position to explain how the process works and what it delivers. Any resistance we encounter generally takes one of two forms: verbalized philosophical difference on the value of the process and how the feedback should be used (see the discussion in Chapter Twenty-Three); and passive resistance in not returning forms, possibly because of survey burnout (see Chapter Twenty-Five) or concerns of lack of anonymity or retribution. These issues are not unlike those experienced by other organizations, and the amount of resistance we receive is minimal.

Managing a process that is loved by some and disliked by others is an interesting challenge. Our best advocates of the process are senior line managers (not just human resources) who describe to others how and why they value multisource feedback. Thus, through word of mouth our process grows in perceived value, in addition to scope and scale. The fact is that business executives who dislike the nuisance of data collection are typically very pleased when the reports appear.

The biggest political reality has to do with whether the company will or will not allocate financial resources for this initiative. It is noteworthy that, despite ups and downs in our business cycle, our MSF process has been funded and continues to expand, almost certainly because of its perceived value among top executives in the organization.

As our process grew to accommodate new business partners (additional senior leaders), we experienced some unexpected political issues. Things we considered to be mundane truly mattered to key players, from the order of distribution of reports (who gets reports first) to the name of the MSF process itself. ("Multiperspective feedback" is now called "360-degree feedback" at Sears.) Decisions to please our stakeholders were easy; clearly, these issues were not among the process nonnegotiables as we defined them. As in any political situation, one must learn to pick one's battles.

Lessons Learned

22. Be able to effectively justify the process. Link both the content and the value of the process to important organizational outcomes to increase the likelihood that the process survives even when resources are limited or when champions of the process change.

23. Everyone has a point of view. Be ready to listen to it.

24. Clearly define when decisions are made and who makes them. Be open to ideas on improving the process, but hold firm when necessary. Pick the battles that matter.

25. Build your reputation as a provider of exceptional customer service for individuals at all levels of the organization.

26. Never underestimate the importance of having a champion at a very senior level (also the first of the lessons learned that we list in this chapter). When the chairman stands behind the program, a loud message about its importance is heard throughout the organization.

Is It Worth It?

Worth or perceived value of an object or process is usually assessed in the eye of the beholder, which is why the final section of this chapter is devoted to the feedback that we have received about this process. The evolution and demand for MSF at Sears has been driven by ratees and their managers, an important testament to its perceived worth in the organization.

First, many managers now feel as if they cannot do a good, accurate job of performance review without it. Second, managers are requesting that this information be used in other human resource processes, such as in selection and promotion decisions and succession planning. They see the information as valuable input about performance, not only relevant for performance review.

Third, our business leaders view the costs associated with this process to be a small price to pay for such valuable information. Even through times of severe cost-cutting measures, MSF has not gone away. On the contrary, the process has continued to grow.

Finally, in addition to the sheer increase in number of participants, the population of feedback recipients continues to grow more diverse. Managers in technical environments are now included in the process, and requests for additional participants spread downward and laterally throughout the organization each year.

Lessons Learned

In order to maintain (and grow) perceptions of value in the organization, we have a few more lessons.

27. Provide cost-benefit analysis for stakeholders in the process. It is important to help human resource and business partners stay abreast of the costs and benefits of the process among other organizational, cultural, and environmental issues, and to understand where an MSF process makes sense and where it does not. No matter how good the tool, there are instances where it is not the right solution for the problem at hand.

28. Offer continuous process improvements. What is an excellent product today may need considerable enhancement to be

valued by tomorrow's audience. Multisource feedback is not exempt from today's environment of fast-paced change; organizations want things that are better, are faster, and cost less than yesterday's product. Process improvements must minimize administrative headaches for all participants and managers of this process.

Some Final Thoughts

If we're asked to update this chapter in ten years, it's highly likely we'll have many changes or process improvements to report. The rumblings afoot today might predict:

- Doing away with this process because managers have found more direct, immediate ways to give and obtain performance feedback
- Growing an entirely different approach "for development only," with less focus on performance review input
- Combining this process with the corporate attitude survey to save data collection time

The challenges for internal MSF professionals are to listen, learn, be open-minded, and be flexible—but to never lose sight of the importance, integrity, and value provided by a process like the one Sears uses today.

CHAPTER 25

Evolution of Multisource Feedback in a Dynamic Environment

Robert A. Jako

It seems safe to say that multisource feedback (MSF) has passed the test of time, in contrast to "quality circles," "self-managed teams," and other overnight fads. MSF has been discussed, implemented, changed, denigrated, and sustained in organizations widely for a solid decade now. It is in a sense a celebration of MSF's success to be able to look retrospectively at what indeed sustains a process, rather than guess about it at this point in time.

Many of my observations require a brief framing in light of the unusual organizational context in which I have worked for the last few years. I've been implementing and sustaining MSF in the country's largest medical group, consisting of thirty-five hundred physicians who are both employees and shareholders of their professional services corporation. Based on comparison with peers in similar roles in a variety of industries and organizations, I've had the unique pleasure of developing a keen and comprehensive awareness of the potential for pushback. Physicians are who they are because of their strong commitment to caring for patients. Providing feedback to one another does not on its own make it onto their radar. Communication is between doctor and patient. Performance is measured by how the patient responds. These physicians are smart; they require facts, evidence, and proof to be swayed into engaging in an activity such as MSF.

MSF's failure would be guaranteed without the sincere commitment of top leadership, which I have had. The technology and facts do not sell themselves. People ultimately need a little faith to start this kind of process, and that faith is generated through effective leadership.

All of this framing implies that my prescriptions are generally conservative (that is, will work in the direst of circumstances), they assume some leadership support, and my concerns may be a bit exaggerated compared to most.

Conceptually, examining the sustainability of an MSF process can be thought of as simply adding a time dimension to the Process Model of Multisource Feedback proposed earlier (see Chapter One). Each component identified in the model can change from year to year in a sustaining process. An example of the time effect is poor rater training in year 1, which doesn't affect readiness in year 1 but very well may do so in year 2. A more subtle example is changing the instrument design in year 2, which affects response rate in year 2 (inability to follow up on issues raised in year 1, incremental cognitive and time demand to relearn the rules for accurately rating), use of feedback in year 2 (changing the standards, bait-and-switch development goals), and therefore readiness in year 3. Therefore the practice of sustaining an MSF process consists of examining a series of process models, each one filled in according to the decisions and actions of a specific feedback reporting cycle, in order to see what led to what, which downturns were outweighed by a corresponding upturn, and ultimately what had the most beneficial lasting effects.

This chapter is intended to highlight significant aspects of MSF that arise over repeated cycles in a given organizational context, and that are germane to the program's evolution.

Assumptions

There are a few givens related to MSF that should be articulated in order to gauge what else is changing around them. The first is the whole notion of whether an MSF program should indeed continue indefinitely. One can implement MSF as a process in itself, based on the belief that this kind of instrumentation, anonymity, reporting, and control over what kind of feedback is conveyed is in itself a legitimate practice for sharing (top-down) a model of performance, and sharing (bottom-up or side-to-side) accurate observations of behavior per the model.

However, MSF can also be implemented as a project, with an end point logically being that organizational members learn first how to constructively share their observations of others' performance; second, how others' perceptions of their performance are not necessarily equal to their own; and third, how to be sensitive to such cues as unique and relevant information. Each of these philosophies requires the same process of monitoring for sustainability, but with specific and material differences (for example, a reduction in response rate is uniformly unfavorable in a "process program," while it requires detailed follow-up and could be potentially favorable in a "project implementation").

A second assumption on which sustainability is based is that the work remains sufficiently based on human interactions to justify MSF. Jobs with limited human interaction are generally not fertile soil for high returns on MSF. By the same token, as many interactions become automated or in some other way predictable and systems-based, the possibility looms that with some managerial work being simplified, the same effect could occur organization-wide and therefore reduce the need for MSF.

A third and final assumption is a shared norm regarding how frequently feedback should be exchanged, and an MSF calendar that fits this norm. In practical terms, this is usually a yearly event, although some have argued that one year is not enough time to incorporate suggestions for behavioral change. This frequency needs to be determined early, and adhered to; people either get fed up with too many reports and survey burnout and say no to the whole thing, or they forget its purpose and assume it must not be important if it's too infrequent. A regular schedule is needed for evolution to be visible.

Challenges to Sustainability

Here are six generic challenges to the sustainability of an MSF program that apply regardless of how adaptively designed the process or program is.

Leadership Turnover

As in my previous remarks in the chapter introduction, if your top leadership does not support the program, it's doomed—appropriately. If you have turnover in leadership and your primary advocate departs, the options are limited. Either you find a new advocate of the current process, or you can try to adapt the process to whatever your new leadership advocates.

Selling, Not Telling

Leaders have to *sell* people on how to do it, not just tell them. Telling gradually leads to your program's demise. People go through the motions, but not with the sincerity needed to make the feedback worthwhile. If recipients of the feedback are not enthused, they will not respond. The lack of results produced by the process in turn validates the leader's failure to sincerely support it.

The Silent Majority

The notion of the silent majority is a practical corollary of the squeaky wheel getting the grease, being that you need to have your satisfied participants squeak. The general tendency is that those who find the system valuable do not speak up about it. Those who get highly positive feedback are generally of the type who don't want to be perceived as praising a process that benefits them in this way. This can often be the majority of people participating.

Conflicting Messages

The problem of conflicting messages is related to selling-not-telling. If the MSF process is not integrated with the rest of operations, it runs the risk of being compartmentalized as "fluff." Integration can be as simple as making sure the performance dimensions assessed are also used to organize the training and development resources offered by the company, or even simply paying for the time required to complete feedback surveys. Integration can go as far as linking the company's compensation program to the MSF outcomes, or improvement in outcomes over the years. In some way, the MSF process must demonstrably tap into the organization's fuel line. If leaders are not willing to have that, problems with selling it are likely to emerge as well.

Survey Burnout

Survey burnout is a particular problem if you are involved in peer feedback; if you need to complete feedback surveys on large numbers of people; or if you allow feedback recipients to designate their survey respondents without any checks (the tendency is for "more is better" to prevail), resulting in the same problem. If this is a problem, time can be paid for, or some rules can be devised to keep the number of surveys manageable. Some organizations have tried approaching this through random sampling of survey populations. The bottom line is that if the survey respondent receives forty-five surveys in the mail, there is a good chance none of them will be completed.

Vendor Relations

It's safe to say that if client and vendor do not communicate regularly and honestly, the relationship is headed for failure. Over time, these two parties have expectations that may tend to conflict because of natural market forces. The client expects that over time the relationship and work will regularize, and costs will decline as more streamlining opportunities are discovered. The vendor, by contrast, often loses money early on, banking on the streamlining as the means to make up for earlier losses (see Chapter Ten for more detail on successful client-vendor relationships). In terms of sustaining an MSF process, vendor relations translate to kept promises and credibility, internally.

Other Challenges

There are assuredly other challenges we each face, with equally grave implications. Hopefully these six serve to generate thought about more. Just as we assess risk for virtually every other significant organizational activity, such pitfalls need constant monitoring for an MSF program to be sustained.

Sustainability Factors

This section is intended to cover some of the pivotal keys to sustaining an MSF process. It's important to keep in mind, however, that *sustaining* does not connote forever, as much as it does avoiding ending a process prematurely. MSF is obviously not a sound investment for all organizations; correspondingly, as organizations change the appropriateness can also diminish. Although the challenges I have just reviewed were traps we can fall into, sustainability factors are pivotal aspects of communicating, administering, and maintaining an MSF program—keys to its continued success, or its accidental death.

Purpose

The initial purpose for implementing an MSF process can play a persuasive role in sustainability. Purpose shapes employee perception of how long the program will be around. For example, a program introduced as an intervention intended to improve managers' sensitivity to their subordinates' views is expected to come and go quickly (probably within a year). By contrast, a program introduced as a redefinition of managerial obligations to their people is expected to stay. At the outset, it is prudent to consider every conceivable purpose for MSF as it potentially evolves in the organization (consider all purposes discussed in Chapters Seventeen through Twenty-One), and then to communicate a core theme that spans all of these purposes.

An unfortunately common example of the impact of communicated purpose is found in organizations that introduce MSF as a tool for performance development, and then eventually tie compensation, or other administrative decision making, to the outcomes. The worst-case scenario is an employee perception of a bait-and-switch, the suspicion being that the link to compensation was always intended, and the introduction as a developmental tool was just a foot-in-the-door sales tactic. This perception can be a mortal blow to the credibility of an MSF program intended for any purpose, as well as a dent in trust in leadership.

Many organizations circumvent this by introducing MSF as developmental, with the caveat that it may eventually be tied to administrative decision making if the data appear to be sufficiently reliable. Another approach is to compartmentalize the purpose of MSF to the immediate outcome: that participants get feedback from the people with whom they work. This approach leaves the potential uses for feedback on another plate.

Psychometric Virtues of MSF and Selling the Program

Just about any internal consultant or practitioner can recall an example—hopefully humorous—of a project implemented with no clear (or with an unclear) connection to the organization's strategies or objectives, and how it eventually faded away without discussion. Overemphasizing the measurement virtues of MSF maximizes the likelihood that MSF falls into this category of memory. Overemphasizing measurement is also probably the predominant cause of the fad contingent of organizations that implement MSF (and then fail to sustain it).

This is a subtle factor, since good measurement practices and data policies are a necessary and functional part of sustaining any MSF program. Additionally, most successful managers have a strong appetite for data and can add pressure to measure and report before determining the logical and strategic approach. In forming the program's purpose and building communication plans, it is important to review the relative importance placed on measurement virtues to ensure that they are presented as a means rather than an end, and that the various bells and whistles now available (for example, Internet processing and reporting) do not distract the participant from the actual reason the organization has opted to implement MSF.

Ultimately, measurement itself represents a cost, and it is difficult to sustain a cost without a clear return. It is good that we can measure accurately, but if the existence of the measure has not been validated in terms of some real, organizationally valued outcomes, it is probably riding on a temporary honeymoon with the virtues of more or new data.

Political Compromises

Implementing MSF typically implies widespread communications, new HR practice agreements, potential policy additions or revisions, as well as substantial behavior change. Undoubtedly, views differ, experience varies widely, and discussion arises regarding how to refine the process to the betterment of all. Compromises can be problematic, because they tend to represent the midpoint between the positions of two parties who differ on a specific aspect of the program (how often to survey, survey length, and so on) rather than the fundamental purpose of the program. If a program is designed as a system, these midpoint compromises on specific aspects of the program have a good chance of undermining some other aspect of the program. Therefore such compromises require careful analysis.

To see how such compromises can go awry, consider an illustration. An organization has already mandated that MSF be used annually for all managers at its twenty divisional offices. It subsequently stipulates that such data can be used as input to decisions about managers' compensation, but this is at the option of local leadership at each of twenty locations. A year later comes the compromise that because receiving feedback annually is too burdensome for the providers and recipients at some locations, the annual *requirement* is adjusted to biennial, although an annual schedule is still preferred.

On the surface, this seems a reasonable compromise; but from a practical standpoint, there are some serious problems. If the leader of a divisional office has already opted to link MSF to compensation decisions, such a decision must have been made on the argument that the data were a valid component of a manager's performance. Now the larger organization has compromised its way into undermining the local leader's position, with a policy that implies that such data are valid only every other year. This situation is not sustainable; it presents a legal liability and an imposition on leadership credibility.

Because political compromises are a given, an inflexible MSF program will not survive, for good reason. However, the MSF experts need to be active participants in such discussions for them to be productive. Thus the balance is between program rigidity and program passivity.

Anonymity: Protecting the Data Quality While Not Discrediting It

Another balance to find is the degree of anonymity, rater error identification, data cleansing, and so on necessary to maximize participants' reception of the feedback report as accurate. There has been a long-standing assumption that MSF programs connote rater anonymity, and it is precisely the protection of this anonymity that leads to the honest feedback that participants provide (see Chapters Eight and Twenty for more on this subject). Again, though, we have a balance, depending on the purpose of the program and the climate in which MSF is implemented.

If the purpose is behavior change in the direction of some specific prescribed model, anonymity has the potential to get in the way of accomplishing the goal in certain climates. The context must be assessed to determine whether participants may discredit their feedback by attributing it to other suspected agendas of the feedback providers, or simply to lack of sufficient attention by the feedback providers. It could be that rater accountability (through identification) is critical to the recipient's feeling that sufficient care and discipline were exercised in responding to the surveys. The other side of the argument is that rater identification can dwarf the response rate and the accuracy and depth of the feedback. Here again is a balance to find when considering the sustainability of a program.

There are a number of devices to draw on in negotiating this divide between anonymity and accountability (for example, rater training, data cleansing, Olympic scoring, and so on). Limited rater identification can also be used, in which a trusted department or individual is the recipient of surveys in a double-envelope approach. This "trust agent" is the only one who can make a connection between who and what was said. Another option further along the continuum is for the data vendor to play this same role, with specific policy regarding the conditions under which the vendor would share information in that regard. The extreme of rater accountability is for the rater to either be specifically identified in the feedback report, or even further, for the rater to hand his or her survey directly to the recipient (or for that matter, have a frank discussion with the recipient over lunch!). This is an area where program rigidity can again limit its sustainability, where the program should be allowed to adapt to the culture and climate in which it's being used if sustainability is the priority.

Standardization Versus Customization

Another area needing assessment, and possibly continuing reassessment, is the degree to which a program should be standardized. The vast majority of programs currently in place are standardized, usually meaning the same survey used for a fairly large category or level of employee, same classes of feedback providers, given the class of feedback recipient (that is, all direct reports, all peers within same office, and so on), and one feedback report format. The general rule is that standardization is good. It yields cost advantages, reduces processing time, increases perceptions of fairness and predictability, and lowers chances of a legal challenge. The need for balance comes when buy-in is a problem. Enabling participants to locally influence the design of the process increases the perceived relevance of the feedback, makes the recipient an owner and an advocate, lowers suspicion of a hidden corporate agenda, and to some degree allows the participant to control what kind of feedback he or she receives. By the same token, this kind of approach increases the chance of error, and of missing important deadlines since the decision making is less controlled.

Customization is a sustainability factor because it can change over time. If trust is low to begin with and a customized approach is used, the control held by the participant may itself soon become a source of resistance if trust is established and the local decision making is seen as an administrative burden. Furthermore, with Internet-based enrollment on the rise, the capacity to customize is likely to become more widespread, and no longer necessarily a radical measure for extremely resistant employee groups. Therefore, the functionality of the level of standardization should be constantly reevaluated to ensure it is providing appropriate returns.

Communications

MSF is typically centered around the recipient, to ensure that he or she receives relevant and useful feedback on performance. The MSF process itself can be framed as a communication process, and as such it is by nature a "local conversation" between the feedback recipient and those with whom he or she has relatively frequent interactions. It is not a communication from corporate offices.

The difference between a top-down evaluation and a one-to-one conversation can best be seen by looking at the comments received on surveys from a number of programs. Some generate comments consistently worded in the third person, as if the respondent is talking *about* the recipient to a higher-level office ("He always does this . . . he never does that"). Other programs consistently produce comments worded in the second person, that is, *to* the recipient ("You do a great job in this area . . . you do too much of that"). This latter symptom says much about how the program is perceived. Its sustainability is influenced by both the fit between this tone and the one sought, and between this tone and how communications about the program are structured.

The Medium

Several media are now available for collecting performance feedback. Telephone touch-tone entry, Internet, internal e-mail system, good old paper, and probably many others (I'm waiting another week for the Palm Pilot version) all constitute perfectly functional methods of collecting data. However, there are nuances to each that affect sustainability, depending on how well it fits the organizational context and MSF program characteristics. For example, in low-trust situations, electronic media such as Internet and e-mail pose a real concern that respondents can be identified; thus these may be approaches better used after trust is established through anonymity.

If respondents are expected to complete MSF surveys on their own time, it is particularly important to tailor the medium to what is most convenient for them; this may be electronic or paper-based, depending on the degree to which employees are computer-literate or computer-dependent. The fit of the medium affects response rates, which affect the quality of feedback and the overall sustainability of the program.

Tolerance for Alternative Approaches

A final factor to consider is how to work with managers who implement their own MSF processes. If the main program is tightly defined in terms of the competencies and format of a specific survey, managers who want to implement something different are on their own, and their success or failure is not attributable to the organization's MSF program. In such situations, managers' activities of this sort should probably be strongly discouraged. Sustainability becomes an issue, however, when you consider that over time managers become more and more familiar with the process, technology, methods, and options. As they learn by participating, they also gain the ability to consider how the process could be modified to better meet their needs. This is why MSF purpose needs to be defined carefully, to enable or discourage this kind of evolution, and to create a basis for responding when ideas of this kind emerge.

Adaptation to Organizational Change: A Case Study

The Permanente Medical Group dramatically changed its physician compensation program in the mid-1990s; part of this change was to link MSF to the overall assessment of the physician's performance (which in turn related to the physician's pay). MSF had already been established in the medical group for several years as a developmental program—not evaluative—so this change represented a serious challenge to the sustainability of many of the program's existing virtues. I briefly describe this transition as a case study in adaptation to organizational change.

The developmental MSF program had been in place for four years. It was a highly customized process, in which medical centers chose their implementation schedule, and departments within medical centers designed their own systems (who rated whom, what was rated, and how it was reported). The general goal of the program was to increase physicians' professional satisfaction. There was compelling information indicating that performance feedback was a key driver; the program was designed to ensure that physicians received feedback on their performance as members of a large organization (service, consultation, collaboration, team involvement, and so on), as well as on their clinical skills. The program enjoyed a high degree of buy-in and support.

With the new compensation program came an exhaustive search for new data-based performance measures on which pay could be based. A large number of physicians and leaders worked on this problem and gradually recognized that much of physician performance (particularly in the areas of clinical excellence and citizenship behavior) could not be adequately "counted," and the current state of the art was still a physician's expert opinion of a fellow physician. Thus the focus shifted to MSF as a basis for pay decisions. After a long series of discussions and decisions, it was ultimately concluded that MSF was to be a major component in the new pay system. With this decision came the need to manage the transition of a successful developmental feedback program to a successful evaluative one.

The first change was to standardize. Pay could not hinge on standards differing by department or medical center. Over a period of two years, hundreds of surveys in use were consolidated into one single-page, twenty-item survey. A significant aspect of survey design was scaling, for it had to give the rater a clear understanding of the lines differentiating exceptional from fully performing from substandard. Previously, the scale had been individually interpreted; the individual would look for his or her relative strengths and weaknesses. Now it was more normative, with standards implied by the survey scale.

The next major challenge was communications: how to reconcile the virtues of anonymous developmental feedback with the need for unbiased opinions regarding, ultimately, how the physician should be paid. The basic strategy was simple sincerity, explaining to participants that they themselves were the best measure of physician performance, and that pay had to be linked to the best measures available in order to be fair. It was up to them to make MSF a valid basis for pay decisions, and they directly controlled the quality of the data.

The next change was in schedule. To support compensation decisions, results had to be on schedule. This was a totally new aspect of the feedback program. Over a three-year period, we have seen the physician leaders gradually learn that it is up to them to compel others to complete surveys on time, so as to receive results in time to use them. There has been steady progress in the area of compliance with deadlines. In summary, the program survived, but only after being literally reinvented to support a new purpose.

There are a few keys to managing an MSF process through a change like this. First, it is clear that the core thread tying these two programs (before compensation and after) together was that the job of physician is far too complex to count exclusively, and ultimately the best, most comprehensive measure of physician performance is physician expert opinion of fellow physician. Focusing on a core thread helps participants see continuity with change, rather than the end of one program and the beginning of another.

Second was an objective audit to analyze how the current process supports—and how it undermines—the new strategy or direction being proposed, and incorporating this information into the new design. Subtleties are missed unless this mechanical process is done.

Third is sincerity and simplicity in communications without much candy-coating, showing where new business pressures create a need to change practices. Fourth is devoting sufficient time to managing the data processing vendor through such a change. This can literally be as much time as is needed to start up a process.

Conclusion

This chapter seeks to make it clear that sustainable MSF programs are pretty simple in purpose. When you get right down to it, MSF at its best is simply a repackaging of the truth that surrounds us every day. MSF is gathering the truth, summarizing it, and reporting it through a loudspeaker (in that the recipient hears from everyone with whom he or she works, all at once). With this as its basic goal, the practice can be sustained with good reason in a variety of organizational contexts.

Sustainable MSF is inherently adaptive. The minute the program becomes rigid, whether because of being too method-bound, glued to an outdated performance model, or tied to an inappropriate implementation calendar, it is dysfunctional and headed for extinction by definition, which is probably for the best. MSF does not stand on its own as an organizational strategy, or as a definition of performance. It's simply a means of moving information for some organizationally desired effect.

In addition to moving information, amplification is another important effect of MSF. It delivers information with much greater impact than the information would have if it were gradually delivered by various individuals over time. There is no time to make attributions for why something was said in isolation; it's all there at once. If the organization is having problems, or if morale is low, feedback amplifies this sense. Conversely, if the organization is growing and people are developing, feedback amplifies this climate likewise.

Hopefully, at this point it is clear that MSF's value is not assured. Its value manifests in support of strategy, and therefore sustaining MSF is not always a desirable effect. The notion of sustainability needs evaluation according to the program's support of strategy.

Although there is plenty of practical noise to prevent it from ever occurring, theoretically a well-run MSF program will eliminate itself in time, as participants learn the virtues of two-way communication about their own performance and others'. As familiarity with the language of performance (as it appears on the survey) and trust in the implications of such communication grow, there should be less need for MSF "programs" as the process becomes an accepted way of behaving in the organization.

Referring back to the Process Model of Multisource Feedback proposed in Chapter One, we can see that this evolution can be thought of as a series of cycles viewed over time, in which each cycle is followed by an increasingly simpler cycle. For example, year 2 might not have readiness evaluation or rater training; year 3 might not have user training, and so on until, you have nothing left but the participants, fully capable of two-way communication about effective performance.

It's an ironic way to conclude a chapter on the evolution of multisource feedback, but I hope that noting the trend, if not the outcome, provides a comprehensive and real definition of MSF's potential in organizations.

CHAPTER 26

Organizational Integration

Michael M. Harris
Laura Heft

In this chapter, we discuss some of the key purposes for having a multisource feedback (MSF) system, such as creating accountability and improving communication, and how those purposes are determined by the organization's internal environment or context. Thus, this chapter is predicated on the assumption that the appropriate goals and purposes of an MSF system are determined, at least in part, by the organizational context. We use the term *context* here in reference to the organizational life cycle and human resource career system.

To that end, we begin by discussing some key MSF goals and purposes. Following that section, we introduce the organizational life cycle and the human resource career system model and discuss how each of these perspectives affects the appropriate goals and purposes of an organizational MSF system. Finally, we describe an organization that has used an MSF system for some of the purposes discussed in this chapter.

MSF: Goals and Purposes

Just as there are numerous goals and purposes for a traditional performance management system, an organization may use an MSF system for various reasons and purposes. We address six such reasons and purposes in more detail:

1. Clarify and drive organizational mission and vision
2. Create accountability
3. Serve as an aggregate metric
4. Change organizational culture
5. Improve communication
6. Serve as a human resource management tool

Clarify and Drive Organizational Mission and Vision

One of the most powerful ways MSF can be used is to clarify and drive the organization's mission and vision (see Chapter Four for more on this subject). In developing an MSF form, top management is forced to articulate the competencies that should be measured. Through this process, these leaders must carefully consider what it is that employees should be doing. As a result, employees who participate in the MSF process become more aware of and focused on critical competencies. For example, an organization with a mission of designing innovative products could implement a quarterly MSF system to provide continuous feedback regarding risk taking and creativity. Interestingly, while those being rated become more aware and focused on the key competencies, those completing the ratings also become more aware of what the organization desires from its employees and how it relates to the organizational mission and vision.

Create Accountability

MSF systems can reinforce and create additional kinds of accountability for individual employees. Traditionally, employees are accountable primarily, if not solely, to their immediate supervisor (see also Chapter Twenty). Implementing an MSF system, however, can substantially change this by having other parties, such as peers, subordinates, and even customers, provide ratings. Although from an employee's perspective this change in accountability may be good (the supervisor doesn't get along well with the employee) or bad (the supervisor gives ratings that are more positive than is deserved), increasing employees' accountability to incorporate key constituencies is likely to be an effective tool from the organizational standpoint.

Serve as an Aggregate Metric

In an organization where group or individual goals are set for employee performance, the MSF process can be used as an aggregate metric to assess skill level attainment (for example, see Yeung and Berman, 1997, on how Eastman Kodak uses MSF to assess leadership competency). The research and development division of an organization, for instance, may have specific goals for improving creativity and the number of new product ideas generated. Since part of this goal (improving creativity) is difficult to quantify, one way of measuring success is to use the aggregate of the department's creativity competency level on the MSF instrument. The division may then set an objective to raise the aggregate creativity rating from 3.75 to 4.25. Of course, one would need to be careful not to create a situation where ratings are artificially increased just to meet this goal. Alternatively, an organization may set minimum performance standards for employees. MSF participants who score below the standard would therefore be targeted for a performance management and development program.

Change Organizational Culture

MSF can also be used to create culture change in organizations and groups (see Chapter Nineteen for more detailed examples). The MSF system could be one of the supporting interventions employed. For example, MSF could be instituted to create a participative management style, generate wide accountability for performance, or reinforce a team culture (coworkers are now involved in evaluations). If organizations with existing MSF systems undergo change, the system may be altered to reinforce or support the change initiative. For example, in systems where MSF is used only for development, the process could be altered to use MSF for decisions about rewards. The process change could be used to demonstrate the division's commitment to personal accountability and data-based decision making in all areas.

Improve Communication

When an MSF system is implemented, it sets the stage for improving communications. Employees who participate in MSF systems grow accustomed to giving and receiving feedback. Employees who become comfortable giving and receiving feedback in a formal system may be more likely to increase the frequency and effectiveness of their feedback in informal communications as well. Using MSF to improve communications can be particularly effective if it is implemented in an intact workgroup and all employees simultaneously participate. As with any other systematic change, however, there are repercussions, and the results may at first be more confusing than before (see Stout, 1998, for an example of a small, family-owned business that used an MSF system).

Serve as a Human Resource Management Tool

We would be remiss in this chapter if we did not mention use of MSF systems as a human resource management tool. Most practitioners have focused on MSF as a vehicle for *developing* employees. Some, however, have used MSF for salary raises and staffing *decisions*. Use of an MSF system for decision purposes is quite controversial (as discussed in detail in Chapters Twenty-One and Twenty-Three). We discuss later in this chapter how the organizational context affects whether the focus of the MSF system should be on developmental uses, or on human resource management decisions (for example, pay raises).

Organizational Context and MSF Systems

So far we have assumed that MSF can serve diverse purposes, ranging from improving communication to changing the organizational culture. We have also alluded to some ways in which the MSF system may vary, depending on the context. Similarly, although we presented six goals of an MSF system, it seems reasonable to expect that some of them are more important than others, depending on the organizational context. This section discusses in detail the interaction between organizational context and the goals of an MSF system. We first describe the appropriate goals of the MSF system using an organizational life cycle framework.

Organizational Life Cycle Model

According to the life cycle model, organizations commonly experience a set of distinct stages as they mature. This framework assumes that each stage ends with a particular crisis, which must be solved before the organization can reach the next stage (see Greiner, 1998). We summarize the first four stages, along with the crisis that occurs in each, and suggest the key goals of an MSF system for each stage in Table 26.1.

Stage One: Creativity

A startup organization is usually founded by a technical or entrepreneurial person, or a small group of people. The members of this new organization share a common vision, even though it may not be written down or even completely understood. The founders are generally experts in a technical or business skill. They have little interest in and often limited skill at managerial competencies, such as delegation. The organization is small and the founders frequently hire family and friends. As a result, communication is frequent and informal and flows easily. Another advantage is that the organization can respond rapidly to customer and marketplace feedback. Such organizations may be highly successful at first.

Table 26.1. Organizational Life Cycle Stages and MSF System Goals.

Stage	Crisis	Goals of MSF System
Creativity	Lack of direction	Improve communication Drive mission and vision
Direction	Lack of autonomy	Change culture by empowering employees
Delegation	Lack of control by top management	Create accountability Serve as aggregate metric
Coordination	Red tape	Change culture Serve as alternative MSF system

The same forces that lead to initial success, however, soon become problematic. As the business grows, more employees must be hired. These new employees are less likely to be friends or relatives and therefore are less committed to the founders' purpose. To be as efficient and productive as possible, increased specialization must take place.

In the human resource field, certain legal requirements are imposed on organizations as they become larger. The founders soon begin to experience frustration as their contact and communication with employees becomes more limited. The founders begin to raise questions about the direction of the firm and develop a concern that there is no longer a shared vision and mission. The crisis that develops is a lack of direction.

An MSF system may be quite useful to an organization as the crisis brought on by lack of direction begins. Implementation of an MSF system helps increase the amount of communication. At least as important, the MSF system offers the means for driving organizational mission and vision. Not only does it enable employees to better understand what they are expected to be doing and why; the process of designing the MSF system helps the founders carefully examine the organizational mission and vision.

Stage Two: Direction

If an organization is to successfully navigate past the crisis of the previous stage, a clear sense of direction must materialize. One result is likely to be a formal organizational structure, with separate departments and formal job descriptions for each position. Second, formal budgets and work standards are articulated, and mechanisms are implemented to facilitate communication between management and employees. Finally, identification and articulation of the organization's mission and vision occurs.

The forces that enable the organization to succeed at this stage, however, eventually lead to a new crisis, namely, a perceived lack of autonomy. That is, as employees develop expertise in the knowledge of particular products or markets, they find that the highly centralized nature of the organization restricts their ability to make good decisions. Thus employees feel they lack the control needed to be effective in their jobs.

Here again, implementation of an MSF system may be helpful, particularly in supporting a changing organizational culture. In an organization that has been emphasizing a hierarchical management system, it is likely that performance management activities are performed solely by an employee's supervisor. Moreover, it is likely that the focus has been primarily on evaluation, rather than development. Implementing an MSF system that provides feedback from multiple sources and focuses on developmental activities helps to signal and reinforce greater empowerment of employees.

Stage Three: Delegation

If the organization is able to reach this stage, it has adopted some kind of decentralized organizational structure and given much more autonomy to plant managers, regional managers, and other business unit managers. Communication from the top levels is far more limited, as decentralized decision making spreads throughout the organization.

These changes, however, soon create a new crisis. Plant, regional, and other business managers enjoy their new autonomy, but senior management becomes increasingly concerned about its own lack of control. Sensing insufficient accountability on the part of their employees, top management feels a need to rein in unit managers. This leads to a new crisis: a perceived lack of control.

We assert that to address this crisis, an MSF system has two major goals: creating accountability and serving as an aggregate metric. Although senior management seeks greater accountability *from employees,* using an MSF system creates greater accountability *to a variety of parties,* including peers, subordinates, and possibly customers. In this way, using an MSF system can ultimately create a greater sense of accountability to top management. Top executives' fears that they have given up too much control may be alleviated by their ability to review general trends in MSF ratings (even if they are not given the results for specific managers). Second, using MSF can provide an aggregate metric for rating behavioral aspects of performance, thereby introducing a potentially important, yet different, way for top management to assess performance of the decentralized units.

Stage Four: Coordination

If the organization is to succeed at this stage, it is effective at achieving a balance between decentralized decision making and coordination between units. Among the common tactics used here is implementing procedures to promote control and review of line managers. As we have noted, part of the solution may be to implement an MSF system, in addition to detailed business reports for corporate headquarters. Thus, managers retain some autonomy, while at the same time becoming more accountable to headquarters.

Eventually, however, yet another crisis emerges, this one over the amount of red tape and reporting requirements for top management and the unit managers. Each party perceives that its effectiveness is reduced by the proliferating number of rules and regulations. Indeed, the organization may simply have become too large and unwieldy for any simple system to work. The way to resolve this crisis is to eliminate extraneous rules and regulations and to learn to work effectively with a minimum of formal oversight and reporting. In essence, the challenge is to become more like the stage one organization, even though the company may be relatively large.

How is this crisis solved? By creating a culture where employees work collaboratively to solve conflicts and where information sharing is common. In other words, informal procedures replace red tape. We therefore question whether introducing a traditional, formal MSF system is regarded as a help or a hindrance. That is, having yet another form to complete may simply be viewed as part of the problem. An informal approach to multisource feedback may be far more effective.

When a major problem arises, for example, the consultant might use an approach where narrative comments are gathered from various constituencies and then fed back to the relevant parties. Rather than using formal ratings, a series of open-ended questions to key parties might produce more useful information. Thus, at this stage of an organization's life careful thought must be given to the function of the MSF system, as well as to how managers perceive it.

Human Resource Career Systems

The human resource career systems model is another useful approach to understanding organizations and their human resource practices (see Sonnenfeld and Peiperl, 1988). In this perspective, an organization's business strategy drives the career system. This typology assumes that the organization's business strategy has determined the career system that is used. Moreover, there are four major business strategies: prospector, defender, analyzer, and reactor. We begin by briefly describing each of these business strategies and then reviewing the corresponding career system. We conclude each section with a discussion of the goals of an MSF system. A summary of these systems and the implications for MSF is in Table 26.2.

Prospector Strategy

Organizations that adopt a prospector strategy focus on innovation and development of new business opportunities. Many consulting firms use a prospector strategy. Internet companies such as Amazon.com also use it. As suggested by the term *prospector*, these organizations are continuously on the forefront of new, cutting-edge products or knowledge. Most important, because such organizations are always entering new businesses they need employees

**Table 26.2. Career System Typology
and MSF System Goals.**

Career Strategy	Business Emphasis	Goals of MSF System
Prospector	New businesses	Change culture
Serve as aggregate metric
Drive and clarify mission and vision
Defender	Monopoly	Serve as an aggregate metric
Analyzer	Combination of new business and monopoly	Serve as major tool for development
Reactor	Declining business	Serve as tool for termination decisions
Drive and clarify mission and vision
Change culture

who already have the necessary competencies to be successful. Human resources focuses on finding, attracting, and retaining the highly qualified candidates (or "stars"). Candidates may be hired at any point in their careers; internal promotions are less important.

Performance is frequently based on measurable factors, such as sales or number of hours billed, and subjective measures are now less important. In short, organizations that emphasize the prospector strategy have little time for careful development of their employees; rather, they seek out applicants who have proven to be successful elsewhere and can deliver independently on the organizational strategy.

In the absence of much emphasis on development, we believe that the major purposes of introducing an MSF system are to change the culture of the organization, drive a revised mission and vision, and serve as an aggregate metric. A prospector organization traditionally is likely to emphasize individual contribution and highly specialized work. Such organizations, however, have by necessity changed to more of a teamwork environment and to a greater focus on customer satisfaction.

To help reinforce those changes, the MSF system would be useful in changing the culture, while driving the revised mission. The MSF system serves at the same time as an aggregate metric for measuring effectiveness in these new areas (for a similar and more detailed example, see Chapter Nineteen, the section "Consultants Developing Consultants").

Defender Strategy

Organizations that adopt a defender strategy focus on a narrow, well-defined product or service, emphasizing consistency and continuity. Such organizations have a monopoly or near monopoly on their business. Public museums frequently use a defender strategy. In the past, most utility companies used it as a business strategy, but greater deregulation has forced them to adopt new strategies in many cases.

For this kind of strategy, changes are typically small and incremental, and the emphasis is on creating public goodwill and reliability. Organizations relying on this strategy therefore concentrate on selecting and retaining employees who develop long-term commitment and loyalty, which reflects their emphasis on consistency and continuity. Accordingly, employee development focuses on employee commitment and preparing for movement through a clearly defined set of progressively higher jobs. Performance, as well as promotion, is based heavily on such things as contribution to the group, commitment to the organization, and organizational citizenship behavior. Employee development has a strong general (as well as job-specific) content.

We suggest that an MSF system plays an important role as a human resource tool in the defender organization. First, employees of this kind of organization enjoy much general development; an MSF system can be very helpful in assessing training needs. Second, given the emphasis on highly subjective components, such as commitment and loyalty, MSF ratings by peers and subordinates may constitute an important evaluative tool. Third, with emphasis on the contribution to the organization as a whole, it is reasonable to have different constituencies involved in the performance management process. For organizations that wish to minimize the evaluative component, this application might be reserved for employees below a certain minimum rating, who then need to undergo some kind of remedial program.

Analyzer Strategy

The third strategy, the analyzer approach, is adopted by organizations that wish for a blend of the prospector and defender approaches. Organizations following the analyzer strategy use a mix of new business and consistency in the product or service. Consumer product firms typically emphasize this strategy. The organization is always searching for new business opportunities, but there is a core, stable business focus.

The type of employee that this organization desires to have is therefore a blend of the types found in the prospector and defender approaches. Employee training and development are critical, as the organization strives to maintain continuity among its employees, while preparing them for new skills and businesses. Indeed, employee development is often deemed a major strategic advantage of such firms. Training must therefore be extensive and focus on preparing for changing needs. Skill development is at least as important as employee commitment.

For the analyzer organization, the MSF system plays a major role as a human resource tool. Much of the original thinking about MSF systems probably took place in the context of analyzer organizations. Moreover, unlike the case with the defender organization, we assert that in this instance the MSF system should be used primarily, if not solely, as a developmental tool. Given the importance of employee development to the success of such a firm, we believe that using the MSF system for decisions (say, salary increase) is at the expense of the developmental uses of the system.

Reactor Strategy

The fourth strategy, reactor, is adopted by organizations that are in the process of a business setback and consolidation. The health care industry has served as an example of this strategy in the last few years. Organizations using a reactor strategy are generally consolidating the size of their workforce, while hiring and retaining a set of highly selective turnaround experts. Employee development in such organizations is practically nonexistent, given their limited resources (both financial and in terms of time) and their need to hire employees with numerous skill sets. A reactor strategy therefore involves two simultaneous human resource foci: reducing the workforce and hiring selected expertise to successfully change the organization's direction.

We assert that MSF systems can play two roles in a reactor organization. One way MSF might be used is to help decide whom to terminate from the workforce; it should be recognized, however, that this is a controversial way to use an MSF system (see Chapter Twenty-One). Alternatively, or in addition, the MSF system might be used as a means of changing the organizational culture, and for clarifying and driving the new mission and vision. To use the same system for these dual purposes may, however, be problematic. If employees perceive that the MSF system served in terminating coworkers, for example, then use of the same system for developmental purposes may be seriously compromised. Thus, organizations using the MSF system for the dual purposes of terminating and developing employees should carefully consider the problems that may arise.

We turn now to a brief case study of an organization that has used an MSF system in a number of ways suggested in this chapter.

Case Study: GuildMaster

GuildMaster was founded in 1982 as a company that purchased, restored, and marketed Spanish antiques. At that time, independent contractors were paid to drive throughout Spain in search of antiques, which the company then received, repaired, and sold in Springfield, Missouri. The founders, Jim and Ellie Parsons, found that it was not easy to obtain the antiques, and it was often difficult to sell them in Springfield. Within a few years, GuildMaster was purchasing and designing new furniture.

By the late 1980s, the company began to manufacture its own furniture. Early on, GuildMaster earned a reputation as an innovative, high-fashion manufacturer of furniture. But by the mid-1990s production began to falter, and the company experienced problems owing to a lack of direction and formal processes. Jon Baker, an experienced executive and consultant, was hired by Jim Parsons to help change the organization. In short, GuildMaster was probably reaching its first crisis in stage one.

Baker brought the structure and direction that the organization needed. In addition, he worked to change the entire culture of the organization, which had been characterized by a great deal of mistrust of top management, to one in which there was a high level of trust between employees and top management. To that end, he introduced an MSF system, which afforded a means of giving feedback effectively.

To begin the MSF process, Baker first had employees complete a 360-degree feedback rating for him, which included a question as to whether he should stay on with the company or leave. Clearly, by having all the employees rate him, Baker was creating an effective communication process as well.

The basically guiding philosophy of the company is that employees must produce results (such as production goals) while maintaining a set of shared values. There are five values that each employee must demonstrate:

1. Positive attitude
2. Team spirit
3. High moral character
4. Hard work
5. Customer and quality orientation

The values are measured by the MSF form, which contains multiple items under each category, as well as a section for narrative comments. Each item is rated on a 5-point scale, where 5 means "almost always" and 1 means "almost never." For new employees, the MSF form is completed after ninety days. New employees first meet with their team leader to review the ratings and develop an action plan to work on shortcomings. New employees then meet with their team members to share their ratings and to discuss their action plan. Every employee is evaluated on the MSF form in January.

The primary use of the MSF system is for developmental feedback to improve performance. Weaknesses are addressed in the form of an action plan, which the employee then works on implementing throughout the year. The MSF system also can be used indirectly for the company's profit-sharing plan. Specifically, each employee sets both individual and team goals and receives a share of the bonus pool for each goal met. The goals can come from the MSF action plan that was created. It should be emphasized, however, that the MSF ratings do not affect the amount of bonus received. Hence, the MSF system is used primarily for developmental purposes, though indirectly it may be used for decisions.

Conclusion

By way of a summary, we conclude with three key suggestions for practitioners considering use of an MSF system.

First, consider the goals of the MSF system. Make sure that you are able to achieve the goals with the system you have designed.

Second, consider the organization's life cycle stage and human resource career system. Be sure that you are implementing an MSF system that is compatible with them.

Finally, the role and nature of the MSF system may need to change as the organization's strategy, mission, or vision changes. Don't forget that the MSF system is intended to help achieve certain business objectives. As the organizational context changes, the MSF system may need to change as well.

References

Greiner, L. "Evolution and Revolution as Organizations Grow." *Harvard Business Review,* May–June 1998, pp. 55–67.

Sonnenfeld, J., and Peiperl, M. "Staffing Policy as a Strategic Response:

A Typology of Career Systems." *Academy of Management Review,* 1988, *13,* 588–600.

Stout, H. "Self-Evaluation Brings Changes to a Family's Ad Agency." *Wall Street Journal,* Jan. 6, 1998, p. B2.

Yeung, A., and Berman, B. "Adding Value Through Human Resources: Reorienting Human Resource Measurement to Drive Business Performance." *Human Resource Management,* 1997, *36,* 321–335.

CHAPTER 27

Cross-Cultural Issues in Multisource Feedback

Stéphane Brutus
Jean Brittain Leslie
Dana McDonald-Mann

So you're thinking about going international with multisource feedback (MSF). Well, join the rest of the world! The emergence of MSF in the international context constitutes the next frontier in the area of performance management. Make no mistake about it, though: MSF is an American product. You need not look further than the cultural dynamics at work in North America today for an explanation for the emergence of MSF.

The democratization and hierarchical flattening of organizations has been a primary influence on the popularity of MSF. Organizations that were once formed of formal and rigid hierarchies are slowly becoming democratic, flat, and open workplaces. Casual Fridays, open-door policies, and managing-by-walking-around offer some concrete evidence of this movement. As layers of management disappear and the span of control increases, appraisal duties are shifting from being the task of supervisors to one for coworkers. Additionally, the emergence of MSF in the early 1990s stems directly from advances in information systems technology. The technological underpinnings of MSF, necessary to process the data generated, cannot be dissociated from the management phenomenon that MSF has become.

Expanding management practices that enjoy demonstrated success in the United States (such as MSF) into the international arena is a common trend among organizations. When management practices are transferred from one cultural context to another, their effectiveness is assumed to be universal. In this chapter, however, we challenge this assumption and question the presumed universality of MSF. We do this by dissecting MSF into its component parts and by analyzing the cultural influences at play on these components.

Here, *culture* is defined as a set of basic assumptions shared by individuals with the same cultural origins (Hofstede, 1980). The chapter is broken into three sections. We open the discussion with the backbone of MSF, or assessing individual performance in different cultures. We then take a look at the contingencies related to using this information (feedback) in cross-cultural settings. Finally, we offer a set of recommendations for those interested in going international with MSF.

Assessing Individual Performance Across Cultures

In this first section, we explore the influence of culture on assessing individual performance via multiple raters. Specifically, we discuss philosophical differences in views of development, selecting and designing an appropriate behavioral model, psychometric and translation issues, legal matters, concern about anonymity, and cultural effects on ratings.

Philosophical Views of Performance Management Practice

Why use MSF in the first place? Many will say that MSF is a great tool for decision making. The belief that organizational decisions need to be based on job-related information, such as that provided by MSF, is well accepted; in many countries, this principle is even enforced by legislation. The fact that much of the literature on MSF focuses on measurement issues is symptomatic of our reliance on accuracy and precision. But this approach to organizational decision making is far from universal. Factors such as gender, family background, and religion are commonly used in different parts of the world to decide who gets the job or the promotion. Relying on some characteristics at the expense of others is a mere artifact of complex and consistent cultural systems. In the next section, we attempt to show how many aspects of MSF, such as reliance on objective and job-related information, are culturally bound.

Selecting and Designing an Appropriate Behavioral Model

MSF, as a process, begins with assessing individual performance according to an established and accepted behavioral model (see Chapter Four). In deciding to use an MSF instrument internationally, one needs to question whether the behavioral model of the instrument selected is appropriate in the country or culture of interest (Leslie, Gryskiewicz, and Dalton, 1998).

When deciding on a behavioral model, an organization can select an existing model (that is, one that was not designed with the new culture in mind) and apply it across cultures. In this case, a constant set of performance expectations is laid out in all locations (for example, "Decision making through consensus is what is valued in our organization"). This *uniform approach* puts the emphasis on corporate control and coordination by placing "organizational" culture above "national" culture (Milliman and others, 1998). However, certain cultural factors are deeply rooted, and issues may arise if national cultures are discounted.

When MSF was used in a large paper company in India, derailment factors were assessed for a group of managers. One factor focused on the extent to which managers relied too much on their superiors. Although overreliance on a superior has been found to be linked to managerial derailment in the United States (McCall and Lombardo, 1988), it was discovered (after the fact) that the same tendency is perceived favorably in India, indicating a loyal and stable employee. This example points to the challenges and potential pitfalls associated with using uniform behavioral models.

A recent study found that congruence between management practices and culture leads to increased organizational performance (Newman and Nollen, 1996). An organization willing to adapt to a local culture chooses a *contingent approach,* consisting of tailoring the behavioral model to the culture at hand. This is done by conducting an assessment of the country or culture of interest and adapting the content of the behavioral model so as to make it "understandable" within the new cultural context. Although adopting this strategy offers a better understanding of cultural nuances, it sometimes precludes the organization from making direct comparisons across countries and cultures.

Psychometric and Translation Issues

Adapting existing instruments could be considered a combination of the approaches outlined in the previous paragraph. Note that we use the term *adaptation* instead of the more common *translation*. The process of adaptation refers to more than just working toward a common language instrument. It includes determining whether or not the instrument can measure the same construct in numerous languages or cultures and deciding on appropriate modification when needed.

Translating the instrument is one of the many steps involved in adaptation. MSF instruments often contain items or questions that use business jargon; it is particularly difficult to convey this in other languages. Adjectives such as *extroverted, engaging, versatile,* and *robust* are commonly used to describe managerial behavior in English, but these may take totally different meanings when translated in other languages. For example, an implementation MSF in India revealed that the performance item "Surrounds himself or herself with good people" was interpreted by some Indian managers as meaning "Surrounds himself or herself with people of integrity and of high morals." The intent of the item, of course, was to assess the extent to which one is surrounded with high performers—a subtle but important difference.

The statistical tools pertaining to measuring psychological constructs have evolved tremendously in the past decade. They allow evaluation of the quality of the adaptation process. Several statistical techniques are available to examine the equivalence of versions of the same survey in various languages. These include item response theory analyses (see Ellis, 1991), Mantel-Haenszel procedures (see Holland and Thayer, 1988), and logistic regression procedures (see Rogers and Swaminathan, 1993). Note these procedures require relatively large samples of data (two hundred or more), but they provide useful information on sources of bias or inequivalence such as true cultural differences in the theoretical constructs (scales and items), poor translation, or measurement aspects of the instrument (format).

The translation can be corrected, and the instrument format improved, but scales and items that show inequivalence should be removed from the instrument unless a good argument can be made for retaining them. If overlooked, this inclusion can have negative consequences on performance assessment because it casts doubt on what the obtained information really means, which in turn makes using this information inadvisable.

Rating Tendencies

Although language differences represent a major obstacle to cross-cultural implementation of MSF, using rating scales also presents a significant challenge. Most, if not all, MSF instruments are based on numerical rating scales. Geert Hofstede (1980) was among the first cross-cultural researchers to report differences in rating patterns by nation. In his seminal study of cultural values, Hofstede found that people from certain countries—notably Venezuela, Peru, Taiwan, Singapore, Mexico, and Greece—tend to respond to questions with the lower end of the scale. In these countries, using extremes on a response scale may be considered boisterous and even in poor taste (Hui and Triandis, 1989). By contrast, research indicates that North Americans (Chen, Lee, and Stevenson, 1995) and Hispanics (Marin, Gamba, and Marin, 1992) tend to respond in extremes when making their feelings known.

Although the research on cultural rating patterns is inconclusive, there are several practical considerations to take into account. It is important to recognize that people around the world vary in their level of exposure to standardized surveys. As stated earlier, the educational experience of North Americans produces substantial familiarity with standardized testing and rating scales. In other parts of the world, however, using these assessment methods may be more a novelty; greater emphasis may be placed on other forms of assessment (say, written essays) or testing may not be used at all. Lack of familiarity with the format used in MSF may lead to unwanted bias.

In summary, the best way to ensure quality adaptation of an MSF instrument is to determine construct equivalence, perform a translation of quality, and then empirically establish equivalence of the scales and items. The purpose of the adaptation process is to empirically establish the equivalence of the versions of the MSF instrument. Many advanced statistical techniques are available to allow the design team to distinguish between such possible sources of bias as true cultural differences in the theoretical constructs (for example, overreliance on a boss has a different meaning in India than in the United States), poor translation ("good people" in India and in the United States), or measurement aspects of the instrument (different use of the rating scale).

Legal Issues

As will be clearly stated in Chapter Twenty-Eight, using MSF for decision-making purposes requires adherence to specific legal parameters. Although guidelines such as demonstrating validity simply represent good practice and should be applied whenever MSF is used, the legal guidelines overseeing performance appraisal practices vary greatly around the globe. American managers, for example, may be accustomed to answering questions about race or ethnic identity, but in the United Kingdom this information is considered sensitive and personal (and covered by the Data Protection Act of 1998). The International Test Commission has published a set of guidelines for adapting tests (see Hambleton, 1994; and van de Vijver and Hambleton, 1996) that apply sound principles for any country or culture; however, there exists no international professional organization to hold members to these standards.

The Issue of Anonymity

A vital element of the MSF process is the guarantee of anonymity given to raters. This protection allows raters the freedom necessary to evaluate others without fearing retribution if the evaluations are negative in nature. Of course, granting anonymity to raters is useful only to the extent that the offer of protection is taken seriously. In other words, it is not anonymity per se that allows ratings to be honest but rather the belief that anonymity is present! Protecting anonymity in management practices has a solid history in North America (think of culture surveys), but it is relatively unheard of in other places.

Despite good-faith efforts, raters from certain cultures may never feel protected by anonymity when rating coworkers. In these circumstances, implementation of MSF should be accompanied by extensive communication of, and strict adherence to, the procedures required to ensure anonymity. Even then, suspicions may persist. If raters believe that their identity will be revealed to the ratee, the validity of their ratings is compromised, regardless of the procedures in place.

Culture and MSF

At this point of the chapter, we introduce a series of cultural dimensions to explain in more detail the interplay between culture and MSF. These dimensions, coined by Hofstede (1980), are well known and extremely useful in understanding the attitudes and behaviors of people from diverse cultural backgrounds. In this section, we use two of Hofstede's dimensions, "individualism" and "power distance," to explain how raters from different cultures may react in completing an MSF instrument.

As stated earlier, certain aspects of MSF make it compatible with cultures in which individual achievement and recognition take precedence over the collectivity. Individualistic cultures include, among others, the United States, Canada, and Germany. (While MSF involves many members of a work unit, as compared to traditional performance appraisal system with only a supervisor doing the evaluation, that does not make it a group process per se.)

Everything about the MSF points to a single individual (that is, the one who is the target of evaluation). The many raters involved still provide their ratings, individually, to the targeted person. Clearly, MSF is aimed at individual assessment, individual development, and individual decision making. Although, managerial sciences have always wrestled with the link between individual performance and group or organizational performance, in individualistic cultures we accept this link de facto. However, this assumption is likely to break down in collectivist cultures such as Japan and China. In these countries, the concept of performance lies at the group level, and the distinction between individual performance and group performance is problematic.

Power distance, which refers to the extent that people accept inequality and power differentials between individuals, is another cultural factor closely tied to MSF. In high power-distance cultures, such as the Philippines and Mexico, respect for hierarchical differences is deeply rooted and serves as a strong guideline by which people relate to one another. Deference to one's supervisor is common in high power-distance cultures. Such regard for the hierarchy is not the norm in low power-distance cultures such as the United States or Canada. MSF has very little consideration for hierarchical "rights." In principle, all rating sources are equal in MSF. The message sent by the process is that everybody who can form an educated opinion about a coworker's performance can and will be heard by the organization and by the focal individual. Although this democratization of relations within the workplace fits well in a low power-distance culture, a rater from another culture may react differently to this situation.

Feedback Across Cultures

This section focuses on the cultural issues specific to using multisource ratings across cultures. We discuss issues such as the logistics of using MSF internationally and provision of feedback to managers from differing cultures.

Logistical Issues

As a performance management system, MSF is extremely complex (see Chapter Twenty). Of course, this process is even more complex when used internationally. Basic issues such as survey distribution, survey collection, and even scoring can lead to a disastrous situation. One of the authors implemented MSF in a large global organization; it required negotiating logistical challenges at every turn. First, getting MSF packets to the participants presented challenges because most had special language requests. For example, one participant might need all French; another all Italian; a third three French forms, three Italian, and four Mandarin Chinese; and so on. In total, at least half of the packages needed customized language combinations.

Secondly, getting these forms to and from participants throughout the world is not only very expensive but also difficult to manage. Regular international mail is notoriously slow and unreliable; therefore, the more expensive option of international express carrier is necessary. Difficulties in gathering the data, of course, had implications for the subsequent waves of administration. Surprisingly, many other difficulties began to surface only after the data were in. Upon receipt of their feedback reports, many participants noted that they did not have complete data. Of course, international express carriers were not used by all participants or their raters; therefore tracking data was often impossible. The story behind the story: plan well in advance, and expect the unexpected when going international with MSF.

Feedback Customs in Various Part of the World

Communicating performance information to the employee—the feedback process—is a very important step in MSF. This is particularly important when MSF is used for a developmental purpose; the individual must accept the information offered and use it appropriately. Cultural variation in how people give and receive feedback is large. Wide variation is also found *within* a culture; experienced users of MSF will surely attest to the many ways people from the same cultural background react to their evaluations.

This variation is even more pronounced when introducing a cross-cultural dimension. Feedback processes have deep roots and are reflected at many levels of a society, from how children are evaluated in the educational system to organizational systems of performance management.

Before discussing the implications of giving feedback in different cultures, let's look at MSF for what it is: a unique feedback process. For one thing, the volume of information conveyed in MSF is enormous; a typical MSF report spans dozens of pages. Secondly, the type of information favored in these reports is mostly objective and quantitative in nature (ratings, graphs, statistics, and so on).

Finally, as stated in the previous section, MSF information always focuses on individual performance. In this section, we use the same cultural dimensions (individualism, power distance) and introduce an additional one—tolerance for ambiguity—to explain how individuals with differing cultural backgrounds may accept and react to feedback in varying fashion.

Delivering Individual Feedback in Various Cultures

The need to convey performance information to employees is common to all organizations, whether Chinese- or American-based. A subtle comment to a third party, a written evaluation, a face-to-face discussion, these are all examples of the manner in which performance feedback can be given.

Feedback in the workplace can take many forms; MSF contrasts drastically with how feedback is used in certain countries. Just as collectivism influences *evaluation* of others, it is also likely to influence *reception* of evaluation. If asking subordinates to rate a supervisor is inappropriate in a specific culture (a rating issue), it is likely that, in the same culture, giving managers feedback from their subordinates is just as inappropriate (a feedback issue).

It follows that the usefulness of individual assessment in collectivist cultures may be limited because feedback recipients may not be used to (or comfortable with) receiving information that distinguishes them from their collectivity. Also, individuals in high power distance may be likely to focus exclusively on a supervisor's feedback while dismissing the information from raters of lesser hierarchical status.

Tolerance for ambiguity is another cultural dimension that influences the feedback process. By nature, MSF information is objective, relying on rating scales, graphs, comparative norms, and indication of rater variance. This format leaves little ambiguity as to the content of the message; in certain cultures such as Japan, this straightforwardness is not typical. Some cultures have high tolerance for ambiguity, whereby subtle and indirect forms of communication are accepted. In North America, where tolerance for ambiguity is low, straightforwardness in communication is valued.

As a result of this cultural variance, acceptance of MSF is likely to differ around the world. Keep in mind that the most accurate and extensive assessment tool is useless for developing a group of employees if they choose to disregard the information. The point is that, in certain cultures, individuals may have a tendency not to use the information to its full value; one has to pay close attention to the feedback process by monitoring recipients' reactions to it. Expect to spend considerable energy getting the feedback through and addressing questions and concerns in these cultures. For example, when implementing MSF in an Eastern European organization, an additional day was scheduled for the development planning phase following feedback administration because managers in that culture were not used to focusing on their own development.

The Cross-Cultural Relevance of Self-Awareness

One of the goals of MSF is to increase the level of participant self-awareness. In recent years, self-awareness has become a defining characteristic of effective leadership (Konger and Benjamin, 1999). By measuring how others perceive a manager's effectiveness and contrasting this information with self-evaluation, we observe the extent to which this particular manager's self-image, or level of self-awareness, is congruent with that of others (see Chapters Thirteen and Nineteen).

This operationalization of self-awareness brings forth the interesting, but rarely mentioned, assumption that in MSF others' ratings always represent "true" performance against which self-assessment is contrasted. To a certain extent, it is as if self were being defined through the eyes of others. Issues of self and self-definition are often greatly influenced by cultural factors, and often rooted in religion and philosophical thought. For example, in Buddhism and Taoism, the definition of self is inner-directed and achieved by processes such as meditation and reflection. In this case, using external benchmarks, such as evaluations of others, to guide the self-discovery process may be inappropriate.

Conclusion

Most of the material used in this chapter is based on a combination of logical arguments combined with our own experiences with using MSF internationally. Although MSF is currently being used in most parts of the world, a survey of these practices is not yet available. For this reason, we were cautious in making any claims about use or misuse of MSF in other cultures; these specific issues just cannot be answered yet. However, what we do know is that MSF is a process that follows a set of specific "cultural rules."

In this chapter, we have defined these rules and attempted to highlight why and how applying MSF in another cultural context may lead to some issues. We do believe, however, that most of these issues can be resolved by paying particular attention to the process. In the final section, we propose a series of recommendations on how this can be achieved.

Recommendations

First, choose or design an instrument that is psychometrically sound. Ensure that the validity of the MSF instrument has been established—if possible, in the country or culture of intended use. Here are recommendations that pertain to collecting MSF ratings:

- Consider the language that you plan to use. It is very important to scrutinize the translation process.
- Expect participants to question the translation, especially people who are bilingual or multilingual. You need to have expert information available to defend the quality of the translation.
- If using the English version of the instrument, think about how doing so can undermine the credibility of the process.
- Prepare for varying levels of fluency among *both* the feedback recipients and their raters (particularly at lower organizational levels).
- Use professional translators. Although costly, a professional translation is important because of the subtlety of language.
- Ensure that you have a detailed account of the procedures used to translate the instrument.

The next recommendation is, of course, to understand the culture. As discussed throughout this chapter, it is critical to understand the cultural context in which you are using MSF. Work with local professionals or "cultural experts" to better understand the cultural dynamics in place.

- Investigate local legal requirements pertaining to performance appraisal systems in the targeted culture.
- Find out how individual feedback is viewed.
- Research how the multisource process will be accepted.
- Learn the history of testing and assessment.
- Understand how the feedback needs to be conducted.
- Understand and consider cultural effects on ratings.

Third, attend to process issues, such as providing rater anonymity, communicating purpose or guidelines, and distributing and collecting materials; they are all important regardless of the culture. Using MSF internationally adds significant complexity to process issues.

Understand how anonymity is viewed in the targeted culture. If necessary, train international raters on using response scales and on evaluating individual performance prior to implementation. Rater training has been found to significantly increase the validity of performance ratings.

Understand how process outcomes are interpreted. Ask yourself:

- Will the process outcomes be the same in all cultures used? If so, are these outcomes equally useful in all cultures where MSF is used?
- Is the feedback for the purpose of self-awareness, and will it remain confidential? If so, you need to understand what confidentiality means within the cultural context in which you are working.
- Do the participants actually believe your assurances of confidentiality?
- Is individual self-awareness from a behavioral perspective valued within the cultural context you are working in?

References

Chen, C., Lee, S., and Stevenson, H. W. "Response Style and Cross-Cultural Comparisons on Rating Scales Among East Asian and North American Students." *American Psychological Society,* 1995, *6,* 170–175.

Ellis, B. B. "Item Response Theory: A Tool for Assessing the Equivalence of Translated Tests." *Bulletin of the International Test Commission,* 1991, *18,* 33–51.

Hambleton, R. K. "Guidelines for Adapting Educational and Psychological Tests: A Progress Report." *European Journal of Psychological Assessments,* 1994, *10,* 229–240.

Hofstede, G. *Culture's Consequences: International Differences in Work-Related Values.* Thousand Oaks, Calif.: Sage, 1980.

Holland, P. W., and Thayer, D. T. "Differential Item Performance and the Mantel-Haenszel Procedure." In H. Wainer and H. I. Braun (eds.), *Test Validity.* Mahwah, N.J.: Erlbaum, 1988.

Hui, C. H., and Triandis, H. C. "Effects of Culture and Response Format on Extreme Response Style." *Journal of Cross-Cultural Psychology,* 1989, *20,* 296–309.

Konger, J. A., and Benjamin, B. *Building Leaders: How Successful Companies Develop the Next Generation.* San Francisco: Jossey-Bass, 1999.

Leslie, J. B., Gryskiewicz, N. D., and Dalton, M. A. "Understanding Cultural Influences on the 360-Degree Feedback Process." In W. W. Tornow and M. London (eds.), *Maximizing the Value of 360-Degree Feedback: A Process for Successful Individual and Organizational Development.* San Francisco: Jossey-Bass, 1998.

Marin, G., Gamba, R. J., and Marin, G. V. "Extreme Response Style and Acquiescence Among Hispanics." *Journal of Cross-Cultural Psychology,* 1992, *23,* 498–509.

McCall, M. W., Lombardo, M. M., and Morrison, A. M. *The Lessons of Experience.* San Francisco: New Lexington Press, 1988.

Milliman, J., and others. "The Impact of National Culture on Human Resource Management Practices: The Case of Performance Appraisal." *Advances in International Comparative Management,* 1998, *12,* 157–183.

Newman, K., and Nollen, S. "Culture and Congruence: The Fit Between Management Practices and Cultures." *Journal of International Business Studies,* 1996, *4,* 753–779.

Rogers, H. J., and Swaminathan, H. "A Comparison of Logistic Regression and Mantel-Haenszel Procedures for Detecting Differential Item Functioning." *Applied Psychological Measurement,* 1993, *17,* 105–116.

van de Vijver, F.J.R., and Hambleton, R. K. "Translating Tests: Some Practical Guidelines." *European Psychologist,* 1996, *1,* 89–99.

CHAPTER 28

Legal and Ethical Issues in Multisource Feedback

H. John Bernardin
Catherine L. Tyler

The purpose of this chapter is to discuss the major legal and ethical issues related to using multisource feedback (MSF). We first discuss the limited case law related to MSF and then present a set of MSF system prescriptions for avoiding, or ultimately winning, legal complaints related to MSF. Although the case law is continually evolving and often confusing, some appraisal practices are clearly viewed more favorably than others by the courts. We conclude with a discussion of the major ethical issues related to MSF.

MSF becomes a potential legal issue whenever the resultant data from the MSF are used for any type of personnel decision (Bracken, 1994). Thus, if an organization rewards, punishes, selects, promotes, transfers, lays off, or fires people on the basis of data from an MSF system, the system could fall under the scrutiny of the courts. MSF poses much less of a legal problem if its purpose and use is strictly employee development. Whether MSF appraisals are designed to predict future performance or to assess past performance, the appraisal process could be scrutinized by the courts under a variety of legal claims.

There are a number of methods for seeking redress through the courts (Malos, 1998). The two major sources of federal lawsuits involving performance appraisal are Title VII of the Civil Rights Act and the Age Discrimination in Employment Act (ADEA). Tort litigation related to unlawful discharge claims and defamation of character are becoming more common and often involve judgments of employee performance (Malos, 1998).

The plaintiff may attempt to meet part of the prima facie burden in Title VII or ADEA cases by employing an "expert witness" who critiques the appraisal system and process. Psychologists routinely serve as expert witnesses on both sides of court cases involving allegations of discrimination related to performance appraisal practice. The main focus of expert testimony on the plaintiff's side concerns the "job relatedness" of the appraisal system and its susceptibility to various forms of bias (Bernardin, Hennessey, and Peyrefitte, 1995). This testimony is often submitted along with adverse impact statistics.

MSF and the Courts

We did not find any cases dealing specifically with use of MSF. Almost all industrial-organizational psychologists will agree that MSF systems are less susceptible to bias than are single-rater systems. Thus, all other things being equal, if a personnel decision is based on MSF data, it is relatively more defensible than one based on a single rater. Williamson and others (1997) found that using multiple interviewers (as opposed to one) was significantly correlated with a verdict in favor of the defendant in discrimination cases. Malos (1998) reviewed recent cases and past legal reviews on appraisal and then included "multiple, diverse and unbiased raters" as a "procedural recommendation."

An interesting and related issue for future litigation is whether the strong arguments supporting incremental validity for MSF are offered in criticisms of a single-rater appraisal system, with the implied assumption that had the organization only used an MSF system, the deleterious decisions or the adverse impact would not have occurred (see Chapter Nine for more on the issue of validity). This argument may now have weight, at least in the Third Circuit Court of Appeals in light of the 1999 decision in *Lanning* v. *SEPTA* in which the Third Circuit concluded that the organization "failed to search for an alternative test that would have less adverse impact" (Sharf, 1999). Such an argument is likely to be introduced in the recent class-action Title VII lawsuit against Coca-Cola (*Abdallah* v. *Coca-Cola Co.*, 1999).

We could not locate any published studies that indicate less adverse impact would be obtained with a multirater system compared to a single-rater system. However, Edwards and colleagues (Edwards, 1992; Edwards, Ewen, and Verdini, 1995) report data indicating favorable results for women, older workers, and minorities. Edwards and Ewen (1996) note that "single-source biases tend to result in lower performance scores for protected classes, such as gender and racial minorities, when the preponderance of super-' visors are, probably, white males" (p. 195).

Courts have ordered multiple-rating systems as redress for discrimination. A judge ordered the Mobile, Alabama, police department to use MSF for each officer being rated. Two of the five raters were to be selected by the person being rated (Cascio and Bernardin, 1981). Numerous other cases involving all types of employment decisions indirectly support the superiority of a multiple-rater assessment system (for example, Veglahn, 1993; Williamson and others, 1997). The courts also consider the independence of ratings by more than one rater. In a case involving the use of appraisals for promotion, three evaluations of a plaintiff were done on the same rating form. It was obvious that the ratings made by the second and third raters were done with knowledge of those of the first rater; the three ratings of the plaintiff were identical. The court, in the context of other evidence indicating that the first rater might have been biased, concluded that the rating process was not an objective measure of the plaintiff's ability and that the lack of independent ratings nullified the incremental objectivity in the multiple-rating process (*Loiseau* v. *Department of Human Resources,* 1983). Obviously, the key here is independent MSF.

Other cases have made reference to the great power exercised by evaluators as they weigh the fate of their subordinates (Barrett and Kernan, 1987; Martin and Bartol, 1991). This is particularly disturbing to the courts when virtually all supervisor raters are white males and adverse impact has resulted from decisions based on their ratings (Kleiman and Durham, 1981).

The courts have been particularly critical of ratings made by first-line supervisors (for example, *Baxter* v. *Savannah Refining Corp.,* 1974). The "unfettered discretion" allowed for store managers in making promotion decisions at Circuit City appeared to play a major role in the 1997 Title VII jury verdict in favor of the plaintiffs in *McKnight et al.* v. *Circuit City Stores.* Most appraisal systems require a supervisor of the rater to review an appraisal and sign off. The only way this can be construed as a multiple-rater system is if the second evaluator has independent sources of information about a ratee and it can be documented that, on occasion, the reviewer in fact changed or contested an appraisal made by the first rater.

Both the case law and the research literature on appraisal and assessment seem clear on the issue of the relative validity of MSF versus single-rater systems (see Chapter Nine for more on this argument). Using more than one rater and different rating sources can diminish the influence, idiosyncrasy, and effects of bias of any single rater and probably increases the validity of the decision making. The courts are likely to see expert witness testimony reflecting this view in future EEO cases. But there is no question that other elements of an appraisal system are also related to legal outcomes and that these variables probably apply to MSF as well as single-rater systems.

Our review of more than four hundred court cases brought under Title VII, the ADEA, the Equal Pay Act, the Family and Medical Leave Act (FMLA), and numerous state statutes, plus a number of published papers on performance appraisal and litigation, has revealed what we regard as "prescriptions" for a sound, defensible MSF system (for example, Austin, Villanova, and Hindman, 1996; Bernardin and Cascio, 1988; Cascio and Bernardin, 1981; Eyres, 1989; Feild and Holley, 1982; Malos, 1998; Martin and Bartol, 1991; Miller, Kaspin, and Schuster, 1990; Rosen, 1992; Werner and Bolino, 1997).

Although these prescriptions were derived from our study of the characteristics of appraisal systems that distinguished the outcomes of the litigation, we propose that the greater the number of prescriptions incorporated in an organization's MSF system, the greater the probability that the organization can win a lawsuit.

Legally Defensible Appraisal Procedures

Attention to several procedural aspects of performance appraisal will increase the legality of an MSF system and may increase vulnerability to negative legal outcomes. Several prescriptions relating to procedural issues follow.

Basis for Personnel Decisions

Personnel decisions should be based on a formal, standardized performance appraisal system. The organization should establish formal MSF procedures whenever the MSF is to be used for personnel decisions. In one of the most frequently cited cases (*Rowe* v. *General Motors Corp.*, 1972), ratings made solely by white supervisors were based on "vague" and "subjectively defined ability, merit and capacity." The court ordered General Motors to develop formal procedures for promotional decisions.

Most ADEA and Title VII cases are based on allegation of disparate treatment regarding personnel decisions or policies (for example, *Cosgrove* v. *Sears, Roebuck & Co., 1993; Lilly* v. *Harris Teeter Supermarket*, 1983). If the *application* of the policy differs as a function of the race, sex, age, or religion of the employee, the organization could have a problem. This was precisely the issue in a recent case involving Wal-Mart where an African American plaintiff was able to show that a written policy was applied in his case but not applied to whites (*Stalter* v. *Wal-Mart Stores*, 1999).

Most of the cases we reviewed have involved alleged violation of Title VII or the ADEA. However, there are many other avenues for litigation related to appraisal (Malos, 1998). In their monograph on wrongful discharge cases, Lorber, Kirk, Kirschner, and Handorf (1984) state that "employee evaluations are among the first company documents demanded by employees bringing wrongful discharge actions . . . evaluations may have a serious negative impact on employers involved in wrongful discharge suits as well as other types of employment discrimination litigation" (pp. 23–24). We support a formal system of performance appraisal with most of the prescriptions we have discussed above. One review concluded that the more the "procedural and fairness safeguards, the safer the system will be in court" (Ashe and McRae, 1985, p. 902).

Uniformity in process and procedure is more problematic for MSF systems where the number of raters and rating sources may differ for ratees. However, such procedures for data collection and participation should be as uniform as possible with any differences not correlated with protected class characteristics.

Formal Communications

Specific performance standards should be formally communicated to employees. There are cases in which a company developed performance standards, documented them in a written position description or performance appraisal, and then neglected to convey the standards to its employees (for example, *Donaldson* v. *Pillsbury Co.*, 1977). Recipients of MSF should be aware of the criteria on which they are being assessed when the data take on administrative significance. There should be no secrets regarding criteria. Most MSF systems do communicate the criteria for evaluation prior to the appraisal period.

Review and Appeal of Results

Employees should have an opportunity to review and appeal their appraisals.

Werner and Bolino (1997) found a statistical relationship between case outcomes and a provision allowing employees to review appraisal results. When MSF is used for decisions, the ratee should be allowed an opportunity to review and respond to the appraisals. It may be advisable to have a formal employee sign-off line on the report, where it can be acknowledged that the appraisal was reviewed on a certain date. Numerous cases also underscore the importance of an internal appeal process regarding appraisals (Bernardin and Cascio, 1988).

The applicability of the appeal prescription to MSF is problematic, particularly given the anonymity requirement for raters. At one Fortune 500 company that uses MSF as one source of data for performance bonuses, the employee can appeal the recommendation to the administrating HR department on the basis of special circumstances, including the characteristics of a work setting that can affect ratings from one or more sources and are beyond the control of the ratee, or considerations of source participation or representation.

Appeal mechanisms can (and should) be put in place regarding the process and procedure of data collection for MSF. There are occasions when there is a breakdown in the processes of administration of an MSF system; this can affect ratings. One Fortune 500 retailer used professional customers as a source for the MSF systems. Accusations of fraud in this data by several store managers led to an investigation of this rating source and an adjustment in some manager ratings. An appeal process should be available for this sort of problem.

Legally Defensible Appraisal Content

In addition to procedural issues, attention must be given to content issues in MSF. Several prescriptions regarding content issues follow.

Basis in Job Analysis

Performance appraisal content should be based on a job analysis. Some courts have found use of ratings to be discriminatory if the content of the rating instrument is not based "on a careful job analysis" (Schneier, 1978, p. 25), but there is no clear legal mandate to have a well-documented job analysis as the basis of an appraisal instrument or process. There are many cases in which a purely subjective performance appraisal was used as the basis of a personnel decision that the organization successfully defended. The courts appear to be more tolerant of subjective appraisals at higher levels of employment. As Rosen (1992) states, "If an objective appraisal system has been established closely related to the job requirements, however, and if a consistent, good faith effort has been made to judge workers by it, those efforts usually will be rewarded with a finding in the company's favor" (p. 115).

Avoiding Character Traits

Appraisals based on ratee traits should be avoided. Some MSF systems call for ratings on traits or competencies labeled as drive, motivation, initiative, cooperation, personal maturity, dependability, and attitude. Given evidence of adverse impact in ratings resulting from such a format, the courts have generally not rendered favorable decisions (Bernardin and Cascio, 1988; Feild and Holley, 1982; Malos, 1998; Williamson and others, 1997). However, although we could locate numerous cases involving trait ratings made by supervisors, we found no cases contesting MSF that involved such terms. We feel safe in recommending that, regardless of the purpose of the MSF system, one avoid trait-based formats with no behavioral definition.

Legally Defensible Documentation of Appraisal Results

A thorough written record of evidence leading to major decisions should be maintained (for example, performance appraisals and counseling to advise employees of performance deficits and to assist employees in making needed improvements).

Malos (1998) and Austin, Villanova, and Hindman (1995) present several cases that emphasize the importance of providing performance counseling to assist poor performers prior to termination. For example, in *Stone* v. *Xerox* (1982), it was established that Xerox offered a one-month program of performance improvement. The key to this prescription is to document the counseling effort. Again, though the many cases supporting this prescription involved termination based on single-rater judgment, using counseling to augment MSF feedback makes good sense.

Several cases have cited the need to justify a number on a rating form with details of what a person did or did not do. Thus, if an adverse personnel decision is made on the basis of an appraisal, documentation is helpful to "explain" a rating. Without compromising confidentiality, such documentation could be made in the form of a record of critical incidents, with the date, time, witnesses, and details noted. Of course, such documentation must be compatible with numerical ratings if the ratings are used for personnel action. Also, the open-ended comments made by partners in *Price Waterhouse* v. *Hopkins* (1989) formed the crux of the sex discrimination lawsuit against the company.

Documentation can be useful with MSF, but it should be restricted to job-related behavior and performance. Obviously, the detail of the documentation could compromise the key anonymity condition for raters. Assuming there is no regulatory requirement for identifying raters, it is preferable to eliminate copious detail so as to not compromise anonymity.

Legally Defensible Raters

Another important issue in MSF is selection of appropriate raters to conduct the appraisals. Several prescriptions regarding rater selection follow.

Training and Instruction for Raters

Raters should be given written instructions and training on how to conduct appraisals properly to facilitate systematic, unbiased appraisal.

In *McKnight et al.* v. *Circuit City Stores* (1997), the lack of procedures or guidelines for supervisors to follow in making promotional decisions played a key role in the finding for the plaintiffs when combined with the adverse impact. Several reviews support this finding (Feild and Holley, 1982; Werner and Bolino, 1997; Williamson and others, 1997).

MSF raters should be informed of antidiscrimination laws and made aware of legal and illegal activity regarding decisions based on appraisals. Training programs that explain relevant laws and litigation help establish a posture of fairness. More important, such training could keep the organization out of the courtroom by preventing violations. Many companies using MSF include brief legal tutorials and proscriptions against biased ratings. Nothing in the case law precludes more efficient written training content that could accompany other MSF materials.

Observation by Raters

Raters must have the opportunity to observe the ratee first-hand or to review important ratee performance products.

There have been several cases in which it was shown that the evaluator had little first-hand information about the ratee (see *Schechtman* v. *Jefferson Ward,* 1985). In *Brito* v. *Zia Co.* (1973), the court was disturbed that raters had spent little time making first-hand observations of subordinates, despite the fact that such observations were the sole source of information on which to base ratings. The court recommended an MSF system for future decisions. In addition, the problem of observability underscores the need to consider other sources for appraisal besides the usual immediate supervisor, assuming these other sources are indeed either in an observable position or qualified to assess a ratee's products or services without observation.

Ethical Issues and MSF

Longenecker and Ludwig (1990) point out that a procedurally sound system alone does not necessarily produce effective, accurate, ethical performance ratings. Deliberate inaccuracy is a critical issue in performance appraisal, be it single-source or multisource. In Chapter Nine, Murphy, Cleveland, and Mohler describe some of the motives behind deliberate inaccuracy in performance appraisal and propose that accuracy should be a general principle guiding the process at both managerial and organizational levels. One ethical principle that derives from their discussion is that assessments provided in any appraisal context should simply reflect a rater's best judgment about the ratee and the dimension, factor, behavior, or outcome on which the ratee is to be assessed. In the end, overrating or underrating for some other motive creates more difficulties than it solves and should be explicitly proscribed in an ethical statement.

This principle certainly applies to MSF systems. In fact, ethical breaches in the form of deliberate rating distortion may be common with some MSF systems, particularly where the data have administrative significance. One company uses this statement regarding the issue of deliberate rating distortion: "It is unethical to evaluate someone's performance lower or higher than that person deserves based on actual performance. There are no circumstances in which deliberate distortion in evaluation is ethical or acceptable." We would recommend adding "judgment of potential" to this statement since an MSF system might ask for judgment of a person's potential for other another job.

Anonymity and Confidentiality

Many authors note the importance of anonymity and confidentiality in an MSF system (for example, Dalessio, 1998; Edwards and Ewen, 1996). Edwards and Ewen (1996) make the strong assertion that "360-degree feedback systems must guarantee absolute anonymity to respondents and confidentiality to employees regarding their feedback, or the process will fail" (p. 157). Typically, such information has been confidential, with only the ratee, the supervisor, and some higher-level managers having access to the information. Safeguards to ensure confidentiality must be part of a multisource feedback process (Edwards and Ewen, 1996).

Of course, this recommendation must be reconciled with any procedural rules stipulated in civil service guidelines or collective bargaining agreements requiring that some (or all) data be published and that both raters and ratees be identified if ratings lead to personnel decisions. Under such conditions, it may be advisable not to use MSF for any administrative purpose. One company uses this statement regarding ethics and confidentiality: "It is unethical to identify or attempt to identify those participants in the upward appraisal program. All such ethical breaches should be reported to the HR department immediately."

In general, information should be gathered on the potential or actual procedural justice related to an MSF system. Questions as to whether participants believe information remain confidential and whether raters remain anonymous are particularly important (Bracken and Timmreck, 1999; see also the Appendix to this volume).

Cultural Issues

Brutus, Leslie, and McDonald-Mann (Chapter Twenty-Seven) offer suggestions for MSF implementation that can help with issues of cultural sensitivity and minority resistance. Prior to implementing an MSF process, make a determination of procedural fairness issues and item and instrument acceptability as a function of participant ethnicity and gender. Where differences are found, take steps to understand and eliminate such potential sources of difficulty before the MSF is implemented, particularly if MSF takes on administrative significance.

Determining if assessment instruments are understood and accepted is another important step. It should also be determined if the employees accept the idea that soliciting information from supervisors, peers, clients, and others is appropriate and useful. Testing these responses as a function of the ethnicity and gender of the respondents gives administrators a sense of how well the MSF system will be received.

We believe it is professionally unethical and irresponsible to recommend or implement an MSF system for administrative purposes if there is no sense of potential problems and perceptions of potential procedural justice from the perspective of a multicultural workforce. If you are purchasing an MSF instrument, the authors of Chapter Twenty-Seven suggest that test manuals be reviewed to determine if appropriate, culturally sensitive normative comparisons are available, and if adaptation procedures are appropriate and sufficient for the intended use.

Another important point to investigate is whether there is evidence of ongoing international research to address cultural issues. When selecting an MSF instrument for use with a multicultural organization, Brutus, Leslie, and McDonald-Mann (Chapter Twenty-Seven) suggest looking for evidence to support a claim of comparability (for example, the translation process), administration instruction in the target language, and evidence that the testing techniques (such as answer formats, conventions, and procedures for instructions) and presentation are familiar to all participants.

Training

Many authors identify training as a crucial element of a successful MSF process (for example, Dalessio, 1998; Waldman and Atwater, 1998; see also Chapter Eight). Training is important not only for proper implementation of the system but also for helping avoid legal and ethical problems. Training is important for raters and ratees alike, so that mutual understanding of the process, forms, and expectations is clear. Training can also increase the validity of the ratings.

Those giving feedback also need specialized training to ensure that it is ethical, legal, and effective. Axline (1996) argues that a major ethical concern is with the ratee's self-esteem. The person giving the feedback needs to be able to give competent, constructive feedback and assist participants through the often unsettling period resulting from the MSF process and receiving feedback (Kaplan and Paulus, 1994). Outside consultants are often recommended (Waldman and Atwater, 1998), but they too must be aware of and concerned with legal and ethical issues of MSF.

Training ratees on how to use the results is another important element of a successful and ethical MSF program. Research has found that managers who met with direct reports to discuss their feedback results improved more than managers who did not (Walker and Smither, 1999). This research also found that managers improved more in years when they reviewed the feedback of prior years with direct reports than in years in which they did not.

In the next chapter of this volume, Waldman and Atwater note the critical role of offering training to raters and feedback givers on how the instruments are used and how feedback is to be presented. Raters need training in possible cultural influence on using response scales, possible cognitive bias (attribution error, anchoring), and rating errors (for example, leniency).

Training on pertinent ethical codes is also important. The American Psychological Association has published ethical guidelines, many of which are directly applicable to the MSF process (Lowman, 1998). Sections pertaining to MSF are the relationship between ethics and the law, record maintenance, confidentiality and privacy issues, and conflict between ethics and organizational demands.

Summary

The legal prescriptions we have presented are not meant to constitute exclusive ingredients for a defense-proof system of MSF. Rather, they are the most obvious implications that can be drawn from case law and applied to MSF systems. We believe each prescription is compatible with sound personnel practice and case law, and that the set of prescriptions can serve as a checklist for MSF systems whenever data are used for personnel decisions (Malos, 1998). We also believe the ethical issues we have covered constitute a set of guidelines for developing and implementing MSF for personnel decisions.

Given the abundance of positive writing about MSF, it is not inconceivable that MSF results designed for employee development and given only to the ratee could be offered as evidence by a ratee-plaintiff to support a claim of bias on the part of a single rater whose judgment led to a deleterious outcome. An organization may have some difficulty explaining great discrepancies between a single supervisor's assessment that led to a termination and the results of a well-crafted, confidential, state-of-the-art MSF system.

Expert testimony reflecting the view that MSF is more valid than single-rater systems should also become more common, particularly on behalf of plaintiffs in class-based, disparate-impact cases where adverse impact statistics are presented. Future expert testimony regarding the susceptibility to bias of the challenged, single-rater appraisal system is likely to include arguments for the incremental validity of MSF systems (Bernardin, Hennessey, and Peyrefitte, 1995; Edwards and Ewen, 1996).

However, we do not argue here that the prescriptions we have presented are necessary requirements for fair and valid MSF data; nor do we argue that an MSF system necessarily results in less adverse impact against a protected class and is thus the alternative measure that organizations should seek out in lieu of single-rater systems. The ethnicity, gender, and representativeness of the participating raters will probably be raised in future litigation in the context of procedural differences (see Chapter Seven for more on rater selection). There is some indication that there may be smaller differences in mean ratings as a function of a protected class characteristic if an MSF system is used versus a single-rater system (Edwards and Ewen, 1996). More studies, including adverse impact analyses, are on the horizon, along with the inevitable case law related specifically to MSF systems as more companies rely on them for personnel decisions.

References

Abdallah v. Coca-Cola Co., WL 527835 (N.D. Ga.), 1999.

Ashe, R. L., and McRae, G. S. "Performance Evaluations Go to Court in the 1980s." *Mercer Law Review*, 1985, *36*, 887-905.

Austin, J. T., Villanova, P., and Hindman, H. D. "Legal Requirements and Technical Guidelines Involved in Implementing Performance Appraisal Systems." In G. R. Ferris and M. R. Buckley (eds.), *Human Resources Management: Perspectives, Context, Functions, and Outcomes*. St. Paul, Minn.: West, 1996.

Axline, L. L. "Viewpoints: The Ethics of Performance Appraisal." *S.A.M. Advanced Management Journal*, 1996, *61*(1), 44–45.

Barrett, G. V., and Kernan, M. C. "Performance Appraisal and Terminations: A Review of Court Decisions Since *Brito* v. *Zia* with Implications for Personnel Practices." *Personnel Psychology*, 1987, *40*, 489–503.

Baxter v. Savannah Refining Corp., 350 F. Supp. 139, 1974.

Bernardin, H. J., and Cascio, W. F. "Performance Appraisal and the Law." In R. Shuler, S. Youngblood, and V. L. Huber (eds.), *Readings in Personnel and Human Resource Management*. St. Paul, Minn.: West, 1988.

Bernardin, H. J., Hennessey, H. W., and Peyrefitte, J. "Age, Racial, and Gender Bias as a Function of Criterion Specificity: A Test of Expert Testimony." *Human Resource Management Review*, 1995, *5*, 63–77.

Bracken, D. W. "Straight Talk About Multirater Feedback." *Training and Development*, 1994, *48*(9), 44–51.

Bracken, D. W., and Timmreck, C. W. "Guidelines for Multisource Feedback When Used for Decision Making." *Industrial-Organizational Psychologist*, 1999, *36*(4), 64–74.

Brito v. *Zia Co.*, 478 F.2d 1200 (10th Cir.), 1973.

Cascio, W. F., and Bernardin, H. J. "Implications of Performance Appraisal Litigation for Personnel Decisions." *Personnel Psychology*, 1981, *34*, 211–226.

Cosgrove v. *Sears, Roebuck & Co.*, CA 2, No. 92-7197, 1993.

Dalessio, A. T. "Using Multisource Feedback for Employee Development and Personnel Decisions." In J. W. Smither (ed.), *Performance Management: The State of the Art in Practice*. San Francisco: Jossey-Bass, 1998.

Donaldson v. *Pillsbury Co.*, 554 F.2d 885 (8th Cir.), 1977.

Edwards, M. R. "In Situ Team Evaluation: A New Paradigm for Measuring and Developing Leadership at Work." In K. E. Clark, M. B. Clark, and D. P. Campbell (eds.), *Impact of Leadership*. Greensboro, N.C.: Center for Creative Leadership, 1992.

Edwards, M. R., and Ewen, A. J. *360-Degree Feedback: The Powerful New Model for Employee Assessment and Performance Management*. New York: AMACOM, 1996.

Edwards, M. R., Ewen, A. J., and Verdini, W. A. "Fair Performance Management and Pay Practices for Diverse Workforces: The Promise of Multisource Assessment." *ACA Journal*, Spring 1995, pp. 50–63.

Eyres, P. S. "Legally Defensible Performance Appraisal Systems." *Personnel Journal*, 1989, *68*(7), 58–62.

Feild, H. S., and Holley, W. H. "The Relationship of Performance Appraisal Characteristics to Verdicts in Selected Employment Discrimination Cases." *Academy of Management Journal*, 1982, *2*, 392–406.

Kaplan, R. E., and Paulus, C. J. *Enhancing 360-Degree Feedback for Senior Executives: How to Maximize the Benefits and Minimize the Risks*. Greensboro, N.C.: Center for Creative Leadership, 1994.

Kleiman, L. S., and Durham, R. L. "Performance Appraisal, Promotion, and the Courts: A Critical Review." *Personnel Psychology*, 1981, *34*, 103–121.

Lanning v. *SEPTA*, 3d Cir., June 29, 1999.

Lilly v. *Harris Teeter Supermarket*, 720 F.2d 326 (4th Cir.), 1983.

Loiseau v. *Department of Human Resources*, 567 F.Sup. 1211 (D. Ore.), 1983.

Longenecker, C., and Ludwig, D. "Ethical Dilemmas in Performance Appraisal Revisited." *Journal of Business Ethics*, 1990, *9*, 961–969.

Lorber, L. S., Kirk, J. R., Kirschner, K. H., and Handorf, C. R. *Fear of Firing*. Alexandria, Va.: ASPA Foundation, 1984.

Lowman, R. L. (ed.). *The Ethical Practice of Psychology in Organizations.* Washington, D.C.: American Psychological Association, 1998.

Malos, S. B. "Current Legal Issues in Performance Appraisal." In J. W. Smither (ed.), *Performance Management: The State of the Art in Practice.* San Francisco: Jossey-Bass, 1998.

Martin, J., and Bartol, K. M. "The Legal Ramifications of Performance Appraisal: An Update." *Employee Relations Law Journal,* 1991, *17,* 257–286.

McKnight et al. v. Circuit City Stores, 73 FEP cases (BNA) 847, 1997.

Miller, C. S., Kaspin, J. A., and Schuster, M. H. "The Impact of Performance Appraisal Methods on Age Discrimination in Employment Act Cases." *Personnel Psychology,* 1990, *43*(3), 555–578.

Price Waterhouse v. Hopkins, U.S. 8-1167, 1989.

Rosen, D. I. "Appraisals Can Make—or Break—Your Court Case." *Personnel Journal,* 1992, *71*(11), 113–116.

Rowe v. General Motors Corp., 457 F.2d 348 (5th Cir.), 1972.

Schechtman v. Jefferson Ward, 16 FEP Cases 902, 1985.

Schneier, D. B. "The Impact of EEO Legislation on Performance Appraisals." *Personnel,* July 1978, pp. 24–35.

Sharf, J. C. "Third Circuit's *Lanning v. SEPTA* Decision: 'Business Necessity' Requires Setting Minimum Standards." *Industrial-Organizational Psychologist,* 1999, *3,* 138–149.

Stalter v. Wal-Mart Stores, 195 F. 3d 285 (7th Cir.), 1999.

Stone v. Xerox Corp., 685 F.2d 1387 (11th Cir.), 1982.

Veglahn, P. A. "Key Issues in Performance Appraisal Challenges: Evidence from Court and Arbitration Decisions." *Labor Law Journal,* 1993, *44,* 595–606.

Waldman, D. A., and Atwater, L. E. *The Power of 360-Degree Feedback: How to Leverage Performance Evaluations for Top Productivity.* Houston: Gulf, 1998.

Walker, A. G., and Smither, J. W. "A Five-Year Study of Upward Feedback: What Managers Do with Their Results Matters." *Personnel Psychology,* 1999, *52,* 393–423.

Werner, J. M., and Bolino, M. C. "Explaining U.S. Court of Appeals Decisions Involving Performance Appraisal: Accuracy, Fairness, and Validation." *Personnel Psychology,* 1997, *50,* 1–24.

Williamson, L. G., and others. "Employment Interviews on Trial: Linking Interview Structure with Litigation Outcomes." *Journal of Applied Psychology,* 1997, *82,* 900–912.

CHAPTER 29

Confronting Barriers to Successful Implementation of Multisource Feedback

David A. Waldman
Leanne E. Atwater

The purpose of this chapter is to identify barriers to effective implementation of multisource feedback (MSF) and to suggest strategies that can be used to overcome them. Our goal is to raise awareness on the basis of our experience and systematic research. We begin by specifying a taxonomy of barriers.

Taxonomy of Barriers

We begin with the assumption that MSF is a dynamic process involving more than just surveying and feedback. Specifically, strategic and planning dimensions come into play prior to survey and feedback activities. Furthermore, follow-up occurs after the delivery of feedback. Thus, barriers to effective implementation of an MSF process can be categorized in terms of the following:

- Inadequate strategy or planning
- Poor implementation
- Lack of appropriate follow-up

Inadequate Strategy or Planning

Early on, an organization should consider its own reasons for pursuing MSF and then carefully plan an implementation strategy accordingly. Without such careful reflection and planning, implementation and the potential for positive effects are compromised.

Reflection should begin with explicit articulation of the motivation on the part of decision makers for introducing MSF. It may seem obvious, but the motives can actually be somewhat complex. The most obvious and logical motive is that decision makers believe MSF helps improve the performance of organizational members. They may also hope that it will further the overall development of the organization, for example, change the organization's culture to one that values employee input and feedback.

However, other motives exist. For example, in an initial interview with a recent client pursuing the possibility of MSF implementation in his organization, we probed as to the reasons for his interest. Much of the conversation seemed to revolve around his desire to know whether competitors had also implemented MSF. We understand such an interest, but we argue that if the desire to keep up with the Joneses is one's primary motive, an initial barrier has already been placed on the road to successful implementation. That is, decision makers, who are inevitably needed as champions, must be able to clearly articulate how implementing MSF reflects their own values or principles as leaders, not just reaction to competitors' practices.

We also argue that MSF is more than a device for individual development; rather, it represents an organizational change intervention (see also Chapter Nineteen). Failure to recognize relevant organizational factors can prove to be quite detrimental to the success of MSF. MSF can affect (or be affected by) the basic underlying norms, beliefs, and values of an organization—stated another way, its culture. Waldman and Atwater (1998) described how many decision makers seek to implement MSF based, at least in part, on the desire to *push* their organizations in the direction of a more adaptive or participative organizational culture. For example, there may be a desire to foster better communication and supplier and customer (internal and external) relations.

MSF may indeed be seen as a mechanism to push the organization in such a direction. Unfortunately, the sheer fact that an organization needs to be pushed in this manner suggests that prospects are high for implementation failure. For example, a prevailing cultural norm or value of being slow to accept change could cause managers to fail to complete surveys or use MSF to pursue developmental goals.

Along similar lines, MSF may not be in line with the organizational reward systems, thereby resulting in another barrier to effective implementation. At its core, MSF attempts to give individuals information about relationships and behaviors involving others in their work settings. Examples include leadership and customer-supplier relationships. If the reward system (performance appraisal, promotion procedures) does not reinforce the relationships and behaviors, we should not expect most feedback providers and recipients to take MSF very seriously. That is, we should not expect them to complete the survey, carefully evaluate their feedback report, take steps to make improvements, and so forth. In an organization in which raises are based on seniority, for many employees there is little incentive to use feedback for performance improvement because "it doesn't matter."

At the same time, we are not strong proponents of using the data generated through an MSF process for evaluative purposes (see Chapters Twenty and Twenty-Three for more on this issue). Waldman, Atwater, and Antonioni (1998) discuss the game playing and implicit and explicit quid pro quo behavior that can occur if MSF is used directly for an evaluative purpose, as when the scores obtained through the survey are used to determine who should be promoted to a higher managerial level. In a later section of this chapter, we describe strategies that can be used to ensure that MSF is in line with the organizational reward systems, while simultaneously not using MSF data directly for an evaluative purpose, at least in the early stages of implementation.

Finally, imagine that you work in an organization with the push type of culture we've already characterized (perhaps it's not too hard to imagine). You arrive at work one morning and find a number of surveys in your mailbox, requesting that you rate the behaviors of several of your coworkers and your supervisor. You are not given much information about the purpose of the ratings or how confidentiality is to be assured. You perceive that if you rate people honestly, it will only come back to haunt you. To make matters worse, you are only vaguely familiar with some of the people you are being asked to rate as coworkers and do not feel comfortable rating the behaviors depicted in the survey. Your likely reaction is to offer less than honest ratings, or simply throw the surveys in the circular file.

This scenario is not unrealistic, and it shows how inadequate information and preparation from the point of view of the participant can be a significant implementation barrier. Participants, including both feedback providers and recipients, who are not cognitively and motivationally prepared are not likely to foster an effective MSF process. In sum, a number of factors come into play prior to implementing MSF that can ultimately affect its success. We now turn our attention to the actual implementation.

Poor Implementation

There are several implementation barriers that we wish to highlight. First, we are concerned about the lack of customization that often accompanies an MSF process, an issue addressed in more detail elsewhere (see Chapters Five and Six for more). In short, standardized surveys are often pulled off the shelf with little attempt to tailor them to the needs or "language" of the client organization. If you believe the old adage that you get what you measure, then careful attention to what is measured is important since it drives behavior.

Second, we view some commonly used procedures as potential barriers. One is to have the targeted feedback recipient select raters. The obvious problem with such a strategy is that the recipient either intentionally or unintentionally selects raters who are most likely to provide positive ratings, while others are avoided. We feel that, at least in the case of upward feedback (as from subordinates), a more desirable strategy is to have all potential raters provide feedback. Unfortunately, in following our own advice, we have found that client organizations may not have the most up-to-date information regarding who reports to whom. The end result is that a number of individuals may be sent surveys to be filled out on supervisors to whom they do not report, or perhaps have not reported to in quite some time.

Third, the state of mind of the participant (provider and recipient alike) represents a potential implementation barrier. Related to the organizational culture concerns already mentioned, we find cause to worry about such issues as cynicism and lack of trust, which can lead to lower response rates or manipulation of ratings. Cynicism is common today in society in general, and organizations in particular. Indeed, a phenomenon may be developing in many organizations whereby individuals have grown both weary of and cynical about change initiatives such as MSF.

Organizational cynicism (see, for example, the work of Vance, Brooks, and Tesluk, 1995), develops from at least two key factors. First, members observe some new change initiative in the organization (say, total quality management). The initiative may appear to be a knee-jerk reaction to problems such as customer dissatisfaction, inefficiency, and so forth. Subsequently, after the initial excitement and hoopla wear off, it becomes apparent to people that other priorities or day-to-day pressures have come to the forefront, and management commitment to the change strategy has begun to waver. Second, because of the wavering commitment, little return on investment is realized, and management undertakes another knee-jerk reaction whereby the initiative is watered down, cancelled, put on hold, or replaced by yet another new initiative. This scenario could be accentuated by replacement of the original decision makers who approved the MSF process, and the new decision makers either do not approve of the original change strategy or simply desire to initiate their own pet program.

So what does all of this have to do with subsequent implementation of MSF? Unfortunately, individuals' memories are not short, and they often remain with the organization much longer than top managers do. Failure to appropriately or fully implement prior initiatives can create a pessimistic or cynical viewpoint with regard to new initiatives. Managers who advocated the prior initiatives appear incompetent, lacking in personal commitment, or both. Past implementation failures then embody a self-fulfilling prophecy. A feeling is likely to exist in the organization that any new initiatives (such as MSF) will probably not realize promised improvements or will not be followed through, so "Why should I even bother to participate?" Recent research has shown how organizational cynicism diminishes the effectiveness of upward feedback processes (Atwater and Waldman, 1999).

Accentuating this problem is the whole issue of lack of trust. A problematic organizational culture, such as what we described earlier, engenders lack of trust and fear of retribution. In such an instance, even if people participate in the MSF process, they may be less than honest in giving poor ratings. To make matters worse, people may see (or just hear rumors about) breaches of confidentiality. In one organization in which we recently implemented upward feedback, a supervisor went back to his subordinates and had individual discussions with them, hoping to get additional feedback. The supervisor did not know how any individual subordinate rated him, and one of his subordinates misunderstood the general nature of discussion and thought he had seen the survey she completed. This rumor about a breach of anonymity then spread like wildfire until we got word of it and personally intervened to explain the situation to the subordinate. This was the only such instance, but it is easy to see how just one or two situations, if not managed properly, can create a barrier to effective feedback.

Finally, cross-cultural situations also present a special implementation challenge. The concept of rating others at work may seem common, straightforward, and acceptable to Americans. However, this is more likely in Western cultures, as compared to other cultures in the world. To cite one example that we experienced recently in an M.B.A. class, a manager from India (a high power-distance culture wherein a large difference in status exists between supervisor and subordinate) was not comfortable asking his subordinates to complete surveys about him, even though this was a developmental process and there was absolutely no evaluative purpose in the use of these data. To participate in the class exercise along with the other students, the manager completed all of the surveys about himself (identically) and returned them as if his subordinates back at work had completed them. Clearly, there was no learning to be gained from his feedback report, but he did save face by not asking his subordinates to evaluate him. (For more information on cross-cultural issues in MSF, see Chapter Twenty-Seven.)

Lack of Appropriate Follow-Up

Barriers to effective MSF exist even after the actual implementation. Some of them affect the feedback recipient, while others are more organizational. First, regarding recipients, the most common problem that we have observed is lack of follow-up on the part of recipients once the MSF is formally delivered. In other words, merely receiving a report does not magically result in behavior change.

Lack of follow-up is also a problem on the part of management decision makers who control whether or not resources are devoted to MSF. Too often, commitment is inadequate, and there is too much of a short-term, flavor-of-the-month taste left in the mouths of initial participants. In other words, they complete one cycle of surveying and feedback and then drop it. As a result, those individuals who receive feedback suggesting areas where improvement is needed and who try to make changes never get to see whether their efforts are noticed by others. As mentioned earlier, such action (or inaction) only serves to foster the buildup of organizational cynicism.

Another potential barrier to MSF is the purpose for which ratings are used. The issue of how, or even whether, to make MSF evaluative in nature (say, input for reward decisions) continues to be controversial in the literature (see Waldman, Atwater, and Antonioni, 1998). We contend that, somewhat paradoxically, both too much and too little evaluative usage can be barriers. As already mentioned, if MSF is used initially in an evaluative mode, the likelihood of suspicion and game playing with regard to ratings is high. On the other hand, if MSF is repeatedly implemented over time and there are no evaluative implications, many people are likely to get frustrated. Raters of individuals who repeatedly receive poor scores are liable to become frustrated with the process, and perhaps discontinue their input, if it appears that no changes are being made and their ratings are put to no evaluative use (see also Chapter Sixteen).

Finally, at the organizational level, a continuing barrier to effective MSF is the paucity of research done in an attempt to understand its impact. That is, we continue to see very little, in terms of both theory and research, with regard to how MSF may affect such organizational-level phenomena as attitudes, culture, customer satisfaction, turnover, and performance. Moreover, we fear that the eventual outcome of this lack of research could be the demise of MSF as a development tool.

Strategies to Overcome Barriers

The barriers to effective MSF that we have described are formidable, but they can be prevented or controlled. We now turn our attention to strategies that help ensure these barriers are minimized.

Organizational Strategies

We recommend that decision makers have a clear purpose in mind before implementing MSF, and that the purpose be in line with other organizational initiatives or values. In other words, motives such as keeping up with the Joneses are insufficient and likely lead to difficult implementation. Instead, it is best if the MSF is seen as complementing broader initiatives such as total quality management or other customer-based strategies. It is also best if management has clearly articulated values in line with MSF, such as those emphasizing employee development, leadership, customer-supplier relationships (which we describe next), and continuous improvement. If such values are clearly articulated, MSF can be used as a mechanism to push the organizational culture in the direction of the values.

Second, it follows that decision makers must be committed to more than one iteration of MSF. Unfortunately, we have seen too many instances of only one iteration, with feedback recipients going through a single round of surveying, receiving feedback, and seeing data depicting needed improvement—but then, because of wavering managerial commitment, the MSF program is dropped. Recipients have no opportunity to see whether effort to make changes and improve has actually been successful. The upshot is additional fuel for the fire of organizational cynicism and skepticism regarding change efforts.

Third, evaluation and reward systems must also be conducive. Even if higher-level decision makers are proponents of MSF, espouse relevant values, and commit to multiple implementation, MSF will not be successful if managers at lower levels do not recognize and reward the behaviors on which feedback recipients are being rated. Does this mean we suggest that MSF be made known to respective managers of feedback recipients, and also be made evaluative?

The answer is yes and no. It is possible to evaluate and reward people in areas assessed in MSF processes without actually using MSF data. For example, such data typically include information pertaining to leadership behaviors and abilities. These data can be used strictly for developmental purposes, while other mechanisms (say, assessment centers) can be used to evaluate and promote individuals with leadership capabilities. In this way, if leadership is recognized as important for promotion, individuals should be motivated to develop those skills and abilities.

Furthermore, we believe that any attempt to make actual MSF data evaluative should be gradual. That is, initially, such data should be strictly developmental and supplied confidentially to the feedback recipient. Thus the recipient has a chance to make changes suggested by the feedback. In later administrations, MSF results can be shared with one's supervisor, perhaps at the discretion of the feedback recipient. However, the emphasis at this point should still be developmental, with the supervisor serving as a coach to help the feedback recipient plan improvements and to direct the individual toward appropriate training opportunities (we discuss this in detail later).

Eventually, it may be possible to use the actual ratings for evaluative purposes, although as outlined by Waldman and Atwater (1998) we propose that the primary goal should be to identify individuals who repeatedly score at the low or high end of the distribution. In other words, evaluative action based on MSF data should only be directed toward individuals with extremely poor or negative ratings.

Actual Implementation

Several points should be made with regard to actual implementation. First, we propose that any implementation involve a customized survey process, to fit the particular needs of an organization.

Recognizing the benefits of standardization (items and scales that measure established theoretical constructs), we feel that the benefits of customization take precedence. If individuals are being asked to tailor their behavior in line with feedback on the survey, it is important that the specific behaviors relevant to organization success be included. If meeting a schedule and staying within budget are critical for the organization's success but the items included on the feedback report emphasize only customer and employee satisfaction, then bottom-line results may be compromised for less critical outcomes. In other words, *be careful what you measure.*

Second, insofar as possible, the group of feedback providers should include all relevant individuals with whom the recipient comes into contact, and the recipient should not be asked to choose names for feedback providers. In the case of upward feedback, all subordinates should provide feedback, not just those who might be handpicked by the feedback recipient. This procedure obviously eliminates the potential bias that can result if the recipient has the opportunity to knowingly or unknowingly pick only those raters with whom she or he has a favorable relationship. We realize that with regard to peer or customer ratings, choosing all possible feedback providers may create an overwhelming rating task for numerous individuals in the organization. Under such circumstances, a representative from human resources (or perhaps a supervisor) could help the prospective recipient pick a sample of potential raters.

Third, anonymity is important if one hopes to maximize the amount of honest feedback provided. Many individuals, particularly subordinates who may fear retribution, are reticent to provide honest, negative feedback if they believe their answers or comments will be identified. For this reason it is important to have numerous raters in a rater group. In the case of superiors or managers, anonymity often cannot be guaranteed (suppose a recipient has only one manager), and the raters should be aware that their responses are identifiable.

Fourth, we suggest ensuring that the nature of implementation efforts and the purpose of MSF be effectively communicated across the organization. Most organizations have formal means of communicating a new initiative, such as e-mail and company newsletters. Face-to-face information sessions with potential participants (that is, feedback providers and recipients) can also be worthwhile in quelling concerns regarding confidentiality, the purpose of the feedback, the potential for being surveyed to death, and so forth. We have found such information sessions helpful in terms of getting an MSF process off to a good start.

Fifth, the actual implementation must take into account the potential for the sorts of cross-cultural differences mentioned earlier. If feedback providers and recipients are from cultures that might not encourage a practice such as MSF, special care should be taken to work with these participants to discuss the purpose of MSF, confidentiality, and uses for the data. Indeed, MSF may not even be appropriate at some international sites outside of the United States.

Finally, we encourage more organizational-level analysis of MSF implementation efforts. With few exceptions (Smither and others, 1995), we know incredibly little about how MSF affects (and is affected by) organizational processes and outcomes. Our fear is that without such research and evaluation efforts, MSF is likely to be poorly implemented and eventually die like just another management fad.

Group and Individual Strategies

Strategies are also relevant that focus specifically on the group and individual levels. First, key cultural values, both within and among groups, must be in line for MSF to achieve success. We propose that one such key value is the importance and breadth of customer-supplier relationships. In other words, it is important for feedback recipients to have a broad view of customer-supplier relationships and the importance of maintaining them if MSF is to have its fullest possible meaning for those individuals (Waldman and Bowen, 1998). Customer-supplier relationships include

- Superiors providing support and serving the needs of subordinates
- Internal lateral service, whereby members *within* a group recognize the importance of teamwork and collegial relationships
- External lateral service, whereby members of separate groups recognize and serve the needs of individuals in groups located further down or along a supply chain

- External service, whereby organizational members recognize that the primary mission of the organization is to serve the needs of external customers

If these values are not highly developed, the MSF data is not likely to be taken seriously. In other words, if a feedback recipient does not view a feedback provider as a "customer," it is not likely that she or he will take the ratings very seriously.

Second, we recommend some degree of training for any individual who may be associated with an MSF program as a feedback provider or rater. Many people may not currently be in a supervisory role, and hence have little experience with the problems associated with rating errors, the importance of offering specifics in terms of behavior when providing write-in comments, and so forth. It is unfortunate when an MSF program results in less than worthwhile information for the recipient because of rating deficiencies on the part of the feedback provider.

Third, we are aware of MSF implementation strategies that simply involve surveying, producing a feedback report, and mailing the report to the feedback recipient. Coaching is the obvious missing link. A feedback report can be easy to read and catchy to the eye, but without follow-up coaching we are not likely to see performance improvement. The job of a coach is to help interpret the data, offer encouragement, make sure the recipient recognizes where problems exist, and devise a developmental plan for making those improvements. It is also important for a coach to help minimize resistance to unexpected negative feedback.

Various individuals can take on the role of coach. Consultants in charge of an MSF implementation can meet in one-on-one sessions or in small groups with feedback recipients. Internal people (say, from human resources) with strong coaching skills can facilitate the coaching process. Eventually, we recommend that the direct supervisor of the feedback recipient get involved as a coach. However, at least in initial iterations of an MSF process, the supervisor should not have actual access to numerical results. Instead, it should suffice for the supervisor to simply understand one or more areas that the recipient feels should be targeted for improvement.

As mentioned above, the feedback recipient should work with a coach to establish a developmental plan. Furthermore, the plan should be honed by having follow-up meetings with feedback providers. Emerging research shows that MSF has a maximum positive effect for the recipient only if this individual looks at the process positively, takes steps to form a developmental plan, and follows up by meeting with feedback providers (Atwater and Waldman, 1999; Walker and Smither, 1999). Even if feedback providers are well trained to provide useful ratings and behavioral comments, it is almost inevitable for the recipient to have some confusion about what the ratings mean after simply viewing a feedback report.

Of course, we recognize that follow-up meetings can be tricky. Feedback providers may fear that confidentiality has been breached. Especially in the case of upward feedback, they may be reticent when face-to-face with the recipient, especially if that person is obviously defensive or accusatory. We suggest that—as is the case in sharing results with one's supervisor—the recipient not share actual survey results in follow-up group meetings with feedback providers. Rather, the recipient should simply name specific areas of developmental weakness for which she or he would benefit from specific behavioral feedback and examples.

Two procedures are possible to elicit this additional feedback. One is for the recipient to be present at the meeting, ask for additional feedback, and simply take notes as specifics are mentioned. A second possibility is for the recipient to introduce the areas he or she would like to improve and then leave the room, letting the group work on its own with an elected facilitator to identify strategies. Once the discussion has taken place with the recipient absent, he or she can rejoin the group for discussion. In this way, no one individual has to take ownership for suggestions that may seem critical. The second option is obviously better if there is fear that feedback providers may not want to speak up with the recipient present, as is often the case with upward feedback.

Fourth, it is essential that training be made available for feedback recipients. MSF often identifies areas that may only improve as the result of attendance in a subsequent training program, such as leadership development. We recommend that the organization recognize ahead of time the likelihood of MSF recipients' needing training to make improvements.

Conclusion

To summarize this discussion, we offer these lists of barriers to successful implementation and strategies for overcoming them.

Barriers

- Inadequate strategic planning
  Unclear motives
  Disconnect with the reward system
  Inadequate preparation for feedback providers and recipients
- Poor implementation
  Surveys that do not fit the organization's goals or priorities
  Self-selected raters
  Organizational cynicism and lack of trust
  Managers' wavering commitment
  Cultural differences
- Lack of appropriate follow-up
  Resources not committed
  Recipients not setting goals
  No incentives to change

Strategies to Overcome Barriers

- Organizational
  Clear purpose
  Organizational values consistent with feedback initiative
  Commitment to at least two cycles of MSF
  Reward system consistent with feedback initiative
  Gradual incorporation of MSF into evaluation
  Customized surveys
  Relevant and inclusive list of feedback providers (for example, all subordinates)
  Effective communication of purpose
  Assurance of anonymity and confidentiality
  Sensitivity to cultural differences
- Group and individual
  Inclusive view of customer and supplier relationships (team members as customers too)

Coaching to develop goals and implementation strategies
Training raters
Follow-up meetings with rater groups
Employee development opportunities for feedback recipients
(such as training)

These lists highlight potential barriers as well as preventive strategies and solutions. In our fifteen years of experience with upward and 360-degree feedback interventions, we have certainly seen many individual cases where MSF has been a great source of enlightenment and performance improvement. However, we have also been aware of cases where organizations could have better prepared their employees for implementation. It is our hope that rather than discouraging potential MSF users, this chapter will help managers make the best use of the process, and that it results in the greatest return on investment for your organization.

References
Atwater, L. E., and Waldman, D. A. "The Antecedent and Consequent Effects of Organizational Cynicism on Upward Feedback Success." Paper presented at the national meeting of the Academy of Management, Chicago, Aug. 9, 1999.
Smither, J. W., and others. "An Examination of the Effects of an Upward Feedback Program over Time." *Personnel Psychology*, 1995, *48*, 1–34.
Vance, R. J., Brooks, S. M., and Tesluk, P. E. "Organizational Cynicism, Cynical Cultures, and Organizational Change Efforts." Paper presented at the tenth annual conference of the Society for Industrial and Organizational Psychology, Orlando, Fla., May 1995.
Waldman, D. A., and Atwater, L. E. *The Power of 360-Degree Feedback: How to Leverage Performance Evaluations for Top Productivity.* Houston: Gulf, 1998.
Waldman, D. A., Atwater, L. E., and Antonioni, D. "Has 360-Degree Feedback Gone Amok?" *Academy of Management Executive*, 1998, *12*(2), 86–94.
Waldman, D. A., and Bowen, D. E. "The Acceptability of 360-Degree Appraisals: A Customer-Supplier Relationship Perspective." *Human Resource Management Journal*, 1998, *37*, 117–129.
Walker, A. G., and Smither, J. W. "A Five-Year Study of Upward Feedback: What Managers Do with Their Results Matters." *Personnel Psychology*, 1999, *52*, 393–423.

CHAPTER 30

Success and Sustainability
A Systems View of Multisource Feedback

David W. Bracken
Carol W. Timmreck

In 1993, we formed and facilitated a consortium of companies with active MSF processes that has come to be called the Multisource Feedback Forum. In addition to attending semiannual meetings, the members are required to complete a comprehensive questionnaire describing their process. In the intervening period of time, membership has been quite fluid, with only a handful of companies maintaining a presence. The good news is that we have gained detailed understanding of more than forty MSF processes, and in some cases we have witnessed the ebb and flow of MSF within individual organizations.

An early observation regarding Forum members was the extreme diversity in approaches to MSF (Timmreck and Bracken, 1995). This diversity, for example, kept us from being able to create a normative database, such as the Mayflower Group's employee survey database (Johnson, 1996), since it was impossible to create a common method—let alone item content and response scales—that could create comparable data sources. At the same time, we observed that MSF processes were meeting with differing levels of success, at least as indicated by viability. We have had members come and go as their MSF process gained, lost, and in some cases regained, support. We also were privy to anecdotal tales and presentations from members as we attempted to share problems and solutions at our meetings.

The agenda of our Forum meetings is largely dictated by the desires of the member companies. Almost every meeting has in one way or another touched on the debate of using MSF for development versus decision making (such as performance appraisal). As proponents of using MSF for decision making under the right conditions, we are very aware of the critics who maintain that it is impossible to have a successful MSF process under these conditions (Dalton, 1998).

Our experience has been that MSF used for decision making can work but in some cases does not. In fact, our Forum surveys indicated that more than half the members were either using MSF for decision making or were planning to do so, but in about half the cases MSF implemented for such purposes was not sustained (Timmreck and Bracken, 1996). At this point, we were beginning to view sustainability as one facet of our operational definition of *success*.

In 1996, we undertook a modest piece of qualitative research primarily on Forum members. Focusing on those companies that had used MSF for decision making, we conducted structured interviews to systematically collect information on and record the nature of these processes and possible reasons for success (that is, sustainability). As we reported (Timmreck and Bracken, 1997), the reasons that seemed to lead to "failure" (inability to sustain) were varied and often uncontrollable. At the same time, we felt we were beginning to see some themes underlying sustainability, or lack thereof, and began enumerating them in the 1997 article.

Since 1993, we have been conducting workshops at Shell for participants in their MSF processes (which, by the way, are usually used for decision making). Although the Forum involvement has given us unusual insights into MSF at the organizational level, the Shell workshops have afforded us the perspective of the individual participant. Even though the workshop participants are typically receiving their feedback for the first time, we can often see how participants react to their results, initial acceptance of the feedback, and resulting willingness (or lack thereof) to use the feedback as a basis for action planning.

Defining Success

The definition of *success* in an MSF process varies depending on the MSF constituent. For example, success for a rater might be the perception that feedback was accepted and the recipient's behavior improved, and that there were no negative repercussions. The recipient of feedback may define it as receiving feedback that was fair, constructive, valid, actionable, credible, and reliable. The recipient's boss may define success as having access to timely, quality feedback appropriate for use in performance management or development (Bracken, Timmreck, Fleenor, and Summers, forthcoming).

As noted in the Introduction to this handbook, we have adopted a view of MSF that requires sustainability (repeatability) as a prerequisite for success, to the extent that in other forums we have gone as far as to suggest that an MSF process that does not meet this definition of success is not valid (Bracken, Timmreck, Fleenor and Summers, forthcoming): "A successful MSF process creates and/or reinforces focused, sustained behavior change, and/or skill development in a sufficient number of individuals so as to result in increased organizational effectiveness."

This definition comes from the total organization perspective. In it, *focused* is synonymous with aligned or relevant, or what most of us would consider a traditional definition of validity. But as we have just noted, alignment in the sense of having a "valid" instrument is necessary but not sufficient; in fact, we have proposed that alignment happens at multiple points in the successful MSF process (Bracken and Timmreck, 1999; see also the Appendix to this volume).

It should also be clear that we question the value of one-time, ad hoc MSF administrations, or MSF processes targeted at small populations (down to $N = 1$) if we are in the business of helping an organization to be more effective. Even though there is undoubtedly a need and a market for MSF for individuals and small groups, we see it as a totally different application of MSF that needs its own handbook.

MSF as Predictor and Criterion

We recognize that multisource feedback can be related to organization outcomes in different ways. As a *predictor* variable, it can be linked to other outcomes such as performance rating category, pay level, promotion, and so on, in an antecedent relationship (see Chapters Sixteen, Twenty, and Twenty-One). As a *criterion* variable, it can be the measure that "defines" achievement of a desired state, for example, exhibiting organization-valued behaviors; thus it is the measure of usefulness of some screening device or intervention (Byham and Moyer, 1998). The view of behavior change as a criterion measure is consistent with our definition of success, holding that sustained, focused behavior change is all that is needed. This is usually the underlying philosophy of values-based MSF, where the behaviors are derived from company values statements. In this process, the organization believes that encouraging (and sometimes rewarding) behavior that is consistent with some core values creates a competitive advantage, and it therefore follows that employees who exhibit such behavior are "successful."

A Systems View of MSF

Figure 30.1 provides a graphic presentation of a systems view of MSF that is designed to support our definition of success. We also are guided by the theme of this handbook, namely, to identify the factors in MSF design and implementation that are most likely to result in increased organizational effectiveness.

We present this model for a number of reasons. One is to guide future research on MSF systems and the factors that lead to success. At this point, this model is a mix of rationale and research, including research that has been conducted in other arenas (performance management, assessment, organization assessment, individual assessment). This model also serves as the underpinning for recommendations we have made in other forums (Bracken and others, forthcoming; Timmreck and Bracken, 1997) and in the "Guidelines for MSF When Used for Decision Making" (Bracken and Timmreck, 1999), which is offered as an Appendix to the *Handbook*. Finally, the model is a means of integrating many of the issues addressed in chapters of the *Handbook*.

An Inside-Out Perspective

Most of our prior treatments of MSF process have considered sustainability from an "outside in" view—that is, the organizational

**Figure 30.1. Sustainability of a
Multisource Feedback Process.**

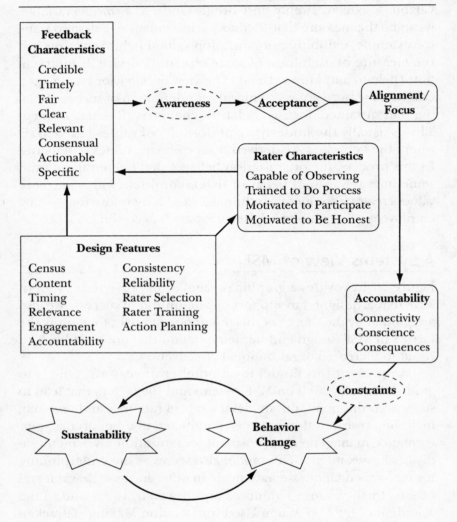

causes and indicators of sustainability (Timmreck and Bracken,
1995, 1996, 1997). This is primarily the focus of the treatment of
sustainability in Chapter Twenty-Four as well. The model in Figure
30.1 is more an "inside out" view of sustainability and success: what
needs to happen *within* the process (versus *to* the process) to increase the likelihood of sustained, focused behavior change. Here
we draw primarily from behavior change research (for example,

Nadler, 1977) and our experiences while interacting with workshop participants, and we apply this knowledge to identifying the features of an MSF process that create behavior change and hence (we propose) are sustained by the organization.

Components of the Model

Acceptance is the keystone of the model, so we start there and work our way backward and forward in describing it.

Acceptance

Acceptance can be defined as "the recipient's belief that the feedback is an accurate portrayal of his or her performance" (Ilgen, Fisher, and Taylor, 1979, p. 356.). Acceptance is a keystone of the model because if the feedback is denied, there is no motivation to change it and hence no behavioral change results. Assuming that there is some gap between the individual's observed performance and the organization's definition of desired behavior (note that we are *not* saying the *raters'* definition of desired behavior), the feedback is in effect creating a "problem" for the individual that must be fully understood and then acted on, which is to say, problem solving (Arnold, 1992).

As noted in the Preface to this handbook, there is a whole area of research that has focused on the characteristics (background, culture, personality) of the ratee and related effects on acceptance of feedback. Given our focus on organization effectiveness, we are devoting attention to the system characteristics that are most likely to create acceptance regardless of (or in spite of) these individual differences.

Awareness

Awareness is the precursor to acceptance. One cannot accept, or change, what one is unaware of. Awareness is the process of bringing information to the consciousness of the individual, as when the emperor became aware through feedback that he had on no clothes. Multisource feedback has the potential of making participants aware of things they were previously blind to. It is a common observation of MSF processes that the feedback is often viewed as unique, a novel experience that captures the attention of most participants. If the feedback is not intrinsically interesting or loses its novelty over time, the organization has the opportunity to get the attention of participants by integrating MSF with other important organization processes, such as staffing, performance management, and succession planning (see Chapter Twenty-One).

We propose in the model that the feedback characteristics are primary determinants of acceptance, and that MSF can be designed to have many desirable characteristics:

- *Credibility.* The feedback should come from credible sources, in this case individuals who have had sufficient opportunity to observe job-relevant behavior and are motivated to present the feedback honestly.
- *Timeliness.* The feedback should, as much as possible, occur without significant delay that might reduce its accuracy. Timeliness speaks to the need, at a minimum, to specifically inform the rater as to the time frame that is relevant (for example, the last year).
- *Fairness.* In this context, the perception (and reality) that the feedback is fair begins with the common standard that is applied to all participants as defined by the content of the instrument and consistent administration.
- *Clarity.* Ambiguity regarding feedback causes hesitation and misdirected actions. Clear, behavioral items presented (in feedback reports) in a manner to promote full understanding of the feedback help advance acceptance.
- *Relevance.* The feedback should be restricted to behaviors that are job-relevant and clearly communicated as being important to individual and ultimately organizational effectiveness.
- *Consensus.* A major rationale for MSF as a cause of behavior change is in the power found in consistent feedback from multiple sources. It is certainly difficult to discount feedback that sends a common message from many reliable observers.
- *Actionability.* The feedback must indicate behaviors that the participant can address through constructive actions.
- *Specificity.* The MSF process should encourage specific behavioral feedback from raters, supported both by behavioral items and by training raters to write in comments that offer insight as to the basis of the ratings.

Rater Characteristics

Even putting aside individual differences in raters, we propose that MSF systems can be designed to increase the probability that raters maximize their performance as reliable, accurate observers and reporters of behavior (see Chapters Seven and Eight). MSF features that address rater performance include the following.

- *Opportunity to observe.* The MSF process should ensure that the rater is selected to be someone with the best opportunity to observe ratee behavior. This is typically accomplished by having the ratee select raters with some form of review by another party (for example, supervisor) or, in the case of managers, including all direct reports.
- *Training.* Rater training, a major theme of this handbook, may be the most seriously neglected opportunity to improve MSF systems, usually under the excuse of "practicality." Rater training can serve many purposes (for example, communication, instructions, reduction of rating errors); rater training in other settings (Levy and Williams; 1998; Woehr and Huffcutt, 1994) has been shown to have the potential to improve rater performance.
- *Motivated participation.* A rater may choose not to participate either by not completing the questionnaire or some other means of being nonresponsive (random responding, selecting all the same rating, and so on). MSF design and implementation should keep in focus the need to keep the rater motivated and engaged in the process on an ongoing basis. Approaches to motivating raters to participate can fall under "carrot" methods (communicating the value of the feedback and the benefit to them as well as to the organization) or "stick" methods (creating rater accountability).
- *Motivation to be honest.* Perhaps the biggest challenge (and criticism) for an MSF process centers on motivating the rater to be honest. As is true for motivating the rater to participate, possible approaches to encouraging the rater to be honest can also fall under "carrot" methods (for example, communicating the value of candid, honest feedback and the cost of dishonest feedback) or "stick" methods (for example, creating rater accountability or discarding suspect responses). Under certain conditions, it appears

that accountability can improve rating accuracy (Haeggberg and Chen, 1999; Mero and Motowidlo, 1995) and that ratees prefer accountable raters (Antonioni, 1994).

Design Features

We propose that all of these precursors to feedback acceptance are ultimately determined by the design and implementation decisions required in any MSF process. We direct the reader to the guidelines in the Appendix of this handbook for our recommendations for decisions that best support the objectives of a successful system. Although the guidelines are presented for use in decision-making processes, we feel that they apply to developmental processes as well. We also suggest that the reader access our other article presenting the rationale for these recommendations (Bracken, Timmreck, Fleenor, and Summers, forthcoming).

Having examined precursors to acceptance, we now turn our attention to aspects of the model that follow acceptance.

Alignment and Focus

Assuming we can create an MSF process that promotes acceptance of feedback, we must ensure that action is taken and that it is in the right direction. Our definition of success speaks to "focused" behavior change, suggesting behaviors that are valued by the organization.

One common mistake is to consider alignment solely in the context of instrumentation, that is, content validity. Such alignment is necessary, but it is not usually sufficient. Since we must admit that an MSF questionnaire creates an imperfect, artificial mode of communication between rater and ratee, we should require that the ratee meet with people who can confirm that he or she has interpreted the feedback accurately and that any proposed actions are indeed "aligned" with organizational values and desired behaviors (Nadler, 1977). These sources, at a minimum, would include the ratee's direct reports and supervisor. Meeting with other raters is certainly desirable but often challenging, yet it creates significant opportunity for the ratee to improve his or her perceived effectiveness (see research reported in Chapters Sixteen and Seventeen).

Accountability

The motivation to take action on feedback can come from within (intrinsic motivators, such as "conscience"), from without (extrinsic motivators such as a tie to another meaningful outcome or consequence for noncompliance), or from some combination of each. Most "developmental" MSF processes rely on the intrinsic motivation of the ratee (Dalton, 1998). Our experience suggests that systems relying mainly on the participant's intrinsic motivation should expect to create significant (observable) behavior change in less than one-third (see Chapter Twenty-Two) of cases. Some organizations seem to find that acceptable. We do not. Part of our rationale lies in the significant costs (hard and soft) of systemwide MSF implementation, and the likely unfavorable cost-benefit ratio if the incidence of change is so low. We would also propose that under these conditions, the figure will drop over time as the system loses momentum and support and ultimately is not sustainable.

Ratee accountability is probably required for a truly sustainable MSF process (London, Smither, and Adsit, 1997). One of the benefits of integrating MSF with other human resource processes, including performance appraisal, is the inherent accountability that is created (see Chapters Twenty and Twenty-Six).

Constraints

Ability and motivation are two necessary components of performance, but so is opportunity to perform. Constraints have been defined as lack of resources, time to practice skills, or information (Peters and O'Connor, 1985). It is probably easy for most of us to think of real and perceived constraints that could prevent the ratee from either taking action or having the opportunity to exhibit modified behavior:

- Access to developmental resources (or lack thereof)
- Type of job assignment
- Low priority given to development
- Low priority given to MSF actions
- Culture or immediate boss not supporting new behaviors

Indeed, research has supported the possible negative effects on intention to change and skill development that are due to perceived or real constraints (Mathieu, Tannenbaum, and Salas, 1992; Williams and Lueke, 1999). Of course, external constraints have already been enumerated in this chapter and others in the *Handbook* as well (see Chapters Three, Fourteen, Fifteen, Twenty-Two, Twenty-Seven, and Twenty-Nine).

Behavior Change

Behavior change implies a change of behavior in the desired direction, that is, behaviors valued by the organization. Our definition of *behavior change* includes skill development, which can include skills and behaviors that are not directly measured by the instrument. We might also include behavior change in raters, such as desirable (aligned) behaviors relating to observing behavior and giving feedback. In fact, many proponents of MSF (see, for example, Dalton, 1998, and Chapter Twenty-Two of this volume) propose that creating these skills that form the basis of a "feedback climate" is the ultimate goal of MSF to the extent that successful MSF eventually goes away and is replaced by ongoing feedback free of questionnaires.

Demonstration of behavior change can be difficult, given the ever-changing workgroup and perspectives of members of even an intact workgroup. One approach that we favor is to ask the raters themselves—meaning, build into the MSF survey an item regarding perception of improvement since the last process. (This also enhances the accountability aspect by informing the participants that they will receive subsequent feedback on their improvement.)

Sustainability

An organization does not support MSF in the long run without evidence of its benefit. Our model indicates that sustainability is likely if behavior change occurs—the bang-for-the-buck notion by which management is the customer, and bang-for-the-effort by which raters are considered as customers. Nonetheless, such notions are contrary to the proposition that MSF should be unnecessary once a feedback climate is achieved.

We argue that a sustained MSF process always has a role in promoting increased organizational effectiveness. On the one hand, constant change in an organization as employees enter, leave, and change roles causes feedback needs to ebb and rise over time. Another type of change is that which occurs outside of the organization, requiring that the organization respond rapidly if it is to be successful (see Chapter Four). Such change probably demands that employees change as well, and MSF processes that have become part of the organization's operating fabric create a means to rapidly communicate and measure progress toward achieving a new set of behaviors (see Chapter Nineteen).

Determinants and Signs of Sustainability

The sustainability of an MSF process is determined by forces that come from within and without, that is, characteristics of the process and the context in which it operates.

Signs of Sustainability

We offer a list as indicators as to whether an MSF process is likely to be supported and sustained in an organization:

- The MSF process is viewed as an ongoing process, with a schedule for implementation by way of repeated administrations.
- MSF is integrated with other human resource systems.
- A sufficient budget is dedicated to MSF.
- MSF is referenced in organization communications and senior management presentations.
- Senior managers model participation in the MSF process and publicly support it.
- Processes are in place to ensure adherence to policies associated with MSF.
- Individuals or groups that do not adhere to MSF policies experience consequences.
- Individuals and groups are recognized and rewarded for positive outcomes associated with MSF (such as participation rates or behavior change).

Threats to Sustainability

Sustainability is threatened for one or more of these reasons:

- No support from senior management, including lack of participation
- Adopting an MSF process from another organization without considering cultural differences
- Approaching MSF as a mechanical data-collection event rather than a process of feedback, engagement, and leveraging data for improved effectiveness
- Only short-term commitment to the process
- Lack of real or perceived relevance to the goals and objectives of the organization
- Lack of trust from one or more constituencies (raters, ratees, management) that promises will be kept (anonymity, confidentiality, adherence to policy)
- Insufficient planning or resources to handle logistical challenges
- Overpromising deliverables, time lines, or expected outcomes
- No real or perceived behavior change on the part of participants
- No real or perceived benefit for any constituency (raters, ratees, management)
- Resistance to change
- Unexpected and uncontrollable changes (new leadership, severe budget cuts, changes in related HR programs)

Value of Sustained MSF

A sustained MSF process has numerous benefits for individuals and their organizations. *Individual* benefits include the following:

- Access to information not previously available
- Seeing that clear expectations for behavior are consistently signaled by the MSF content and prescribed process
- Perceived fairness of treatment over time
- Skill development over time, enabled by feedback on areas identified for improvement
- Being rewarded over time for exhibiting valued behaviors

The benefits of a sustained MSF process to the *organization* include these:

- A workforce aligned with organizational direction and valued behaviors as communicated and reinforced by repeated cycles
- Balanced recognition of results and the behaviors used to get them (a balance of "what" and "how" both being recognized)
- Reinforcement of team-oriented behaviors
- Standardization that creates common expectations across the organization
- A method to quickly change priorities, as the content and process of the MSF signal and reinforce valued behaviors
- Means to identify role models, and to coach or remove nonperformers

Sustainability also ties to our definition of the success of an MSF process through repetition of the model over organizational cycles, typically annually.

Conclusion

We have presented a model for success and sustainability of an MSF process that considers what impact participants and the context of MSF have on the sustainability of the process, to guide the practitioner in making decisions regarding design and implementation. We have also acknowledged and discussed the contextual factors that promote (or prevent) sustainability, along with the corresponding indicators.

One question that the model begs is whether behavior change promotes sustainability or vice versa. In reality, it probably works in both directions, which is good. We need behavior change for a process to be sustainable (or else why bother?), and a sustainable MSF process should in turn continue to promote ongoing behavior change and skill development.

So, why all this fuss over sustainability? You have probably participated in a one-time MSF process as a rater or a ratee, and you probably also have an opinion about the value of the experience. In many cases, such experiences are relatively benign if they don't get in the way of "real" work, or they may be sufficiently novel to draw your attention for a short time.

A more nefarious and (unfortunately) realistic view of ad hoc, one-time MSF processes is that they may cause more harm than good. An MSF process that is not sustained either by design (as with one-time administration) or circumstance (lack of support) can result in one or more negative outcomes:

- It communicates that the content (values, competencies) are not an important organization priority.
- It says that the MSF process is not an important organization priority.
- It expends organizational resources (time, money) with no opportunity to produce documentable benefits.
- It sets up an unrealistic expectation of benefits (behavior change) in a culture that does not support the process.
- It reduces the likelihood that participants (especially raters) are willing to support future MSF processes.

The Preface to this handbook begins with a quote from an unknown source: "Large-scale change occurs when a lot of people change just a little." We don't see how it would make sense to add ". . . just a little *for a while*" any more than we would support organizational change "for a while." We have often looked askance at the anthropomorphic notion of the "learning organization" because it is people who learn (albeit as both individuals and groups). Here we propose that organizations cannot really change unless people change; repeated nonproductive reorganizations, reengineerings, and other surface treatments are testimony to that fact. Processes that do not create sustained behavior change cannot be considered successful under any but the most shortsighted criteria.

References

Antonioni, D. "The Effects of Feedback Accountability on Upward Appraisal Ratings." *Personnel Psychology,* 1994, *47*, 349–356.

Arnold, J. D. *The Complete Problem Solver: A Total System for Competitive Decision Making.* New York: Wiley, 1992.

Bracken, D. W., and Timmreck, C. W. "Guidelines for Multisource Feedback When Used for Decision Making." *Industrial-Organizational Psychologist,* 1999, *36*, 64–74.

Bracken, D. W., Timmreck, C. W., Fleenor, J. W., and Summers, L. "360 Feedback from Another Angle." *Human Resource Management Journal,* forthcoming.

Byham, W. C., and Moyer, R. P. *Using Competencies to Build a Successful Organization.* Monograph. Pittsburgh: Development Dimensions International, 1998.

Dalton, M. A. "Best Practices: Five Rationales for Using 360-Degree Feedback in Organizations." In W. W. Tornow and M. London (eds.), *Maximizing the Value of 360-Degree Feedback: A Process for Individual and Organizational Development.* San Francisco: Jossey-Bass, 1998.

Haeggberg, D., and Chen, P. Y. "Can Accountability Assure the Accuracy of Upward Appraisals?" Paper presented at the fourteenth annual conference of the Society for Industrial and Organizational Psychology, Atlanta, May 1999.

Ilgen, D. R., Fisher, C. D., and Taylor, M. S. "Consequences of Individual Feedback on Behavior in Organizations." *Journal of Applied Psychology,* 1979, *64,* 349–371.

Johnson, R. H. "Life in the Consortium: The Mayflower Group." In A. I. Kraut (ed.), *Organizational Surveys: Tools for Assessment and Change.* San Francisco: Jossey-Bass, 1996.

Levy, P. E., and Williams, J. R. "The Role of Perceived System Knowledge in Predicting Appraisal Reactions, Job Satisfaction, and Organizational Commitment." *Journal of Organizational Behavior,* 1998, *19,* 53–65.

London, M., Smither, J. W., and Adsit, D. L. "Accountability: The Achilles' Heel of Multisource Feedback." *Group and Organization Management,* 1998, *22,* 162–184.

Mathieu, J. E., Tannenbaum, S. I., and Salas, E. "Influences of Individual and Situational Characteristics on Measures of Training Effectiveness." *Academy of Management Journal,* 1992, *35,* 828–847.

Mero, N. P., and Motowidlo, S. J. "Effects of Rater Accountability on the Accuracy and the Favorability of Performance Ratings." *Journal of Applied Psychology,* 1995, *80,* 517–524.

Nadler, D. A. *Feedback and Organizational Development: Using Data-Based Methods.* Reading, Mass.: Addison-Wesley, 1977.

Peters, L. J., and O'Connor, E. J. "Situational Constraints and Work Outcomes: The Influences of a Frequently Overlooked Construct." *Academy of Management Review,* 1985, *5,* 391–398.

Timmreck, C. W., and Bracken, D. W. "Upward Feedback in the Trenches: Challenges and Realities." Paper presented at the tenth annual conference of the Society for Industrial and Organizational Psychology, Orlando, Fla., May 1995.

Timmreck, C. W., and Bracken, D. W. "Multisource Assessment: Reinforcing the Preferred 'Means' to the End." Paper presented at the eleventh annual conference of the Society for Industrial and Organizational Psychology, San Diego, Calif., Apr. 1996.

Timmreck, C. W., and Bracken, D. W. "Multisource Feedback: A Study of Its Use in Decision Making." *Employment Relations Today,* 1997, *24,* 21–27.

Williams, J. R., and Lueke, S. B. "360-Degree Feedback System Effectiveness: Test of a Model in a Field Setting." *Journal of Quality Management,* 1999, *4,* 23–49.

Woehr, D. J., and Huffcutt, A. I. "Rater Training for Performance Appraisal: A Quantitative Review." *Journal of Occupational and Organizational Psychology,* 1994, *67,* 189–205.

Appendix: Guidelines for Multisource Feedback When Used for Decision Making

David W. Bracken
Carol W. Timmreck

For the purposes of these guidelines, *multisource feedback* (MSF) is defined as questionnaire-based feedback to an individual regarding work-related behavior from coworkers (supervisor or supervisors, subordinates, peers, team members, internal customers) and other individuals (such as external customers) who have had an opportunity to observe the behavior. Supervisor feedback is typically not anonymous since it is collected from one person, but feedback from other sources typically is. Participants (ratees) typically receive feedback results in the form of aggregated scores (mean scores), usually reported for each feedback source (peers, subordinates, and so on) and often including write-in comments.

Contributors to this Appendix include Allan H. Church, Mark A. Edwards, John W. Fleenor, Rod Freudenberg, Robert A. Jako, John Kasley, Carey Peters, Vicki Pollman, Lynn Summers, and Alan G. Walker. An earlier version of these guidelines was published in the *The Industrial-Organizational Psychologist* (Bracken and Timmreck, 1999). This version includes revisions based on feedback received subsequently from many individuals. We thank those many contributors for their role in improving this document, and the Society for Industrial and Organizational Psychology for permission to reproduce and adapt it here. Readers who are interested in the research and rationale behind these guidelines can refer to Bracken, Timmreck, Fleenor, and Summers (forthcoming).

Definition of a Successful MSF Process

For the purposes of these guidelines, a *successful* MSF process is one that "creates and/or reinforces focused, sustained behavior change and/or skill development in a sufficient number of individuals so as to result in increased organizational effectiveness."

Note that "behavior change" and "skill development" can be in areas valued by the organization but not necessarily measured directly by the MSF instrument.

Purpose

These guidelines are recommended practices for implementing MSF for decision-making purposes in human resource systems (performance management, staffing, succession planning, compensation), which in turn optimize the likelihood of success (as defined above). These guidelines should be applied to MSF processes that are designed in anticipation of use for decision making even though initial administrations may not include that purpose. Application of these guidelines to "development-only" MSF processes also typically improves the likelihood of success.

MSF used for decision making typically has design considerations that are not found in many development-only processes. For example, MSF used for decision-making processes such as performance appraisal (and resulting outcomes) are conducted for *whole segments* of an employee population (supervisors, all exempt employees, and so on) on a schedule determined by organizational needs (perhaps annually). Such practices place significant demands on the system that most development-only processes do not.

A second point of differentiation of MSF used for decision making regards the issues of *sustainability*. (Although MSF is occasionally used one time for purposes such as downsizing, that practice is outside the scope of these guidelines and may be harmful to other MSF processes.) Many decision-making applications of MSF are repeated events, such as those conducted annually. These processes are dynamic since participants (raters, ratees, management) have experiences that shape their behavior over time.

These guidelines in total *should not* be used as "standards." It would be inappropriate to use the guidelines to determine whether an MSF process is legally defensible. It is unlikely that any MSF process can simultaneously satisfy all of the objectives listed below. The guidelines reflect practices and recommendations that have been shown to optimize the likelihood of achieving success (as defined above). The guidelines should be used to guide decisions in designing MSF processes with an acknowledgment of the ramifications of each decision.

In cases where a guideline is of sufficient criticality as to be required, it is noted as "Essential." Used at the beginning of a paragraph, the bracketed word indicates criticality for all points that follow in that paragraph. When indicated after a sentence, it applies to only that point.

Objectives

These guidelines are designed to support the following objectives. Objectives are referred to in support of recommendations in the sections that follow.

- *Acceptance:* the feedback has characteristics that enhance acceptance by the ratees and their managers. Acceptance is a precursor to behavior change for ratees and to decision making for their managers.
- *Accuracy:* the process ensures that data are collected, processed, and reported with no errors.
- *Actionability:* the feedback (including write-ins) is behaviorally based and within the ability of the ratee to address through behavior change or skill development.
- *Alignment:* the content of the feedback and the process itself are consistent with the organization's strategies, goals, values, competencies, and desired culture.
- *Anonymity:* the process guarantees and delivers real and perceived anonymity for the feedback providers (raters) as a means of maximizing honesty and candor.
- *Census:* the data collected represent a census (as opposed to a sample) of those persons who have the best opportunity to provide reliable feedback, consistent with rater selection policies (for instance, all direct reports, X number of peers, and so forth).
- *Clarity:* participants (raters and ratees) fully understand their roles and how to correctly fulfill those expectations.

- *Communication:* communications regarding the purpose, methods, and expected outcomes of the process form a "contract" with participants on behalf of the organization to fulfill the commitments made.
- *Confidentiality:* a clear policy is communicated stating who may access and use feedback data. It is understood by all participants that data must be accessible to the data processor (internal or external), with clear requirements for data integrity and security. (A confidentiality policy that allows the ratee to keep the results to himself or herself is not considered a requisite for MSF when used for decision making, and in fact it may be a barrier to success.)
- *Consistency:* all processes are administered consistently for all participants (raters, ratees, management). Where procedures necessarily differ, administrators must demonstrate that the inconsistencies do not have a systematic effect on the feedback results.
- *Cooperation:* the task of providing feedback by raters is not so onerous as to affect the quality (for example, honesty) or quantity (response rates) of the observations.
- *Insight:* the ratee is given information of sufficient quality and specificity to ensure that resulting actions are aligned with and responsive to the observations of the feedback providers.
- *Ratee accountability:* methods are used that maximize the likelihood that ratees understand, accept, and use their feedback in the manner intended by the organization.
- *Rater accountability:* methods are used that maximize the likelihood that raters fulfill the role of accurate, honest reporters of observed ratee behaviors, including offering assistance to the ratee in understanding the feedback, guiding action plans, and reinforcing desired behavior.
- *Relevance:* the feedback addresses behaviors and skills that occur within the work setting and are observable by others.
- *Reliability:* the feedback instrument (questionnaire) is designed to generate reliable, quantifiable data based on content design principles and supporting statistical documentation.
- *Timeliness:* methods minimize problems caused by delays between observation and reporting, and between action and feedback by the ratee.

Preconditions

Commitment

A successful MSF process should gain the support of the organization in the form of coordinators (training, workshops, administrators) and endorsement. This support includes participation by all levels of management, including the most senior executives. *(acceptance, alignment)*

Clarity of Purpose [Essential]

The purpose of the MSF process must be clearly and explicitly understood and communicated. In these guidelines, *purpose* must include a statement as to how the feedback is distributed, documented, and used. MSF processes used for decision-making purposes should clearly communicate and support methods to assist ratees in their development as well. *(communication, consistency, clarity)*

Behavioral Model [Essential]

The content of the feedback instrument must be derived from a model (for example, competencies, values, strategies). This model should be translated into behavioral terms. Models may differ according to level or job. There must be full management endorsement and acceptance at all levels as to the relevance and importance of the models. A model not developed specifically for the organization (one that is off-the-shelf) must be reviewed for relevance and accompanied by a technical report documenting its measurement characteristics and (if relevant) the characteristics of any normative data provided. *(alignment, reliability, relevance, acceptance, actionability)*

Instrument Development

Item Construction

Items must be behaviorally based. [Essential] The feedback instrument should be designed (or reviewed) by survey professionals. *(reliability, actionability, relevance)*

Content and Forms

Items must be examined to see that they give various rater groups the opportunity to observe. [Essential] Where items are appropriate for one group but not another (for example, external customers), separate forms containing only relevant content are recommended. *(reliability, relevance)*

Rating Scales

Rating scales should be designed to be consistent with the purpose of the feedback. If the purpose is decision making, the anchors and related training should encourage between-person (normative) comparisons (for example, "in the top 5 percent"). The number of choices should allow for meaningful differentiation in performance, either between ratees or among ratees over time, usually 5 to 9 points. Scales must include an option for raters to indicate insufficient information to respond. [Essential] The use of multiple scales (for example, importance, desired versus observed behavior) should be carefully evaluated for their added value in light of rater overload, quality of information, and reporting complexity. *(reliability, insight, clarity, cooperation)*

Write-In Comments

Raters should be given the opportunity to provide additional feedback to ratees using write-in comments consistent with the purpose of the process. The process should not *require* write-in comments (that is, it should not support extreme ratings). Raters should have a clear understanding as to how their comments are reported (verbatim versus paraphrased) and receive training on how to write good comments consistent with the purpose of MSF. *(insight, clarity, cooperation, actionability, relevance, alignment)*

Pretesting

Prior to initial administration, the tools, policies, procedures, and communications should be pretested with representatives of the anticipated audience (raters, ratees, managers, administrators).

While many methods are available to the practitioner for doing pretests (such as pilots, focus groups, and interviews), the process or processes should allow collection of reactions, suggestions, and identified barriers to successful implementation. Pretests may also be used to collect initial normative data. The pretest should solicit input on:

Purpose

Policies and procedures

Perceptions of anonymity

Perceptions of confidentiality

Rater nomination

Rater honesty

Instructions

Instrument characteristics (such as clarity, observability, and length)

Content relevance

Report format

Resources required for ratees (training, courses, coaching)

Appropriateness for use in decision making

Process communications *(supports all objectives)*

Reliability

Data collected from a pilot or initial administration of the instrument must be analyzed to determine reliability. [Essential] *(reliability)*

Rater

Indices of rater agreement should be analyzed both within and between rater perspective groups (subordinates, peers, customers). Insufficient within-group agreement may indicate the need to increase group size or use alternative groupings (such as peers versus team members versus internal customers). Where feasible, a test-retest reliability check is also desirable.

Inter-Item Reliability

When category (dimension) scores are used, the instrument should be analyzed to determine the cohesiveness of categories to justify calculating category scores. Appropriate analyses can include factor analysis and coefficient alpha when pretest populations are of sufficient size. *(reliability)*

Validity

Validity must be demonstrated. [Essential] The process of demonstrating validity is typically iterative, collecting evidence over time. *(alignment, acceptance, reliability, relevance)*

Content Validity

Most instruments are initially constructed to satisfy requirements for relevance and alignment, reflecting the organization's strategies, goals, values, and competencies. Content should be reviewed repeatedly for relevance over time.

Criterion-Related Validity

As data are collected, the correlation of MSF results with other indicators of individual, group, and organization success should be examined (formal appraisals, sales, customer satisfaction and retention, promotions, turnover, organizational surveys).

Administration

Rater Nomination

Selecting raters is a key factor in the reliability, validity, and acceptance of the feedback results. Policies and procedures for selecting raters must be clearly communicated and applied consistently across the organization (see the following guidelines). [Essential]

Opportunity to observe is a key factor in deciding rater groups and the raters to be selected within a perspective group.

Rater groups that cannot be trained or monitored, or that have insufficient opportunity to observe (perhaps the case with external customers), may not be appropriate feedback providers.

"Opportunity to observe" considers not only working relationships but also length of time; a requirement for minimum time for the work relationship (considering both time and amount of contact during that time) should be specified to ensure sufficient opportunity to observe behavior.

All direct administrative reports (where applicable) should be included as raters.

For other rater groups, enough raters should be selected to enhance the reliability of the feedback. This typically suggests nominating at least the four to six raters per category who have had the best opportunity to observe ratee performance.

For nominations not determined by policy (say, all direct reports), the ratee is the primary source in selecting raters. The nominations must have the concurrence of the ratee's supervisor. [Essential]

The nomination process should include a method to identify cases where a rater is nominated an excessive number of times, which has potential impact on the quality of the feedback. A policy should specify ways to handle this situation. *(reliability, acceptance, clarity, cooperation, census, consistency)*

Rater Training

Once nominated to provide feedback, raters should be trained as to how to perform their role. Training is necessary primarily for first-time participants. Possible topics can include the following:

Purpose of the MSF process

How the feedback is used

How raters were selected

How to complete the rating form

How to be a good observer and rater

How missing data are defined and reported

How to write a good comment

How to avoid typical rating errors

How the feedback data are processed

How the feedback are reported to the ratees

How write-in comments are reported

How to avoid invalid rating patterns
How to properly fulfill the role of rater
Expectations for the ratees
Time line and next steps

Although rater training can be delivered effectively through various media, methods that use face-to-face delivery are preferred. Producing written instructions alone does not suffice as rater training. *(clarity, reliability, consistency, anonymity, rater accountability, acceptance, confidentiality, communication, actionability, relevance)*

Technology

Many technologies exist for administration and data collection of MSF feedback. The best technology is partially dictated by the nature of the feedback instrument (length, branching, open-ended questions and comments) and organizational culture. There are additional issues to consider:

- Perceptions of anonymity for the raters can affect the honesty of feedback. In certain climates, technologies that are not perceived to guarantee anonymity (for example, those that are internally processed) may result in feedback with low reliability because of reduced honesty and candor as well as lower response rates. *(anonymity, reliability, cooperation)*
- Logistics, geography, and resources may require using multiple technologies. If this is necessary, the feedback should be systematically examined to detect any possible bias introduced by a technology (lower or higher scores, lower response rates, incomplete questionnaires, errors in responding). Some work climates may show resistance to using certain technologies. *(consistency, cooperation, accuracy, reliability, timeliness)*
- Any technology must protect the data from access by unauthorized parties. [Essential] *(accuracy, anonymity, confidentiality)*

Timing

The timing and frequency of administration may be dictated by the systems that require MSF data (such as performance appraisal or succession planning).

Annual administrations that are integrated with other HR systems help establish accountability for using MSF results in ways that are aligned with organization objectives and therefore are recommended. *(alignment, timeliness, ratee accountability, acceptance)*

A long time interval (eighteen months, two years) between administrations can lead to problems of timeliness in regard to (1) the time lapse between rater observation and reporting, (2) the delay between behavior and feedback for the ratee, and (3) the delay in receiving feedback (and reinforcement) for actual behavior change on the part of the ratee; such an interval is therefore undesirable. *(timeliness, reliability, actionability)*

Annual census (one-time) administrations can place significant strain on the organization, with possible negative effects on some objectives. Creative solutions should be explored (for example, technologies, formats displaying multiple ratees). *(cooperation, census, clarity)*

Staggering administrations throughout the year may create both real and perceived inconsistencies, affecting acceptance by ratees and perceptions of fairness for all participants. Staggering across a limited time period (say, three to six months) can help reduce real and perceived inconsistency. *(consistency, acceptance)*

Data Processing

The role of the data processor is primarily to ensure total accuracy, along with maintaining anonymity and confidentiality consistent with policy and communications. Other important considerations are timeliness, cost-effectiveness, and customer service. Data processing must be carefully tested and monitored to ensure 100 percent accuracy. [Essential] *(accuracy)*

[Essential] The data (questionnaires and reports) must be totally secure from access by unauthorized personnel. In addition, policies and procedures must clearly state who can see the reported results and under what circumstances. Such policies and procedures should be clearly communicated and agreed to by management to prevent possible abuses. *(confidentiality, anonymity, consistency, communication)*

Data should be maintained according to policy and legal requirements consistent with those applied to other employee performance data (for example, performance appraisals). *(consistency, communication, alignment)*

Note that there are some legal opinions regarding the ability to "guarantee" anonymity in all circumstances. Communications regarding legal anonymity should incorporate local legal guidance. (*consistency, communications*)

Reporting

Report Generation

[Essential] Reliability and anonymity both require specifying minimum group size to report a score (item and category). This is never less than three (3) people, except for self-scores, supervisor scores, and any other agreed-on, one-on-one relationship; the number can be greater. (*reliability, anonymity*)

At a minimum, reports should include for each category and item an aggregate (for example, mean) score, the number responding, and some indication of rater agreement (if score distributions are not displayed). If available, trend scores (prior results) should also be included in the report. (*insight, acceptance*)

Internal normative comparisons (percentiles, comparison group scores) should be in the report, with care taken to ensure that the normative data are relevant, accurate, and up-to-date. If off-the-shelf instruments are used, internal norms should be generated. (*insight, acceptance, accuracy*)

Write-in comments should be reported verbatim, with the possible exception of editing for expletives. Reporting by rater group helps ratees interpret the feedback. (*insight, acceptance, alignment*)

Rater Reliability Checks

Any data "cleansing" performed after processing should be clearly communicated to participants prior to administration. A possible useful method is to identify invalid rating patterns, suggesting that a rater is not fulfilling his or her role as a quality feedback provider. Processes that arbitrarily remove data (such as Olympic scoring) or similarly result in reduced group size are not recommended but may be useful in some instances (as with a climate of ratee distrust and large group sizes). (*reliability, census, consistency, communication, rater accountability, acceptance*)

In cases where a rater is found providing invalid feedback (say, ratings all of the same score), a policy should be set and followed for handling this circumstance. Options include automatic discarding of a questionnaire with an invalid rating, or allowing a rater the opportunity to modify a response. *(reliability, consistency, clarity, communication, rater accountability)*

Online administration can be used to provide real-time feedback to raters regarding their response patterns. *(reliability, rater accountability)*

Feedback reports are typically produced for each ratee. Copies may be given to other sources (manager, human resources) depending on policy, with clear communication of this policy to ratees. *(insight, ratee accountability, communication, consistency)*

Follow-Through

Ratee Training

Ratees should be trained on how to read, interpret, and use their feedback. Best done in a workshop setting, ratee training can include:

How feedback can be used for behavior change

How to read a feedback report

How to identify priority behaviors for improvement

How to create an action plan

How to identify and access development resources

How to conduct a meeting with raters

How to conduct a meeting between ratee and manager

How the data are or should be used

Expectations for the ratee

Other resources can be used to support ratee training, such as written guides, coaches, counselors, mentors, and help centers (perhaps online or telephone). *(ratee accountability, acceptance, communication, clarity, alignment, consistency, actionability)*

Using the Results

How the feedback is used ultimately determines the success and sustainability of the MSF process. Two events are vital to successful implementation and sustained engagement of feedback providers. First, in a decision-making context, *the ratee is required to share results with his or her manager.* (Note that other individuals in the company may be given access to individual results by policy.) This sharing process gives the manager information necessary to fulfill his or her role as a representative of the company. A meeting to discuss results facilitates implementing an action plan for the ratee. [Essential] *(ratee accountability, alignment, acceptance, insight, consistency, confidentiality)*

Second, decision-making contexts typically include repeated administration (perhaps yearly). Raters continue to participate and provide honest feedback only to the extent that they see their effort rewarded through the resulting actions of the ratees. A key event to support this engagement is for the ratee to *share results and action plans with the raters,* particularly direct reports. Sharing results has additional benefits: allowing the ratee to gain further insight into the meaning of the feedback, facilitating rater conversation that enhances his or her understanding and workgroup alignment, and creating an ongoing dialogue with the raters throughout the year. Sharing results with raters, particularly direct reports, should be a clear expectation for the ratee, with significant flexibility as to how results are presented. *(ratee accountability, rater accountability, insight, alignment, consistency, acceptance)*

There are a number of additional considerations:

- Ratees must be given resources that enable them to address the gaps (between desired behavior and actual behavior) identified in their feedback. [Essential] Resources might include internal and external training, job experiences, special assignments, community activities, and various media sources. Coaches can be very effective in aiding both data interpretation and action planning. It is important that such resources be not only available but also easily accessible to those who desire them. *(acceptance, actionability, ratee accountability)*

- The MSF process should integrate ongoing support between administrations, such as interim progress reviews, minifeedback tools, communications, ongoing training, and mentor relationships. *(timeliness, alignment, communication)*

Integrating Results into Decision Making

Once steps have been taken to ensure that the feedback data are reliable and valid, it becomes equally critical to ensure that the data are used appropriately, accurately, and consistently.

- Managers given access to MSF feedback for use in decision making should be trained on how to read, interpret, and use it.
- Formulaic approaches that use mathematical calculations based on MSF scores as the sole determinant in making decisions are not appropriate.
- Policies and practices should be clearly defined and communicated regarding use (and misuse) of MSF. [Essential] Violations of these policies should be monitored and remedied.
- Processes that use MSF results must be scrutinized to ensure that results are not disclosed in a way that violates confidentiality policies. [Essential] *(consistency, alignment, clarity, communication, acceptance, confidentiality)*

Evaluation

Methods should be used to determine whether or not the MSF process is being implemented as prescribed and is having the desired results. Methods available to the user include these:

Focus groups

Interviews

Audits

Surveys

Use of organizational resources to address individual development

Process data (response rates, score trends)

Statistical analyses (rating patterns, adverse impact)

Related organization outcomes *(supports all objectives)*

References

Bracken, D. W., and Timmreck, C. W. "Guidelines for Multisource Feedback When Used for Decision Making." *Industrial-Organizational Psychologist*, 1999, *36*(4), 64–74.

Bracken, D. W., Timmreck, C. W., Fleenor, J. W., and Summers, L. "360 Feedback from Another Angle." *Human Resource Management Journal*, forthcoming.

Name Index

263, 265, 267, 271, 309, 317, 318,
333, 362, 367, 369, 371, 376–377,
384, 458, 462, 473, 475, 477, 487,
493
Sonnenfeld, J., 425, 431–432
Springer, D., 20, 32
Sproull, J. R., 44, 47
Stalk, G., 11, 14
Stevenson, H. W., 437, 445
Stone, J. B., 20, 29
Stoner, J. D., 238
Stout, H., 421, 432
Stringfield, P., 103, 112, 309, 316
Strupp, H. H., 19, 29
Summers, L., 12, 14, 45, 46, 93, 156,
158, 164, 165, 169, 170, 172, 175,
176, 180, 343, 346, 347, 349, 480,
486, 492, 510, xxiii, xxvii, xxxii,
xxxiv
Sundstrom, E., 83, 95
Sundvik, L., 103, 113
Swaminathan, H., 436, 446
Swann, W. B., 107, 113

T
Tannenbaum, S. I., 488, 493
Taylor, M. S., 25, 30, 322, 323, 333,
483, 493
Taylor, S., 309, 317
Tesluk, P. E., 467, 477
Tetlock, P. E., 118, 129
Thayer, D. T., 436, 446
Thomas, M. D., 84, 94
Thorndike, R. L., 21, 32
Thornton, G. C., 132, 139, 147–148
Tiegs, R. B., 320, 333
Timmreck, C. W., 3, 12, 14, 93, 149,
158, 164, 185, 196, 201, 203, 323,
334, 341, 343, 346, 347, 349, 351,
368, 380, 385, 457, 461, 478, 479,
480, 481, 482, 486, 492, 493, 494,
495, 510, xxi, xxiii, xxiv, xxix,
xxvii, xxxii, xxxiii, xxxiv
Tornow, W. W., 27, 32, 48, 62, 309,
317, 372, 373, 377, 378, 379, 384,
385, xxi, xxiii, xxix, xxxiv

Triandis, H. C., 437, 446
Tsui, A. S., 373, 383
Tyler, C. L., 447

U
Ulrich, D., 319, 334
Underhill, B. O., 260, 268, 275, 288

V
Vaill, P. B., 228, 238
Van de Vijver, F.J.R., 438, 446
Van Eynde, D. F., 309, 316
Van Velsor, E., 55, 56, 62, 63, 73, 78,
87, 89, 95, 309, 317
Vance, R. J., 467, 477
Vandewalle, D., 360, 367
Vasilopoulos, N. L., 181, 263, 267,
271
Veglahn, P. A., 449, 462
Vendantam, K., 239
Verdini, W., 39, 47, 449, 461
Villanova, P., 376, 450, 454, 460
Viswesvaran, C., 132, 133, 134, 148
Viteles, M. S., 18, 32

W
Waclawski, J., 12, 14, 79, 82, 87, 88,
90, 91, 94, 301, 304, 306, 309,
316, 317, xxix, xxxiv
Waldman, D. A., 90, 95, 264, 267,
270, 346, 351, 458–459, 462, 463,
464, 465, 468, 469, 471, 473, 475,
477, xxi, xxxiv
Walker, A. G., 256, 265, 266, 267,
271, 309, 317, 362, 367, 458, 462,
475, 477
Walker, S. A., 266, 271
Walt, C., 278–279, 288
Walton, A. E., 366
Warr, P., 103, 113
Waterman, R. H., 27, 31, 231, 237
Watson Wyatt, 269, 271
Webb, W. B., 25, 32
Weick, K. E., 22, 28
Weitz, J., 20, 21, 32
Welch, J., 226

Subject Index

feedback discussion and, 222–226; limitations of, 42–43; migration from, to administrative purposes, 177, 252–253, 318, 323–324, 378–382, 383, 408–409, 414–416; rater accountability problems in, 372, 376–377; rater disagreement and, 145; rater performance improvement for, 115, 116–117, 126; rater selection for, 99–100; self-development approach to, 226–237; separation of administrative decision-making purpose from, 381; for teams, 289–300; tools and resources for, 221–237; validity of rater selection for, 99–100; in vendor-based projects, 161–162; Web-based systems for, 166, 171, 173. *See also* Leadership development; Self-development; individual development

Developmental resources, 230–231, 234, 363, 508

Developmental suggestions, 507–508; in feedback report, 197, 198–199; sample, 198–199

DevelopMentor, 230, 234

Difference scores, 204, 262

Differential/comparative rating sources, 111

Dimension-based multipoint rating scales, 117

Direction stage of organizational maturity, 422, 423–424, 430; in case study, 430; crisis of, 422, 423; multisource feedback goals for, 422, 423–424

Discrimination law, 337, 447–448, 449, 451, 453, 454, 455

Disk-based method, 91, 92

Disparate-impact cases, 459

Distal approach, to corresponding items, 81–82

Distortion. *See* Rater distortion

Distributive justice, 35

Diversity, 401; ethics and, 457–458; norms and, 67, 72. *See also* Cross-cultural issues

Diversity management, need for, as indicator of readiness, 41

Documentation, 451–452; legally defensible, 453–454

Donaldson *vs.* Pillsbury Co., 452, 461

Double-translation process, 83

Downsizing, 338, 429

E

EAdvisor, 230, 234

Eastern European countries, 443

Eastman Kodak, 420

Egocentric biases, 132

Electronic multisource feedback, 8; anonymity and confidentiality in, 158–159, 170, 174–175, 344, 504; customization enabled by, 412; data capture for, 158–159; forms distribution for, 158; infrastructure readiness for, 45–46, 175–176; for on-demand development, 381–382; for performance management multisource feedback, 331–332; planning for, 155, 156; processing written comments for, 160; project management for, with vendors, 155, 158–159, 160–161, 162; reporting in, 160–161; time frame for, 155; Web-based, 165–179. *See also Technology headings;* Web-based systems

E-mail, 165, 472; for on-demand developmental feedback, 381–382; as reminders, 169; uses of, 165; in Web-based systems, 169, 172, 173

Electronics industry, user satisfaction in, 247, 248

Employee loyalty, 427–428

Employee opinion surveys, 39; example of, 40–42

Employee surveys, 8; multisource feedback compared with, xxvi, xxvii, xxviii; of satisfaction with